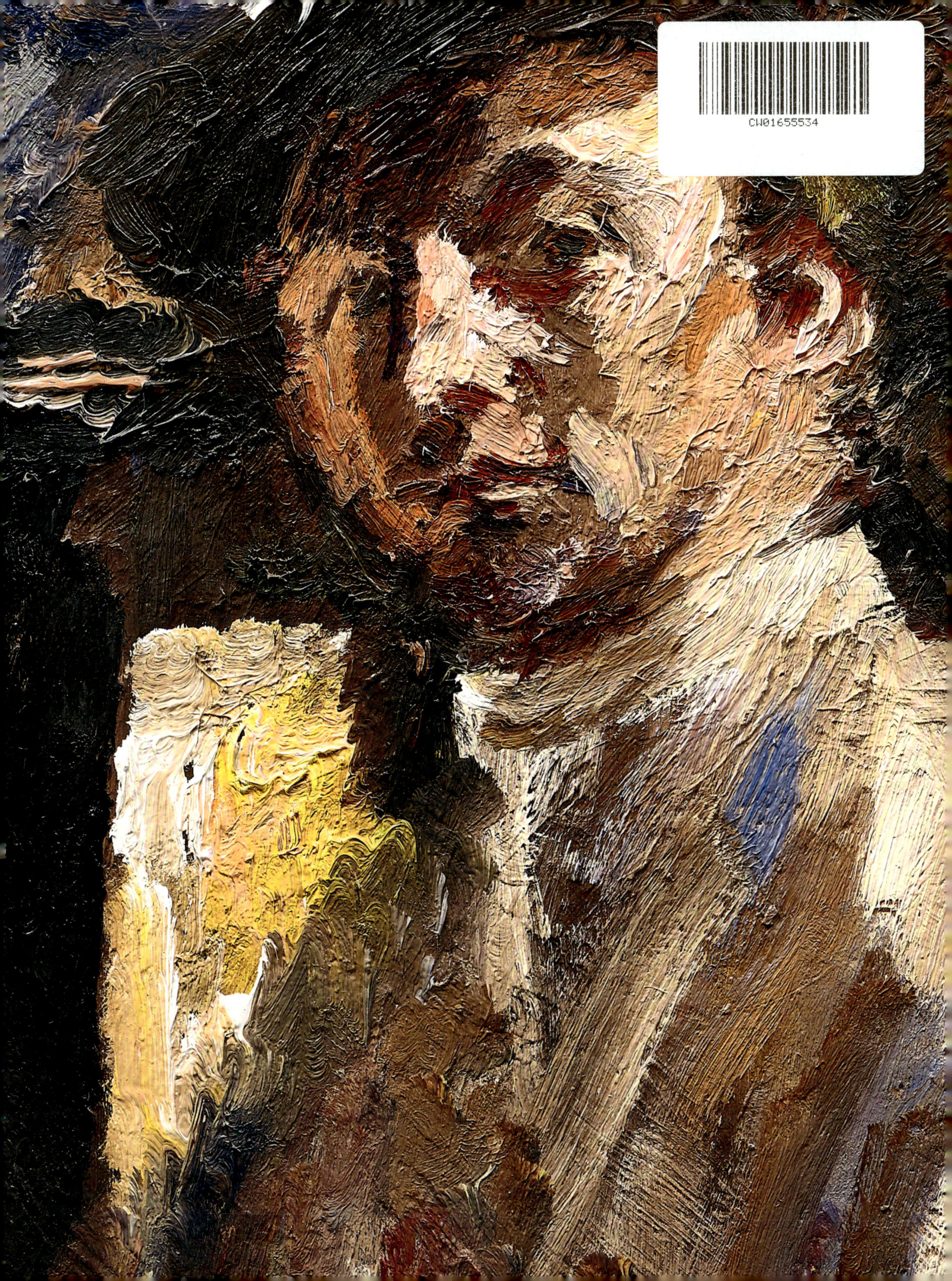

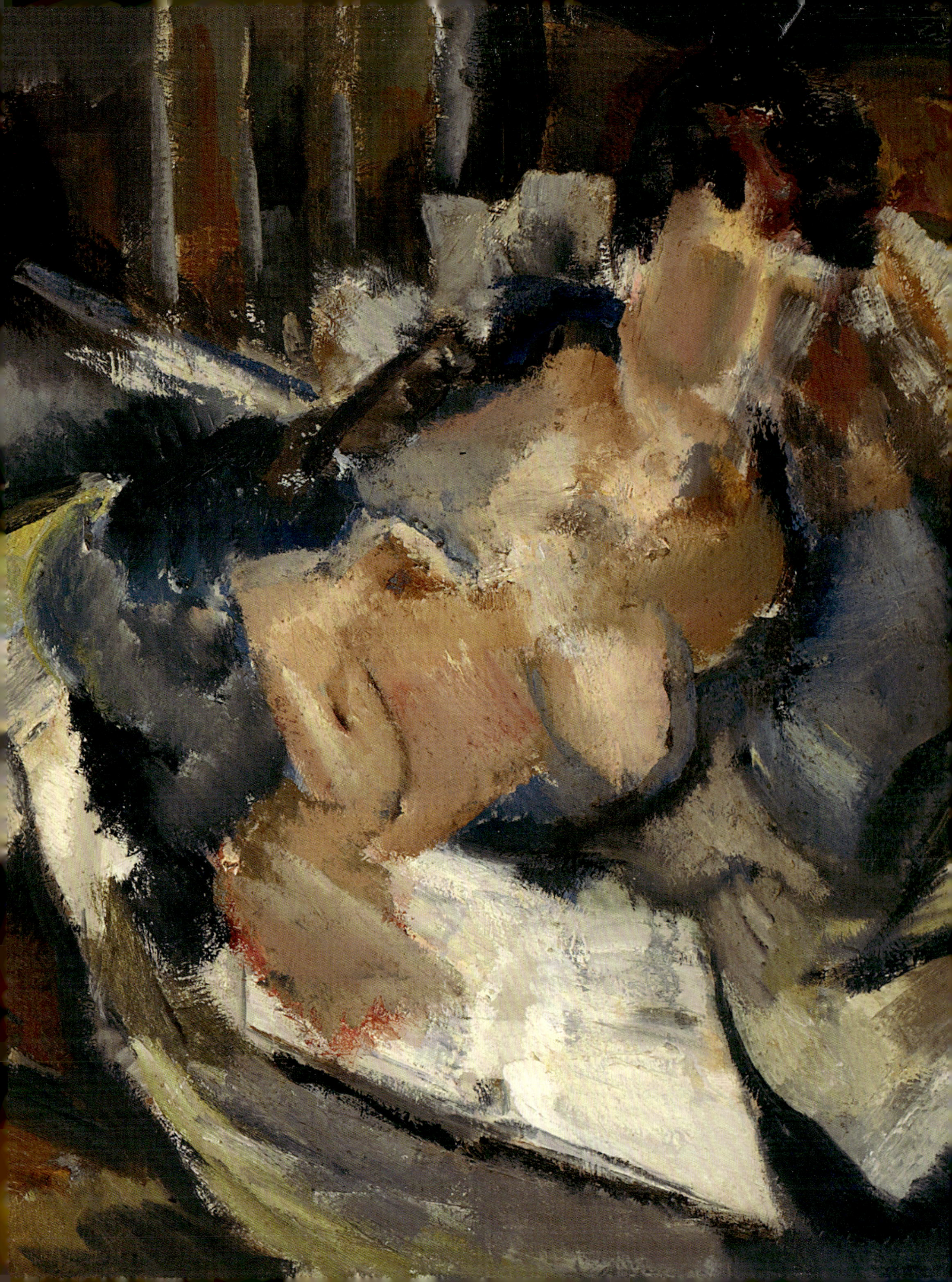

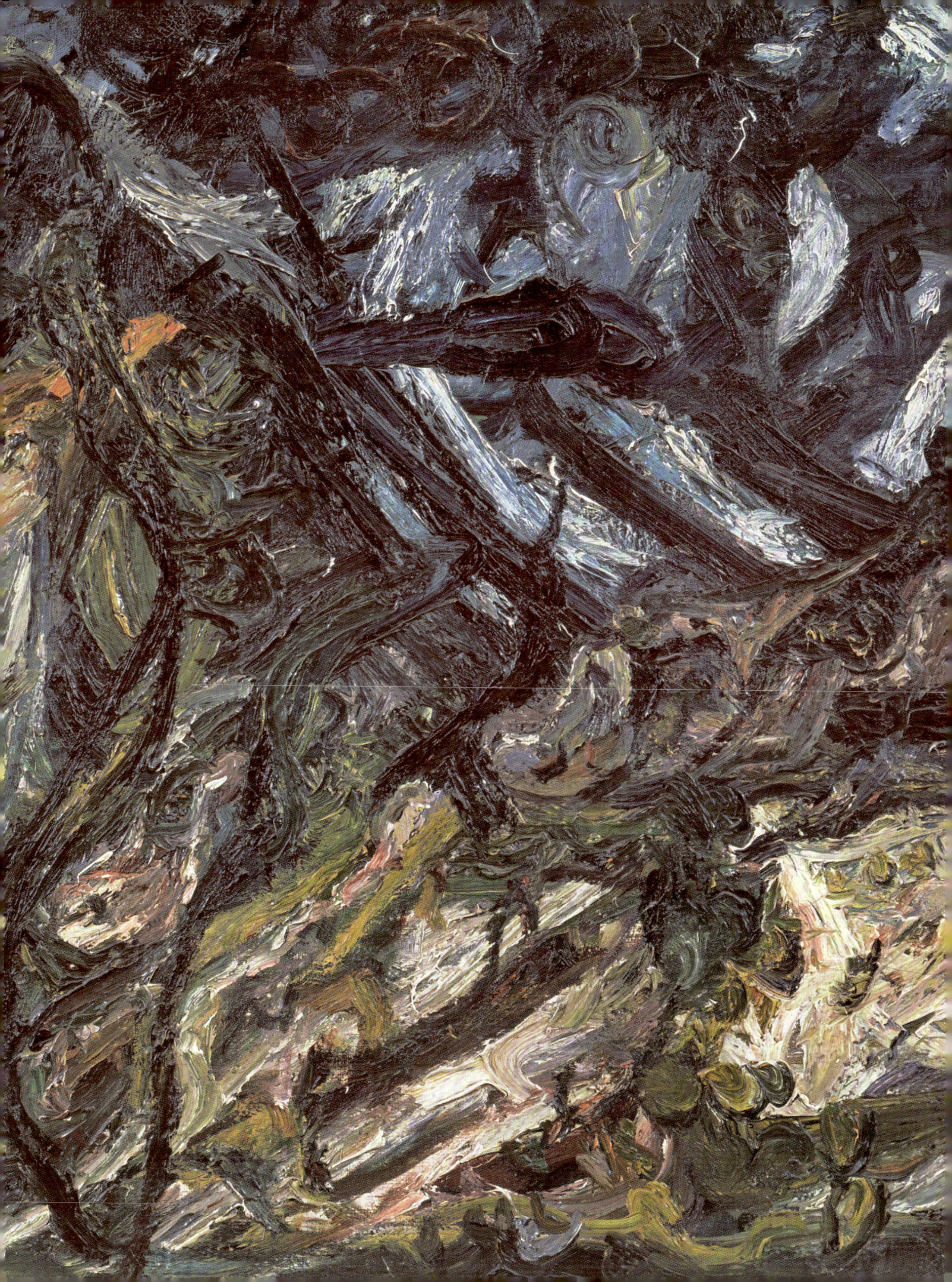

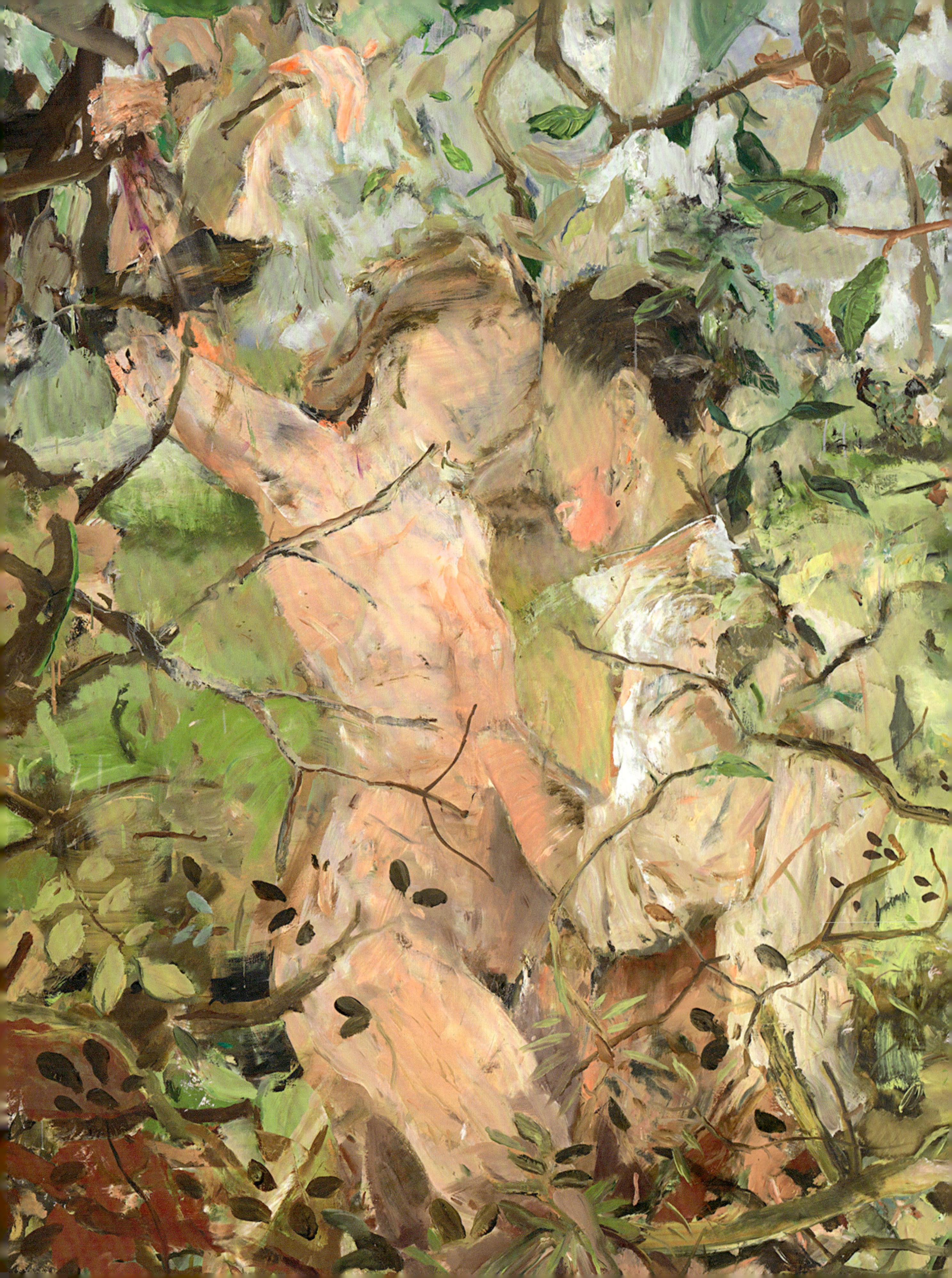

All Too Human: Bacon, Freud and a Century of Painting Life

Edited by Elena Crippa

Tate Publishing

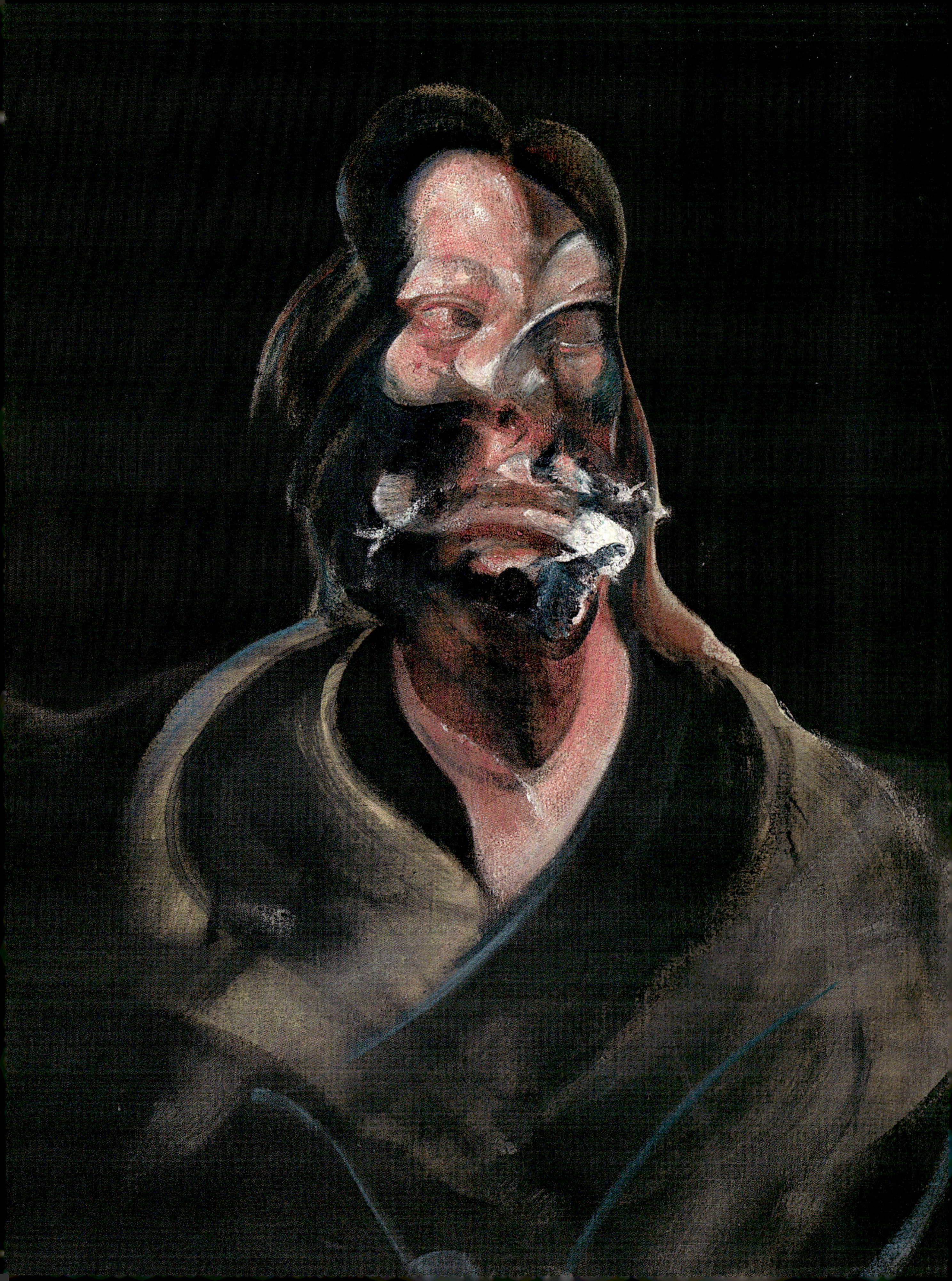

Contents

Foreword

The reinvention of the European tradition of figurative painting – especially paintings of the human figure, clothed and unclothed – is one of the most important contributions British art has made since the Second World War. Each artist associated with this tendency has sought to find new ways of capturing the physical and psychological presence in paint of a single human being, often painted from life, or else a group of people or an environment that reflects the larger dynamics of history and society. It is a tendency that is unusual in modern art for reinventing, rather than breaking with, genealogies of pre-1900 art: the National Gallery's collection has been especially important for these artists. Whether focused on the human figure alone, a non-descript corner of the urban environment, or a larger social drama, that reinvention unmistakably reflected the existential and societal crises of the postwar age.

Most of the artists that form the core of this exhibition emerged in the late 1950s, although Francis Bacon and Lucian Freud, who are represented here in most depth, had been making important work throughout the 1940s. But it wasn't until the 1980s and 1990s that Michael Andrews, Frank Auerbach, Freud, R.B. Kitaj, Leon Kossoff and even Bacon himself achieved the profile, and perception of interrelatedness, they have today. A so-called 'new spirit' in painting – often raw, figurative, large-scale and expressionistic – by both new artists and those previously side-lined (Baselitz and later Picasso and Guston) created a general environment within which this tendency in British painting became better appreciated and understood. The six aforementioned artists became those most often associated with a new label, the so-called 'School of London', a speculative term adopted by Kitaj himself in an exhibition he curated in 1976 called *The Human Clay*. All six have been important to Tate, each having previously been the subject of a solo exhibition.

While known to each other and sharing certain commitments to painting and its relationship to the world, the irony of this 'school' was that its artists were and are highly independent, even isolated, in pursuit of their art. We may think of this as a somehow quintessentially British school of painting, yet only Andrews and Kossoff were born in Britain. The others experienced London, and Britain, to a greater or lesser extent through their first-hand experience of migration and exile: from Ireland, Nazi Germany and the American midwest. As with many art movements, the School of London label, once it stuck, determined the group identity of artists who have some things in common and much else that separates them. It can do a disservice both to those it includes and those it excludes.

All Too Human seeks to tell a broader and longer history of modern figurative painting in Britain. Critically, Paula Rego and F.N. Souza, who came to London from Portugal in 1952 and India in 1949 respectively, both have rooms devoted to their work, and John Deakin, Dorothy Mead and Euan Uglow, also more or less contemporary, also feature. The exhibition begins with the postwar generation's immediate artistic ancestors: Walter Sickert, Stanley Spencer, David Bomberg and

William Coldstream. Bomberg's and Coldstream's influence was direct, through their teaching at the Slade and Borough Polytechnic respectively. Chaïm Soutine and Alberto Giacometti make brief appearances in the exhibition as international influences, further situating this tendency in British art in a global context.

The exhibition also sheds light on the role of women artists in the traditionally male-dominated field of figurative painting, beginning with Dorothy Mead, moving through to Rego's often autobiographical explorations of the experience of women in a patriarchal culture, with a particular focus on her work of the late 1980s and 1990s when she returned to working from life. The exhibition ends with four women artists who develop the tradition of painting the figure by departing in various ways from the precedent of their postwar, and mostly male, forebears. Lynette Yiadom-Boakye's figures appear recognisable, yet they are fictional, while Cecily Brown scrambles bodies in erotically-charged all-over compositions that also speak to the precedent of abstract expressionism. Celia Paul's self-portraits and portraits of those close to her are quietly haunting, while Jenny Saville's intensely observed self-portraits reflect the feminist critique of the female nude in Western art.

I would like to warmly thank Elena Crippa, Curator, Modern and Contemporary British Art at Tate, for the boldness and sensitivity she has brought to conceiving and developing the exhibition. Elena has been supported by a changing team of equally committed assistant curators: Rachel Smith and Hattie Spires in the initial phase, and Laura Castagnini in the past nine months, with the vital support of Gillian Buttimer, Carolyn Kerr, Kiko Noda and Zuzana Flašková.

The exhibition is organised in partnership with the Museum of Fine Arts Budapest. From the outset Dr László Baán, General Director, Csilla Regős, International Exhibitions Manager, and Dávid Fehér, Associate Curator in the Department of Art after 1800, have been enthusiastic and collegial partners. We look forward to the exhibition's presentation in Budapest.

We have been very fortunate to have had the support of many private collectors and public institutions who have been so generous in lending their treasured works to the exhibition. We thank them all.

We are very grateful for the generosity of the All Too Human Exhibition Supporters Circle, including The Garcia Family Foundation, Hazlitt Holland-Hibbert, Victoria Miro, and Robert and Matthew Travers of Piano Nobile. This is in addition to the support lent by Tate International Council, Tate Patrons and Tate Members to whom we also extend our great thanks.

The exhibition has also been made possible by the provision of insurance through the UK Government Indemnity Scheme. Tate Britain would like to thank HM Government for providing Government Indemnity, and the Department for Digital, Culture, Media and Sport and Arts Council England for arranging the indemnity.

Finally, we would like to warmly thank Frank Auerbach, Leon Kossoff, Paula Rego, Celia Paul, Cecily Brown, Jenny Saville and Lynette Yiadom-Boakye for their participation and dialogue, and the enduring inspiration of their work.

Alex Farquharson
Director, Tate Britain

Acknowledgements

This exhibition would not have been possible without the generosity of many lenders. We would like to express our deep gratitude to the following individuals and institutions, as well as those who wish to remain anonymous: Amgueddfa Cymru – National Museum Wales; Arts Council Collection; Birmingham Museum and Art Galleries; British Council Collection; Chatsworth House Trust; Collection Ostrich Arts Limited; The Courtauld Gallery; Danny and Lisa Goldberg; Ferens Art Gallery: Hull Museums; The New Art Gallery Walsall, Garman Ryan Collection; Grosvenor Gallery; Harris Museum & Art Gallery; James Moores Collection; Jane and Kito de Boer; Kunsthaus Zürich; Laing Art Gallery; The Lambrecht-Schadeberg Collection at the Museum für Gegenwartskunst Siegen; Larry Gagosian; The Lewis Collection; Lord and Lady Irvine; Marlborough International Fine Art; Museum of London; The Museum of Modern Art, New York; Nottingham City Museums & Galleries; Pallant House Gallery; Piano Nobile; The Sarah Rose Collection at the London South Bank University; Southampton City Art Gallery; Touchstones Rochdale; The Whitworth, The University of Manchester; Victoria & Albert Museum and Victoria and Warren Miro. We would also like to thank the following institutions who have facilitated the inclusion of artworks currently on loan to them: Casa das Histórias Paula Rego, Irish Museum of Modern Art and Art Gallery of New South Wales.

Many individuals have provided vital contributions to this exhibition through their generous support, advice, encouragement, help with the loans, criticism and research: Catarina Alfaro, Susan Almrud, Jamie Anderson, Paula Aparício, Jake Auerbach, Kate Austin, Oliver Baker, Tracy Bartley, Rebekah Bowling, Charles Bradstock, Ivor Braka, Aude Breusse, Melanie Clore, Cristina Colomar, Tommaso Corvi-Mora, Thomas Dane, David Dawson, Gautier Deblonde, Andrew Dempsey, Emmanuel Di Donna, Esti Dunow, Lisa Edwards, John Erle-Drax, Manuel Fontán del Junco, Georgia Georgallas, Lily Goldberg, Clare Hallin, Martin Harrison, James Holland-Hibbert, Timothy Hyman, Daniel Katz, Christina Kennedy, Theresa Kneppers, Carolin Leistenschneider, MJ Long, Val Long, Lizzy McInnerny, Julie Milne, Richard Nagy, David Nash, Pilar Ordovas, Geoffrey Parton, Justin Paton, Steve Pilkington, Chantelle Pinkerton, Steve Pocklington, Anne Purkis, Andrea Rose, Paul Rousseau, Georgina Rumbellow, Anders and Yukiko Schroeder, Piers Secunda, Nicholas Serota, Rachel Taylor, Robert Travers, Maurice Tuchman, Virginia Verran, Mercedes Vilardell, Alice Whitehead, Oliver Wick, Diana Willkie and Cassie Young. Special thanks are due to Vivienne Lewis and Victoria Miro for their exceptional support. I am personally indebted to Catherine Lampert and Chris Stephens for being so generous in sharing their knowledge, and for their advice and encouragement.

I am grateful to Andrew Brighton, Charlotte Mullins and Gregory Salter for their commitment to the project and the insightful essays they have contributed to the catalogue. Their texts offer compelling and imaginative ways of rethinking and looking with fresh eyes at the works presented in the exhibition and the many relationships connecting specific artworks and artists. Complementing the essays are the short texts on the different sections of the exhibition, for which thanks are due to Katie Campbell, Laura Castagnini, Emma Chambers, Priyesh Mistry and Hattie Spires.

I would also like to thank colleagues from across Tate. As always, an exhibition of the scale of *All Too Human* is only possible because of the vital contribution of highly committed and knowledgeable colleagues from all areas of activities. A special thank you is due to a changing team of assistant curators, each person having brought new energy, passion and insight to the project: Rachel Rose Smith, Hattie Spires and Laura Castagnini. Thank you also to Zuzana Flašková, Curatorial Assistant, and Katie Campbell, who worked on the project as an intern, for their dedication and initiative; and to Kiko Noda, Exhibition Registrar, whose work has been invaluable in managing the complex network of international loans, transportation and insurance. We are indebted for their vital support to Carolyn Kerr, Head of Programme Management, and Gillian Buttimer, Programme Manager. We would also like to express our gratitude to Rebecca Hellen and Helen L. Smith in Conservation; Kate Parsons, Christopher Higgins and Sanne Klinge in Collection Care; Kirsteen McSwein and Sophie Nibbs in Interpretation; Adrian Glew, Darragh O'Donoghue and Victoria Jenkins in Archives; Alessandra Serri in Copyright and Legal; Abi Laughton, Lara Kingsbeer and Georgina Ramkoleea in Marketing; Nicholas Bennett from Design; Cecily Carbone from Press; Lily Bonesso and Saskia Mercuri from Tate Digital; as well as to Joseph Kendra, Isabella Nimmo and Sandra Sykorova, who have put together a stimulating public programme. Special thanks are also due to Liam Tebbs, Juleigh Gordon-Orr, Andy Sheil and the art installation team, as well as to many more colleagues than can be named fully here, in Photography, Advocacy and Events, and Visitor Experience. Thanks are due to Peter Dawson and his team at Grade for their elegant design of the catalogue. The production of the catalogue has been managed with great dedication and distinctive good humour by Emma Poulter as Project Editor, as well as Tate Publishing colleagues Bill Jones, Roz Hill and Emilia Will.

A special thank you to the artists and colleagues who have engaged in the selection of the work and in many discussions pertaining to the overall rationale of the exhibition and its many limits. A group exhibition of this scale, with all its ambitions and constraints, will always fail in its ability to adequately represent the breadth and range of works produced by exceptional artists over sustained careers, while many other important and accomplished painters could have been included. My hope is that the exhibition will provide memorable encounters with individual pictures and stimulate visitors' desire to see more, to feel more.

Elena Crippa
Curator, Modern and Contemporary British Art, Tate

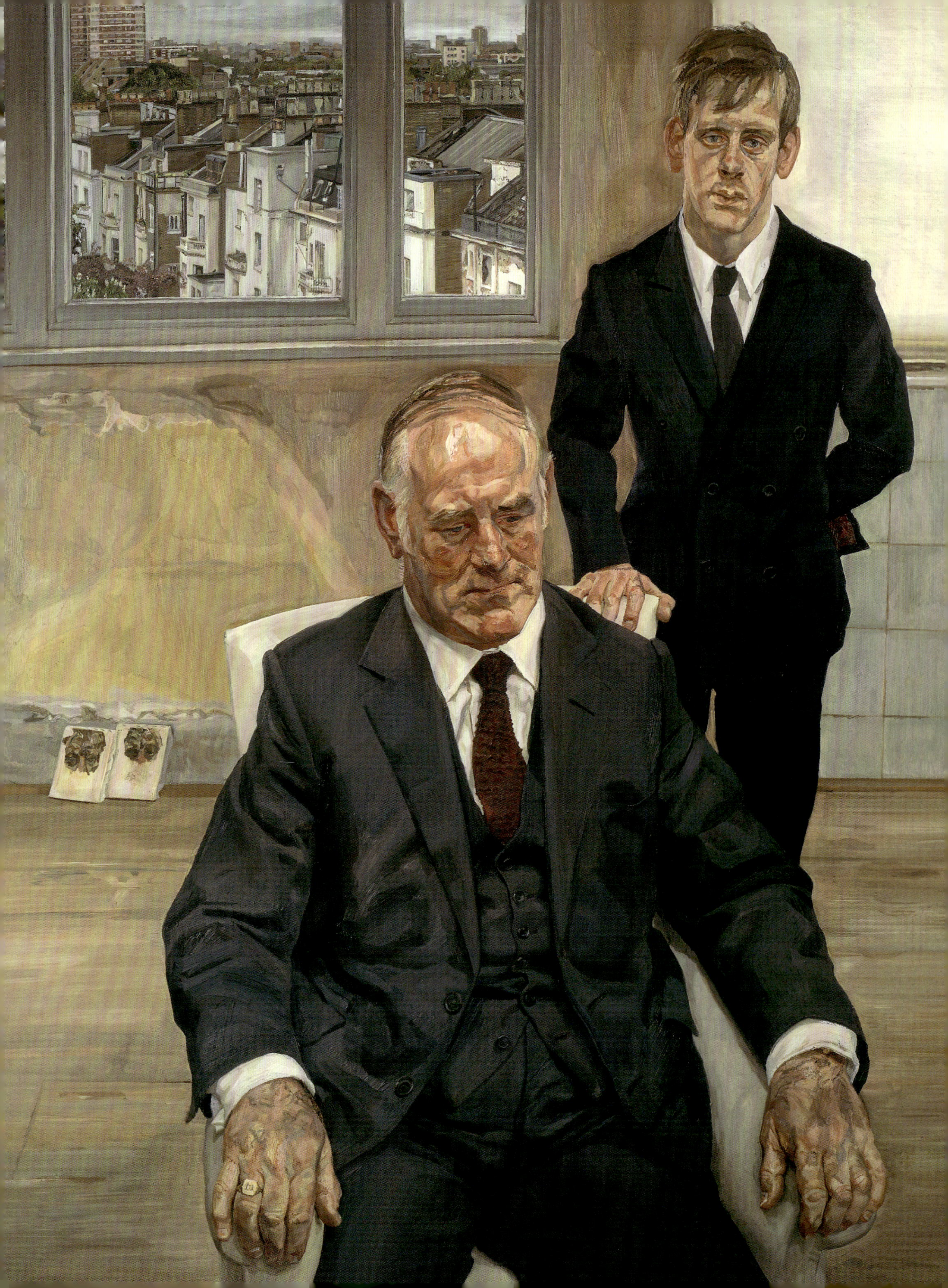

The Embodied Life of Painting
Elena Crippa

Lucian Freud
Two Irishmen in W11 1984–5
(detail)
Oil on canvas
172.7 × 141.6
Private collection

'Everywhere he looked, even at those things and thinkers supposedly representing the pride of our culture and the zenith of humanity, what he saw was not only far from divine but all-too-human.' [1]

This is the way in which the philosopher Richard Schacht summarises Friedrich Nietzsche's thinking at the time of the writing of his seminal book of aphorisms, *All Too Human* 1878. Although the German philosopher continued to yearn for a higher humanity, for a 'free spirit' to emerge from a world lacking in transcendental meaning, he came to realise that any philosophical investigation had to take as a starting point the examination of everything human, and all too human, which underpins our existence.

Nietzsche's sense of disjunction from any major transcendental belief and humanistic or philosophical system of knowledge has remained relevant ever since, and so has his desire to explore our existence by dissecting and scrutinising the raw and factual aspects of life. Since the second half of the nineteenth century, a parallel return to the appraisal of the experience of life in situation has also defined one of the most important chapters in the history of modern painting. It is this story and the way in which it unravelled in Britain that is explored here.

All Too Human is about painting, and takes as its starting point specific and personal facts of life treated with an unsentimental approach that eschews clichés; the result of probity and sustained physical and intellectual engagement. There are portraits of friends, lovers and relatives, and landscapes and cityscapes, mostly familiar places to which the painters return over and over again. There is also a more imaginative – but still real, intimately felt and urgent – representation of personal experiences and concerns, memories, past events, and personal drives and fears coming together to yield complex and powerful stories.

Gathered here are works from the early twentieth century to our time, either produced by artists based in Britain or, as in the case of Alberto Giacometti (1901–66) and Chaïm Soutine (1893–1943), by artists who were based across the Channel but whose work had a great impact on British artists. While the book attempts to represent most of the artists included through a range of their works, it is not representative of the entirety of their output, which was often accomplished over long and sustained careers. Instead, specific aspects, themes or periods of each artist's work have been selected, revealing a series of discrete but interlinked narratives. It also explores a constellation of associations through affinities and specific sources of inspiration, as well as contrasts, collisions and diverging ways of experiencing and rendering one's experience of the world.

While most of the work illustrated was made in the second half of the twentieth century, the first section (pp.66–81) serves as an introduction, presenting work by artists who were active primarily in the first half of the century and whose influence has endured: Walter Richard Sickert (1860–1942), David Bomberg (1890–1957), Stanley Spencer (1891–1959) and Chaïm Soutine. Other sections range from monographic and comparative to thematic presentations, two of which relate to the work as much as to the influential role of Bomberg and William Coldstream (1908–87) as teachers. The final section presents the work of a younger generation of artists and looks at the enduring influence of – as well as departures from – their predecessors' ways of painting: these are Celia Paul (b.1959), Cecily Brown (b.1969), Jenny Saville (b.1970) and Lynette Yiadom-Boakye (b.1977) (pp.194–205).

'To me, Art's subject is the human clay.' [2]
W.H. Auden

The main narrative that has so far framed the history of modern figurative British painting is that of the 'School of London', with Francis Bacon (1909–92), Lucian Freud (1922–2011), Leon Kossoff (b.1926), Michael Andrews (1928–95), Frank Auerbach (b.1931) and R.B. Kitaj (1932–2007) as its major actors.[3] The School of London brings together artists who, in the postwar period, were directly or indirectly linked by friendship and reciprocal admiration. Some of these relationships were important and long-lasting, as signalled by Bacon's many portraits of Freud (p.166), or Freud's portraits of Bacon and Auerbach (p.151), or Andrews's painting of the Colony Room drinking club, one of the venues in Soho where many of these painters used to meet regularly over nearly two decades (p.179). A selection of these paintings have been included here, as testament to the relationships they stand for and to the importance of the artistic milieu they shaped over at least two decades, from the early 1950s.

'It is no part of my claim that there will be no stories to tell after the end of art, only that there will not be a single metanarrative for the future history of art. There will not in part because the previous metanarratives excluded so much in order to get themselves told.' [4]
Arthur C. Danto

While acknowledged, the framing of the School of London is also exceeded. Favouring autobiographical connections over other aspects of the work and its context of production, it is inevitably a history of exclusion as much as inclusion. In particular, it excludes the work of a number of artists who – because of their different background, gender or ethnicity – have not been brought together under the same discourse. For instance, despite Francis Newton Souza's (1924–2002) prominence in Britain between the mid-1950s and the mid-1960s, his work – like that of many other exceptional artists and Commonwealth citizens who moved to the UK after the Second World War – has rarely been foregrounded in the history of modern British art.[5] This is despite the fact that Souza shared so many of the same references as other artists who have more readily been accepted as part of the canon, from his frequent visits to study historical examples of painting and sculptures in museums across Europe to his assimilation of the lessons of Picasso (1881–1973), Van Gogh (1853–90) and Soutine, among many others.[6] This book positions the work of Souza as central to the development of British art in the postwar period. Looking beyond the established narrative of the School of London enables us to explore new and compelling analytical approaches, as the essays here demonstrate.

The theoretical framework underpinning the very idea of the School of London, and more broadly of the strand of 'modern realism' promoted by the art critic David Sylvester, has primarily remained anchored to formalist art theory, in its lack of illustrational concerns, literary references, narrative approaches and psychological insight.[7] Many art critics and curators have installed a great gulf between the work of artists such as Auerbach and Bacon, seen as 'existentialist', and painting that is more explicitly narrative, as in the case of Kitaj or Paula Rego (b.1935).[8] *All Too Human* brings these different approaches together in the belief that they all offer a convincing and imaginative vision of a personal and intense experience of life. Their emphasis moves between perceptive experience and personal and social predicaments. The two are not seen as mutually exclusive, rather as part of the continuous range of our everyday experiences. They both pertain to the sensible and the organisation of the sensible into forms of visibility.

A very broad historical period is covered here, through which artworks have emerged from radically different historical moments. While there is no desire to look at the work as independent from the specific context in which it was made, certain aesthetic concerns are not necessarily tackled (and certainly not resolved) within a generation; they recur across generations and continue to occupy artists and fascinate onlookers. Furthermore, despite the dramatic social and cultural changes that have taken place between the early twentieth century and the present time, an awareness has endured that, under the circumstances set by modernity (of which we are still part), life is always under threat. The philosopher Judith Butler has observed that, under these very circumstances, 'loss, death and what deadens are too much with us, and that to feel the painting's impression on our skin is finally to receive the tactile at the limits of the visual – a triumph for what lives on despite the odds'.[9] As we shall see, beholding pictures of intimate life painted in an enlivened manner is not only an extremely rich aesthetic experience, there is also an ethical dimension, a reflection on prosaic interactions and – as part of them – of each individual's unique and responsible position.

'The plastic arts are gross arts, dealing joyfully with gross material facts.' [10]
Walter Richard Sickert

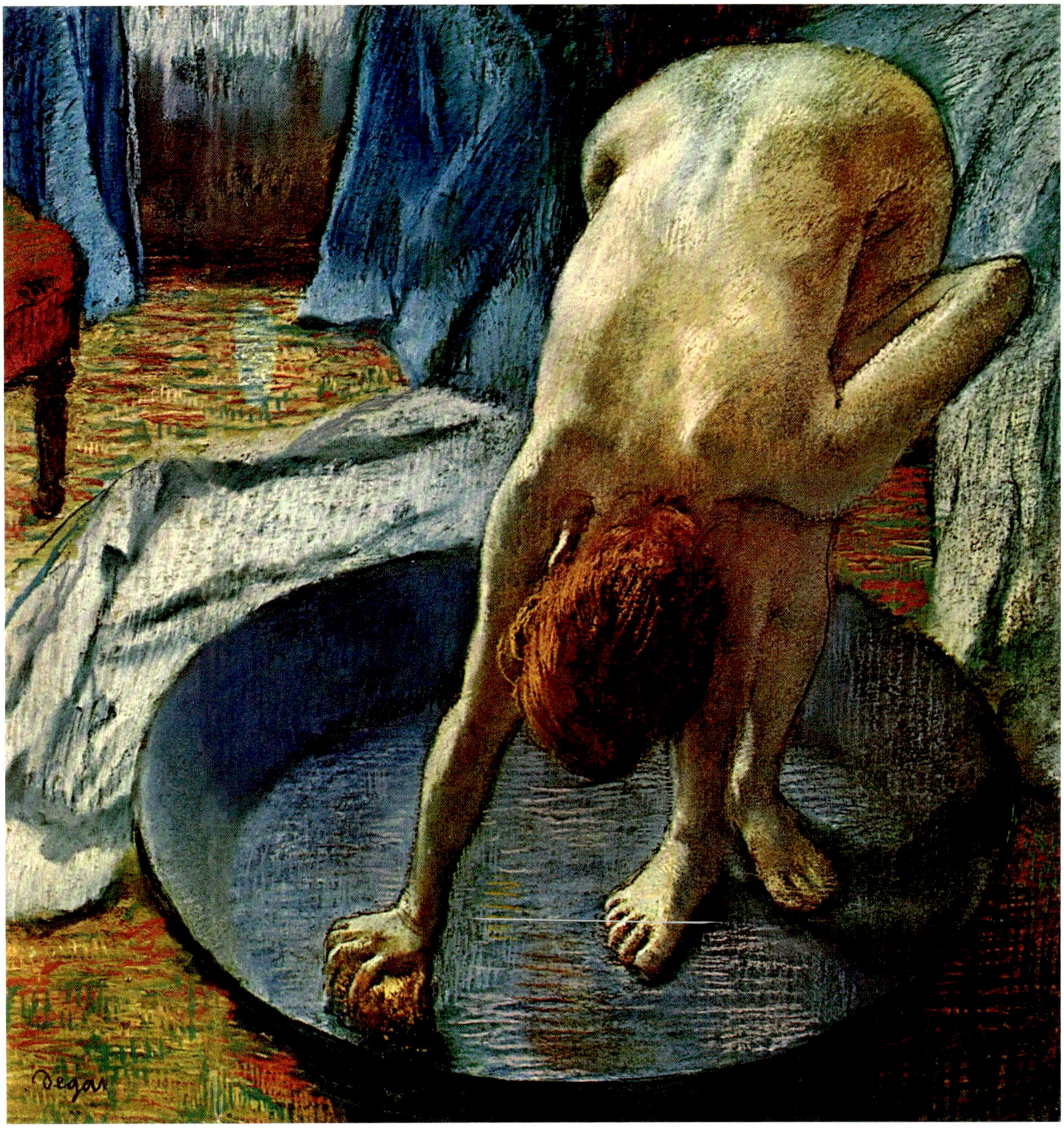

Edgar Degas
The Tub 1885–6
Pastel on blue-grey paper
69 × 69
Hill-Stead Museum – Farmington, Connecticut

'I never visualise a picture before I start. I have an impulse and I try to find a form for that impulse.' [11]
Frank Auerbach

In Britain, the long and multifaceted history of the modern engagement with the representation of life in all its force, enlivened and intensified, could be said to begin with Sickert's voyeuristic pictures of naked female bodies in humble London dwellings (pp.66, 69) and images of the public in music halls (p.70). This is not the modernity of impressionism, of the creation of modern urban myths around recreation, leisure, sexual pleasure and entertainment.[12] Despite the enduring markers of spectacle and consumption, Sickert's pictures belong to a re-engagement with realism that, across Europe – from Edgar Degas's (1834–1917)

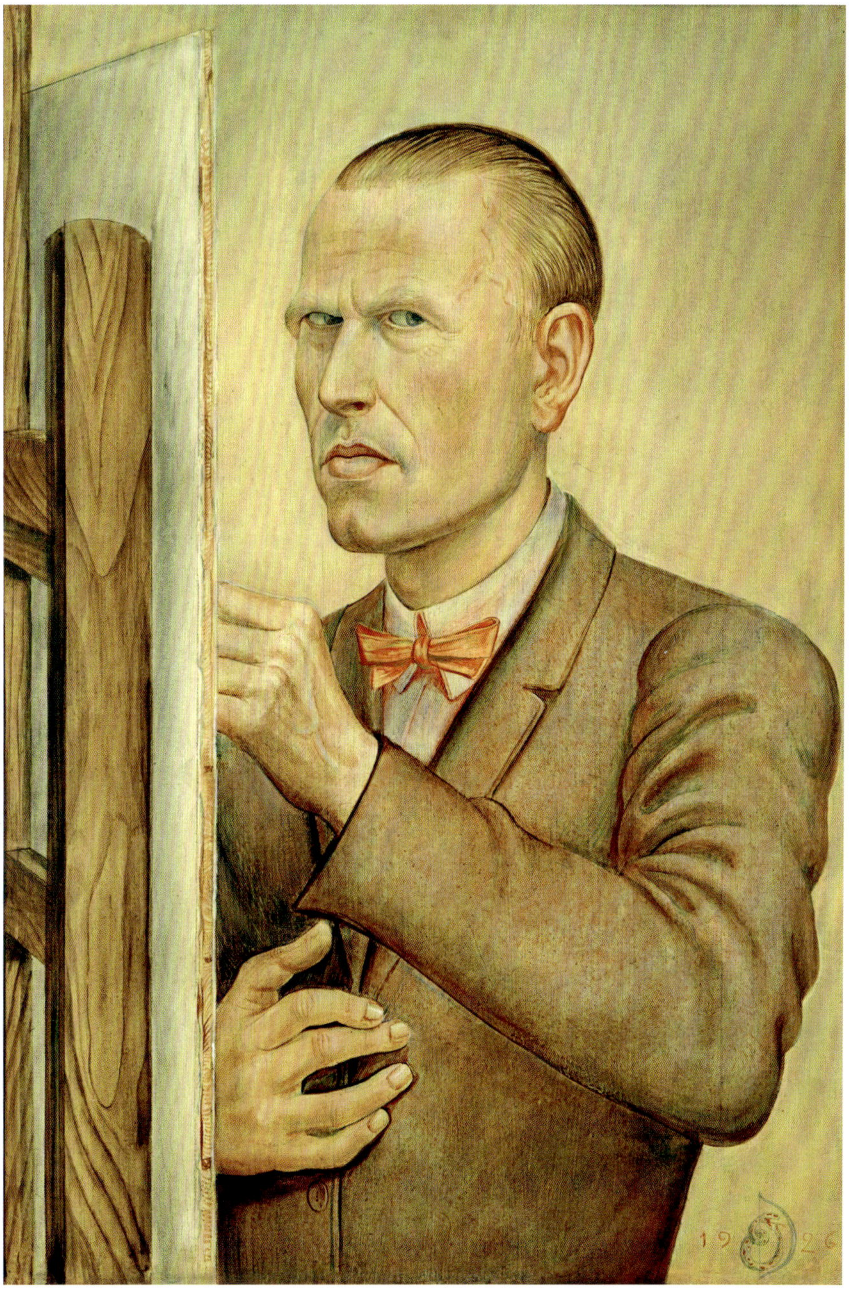

Otto Dix
Self Portrait with Easel 1926
Mixed media on plywood
80 × 55
Leopold-Hoesch-Museum,
Düren

interior scenes, viewed as if peering through a peephole (p.16), to Otto Dix's (1891–1969) abrasive portraits from the interwar period (above) – was defined by an unsentimental objectivity at least as much as by a deep fascination with the act of looking at and participating in the modern world. Spencer's work in portraiture, with its piercing, objective gaze, is also part of this narrative in which desire, voyeurism and surveillance are intertwined (pp.80–1). The same could be said of Lucian Freud's portraiture from the 1940s, the surveilling gaze of the painter registered in the responsive gaze of the sitter, interlocked in the enduring experience of each being exposed (p.104).

Although the term 'realism' has been used in a variety of ways to categorise a range of approaches and styles, in the context of this book it relates to the aim of reconstructing and healing the shattered image that, in cubism and other abstract idioms, was seen by many artists as leading to the loss of any factual, sharable reference.[13] Additionally, it retains a sense of the ordinary and familiar which seems productive in relation to the selection of works illustrated. As the art historian Linda Nochlin has written: 'on the whole, realism implies a system of values involving close investigation of particulars, a taste for ordinary experience in a specific time, place and social context; and an art language that vividly transmits a sense of concreteness'.[14] Nonetheless, 'realism' is here used as a conceptual anchor rather than a precise framing device. In its representation of life, the work of the painters featured ranges broadly between abstraction and more naturalistic executions. An inclination towards realism is also often balanced with a more or less pronounced tendency towards the allegorical and the imaginative, especially in the case of Kitaj and Rego but also in the work of Bacon, Freud and Souza.

'When I talk about sensuality in my own work, I'm very much thinking about the use of paint, the image and the whole action of painting.' [15]
Lynette Yiadom-Boakye

'I want the paint to work as flesh does.' [16]
Lucian Freud

As well as an attachment to the raw facts of life, and indistinguishable from that, at the heart of this selection of works is paint – primarily oil paint – and the way in which it is applied, accrued and moved around on the support. At times this is achieved by building up surfaces that look like substances. Many of the works, by artists as diverse as Soutine, Bacon, Kossoff, Freud and Brown, can be described in terms of the lush, visceral quality of the way in which paint is applied. In many of their works the interlocking of image and painterly gesture carries a sense of becoming, delivering elements of chance or accident that are nonetheless submitted to the control of the artist, often through a long process of marking, erasing, painting over previous executions or even scraping down the entire surface of the canvas in order to begin anew. Other artists, such as Coldstream, Uglow and early Freud, have built up paint slowly in a way that seems more meticulous and less prone to chance. Nonetheless, a sense of becoming is still intrinsically part of their process of making, through accrual, change and the recording of the evolution of the process over time. Both approaches bring together what the philosopher Gilles Deleuze has discussed as the painter's 'sensation' – their vital movement and temperament (and the object) as fact, place or event.[17]

In the 1940s and 1950s, Soutine and Giacometti proved particularly influential among British painters, their work appearing in private collections and exhibitions in London and Paris. The highly animated pictures with a rich impasto that Soutine produced between the two world wars, and the encrusted,

Francis Newton Souza
Mr Sebastian 1955
Oil paint on board
78.8 × 63.5
Kiran Nadar Museum of Art,
New Delhi

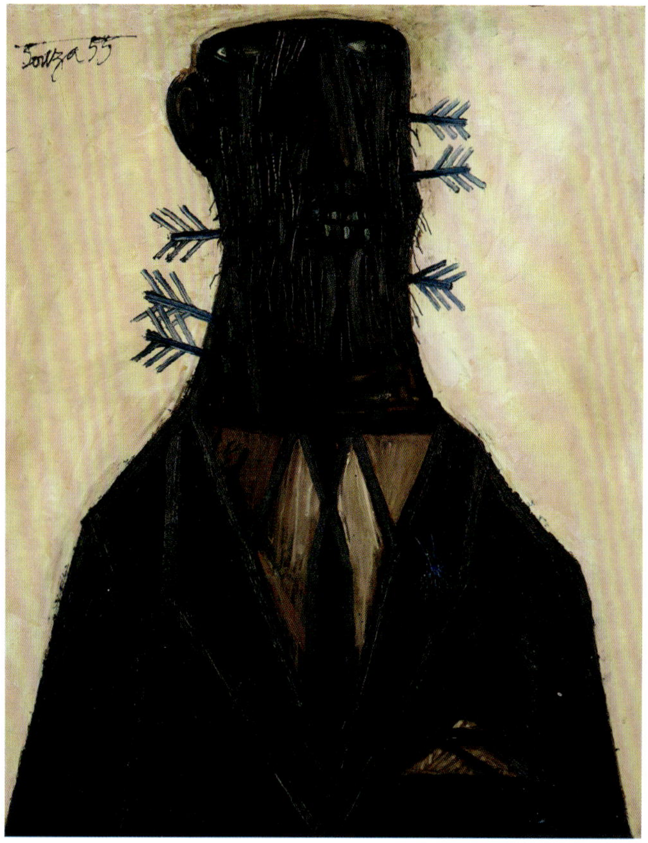

frail figures and heads that Giacometti sculpted through the handling of plaster, were the result of prolonged and intense sessions of working from life, always in the presence of the sitter. The works were manifestations of two equally powerful ways of expressing an intense experience – not just of seeing but also of feeling with one's touch and sense of spatial embodiment. From Bacon to Bomberg and many of his students at the Borough Polytechnic, the distortion of Soutine's figures and landscapes was not something artificially imposed, but the materialisation of an acutely felt sensation through its execution. In the postwar period Giacometti's work was also crucial as an embodiment of the values of existentialism, which shaped its early reception through the writing of the French philosopher Jean-Paul Sartre. Nietzsche's investigation of all-too-human facts of life was reconstituted in the belief that 'existence precedes essence' and in the need for individuals to take responsibility for their choices and actions, in the absence of given principles or beliefs.

If Sartre's variant of existentialism gained particular prominence, it is at least partially due to the way in which it resonated with the experience of the war. It called for a return to the individual's authenticity at a time inevitably defined by the angst and sense of isolation caused by years of systematic annihilation. Bacon and Giacometti have, since the early 1950s, been discussed as exemplary of the postwar, post-Hiroshima time. In many respects, this is also true of the work that many artists represented here produced in the postwar period, from Freud's early work in portraiture and still life (pp.104–9) to Souza's iconography of sainthood as a conduit for the portrayal of the experience of inflicted pain, solitude and endurance (above, pp.95, 101–2).

'In their traditional exhibitionist role women are simultaneously looked at and displayed, with their appearance coded for strong visual and erotic impact so that they can be said to connote to-be-looked-at-ness.' [18]
Laura Mulvey

Despite the thread that weaves through this book, much has changed in the past fifty years in the way we interpret and discuss specific forms of representation. The body, gaze and identity, so central to the themes explored, have been the object of groundbreaking work, particularly on the part of feminist theoreticians and art historians. Since the 1970s, seminal work has been done on the relationship between the construction of gender and the structuring of the gaze, from the art critic John Berger's famous statement that 'men act and women appear' to the film theorist Laura Mulvey's analysis of the passive role of the observed woman, as interdependent with the active role of the male subject.[19] The female nude – or rather the naked body, as per the art historian Kenneth Clark's distinction – passive and subjected to a number of patriarchal constructions, undoubtedly played an iconic role in modern art.[20] It reflected the fragmented and dislocated nature of modern urban life, at a time when industrialisation and the changing status of women under new forms of labour were re-shaping living conditions and gender politics.

As the art historian Griselda Pollock has pointed out, many of the works considered key in the development of modern art are defined by a particular treatment of the area of sexuality: as a commercial exchange.[21] In Sickert's *Nuit d'Été* c.1906 (p.66) and other nudes he painted in the first decade of the twentieth century, and Spencer's portraits of his second wife Patricia Preece (pp.80–1), it still seems that the naked model fulfils the tropes of modern art. Sickert's female subject can be identified with some of the emblematic roles of women in modern painting, such as the prostitute and the working-class girl. In the case of Spencer's pictures, Preece represents the traditional modern trinity of model, mistress and muse, her nudity linked to the painter's creativity and sense of alienation.

Yet, the enduring fascination for these pictures is at least partially due to the complexity and contradictory nature of the signs they inscribe.[22] As the art historian Lisa Tickner has pointed out, the naked female body in Sickert's paintings is also the painted model.[23] Sickert allegorises the relationship between painter and model, the artist identifying with the role of the woman/prostitute, at the hands of the market and at the mercy of the all-consuming activity of painting. Spencer's nudes of Preece are far from the fetishised, 'perfect' types, soliciting male desire. She is not portrayed as passive and defenceless but as knowing and confident. It is possibly in their unresolved narratives and lack of a simple, binary distinction between active, powerful subject and passive, recipient object, that the enduring power of these pictures resides. This is also the case for Francis Newton Souza's *Black Nude* 1961 (p.92) or Francis Bacon's *Portrait* 1962 (p.165), where the figures' faces are ravaged and their sexual organs exposed. Both Bacon and Souza's work of the time seems to share an inner tension between violence and sensuousness, with bodies becoming the sites of both love and abjection.

Importantly, the vast majority of portraits featured – by Spencer, Bacon, Auerbach, Freud, Kossoff and Uglow, all the way to Paul – are of people close to the artists; mostly friends, relatives or lovers, as well as self-portraits. These portraits are not just pictures but the result of an urgent need for contact, the meeting of two subjectivities.[24] In the work of Yiadom-Boakye, although her figures are fictional, the same longing for contact and exchange seems to define most of her 'portraits'. In other cases, following on from Judith Butler's anti-essentialist theory, whereby gender identity is performed in social contexts rather than a given, portraits are often the result of intimate exchanges – where public identity may differ from the identity acted out and mediated by the painter. This is the case in Freud's tender portraits of Leigh Bowery, famous for his outlandish costumes and performances (p.156), or the figure of the businessman, seen in the painter's studio in the absence of the props and context that confer his role and power (pp.152–3).

'Ever since the age of twelve, I have drawn and painted London ... the strange ever-changing light, the endless streets and the shuddering feel of the sprawling city linger in my mind like a faintly glimmering memory of a long-forgotten, perhaps never experienced childhood, which, if rediscovered and illuminated, would ameliorate the pain of the present.' [25]
Leon Kossoff

The paintings in *All Too Human* are not simply defined by their subjects, which represent the intimate reality of the painters' lives; they are pictures that open a view of the world, making onlookers feel embedded within it. Often, this is achieved through the way in which the painter engages with their activity, as the philosopher Maurice Merleau-Ponty suggests, surrendering their body to the world and capturing things in becoming, in their transient nature.[26] If the human body is central to an exhibition dedicated to the rendering of a sensuous, embodied experience of reality, the same can be said of some painters' landscapes or cityscapes. Soutine, Bomberg, Auerbach and Kossoff, in different ways, have all created pictures as the epitome of an embodied situated experience; the painter operating from within the field of experience rather than inspecting it from afar.[27] In their views of hilltops and streets, scenes are enveloped by the continual opening and re-opening of space, the result of being and operating from within the world.

While Soutine only painted in situ, Bomberg and later Auerbach and Kossoff tended to make numerous drawings of the same view before returning to the studio and working on the painting. The resulting pictures are sedimentations of different temporalities, while the act of painting inscribed in the work – through the accumulated layers of paint, visible brushwork or dripping paint – allows the

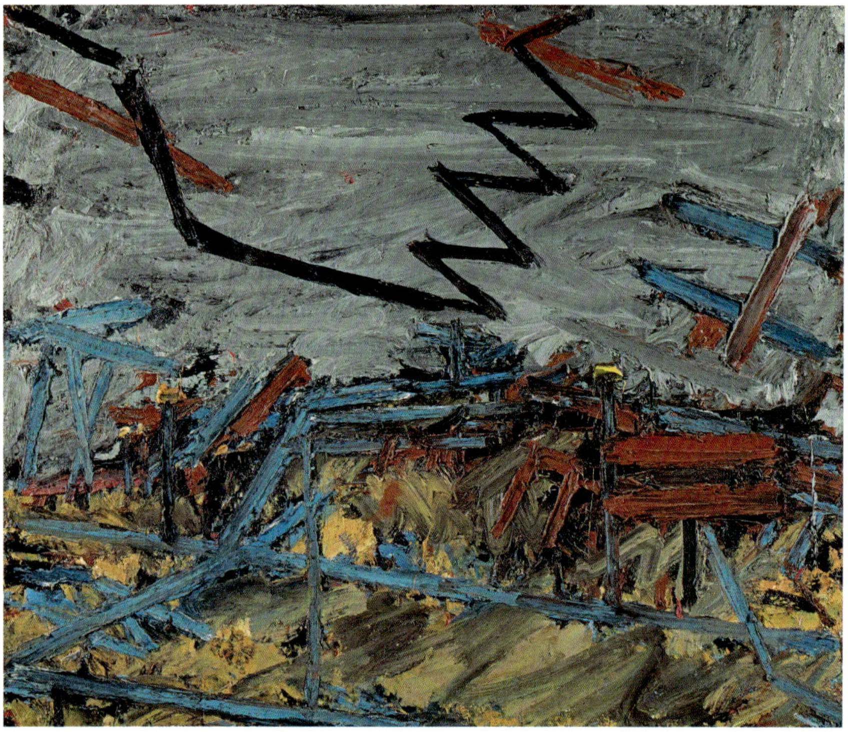

Frank Auerbach
Primrose Hill 1967–8
Oil paint on board
121.9 × 146.7
Tate. Purchased 1971

finished image to retain the sense of change that we experience when inhabiting the world (above, pp.124–39). The eye of the artist and the perceived environment are interlocked, and it is as such that they can be experienced in the final picture. The organic, living singularity of the event of perceiving a specific scene at a particular moment is also understood through its changing nature over time. Rather than pure presence and a sense of totality, we find ourselves experiencing a place that is mutating in time, and is always partial.[28] For as much as we may want to find an essence of people and places, it can only be reduced to a range of appearances encompassing the present, memories and anticipations.

'I think that, if I have the presence of the image there, I am not able to drift so freely as I am able to through the photographic image.' [29]
Francis Bacon

While most of the artists discussed so far primarily drew and painted from life, others reanimated the mechanically reproduced image through the treatment of paint, stretching the expressive potential of the medium. Souza worked extensively from photographs, which often acted as the starting point for an image. Towards this end, he kept and constantly added to a large collection of photographs cut from publications, particularly magazines.[30] He often combined images of places he had known through his extensive travelling into a unified picture, so that the same landscape could include elements seen in Bombay, Barcelona and Rome (pp.98–9).[31] Similarly, Bacon drew from a large range of reproductions that he accumulated over time, of paintings, sculptures, photographs and film stills taken from books, magazines and newspapers, as well as commissioning new portraits by photographers he respected, particularly John Deakin.[32] Both Souza and Bacon combined fragments of images in unified pictures, enabling disparate and at times contradictory ideas and temporalities to come together. In the case of Bacon, the use of photographic sources also enabled him to create the illusion of movement, obtained by condensing in one image different aspects of expressive bodily movements that could not possibly be visible simultaneously. This applies particularly to his mature work, for example, *Triptych 1974–77* (pp.170–1), in which the figure of Bacon's late lover, George Dyer, is seen in three different positions that provide a sense of enlivened dynamism, in dialogue and yet contrasting with the two head and shoulder portraits in the central panel.

'Stories are just as important as if they existed in reality; it makes no difference.' [33]
Paula Rego

A fear of content, of the experienced reality breaching into painting as a self-sufficient and self-referential object, marked one of the most extreme developments of the modern movement, with its influence felt well into the 1970s and beyond. While modernism repelled literary references, which it perceived as illustrative and as such inferior to painting as a formal exploration of its own internal development, there were contemporary ways of thinking that pointed in a different direction. Writing in 1950, the psychoanalyst and writer Marion Milner argued that drawings and paintings could embody both a form of knowledge or reflection on one's specific human situation, and an experience with a medium. For Milner, art could be the expression of 'thinking in the private language of one's own subjective images, as against thinking in the public language of words'.[34] She described 'statements in pictures' as follows: 'not only did they bring so much of the past into a single moment of present experience, they also embraced a wider range of bodily experience than intellectual verbal statements can'.[35]

Among the artists who, with very different ends, adopted a similar approach in their work are Andrews, Kitaj (pp.176–85) and Rego (pp.186–93). Since their early work in the 1950s and 1960s, they not only brought a constellation of disparate, fragmented elements into their images, borrowing from both topical images and the work of the masters, but also took inspiration from a variety of stories, as captured in newsreels, historical accounts and literary texts. Over various periods of their careers, they worked on large-scale figure compositions, unleashing their imaginative vision of life to explore inter-subjective relationships as part of their existentialist, socio-political or feminist concerns. They were, in different ways, preoccupied with human relationships – with the way in which men and women interact as part of small communities or public gatherings; or, more broadly, with the way in which their identities are shaped by historical and socio-political constraints.

In their own, very different, ways Andrews, Kitaj and Rego incorporated into their work both the physical reality of objects and the less material, but in no

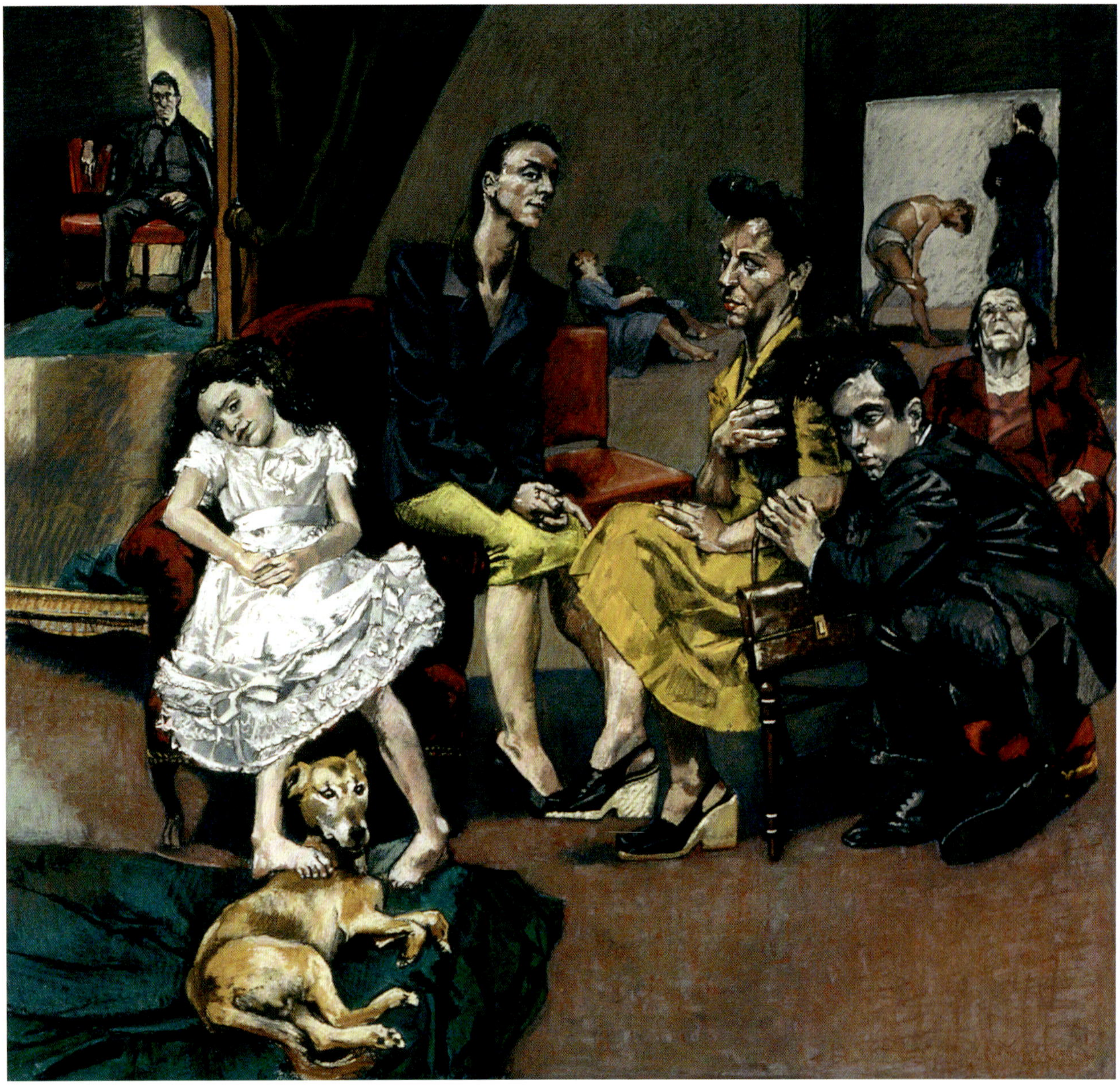

way less present, reality of memories and drives, felt and painted as part of one's physical reality. The men and women they painted vividly, with their expressive postures and gestures, as if coming to life, are inserted in exchanges that move from the ethical plane of the individual figure to the political sphere of human interaction. They do not only explore how we can be with one another, but how we may want, or be able, to live together.

As the artist and writer Timothy Hyman has remarked, Rego, as well as producing enticing and daring pictures, has played a key role: as a role-model for the many female painters who, from the 1970s onwards, had abandoned painting as a masculine activity; and as a leading painter who was able to reclaim the right to paint confessional and imaginative pictures, without fearing the backlash against illustrating and telling stories.[36] Nochlin has discussed the major role that female painters have played, particularly through portraiture, in subverting the laws of modernism through their 'talents as seismographic recorders of social

Paula Rego
The Betrothal: Lessons: The Shipwreck, after 'Marriage a la Mode' by Hogarth 1999 (detail)
See pp.192–3

position, as quivering reactors to the most minimal subsurface psychological tremor'.[37] In different ways, Brown, Paul, Saville and Yiadom-Boakye, as much as Rego, are continuing to pursue this endeavour (pp.194–205).

Brown and Saville extend the identification of paint as flesh and the body, key to the work of Soutine, Bacon, Freud and many others. Brown consistently refers to a range of works by modern and old masters, unmissable for example in *Boy with a Cat* 2015 (p.201), which playfully refers to and subverts Manet's *Olympia* 1863. In this and other paintings by Brown, a voyeuristic urge meets bodies whose physical boundaries are porous, part of a scene in which objects seem to dissolve and mutate. The act of looking becomes an act of searching and experiencing a range of conflicting and coexisting sensations and emotions – from arousing to humorous and unnerving.[38]

In the self-portraits of Bomberg (p.76), Kossoff (p.133) and Freud (p.144), the artists paint themselves gazing boldly ahead, representing their features as much as their daring and uncompromising artistic quest. These paintings belong to a long tradition that encompasses numerous self-portraits by Rembrandt (1606–69), Pierre Bonnard (1867–1947) and Pablo Picasso (1881–1973). Saville's larger-than life self-portrait, *Reverse* 2002–3 (pp.198–9), does not shy away from entering in to dialogue with such an established tradition, taking on a bold and confrontational stance. And yet, at the same time, the head lying on a sheet of glass, the parted lips, the dark and fleshy tones used for the skin, as if revealing hints of her insides, contribute to a sense of frailty and vulnerability.

Paul's *Painter and Model* 2012 (p.194) seems to allude to her experience as a sitter of many portraits – see, for example, Freud's *Painter and Model* 1986–7 (p.64), in which she appears standing as the painter, brush in hand, the naked male model lying in front of her.[39] It also speaks of the activity of the painter, who is at once both aware of the need for solitude and yet longs for close relationships, attentive to the feeblest nuances of one's rich psychological realm. Little prepares viewers for the intense and intimate encounter with Paul and Yiadom-Boakye's figures, often depicted in a bare or sparsely defined environment, their self-absorption and state of semi-suspension adding to the intensity of the encounter. The uncertainty of Yiadom-Boakye's figures – their roles, position and setting – adds a particular complexity, and calls for an understanding of identity that reflects our contemporary world: as manifold and resisting being closed down into tight definitions.

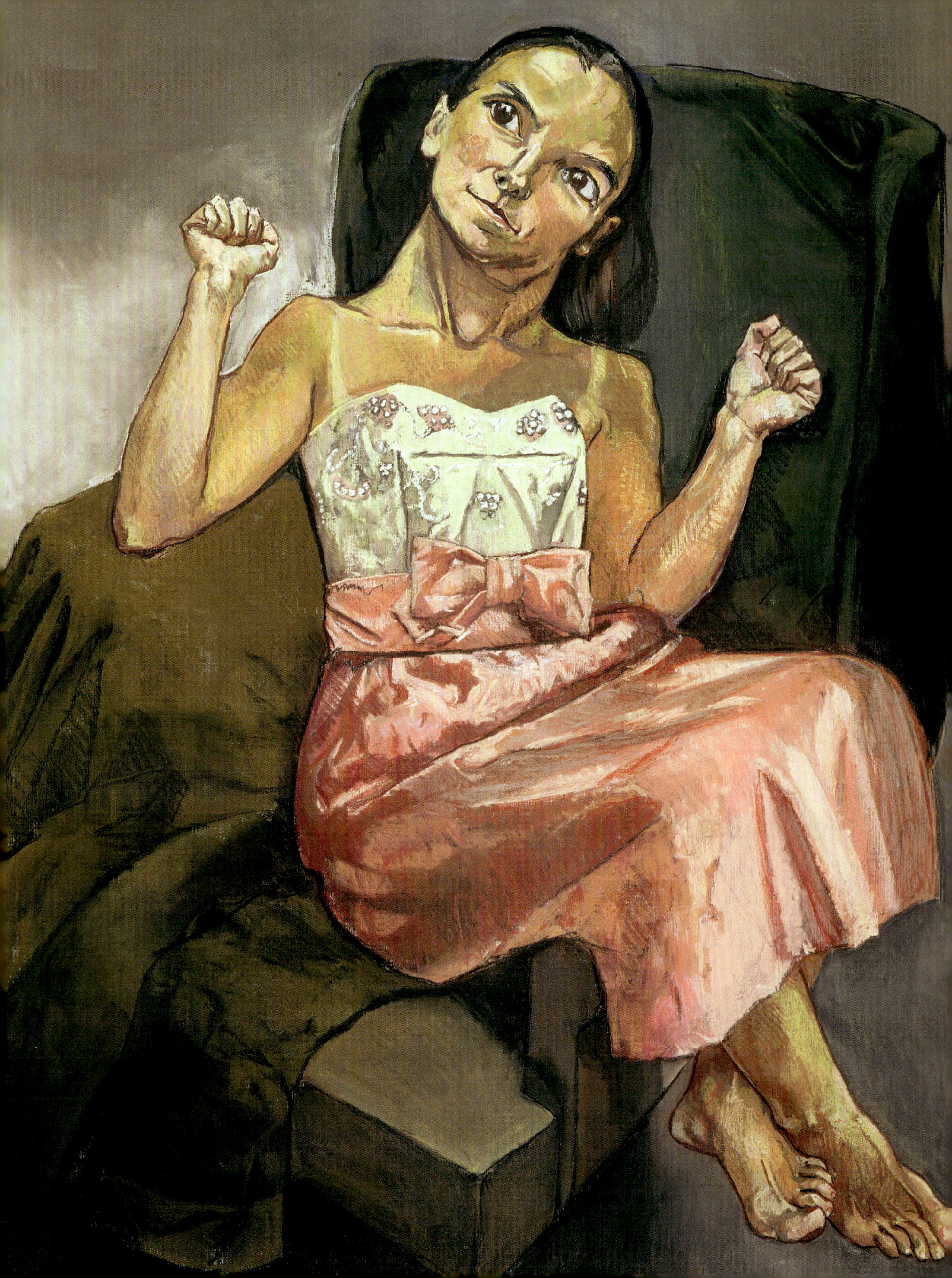

London: Painting in the Time of Modernist Art
Andrew Brighton

'The fate of our times is characterized by rationalization and intellectualization and, above all, by the disenchantment of the world. It is not accidental that our greatest art is intimate and not monumental.' [1]
Max Weber

For the avant-garde in the late nineteenth century the question was no longer 'is this beautiful?' – it became 'is this art?'. 'From this moment on, it was art that was at stake rather than beauty within art.'[2] So argues Thierry de Duve, in *Kant after Duchamp*. If artists address the question of art, then this is an exhibition without artists. It is an exhibition of painters who address the problematics of painting.

There is another related characteristic that links the paintings at the core of *All Too Human*: they do not belong in a curated more-or-less chronological hung exhibition in a public art gallery. The sensibility, the way of making and the kind of attention incited by these paintings, comes from a time before the postwar development of public contemporary art galleries; a time when art historians concerned themselves with dead artists and a curator was a superintendent in charge of a zoo, an archive or an historic museum collection. The places for contemporary painting and sculpture were private, and the art economy depended on purchases made for homes and shared private spaces: clubs, boardrooms and senior common rooms.

At the end of the nineteenth century, the London art market was slow to adopt the Continental idea of *oeuvre*; the idea that a work is to be seen as part of the total body of an artist's production, each work a sentence, paragraph, page or chapter in the story of the artist's development, which is in turn a part of art's larger narrative. Such a view assumes a supervisory discourse: texts and museums that tell the story in which the work features. German public museums and critics pioneered the historicist account of modern art. Against this, in 1933 the British art critic Roger Fry criticised German scholarship as attending to artworks 'almost entirely from a chronological point of view, as coefficients of a time sequence, without reference to their aesthetic significance'.[3] The German model was, however, the model that the American art historian Alfred H. Barr Jr took in creating the exemplar Museum of Modern Art in New York City.

In the German model, the competent art world participant knew about art; they knew the supervisory discourse, and they knew the place of a work within the bigger story. Meanwhile the competent art world participant in Britain was a connoisseur of paintings or sculpture; they distinguished qualitatively between the particular works. For them, each painting had to carry its own aesthetic justification; it had to be its own story. The supervisory discourse of art and what it includes in its pantheon we have come to call modernism, and the best name we have for our local anomalous family is the School of London.

Paula Rego
Dog Woman – Moth 1994
(detail)
Pastel on canvas
160 × 120
Private collection

Kitaj's polemic

R.B. Kitaj, an American painter living in London, deployed 'School of London' in the catalogue to *The Human Clay*, the exhibition he curated for the Arts Council of Great Britain in 1976.[4] 'The bottom line is that there are artistic personalities in this small island more unique and strong and I think numerous than anywhere in the world outside America's jolting vigour.' He went on to say that 'given a fraction of the internationalist attention and encouragement reserved in this barren time for provincial and orthodox vanguardism, a School of London might become even more real than the one I have constructed in my head. A School of real London, England, in Europe...' Kitaj's catalogue essay is written in an 'it seems to me' style. It is a polemic nevertheless, with blood on its knuckles. For instance, his 'provincial vanguardism' carries an accusation that the British art given the most critical and curatorial attention is merely an echo of movements and tendencies that have their origins elsewhere.

Kitaj enlisted paintings and drawings in *The Human Clay* to challenge an enemy: a professional orthodoxy, modernism. It would be difficult or simply irrelevant to place the drawings and paintings he chose in the chronological development of art exemplified in 1976 by the Museum of Modern Art in New York and its mediocre echo at the then Tate Gallery in London.[5] The pre-eminent American art critic Clement Greenberg attributed the aesthetics of modernism to the 'quest for the empirical and positive'. Art looks for its resources of conviction, he said, 'in the same direction as thought'. It was the rise of positivism that gave rise to our 'increasing faith in and taste for the immediate, the concrete, the irreducible'. Pictorial space becomes purely an optical sensation – as, say, in a Mark Rothko painting. Rationalised by curators, this taste became an evolutionary hanging, a progression from impressionism to abstract expressionism and beyond, each work an illustration of the movement towards pictorial non-illusion. What Greenberg's account entails, however, is that there was more at stake than taste, painting or art. To challenge modernism was to resist the dominant positivist modes of thought.

The painters in *All Too Human* sometimes labelled, branded, marketed and collected as the School of London have in common the use of painting's traditional pictorial devices. Herbert Read could assert in 1951 that 'for a painter to ignore the discoveries of a Cézanne or a Picasso is equivalent of a scientist ignoring the discoveries of an Einstein or a Freud'.[6] In his view, these painters were pictorial reactionaries. The means used were often the same as those of the traditionalist paintings to be found on the walls of the Royal Academy Summer Exhibition: colour resembles the local huc of flesh and things; tones from light to dark model form; forms derive from observation, directly from the subject, or from drawings or photographs. To make pictorial space they exploit that enchantment, that irrational compulsion of perception to see in marks on a surface the likeness of things in the world, and to feel and reflect on images as if they were people and things. What distinguished their work from traditionalist painting is that their paintings are reflective; in their various ways they make pictorial enchantment uneasy. If traditionalist paintings offer a happy bridge between pleasing pictorial conventions and things, these paintings offer things figured out of de-habituated devices. They paint in and against disenchantment. Even if these artists paint as if cubism never happened, they do paint in the knowledge that Nietzsche declared that God is dead and thus upon humankind falls the terrible burden of self-creation. Frank Auerbach, for instance, when asked about the relation of his work to international art, wrote:

> I cannot answer these questions because they seem impertinent to my situation. I think of painting as something that happens to a man working in a room, alone with his actions, his ideas, and perhaps his model. He is affected by his circumstances, and by the standards and events of his time, but he seems to me to be the sole coherent unit.[7]

It is a Nietzschean reply. In a world empty of meaning, cultural, social, economic and political life is merely the playing out of given roles. Against this backdrop, the artist creates an authentic self. The 'sole coherent unit' in Auerbach's image is the heroic painter, who rejects the loss of integrity inherent in the bad faith of social and institutional expectations.

School of London?

Modernism claimed to be international, which in the postwar period meant the art dominant in the USA and echoed in the major NATO countries. One of the hopes in Kitaj's polemic was for the idea of a painting grounded in lives lived in a particular place: 'a School of real London, England, in Europe'. It was not only London that had anomalous painters, painters with strong artistic personalities working in conventional pictorial means. Consider, for instance, Giorgio Morandi, Aleksandra Deyneka, Balthus, Edward Hopper, Max Beckmann, Chaïm Soutine, Frida Kahlo, Alberto Giacometti, Ed Ruscha, Bhupen Khakhar and Gerhard Richter. The list could be much longer. What was particular to London? What might be the people, institutions and ideas, the local traditions of skill and sensibility, that inflected painting in London in the time of modernist art?

The realism of Edgar Degas and Édouard Manet, as conveyed to London by Walter Richard Sickert, was influential. Sickert's paintings at the turn of the twentieth century are uneasy and contrived. He refuses the viewer ease both by what he paints and the way he paints it. He puts on paint as if painting from life onto a dark canvas, but in practice he painted from and on drawings transferred onto a mid-toned canvas. He is a bravura filler-in. *The Studio: The Painting of a Nude* 1906 (p.69) is disconcerting. The arm of the painter looms in the foreground, and we see the mirror in which the painter looks at a model whose back is seen in another mirror. In *Noctes Ambrosianae* 1906 (p.70), caricatured faces like illuminated ghouls appear in the dark. It was not only French pictorial realism that was formative in Sickert's work. To take a phrase of the novelist and playwright Émile Zola, Sickert was an 'apostle of the gutter'. He was artist as jaundiced *flâneur* who observed *les fleurs du mal* beneath the city's propriety. In *Nuit d'Été* c.1906 (p.66) a naked woman indecorously sprawled on a crumpled bed with her bared genitals is used as the pictorial fulcrum. His work is too wanton, too unresolved, for easy assimilation to an international history of art.

Sickert is a patriarch who left a troubled inheritance, not least the core contradiction in his work: he was a painter of images who put paint on as if he painted from life. In his wake this anomalous family has two branches – painters of things and painters of images.

Painters of things: a mafia of mysteries

Art is a concept, painting is a practice; painting has mysteries. To be a serious painter requires intelligence to be initiated and constituted in a tacit knowledge of how paint can perform. It is the acquisition of a palette of the eye. The hand learns to move with unconscious certainty and the painter sees the world through an optic that feeds their imagery. The locus of these mysteries of painting was the Slade School of Fine Art in London. Retiring as Professor at the Slade in 1892, the French painter and sculptor, Alphonse Legros, famously accused English artists of painting by drawing and filling in.

When Legros left the Slade, Fred Brown – a co-Francophile and friend of Sickert's – was appointed, and he brought with him Henry Tonks and ways of drawing that came out of the French realism of Jean-François Millet, Jules Bastian-Lepage, Manet and Degas. It was a more linear, direct and analytic draughtsmanship than that which prevailed at other British art schools. Henry Tonks's influence was to dominate the Slade from the 1890s until he retired in 1926, and beyond. Via Tonks and by direct laying-on of hands or ideas there is an apostolic connection to Sickert among this family. Sickert taught David Bomberg, and William Coldstream attended his lectures. Tonks taught both of them, and Stanley Spencer. In turn Bomberg taught Dennis Creffield, Dorothy Mead, Frank Auerbach and Leon Kossoff. During Coldstream's reign as Principal and Professor at the Slade, Michael Andrews, Euan Uglow and Paula Rego were students, and Lucian Freud was a tutor.

Henry Tonks taught drawing, and drawing is taught by showing. Theory is as much use in learning to draw as it is in learning to swim or ride a bicycle – i.e., not much. Lynda Morris summarised Tonks's method, saying that he 'taught his pupils to draw the model at the size it was seen, measured at arm's length (sight

Henry Tonks
Annotated Demonstration Drawings and Study of a Girl's Head c.1908
Pencil and red chalk, with annotations in black ink on paper
38 × 25.3
UCL Art Museum, London

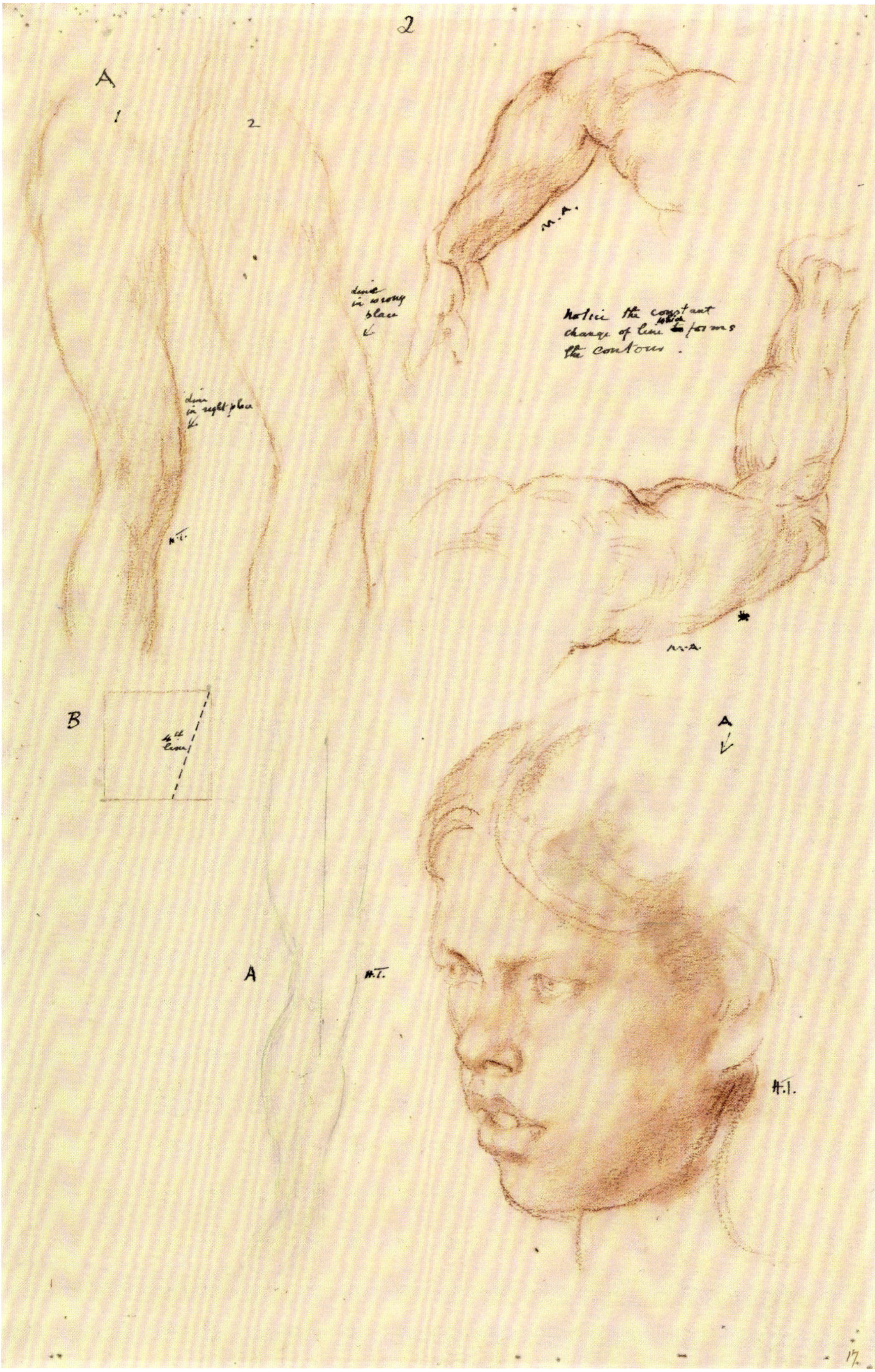
2
A
1
2
line in wrong place
M.A.
notice the constant change of line which forms the contours.
line in right place
H.T.
B
4th line
A
H.T.
M.A.
H.T.
17

size), which enabled them continually to correct the drawing for themselves, against a physical object'.[8] Tonks learned drawing at 'sight size' from Sickert.

The mysteries are then acquired by example not by principle, but Tonks did teach an ethic. To be an artist was a vocation, like being a priest. Drawing was not concerned with appearance, rather it should construct a truthful understanding of form: 'A bad drawing is like living with a lie.'[9] In Tonks's teaching, there was a residue of art critic John Ruskin's idea that by rendering nature accurately a higher spiritual order can be imparted. Painting and drawing as if they can reveal, show or create some order behind or beyond the appearance of things is the enabling assumption for these painters from life. Through this method the painting can take on a life of its own.

Drawing the one-eyed line

Our brains may contrive how we see, but sight shows us more than we can know or remember; not a parade of named things but a passing flood of sensate data. Tonks's solution, his method of drawing, is a way of seeing things as we do not see them. A draughtsman measuring the figure with a pencil at the end of an outstretched arm and conveying that measurement to a drawing to determine, for example, how long is a thigh in relation to the width of the hips, is acting as though the living, breathing model is motionless. Further, the artist draws or paints as if they were seeing with one static eye in a head as still as a camera on a tripod. Drawing as Tonks did, by the accumulation of increasingly decisive lines, there is a sense of motion made by the repeated traces of the chalk or pencil lead across the paper. But painting as if things have edges imparts a chill immobility.

In the 1930s Stanley Spencer made a series of paintings of his lover and eventual wife Patricia Preece. Acuity of observation is their dominant characteristic. His variations in hue and tone give her flesh its own illumination that reveals an imperfect body, delineated from context by hard-edged tonal contrast. Preece's pullover in *Patricia Preece* 1933 (p.80) and the ghostly stuffed black leather chair behind her in *Nude Portrait of Patricia Preece* 1935 (p.81) are without the light that illuminates the flesh. Likewise, in Lucian Freud's work the linear architecture holds the body immobile. Within the still body, skin is given a teeming painterly life of heightened hue and tone, a chafing sea of varicoloured flesh. Like a mind alone, absorbed in itself, the body is pictorially isolated. Only in the absence of flesh, as in *Two Japanese Wrestlers by a Sink* 1983–7 (opposite), or when the tonal contrast between flesh and context is minimal, as in *Girl in a Striped Nightshirt* 1983–5 (p.155), does the painting have an overall life. Spencer and Freud offer forensic images: disenchanted, fascinating, disgusting, beautiful.

Coldstream used Tonks's method of drawing, with its contradictions, to draw in paint. The game of measuring is explicit; small grid lines map the relative locations in the complex asymmetry of forms. As he put it, 'This process, I

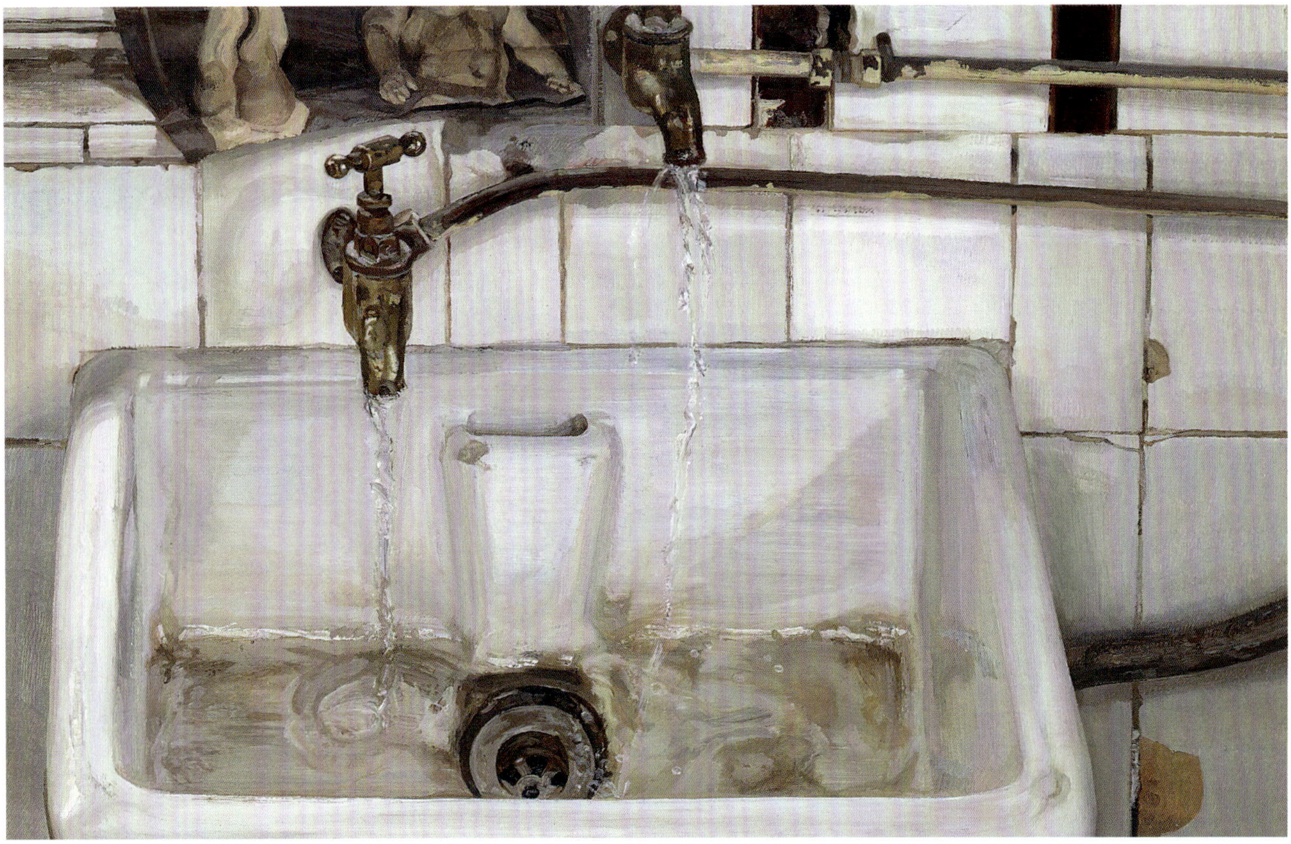

Lucian Freud
Two Japanese Wrestlers by a Sink 1983–7
Oil paint on canvas
51 × 78.3
The Art Institute of Chicago, Illinois

suppose, is to get something on the canvas you can believe in.'[10] The philosopher A.J. Ayer, a fellow professor at University College London, said Coldstream was the only logic positivist he ever met. Ayer's influential exposition of logical positivism, *Language, Truth, and Logic*, was published in 1936. He argued that statements about aesthetic or ethical values are meaningless; they can be neither logically necessary nor empirically verifiable. If the postwar generation was haunted by Nietzsche and existentialism, Coldstream in the late 1930s had to find a way of painting that held off a sense of meaninglessness and social irrelevance. He proceeded like a positivist whose rigorous intellection produces an unintended proof of metaphysical presence. The process of recording bodies and things as if they were inert can animate them; repeated measuring marks index change and approximation. Paint registering shifts in hue and tone becomes plastic; substantial form emerges as if a side-effect of the process. Coldstream paints as if he were just a method; however, the results are intimate, reflexive, tentative, sensual indexes of time embedded in attention to light, hue, place, objects and bodies.

If painting from life can be a means to a vivid pictorial autonomy, a kind of metaphysical presence, then Euan Uglow's paintings remain in the grip of the artist's will. Given fixity, suggestion of movement can be like the crash of a pin drop in a silent room. For instance, in *Georgia* 1973 (pp.116–17) the model would seem nailed in position, mapped in two dimensions. But the sensuality of colour heaves the figure into three dimensions: the cast of the shadows, the hem of the skirt, the red rings at the cuffs are almost diagrammatic renderings of rotundity. The perspective of the blue motif against which Georgia leans refutes flatness.

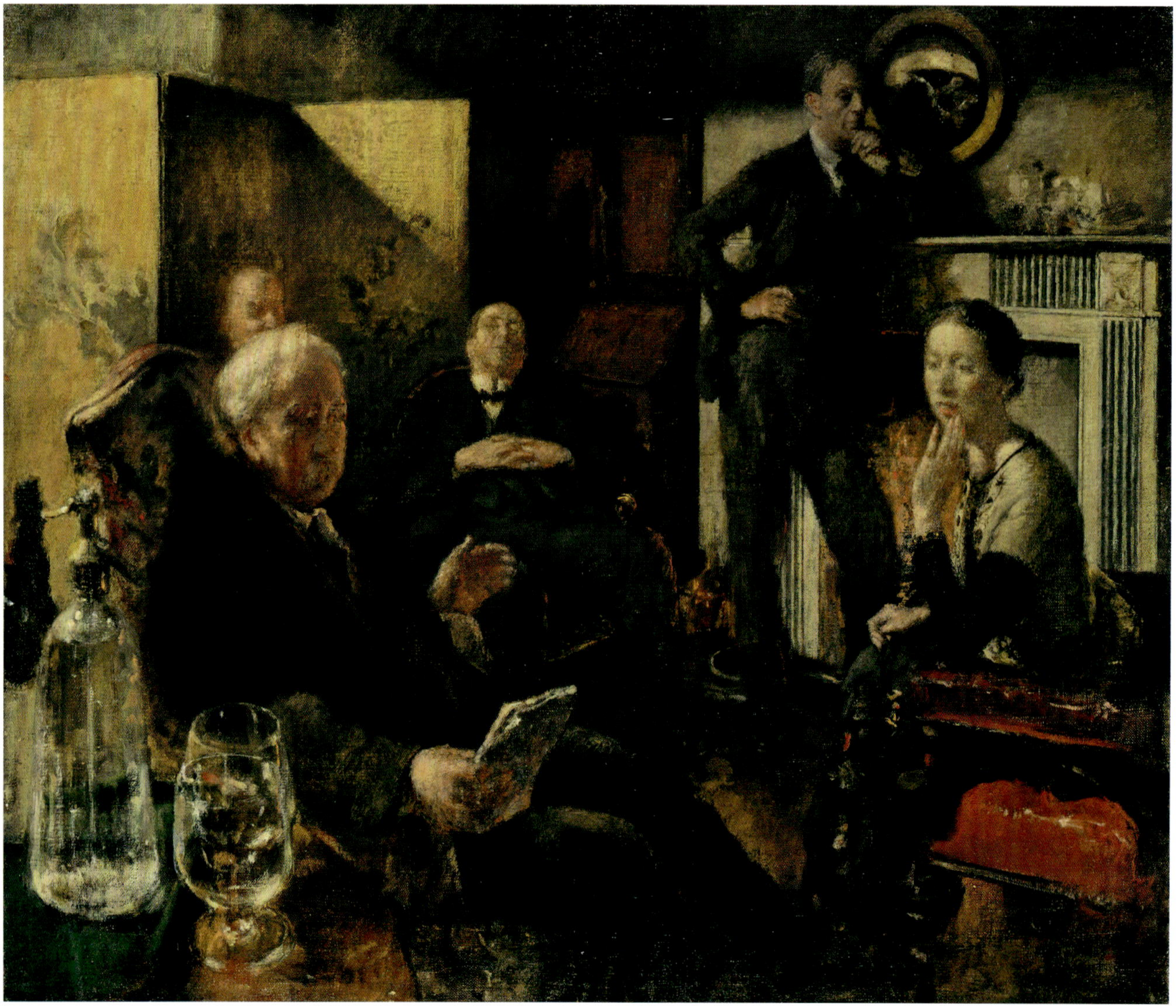

The spirit of the mass

Out of all of Tonks's ethical bombast there emerged paintings as rigorous and demanding as a pair of carpet slippers. He painted like a complaisant club-man; a skin of unfocused painting on a linear architecture (see above). Bomberg in his writing often acknowledged his debt to Tonks, but he was no clubbable painter – for him painting was a priest-like vocation to the point of self-martyrdom. Bomberg took Tonks's ethic beyond pictorial familiarity. He is truthful to the activity of seeing. His paintings record the motion of looking into the buzzing manifold of sight. We do not see a flat screen; there is the wandering centre of gaze surrounded by the blur of peripheral vision. Painting from multiple drawings that embed a sense of place, Bomberg has a still centre of attention. In *Evening in the City of London* 1944 (p.121) it is St Paul's Cathedral; in *The Bridge and the River Tajo, Ronda* 1935 (p.79), the architecture among the precipices. Around these focuses are peripheral energies. At one moment, the brush may describe a sloping plain, at the next the movement of the eye across forms like a blind man's thumb feeling a face, or it might then make an area of darkness. As with Bomberg's

Henry Tonks
Saturday Night in the Vale
1928–9
Oil paint on canvas
51.4 × 61
Tate. Bequeathed by
Sir William Orpen 1932

students, Dorothy Mead, Dennis Creffield, Frank Auerbach and Leon Kossoff, we are not offered a stable pictorial language. Bomberg often talked of working towards 'the spirit of the mass', and he attributed to both his subject and the desired end of his activity a metaphysical presence: 'Style is ephemeral – Form is eternal.' [11]

As I see it, the work of the painters of things aspires to win or lose on the strength of its pictorial transmutation of the activity of looking. It is anti-conceptual in that it valorises otherness; the space between the idea and the reality, between the concept and the dumb sensate presence of bodies and things. In this space it constructs pictorial comprehensions of this other: a comprehension justified by its power as painting and not by resemblance. It assumes a cultivated sensibility formed by past paintings. Time is ill-used reading art history or criticism that could be spent in the National Gallery looking at paintings. In that sense, it is ahistorical and textless. Before a Kossoff or an Auerbach or the other students of Bomberg I would want to gesture to an enquiring companion in silence – it would take a ballet of gesticulations to suggest the complex spatial animations that constitute the chords in these concerts of pictorial form.

Painters of images: figured words

'Speaking for my own life in art, Bacon is arguably the finest painter alive,' wrote Kitaj in his *Human Clay* essay. Bacon and Kitaj are history painters – that is to say, their imagery is informed by literature in two senses. They take from and allude to literary imagery, and we can partly unpack our experience of the work by interpreting their images.

Bacon told David Sylvester in an interview, 'I always feel I've been influenced by Eliot. *The Waste Land* especially and the poems before it have always affected me very much.'[12]Among the books left after his death are four about and one by Ezra Pound: *Literary Essays of Ezra Pound* 1968, edited with an introduction by T.S. Eliot. 'An "Image" is that which presents an intellectual and emotional idea complex in an instant of time,' wrote Pound. Bacon spoke of making images rather than of making paintings, and wanted them to assault 'the nervous system', to have an instantaneous effect. The motifs and the way he worked them resemble those of the poets he admired. Like Pound and Eliot, motifs derived from classical literature and past art are revisited throughout his work. For instance, '*Study after Velázquez*' 1950 (p.82) is one of many paintings derived from a black and white photograph of Diego Velázquez's 1650 *Portrait of Innocent X*, and the Furies from Aeschylus's *Oresteia* recur in his paintings, at least from *Three Studies for Figures at the Base of a Crucifixion* of 1944 onwards. Versions of the Furies disport themselves in *Fragment of a Crucifixion* 1950 (p.47) and *Three Figures and Portrait* 1975 (p.169).

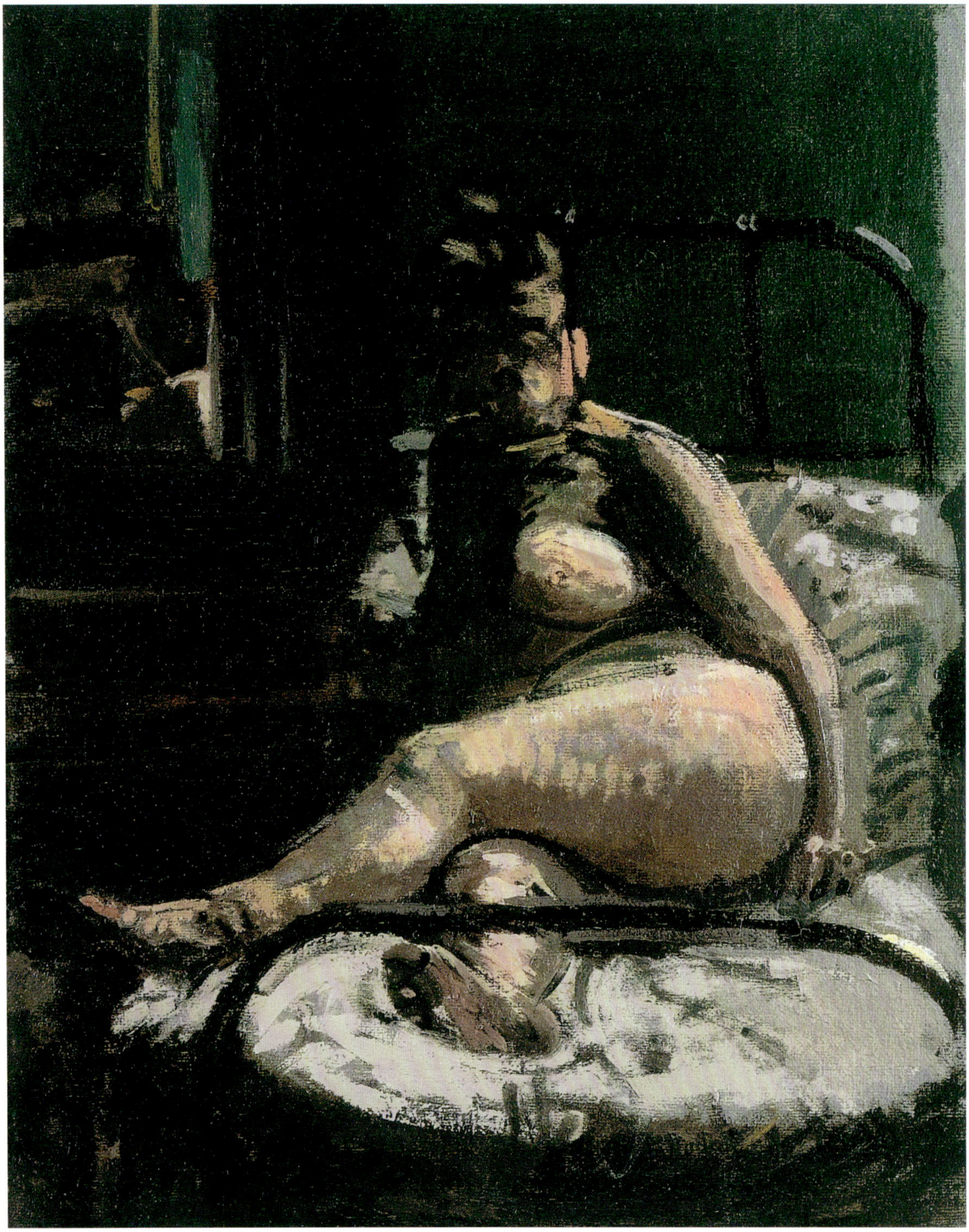

Walter Richard Sickert
La Hollandaise c.1906
Oil paint on canvas
51.1 × 40.6
Tate. Purchased 1983

Francis Bacon
Portrait of Henrietta Moraes on a Blue Couch 1965
Oil paint on canvas
198 × 147
Manchester City Galleries

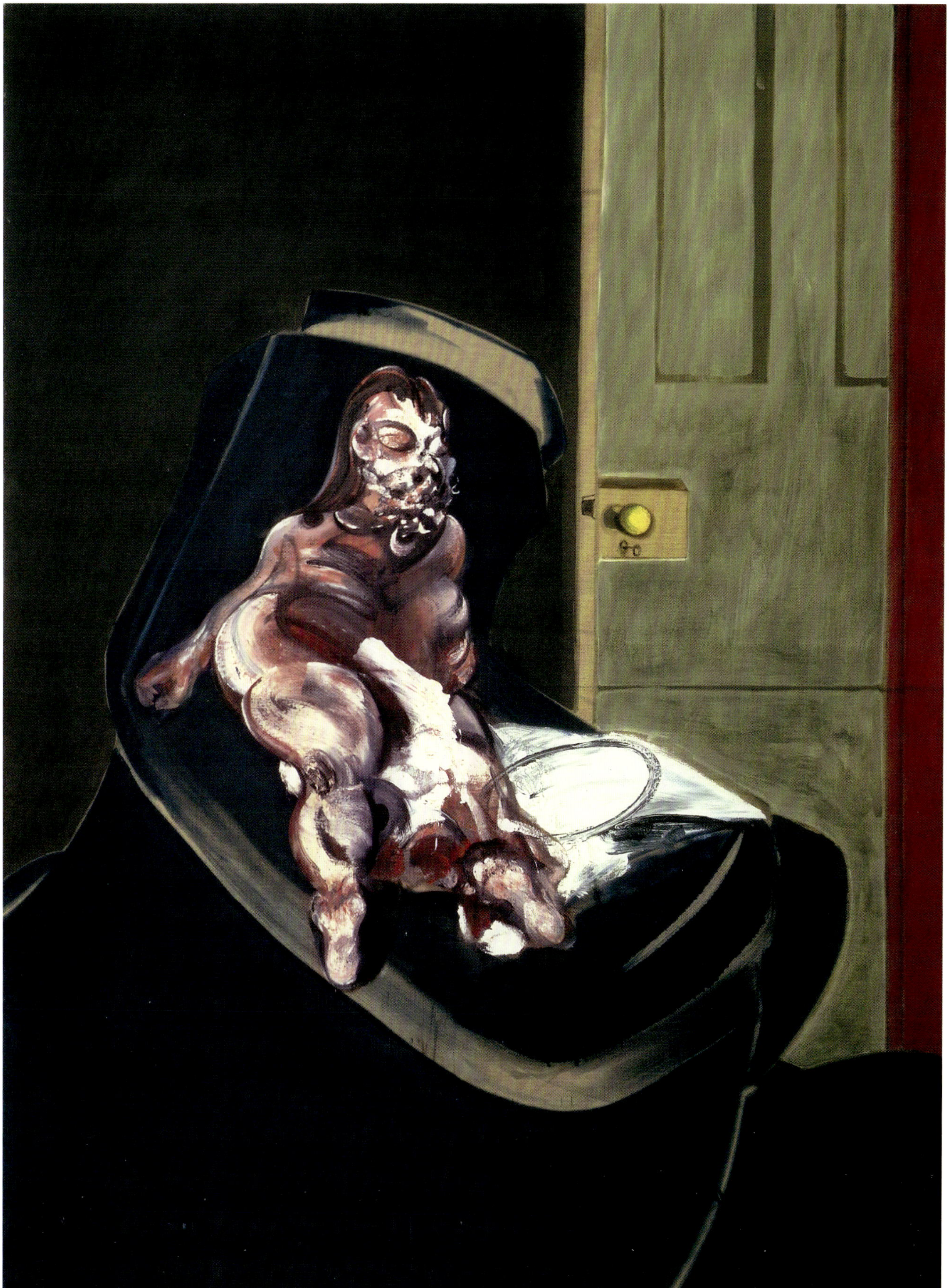

In 1953 the Tate Gallery held a Matthew Smith exhibition, and Bacon contributed to the catalogue. Echoing the 'filling in' charge of Legros, he claimed that Smith was one of the few English artists concerned with painting since Turner and Constable. 'Painting in this sense tends towards a complete interlocking of image and paint, so that the image is paint and vice versa. Here the brush-stroke creates the form and does not merely fill it in.' The Bacon paintings included in *All Too Human* from between 1945 and 1954 come from the years when he was learning to paint in public, and most insistently finding his image in the process of painting. Like Sickert in 1906 Bacon painted into a mid-tone, and like Sickert's ghouls his figures come out of darkness. Sickert's trope of a naked figure reclining is a recurring motif in Bacon's work (pp.36–7). However, Bacon's rendering of light and dark is formed by photography rather than by life drawing and painting – he did not attend art school. Specifically, in '*Study after Velázquez*' he used a black and white photograph of the Velázquez and a still of the screaming nanny from Sergei Eisenstein's film *Battleship Potemkin*. The way the camera records light and dark has become for us – in the age of mechanical representations – the norm for images. We can think we see like film. In Bacon's paintings we recognise the norm within the image, and there is something visceral when that norm is frustrated or fractured.

Kitaj's idea of history was modern. He was a man of the Left; Bacon wasn't: 'Who remembers or cares about a happy society? One remembers a society for what it has created.'[13] Art history and criticism mattered to Kitaj in a way rare to artists. While a student at the Ruskin School of Art in Oxford, Kitaj met Edgar Wind, then Professor of Art History at the university. Wind was an iconographer, concerned with identification, description and the interpretation of Renaissance art informed by contemporaneous texts and artefacts. He was instrumental in moving the great resource of iconographic study, the Warburg Library, out of Germany to London during the Nazi period. While still a student, Kitaj bought the whole run of the *Journal of the Warburg* and it continued to be an iconographic source for his work. If there was a father Kitaj wished to please, it was a future art historian of Wind's kind, a polymathic iconographer.

To force the issue Kitaj intervened in the reception of his work. For instance, in the catalogue to the Tate retrospective he supplied entries for many of his pictures. In the note for *Cecil Court, London W.C.2 (The Refugees)* 1983–4 (p.184) he quotes Sigmund Freud: 'no longer a German. I prefer to call myself a Jew.' Kitaj had identified himself as a diasporic Jew by this time and made that the thematic of his work. He goes on to mention the escape of his father, grandmother and others dear to him from Nazi Germany; that his figures in the painting have been likened to *meshuga* (Yiddish for 'fools' or 'crazies'); Yiddish theatre; Kafka; his own book collecting; Mr Seligmann, from whom he bought in the book alley, Cecil Court; and 'my favourite anti-Semite' Ezra Pound. 'Another day I'll tell who the other people in the painting are supposed to be, whether aesthetes find such midrashic [commentary on part of the Hebrew scriptures] gloss and emendations revolting or not.'[14]

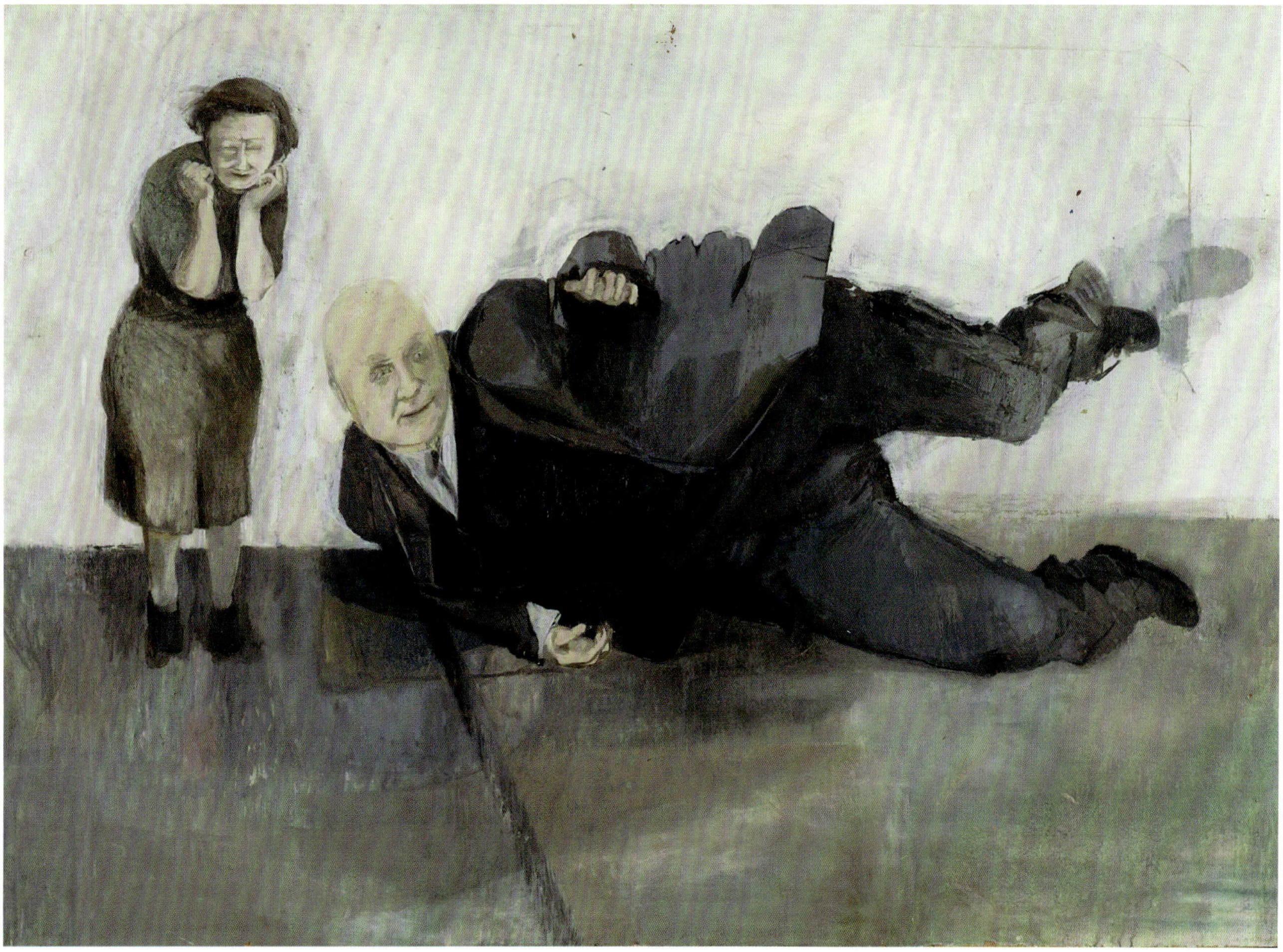

Michael Andrews
A Man who Suddenly Fell Over
1952
Oil paint on hardboard
120.6 × 172.7
Tate. Purchased 1958

Kitaj did make paintings to have texts: 'some books have pictures and some pictures have books', as he once wrote. For Kitaj form followed content; he was a maker of icons for a future time. As part of his insistence that he was a maker of images, a depicter of things, Kitaj called his paintings 'pictures', a solecism in cultivated art circles of a modernist disposition. He painted for the culture he believed we ought to have. The smoking chimney at Auschwitz is a recurring motif in later work, and it appears in the top right of *The Wedding* 1989–93 (p.185). He once told me his ambition was that it become a sign as familiar and specific in its significance as the crucifix.

Post-heroism

Michael Andrews and Paula Rego are both errant offspring of the Slade. They deploy considerable linear draughtsmanship, acquired in the school of sight exploration, but they are image makers. In both cases texts are part of the mulch of ideas and pictures in which the paintings grow. Andrews's *The Deer Park* 1962 (p.180) was partly prompted by reading Norman Mailer's book of the same name, and inflected by his reading of Rimbaud. And in an interview with critic John McEwen, Rego cites texts and films that have been formative for her, from *The Wizard of Oz* to Luis Buñuel's *Los Olvidados*. As she says: 'My paintings are stories, but they are not narratives in that they have no past or future.'[15]

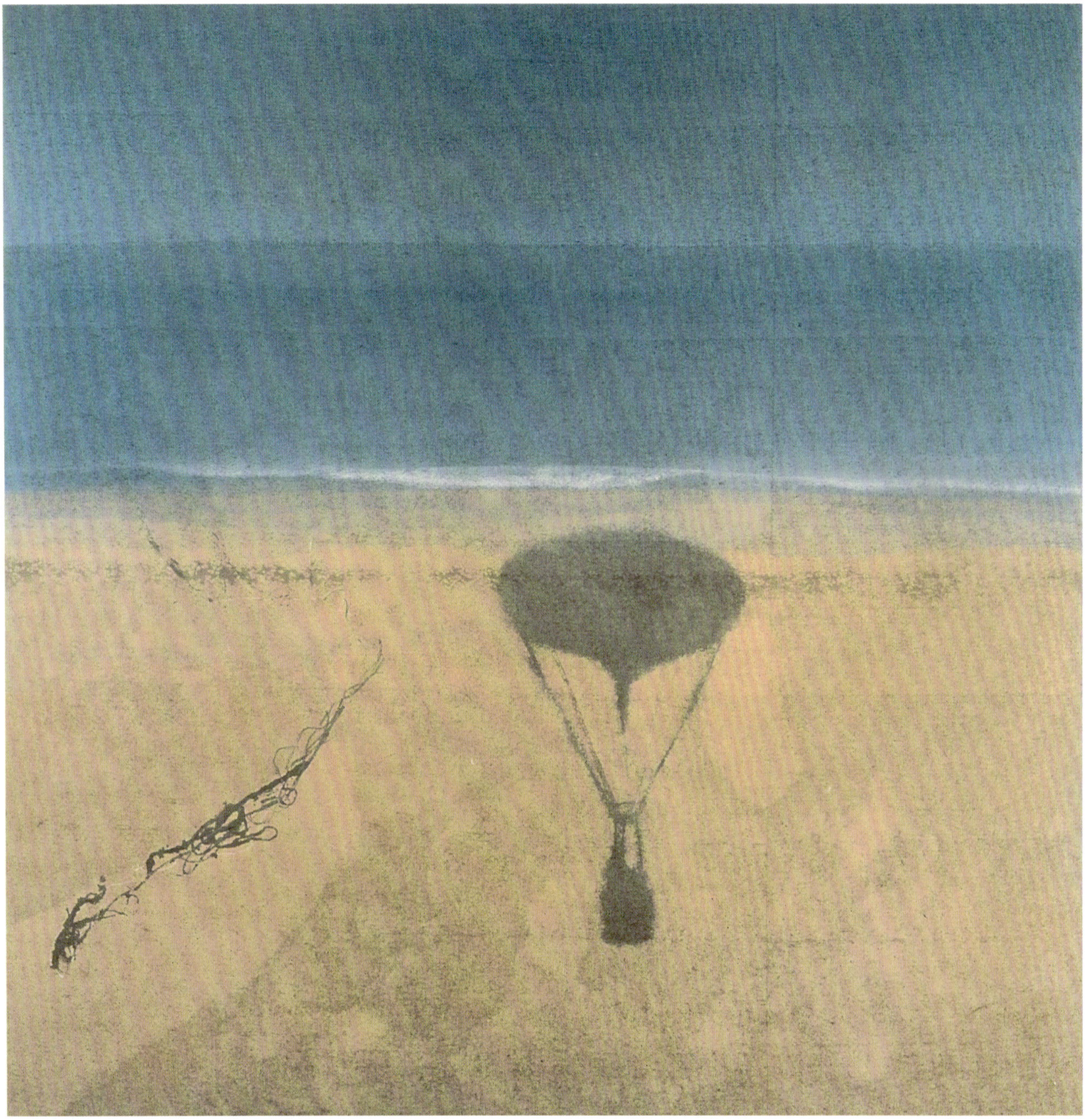

Michael Andrews's 'unique and strong' artistic personality is not overt. His paintings are instantly recognisable but seem to be without a style. Rather he becomes in his later work the Buddhist 'no-self'. As has often been pointed out, his student painting *A Man who Suddenly Fell Over* 1952 (p.39) predicts his interest in things caught as in a glance – people congregated in a bar, a woman's moment of drunken exuberance – and then in his later acrylic painting, a pattern of fish in an aquarium, a momentary surreal light on Uluru (Ayers Rock) and a holiday snap became *Melanie and Me Swimming* 1978–9 (p.176). His work seems to rise above the battle, and many of his later works, such as *Lights VII: A Shadow* 1974 (above), literally look down at their subjects from a high viewpoint. Rather than waging a heroic struggle for the verities of sight he is almost humorous in the way

Michael Andrews
Lights VII: A Shadow 1974
Acrylic paint on canvas
182.9 × 182.9
Private collection

he paints; it is as if he were amused by the way he can make paint flow, spatter, crust and stain into an image.

Paula Rego's pictures are like a risqué joke: they play with your sense of propriety. In Rego's *Bride* 1994 (p.190), among the deliciously rendered white bridal litter, the bride's withering stare presides over her parted knees. There is an ambivalence in Rego's work, and to have a comprehension of it is to become complicit in 'inappropriate' feelings. Against the staid masculine eroticism of the life room, Rego brings her sirens and suggestion of a libidinous misrule. Hierarchy is awry, the second sex is not subordinated, and the male sense of self is imperilled by the threat of demeaning laughter. She paints or draws women, not models – they are not figures devoid of social context, they are persons; uncowed characters, knowing players in patriarchal life games. In its indecorum her work discloses the properties of our social order as anchored in masculine power and desire.

A kind of beauty

Positivist disenchantment is not a condition of disbelief – it is a faith in rationalisation and intellectualisation as the instruments of human betterment. Within this faith aesthetic experience can only be rescued from triviality by attributing progressive agency to art. For example, in modernism as a step in arts historical development, or in Soviet socialist realism as propagator of a classless society, or currently, as a provider of social benefit to the 'excluded', as prescribed in the Arts Council of England's question to artists applying for funding: 'What are the age ranges of the people who will benefit from your activity? Ethnicity of beneficiaries. Disability status of beneficiaries. Social exclusion status of beneficiaries.'[16] In these painters, rejection of modernism was, I suggest, a refusal of the rationalised and institutionalised aesthetics of positivist disenchantment. It gave rise to paintings as enactments of resistant modes of cognition. Their proof is their aesthetic force; their verification is a kind of beauty.

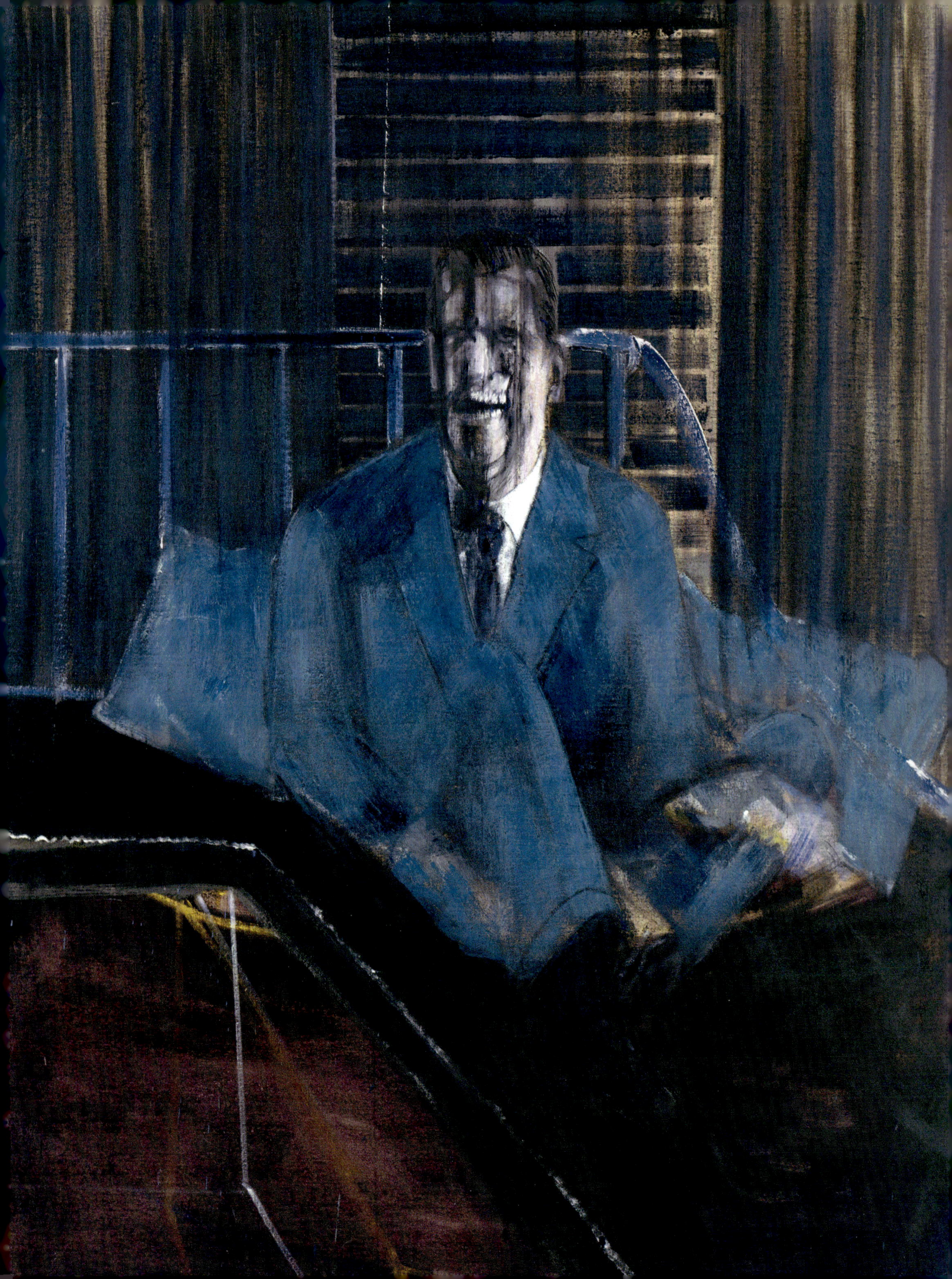

Looking at Identity: Bacon, Souza, Freud

Gregory Salter

Francis Bacon, Francis Newton Souza and the suit

In Francis Bacon's *Study for a Portrait* 1953 (opposite), the painting's lone male figure seems to be folding in on himself. He appears, however, not to have noticed – or, at least, is keeping up appearances. He is dressed respectably: he is wearing a blue suit, white shirt and dark tie, and he has neatly cropped and combed hair. He has been caught mid-conversation. His mouth is open, his teeth visible, in an uncanny expression that seems to have been captured suddenly, like a photograph. His facial features, though recognisable, are blurred; Bacon's daubs of white, lilac and grey have been partially smeared by a set of vertical lines running down his face. He is perched rather uncomfortably on a structure that looks to be somewhere between a bed and a chaise longue, with his body supported by cushions and a set of railings. Though his head, shoulders, arms and upper torso are visible, he seems to be in the process of disappearing into this structure on which he sits – or, alternatively, his body has been purposely and quite jarringly truncated. His hands are not visible, and only one trouser leg protrudes and bends almost like a leg, but there is no foot at its end.

This is a painting that is both attentive to the performance and appearances of masculinity, and seeks to explore its failures and violence. Bacon consistently painted images of suited men in the early part of his career, representing the restrictive uniform of the majority of men in Britain outside of the counter-culture in the postwar period.[1] The figure in *Study for a Portrait* can be considered a precursor to Bacon's 'Man in Blue' series (e.g. p.44), which he painted in the following year and which was reportedly inspired by a man he met and picked up at the Imperial Hotel in Henley-on-Thames. These men glance up, look away and lean in across the seven works in the series, with their shifting looks and positions seemingly echoing the uncertain, heightened process of cruising for queer men like Bacon. In these works, the suit could be read as taking on the quality of a public mask or costume, something that was worn to conceal queerness (at least from those from which queerness needed to be concealed) and give a veneer of respectability. It is known that these were often the type of men Bacon liked to pick up – seemingly heterosexual men who 'could be seduced by money, or by the novelty, or by their own desire for defiance'.[2]

While we might want to exercise caution in attributing a contemporary queer identity to the male figure in *Study for a Portrait*, there are parallels with the look and its relationship to (or its unravelling of) the appearances of masculinity in the 'Man in Blue' series. Bacon knew of the central importance of looking for queer experience, particularly in the postwar period prior to the partial decriminalisation of homosexuality in 1967:

Francis Bacon
Study for a Portrait 1953
(detail)
Oil paint on canvas
152.2 × 118
Kunsthalle, Hamburg

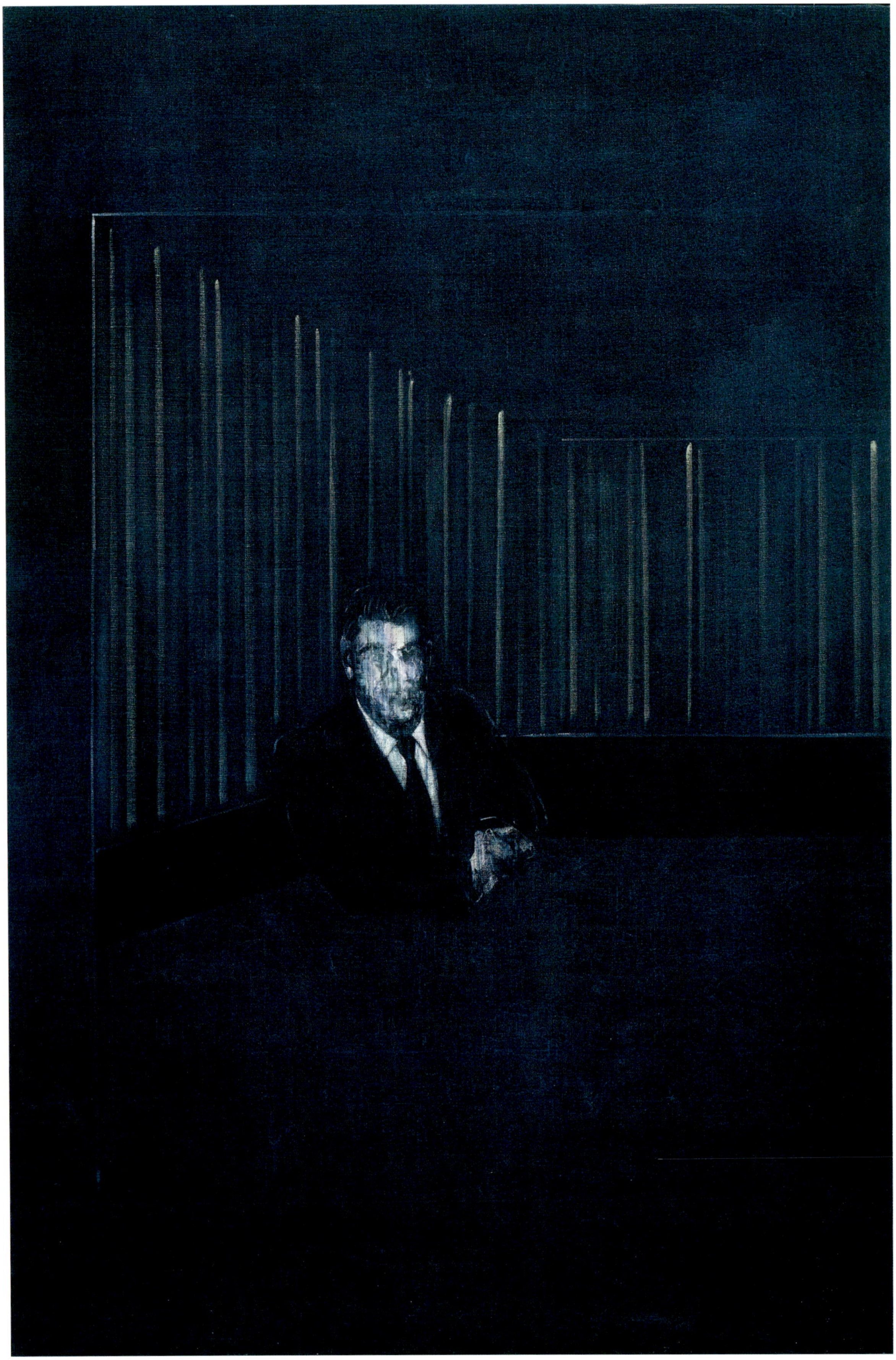

Francis Bacon
Man in Blue V 1954
Oil paint on canvas
198 × 137
Kunstsammlung Nordrhein-Westfalen, Düsseldorf

> Whenever I really want to know what someone looks like I always ask a queer – because homosexuals are always more ruthless and more precise about appearance. After all, they spend their whole lives watching themselves and others, then pulling the way they look to pieces.[3]

The ruthlessness and precision of the queer male gaze is, in Bacon's own terms, a result of the surveillance and self-censorship experienced by queer men in their daily lives. Police raids and arrests were common in the period between the end of the Second World War and partial decriminalisation. We might read *Study for a Portrait* as a reflection on the intersecting nature of these looks: masculinity coheres into the symbolic uniform of the suit under the eyes of the state, but also begins to shift and collapse under the gaze of the queer look.

The suited male figure is also a conduit for the exploration of marginal experience and the wider politics of the postwar period in the work of Francis Newton Souza. The figure in *Mr Sebastian* 1955 (p.19) also wears a dark suit, white shirt and dark tie, though this is a black male figure – one who would face even more of a struggle to 'blend in' than Bacon's queer men. The figure in the painting has been pierced with a series of arrows – a signature of Souza's work at this time – which protrude from his head and his neck. These arrows give the painting its title: they are appropriated from representations of St Sebastian, an early Christian saint who the Romans killed by tying him to a tree or a post and shooting him with arrows. Souza has adapted these arrows and inflicted them on a more ordinary figure – Mr Sebastian, rather than St Sebastian – who appears to endure their onslaught, rather than succumb to the glory of martyrdom.

It is this rigid stoicism that is particularly striking about Souza's works of pierced male bodies like *Mr Sebastian*. While Bacon's male figures appear in the process of shifting and disintegrating, making eye contact or opening their mouths to speak or to scream, Souza's figure appears frozen and still, his shoulders narrow and his neck long and taut. This tension is consistent with the endurance of pain; not succumbing to it. Other elements of Mr Sebastian's body attest to this too. His eyes are perched right at the top of his head and look in both directions at once, alert and on guard. His mouth is a grimace, with his teeth bared, gnashed together – he appears silent, but rigid. This silence is typical of Souza's figures in general: they are often mute, apparently making an effort not to speak, communicate or even cry out.

With his brown skin and smart but inconspicuous suit, Mr Sebastian appears to evoke the postwar figure of the assimilative male migrant. As migrants from South Asia and the Caribbean began to arrive in Britain from the end of the 1940s, assimilation became the expectation of the British government: it was assumed that, over time, they would abandon the culture of their home countries in favour of a Western lifestyle. (The appeal and ease of assimilation varied from individual to individual.) Souza himself was an English-speaking Catholic, though this would not have shielded him from the obvious otherness of his skin and the jarring experience of migration more generally. Before leaving India, he had imagined London as the 'most cultured city in the world', though he was quickly disappointed on arrival:

> I was astonished by the grimness of Britain. Here was the country that was running, only a few years before, an empire encircling nearly three quarters of the globe. Yet there was no joy in it. The people were grim-faced after a prolonged war...[4]

Francis Bacon
Fragment of a Crucifixion 1950
Oil paint and cotton wool on canvas
140 × 108.5
Collection Van Abbemuseum, Eindhoven, The Netherlands

Mr Sebastian appears to register the processes and tensions of assimilation for the male migrant in postwar London. This figure adopts a Western uniform, his eyes pivot with an anxiety about his own performance, and his mouth is gripped in silence, as if to prevent speech that might give him away or to indicate the physical and psychological anguish of this process.

Mr Sebastian may well, in part, be afflicted by the arrows of assimilation, but they also evoke the violence and indignities of discrimination and racial abuse in postwar Britain. From the moment of their arrival and increased visibility in the late 1940s, black migrants were subject to discrimination for jobs and in the workplace; refused service in bars, shops and restaurants; struggled to secure homes; and were subject to taunts and violence in the street. The response of many migrants to this frequent and often daily experience was a mixture of stoicism and silence; a sense of keeping to oneself in an effort not to encourage further incidents.[5] In many ways, Souza's painting feels like another instance of this self-control – Mr Sebastian mutes his voice, seeks to repress any visible signs of pain and emotion, and appears hyper-vigilant. Elsewhere in Souza's art, repression is denied and a sense of impending tragedy is allowed to take shape.

Crucifixions and politics

At the centre of Souza's monumental *Crucifixion* 1959 (p.97) is the body of a black Christ, distorted and brittle in his moment of crucifixion. Souza has painted this figure in black, but also in vivid blue hues on the joints at his knees, hips and shoulders, as well as browns and the occasional slash of red around his eyes, on his face and at his side, where he was pierced by the lance. The head of Christ appears blank and mask-like, with either the pain of suffering or the absence of death. His teeth are visible, again in a grimace which extends across one side of his face, and like his eyes suggests a state between life and death. The head is augmented with ambiguous forms – between plants, feathers, thorns and fish scales – that seem to cling to the face or emerge from it. His body is also caught between human and non-human: his legs and feet appear skeletal, while his arms seem to sprout like thorny branches out of his torso, disappearing abruptly off the edges of the canvas.

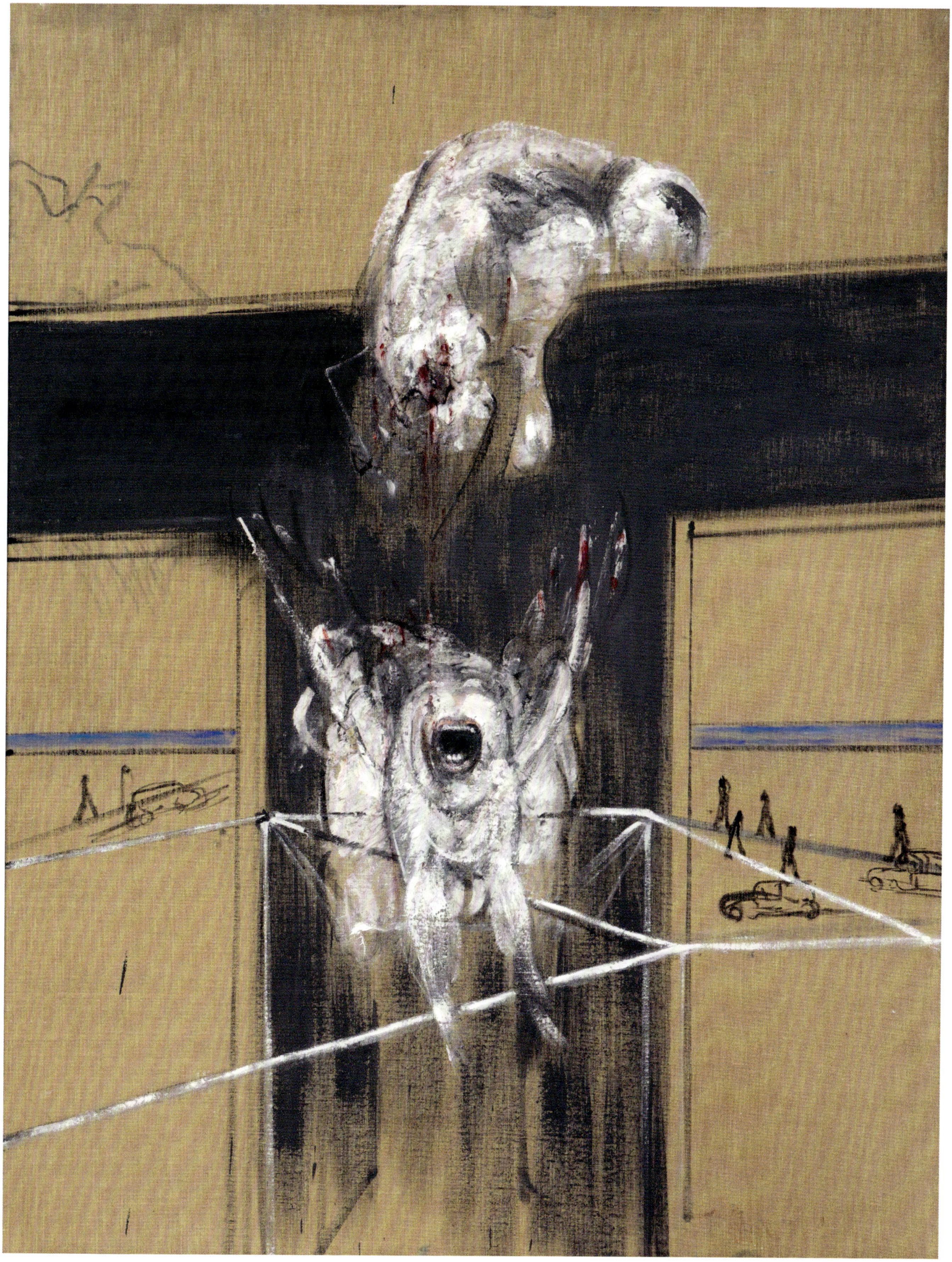

His limbs are pierced with arrows, while nails protrude from his feet. To either side are figures that Souza identified as John the Baptist and a disciple. These two figures are black, too, their faces wearing the grimaces that we have seen elsewhere in Souza's art, and their eyes staring intently and resolutely out at us.

Crucifixion is another example of Souza's engagement with Christian imagery from Western art. He recalled how, at his Jesuit school as a teenager, he was encouraged to copy and admire the work of Heinrich Hofmann, who painted, in Souza's words, 'blood operatic Christs and flaxen-haired shy Virgins'.[6] This work is a denial of that tradition, replacing a dignified, pure, white Christ with the distorted, suffering, lifeless body of a black Christ. It can be read, in part, as a rebellion against the colonial forces that had brought Catholicism to Goa and to Souza's family, and as a reflection on the violence of decolonisation in India that Souza left behind. It seems to also evoke migrants' experiences in Britain. In the summer of 1958, just months before *Crucifixion* was painted, racist violence erupted into riots that swept through North Kensington in London, an area dominated by overcrowded slums occupied by poor black and white households. This would not be the first work by Souza that responded to racial discrimination and violence – 1957's *Negro in Mourning* appears to speak, broadly, to the black struggle in Britain at that moment, for instance – but *Crucifixion* is stark and unapologetic in its depiction of a flayed, black, male body. Here, Souza makes the male body a conduit for the violent legacy of colonialism and racism. It speaks of the histories of struggle and suffering that Souza and others are forced to inhabit: this is a crucial personal (and global) history, and an inherently violent one.

Bacon, of course, explored the subject of the crucifixion extensively throughout his career. However, while Souza's crucifixion – like his *Mr Sebastian* – is a highly visible work that is steeped in the violence, politics and tensions of black migrant experience, a work like Bacon's *Fragment of a Crucifixion* 1950 (p.47) makes explicit the disintegration that was in process in *Study for a Portrait*. A black T-form looms at the front of the picture plane, set in a minimally sketched cityscape of cars and human figures. A dog-like creature is positioned over the top of the cross, gripping a chimera figure in its jaws. This chimera is rendered as part-human, part-bird, and it cries out in agony with a mouth adapted from the screaming mouth of the nurse in Sergei Eisenstein's film *Battleship Potemkin* 1925 (a source to which Bacon frequently and famously returned). Here, the crucifixion has become a battle between the worldly and otherworldly, and the chimera is succumbing to defeat. In the process, however, both figures appear about to be swallowed by the gaping black form of the cross from which they emerge. If Souza's crucifixion made the black body visible to speak to legacies of violence, then Bacon's crucifixion is concerned with undermining the very stability of the body itself, as well as the symbols and ideals it might serve elsewhere.

The male figure is continually subjected to similar approaches in Bacon's art: dissected (as in *Study for a Portrait*), subverted – think of the famous screams of his stranded, hopeless popes – and even attacked. This is the case in the early work *Figure in a Landscape* 1945 (p.85), which is widely accepted to have been based on a photograph of one of Bacon's lovers, Eric Hall, dozing on a bench in Hyde Park.[7] In the painting, the body of Hall and the space of the park have been violently altered and invaded. Hall's body has been destroyed, with only an arm and part of his torso remaining; the legs of his tweed suit hang lifelessly over the bench. The rest of him has been engulfed by a great black space, out of which emerge another set of forms. There is a curved railing, held up on legs, that merges with the bench. Connected on top of this is what has been identified by some critics as a microphone and by others as a machine gun; behind this is a mouth with its lips parted and teeth clenched. Both interpretations suggest photographs as sources: Bacon could be quoting a dictator mid-speech behind a microphone here, or the menacing spectacle of a soldier behind a machine gun.[8] In either case, we are confronted by the disturbing conflation of a photograph of Bacon's partner in a peaceful setting with a horrific image of war – one that would have resonated with Nazism in 1945.

In postwar Britain, queer men were portrayed as figures of corruption and vice at the heart of reconstructive society by the popular press, where they were framed as symbols of the decline of the British Empire, the feminising effects of consumerism and the wartime breakdown of the family unit.[9] In part, then, Bacon's painting is an extreme embrace of the marginal, 'evil' status attributed to queer men. It is also, provocatively, a fundamental destruction of the veneer of respectable masculinity that Bacon pulled apart elsewhere. This was broadly, and memorably, one of his stated aims in painting:

> We nearly always live through screens – a screened existence. And I sometimes think, when people say my work looks violent, that perhaps I have from time to time been able to clear away one or two of the veils or screens.[10]

In allowing the figure of the Nazi to emerge from the figure of a lover, Bacon refuses to construct a division – between temperate, domestic British masculinity and evil, inhuman Nazi masculinity; and, more generally, between 'us' and 'them'.

Francis Newton Souza, Lucian Freud and the female body

Souza performs a very different act of violence through paint in his images of women. In his *Black Nude* 1961 (p.92) a woman stands nude before us, her body picked out in tones of black, brown, orange and blue. Her breasts and abdomen are round and enlarged, her genitalia exposed, and her face takes on the form of a skull-like mask. Her eyes are wide with a look of benevolence, and her teeth are, once again, bared. This vivid, highly sexual but also potentially violent image of a black woman was received by Souza's critics in strikingly similar ways when it

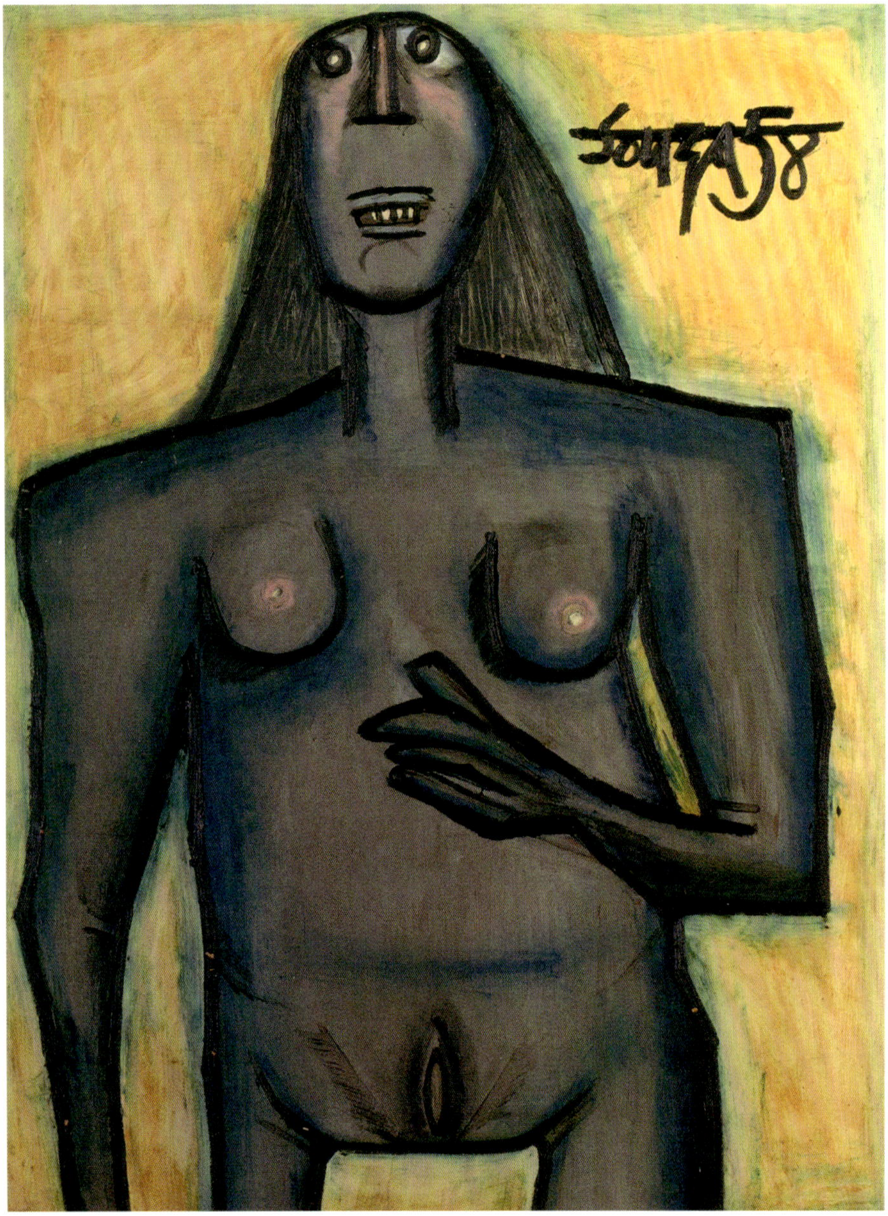

Francis Newton Souza
Miss Universe 1999 AD 1958
Oil paint on board
120 × 90
Private collection

was exhibited in 1961. For Edward Lucie-Smith in the *New Statesman*, *Black Nude* had a 'crude, menacing sexuality' that reminded him of 'Kali, the goddess of love and death'.[11] Perhaps not coincidentally, Kali is often represented with her feet on the male god Shiva in order to demonstrate their co-dependence and her pacification by the reclining male figure. Here, Souza's female figure evoked resonances of threat and sexuality – and provoked, perhaps, a desire to subdue her. The way in which Souza builds this vision of a black female nude out of simplified, stylised forms that had, over the previous 50–60 years, been lifted from non-Western cultures and utilised for the stylistic innovations of modernism, can leave a contradictory impression. This is, on the one hand, Souza re-appropriating the primitivism of white artists and returning it to them in a figure of looming threat, as well as a rejection of the constraints and sanitisation of colonial Catholicism into which he had been born. At the same time it utilises simple or even misogynistic categories – woman as mother, lover and destroyer – to set up this rebellion.

George Butcher, in *The Guardian*, reiterated the comparison with Kali, though he argued that this 'six feet tall...devouring goddess of evil' had been translated into a symbol of nuclear threat, as 'the Mother of man about to devour her offspring'.[12] The nuclear bomb was an obsession for Souza in the late 1950s and early 1960s. In 1958, he had produced a grim vision of a female figure that he titled *Miss Universe 1999 AD* (opposite). This figure has also been depicted completely nude in three-quarter length, though her skin here is rendered in an ashy grey. Years later, he reflected on its sheer pessimism and ugliness, stating that 'in the 1950s and 60s there arose a great fear that the world was on the brink of nuclear war. It would be the ultimate war; to say Goodbye Earth...It's all wrong and will end in ashes. This is why my painting is in grey'.[13] Here, Souza has transformed the superficial grin of a beauty pageant contestant into the skeletal, permanent smile of a post-nuclear-fallout Miss Universe; her hair looks visibly brittle and her eyes are tiny white dots that disappear into sunken hollows. While not all of Souza's reflections on the threat of the nuclear bomb were figured through women – his 1961 painting *Mad Prophet in New York* depicts a bearded priest-like figure who warns of postwar humankind's apparent suicide mission – it is nonetheless critical that he so often transposes women into figures of threat, sexuality and ultimate destruction. In 1964, Edwin Mullins observed that, for Souza, 'it is as if painting were both an act of hate and an act of love, and he himself were torn between disgust and longing, uncertain whether painting is a protective daydream or something unpleasant in his system to be purged'.[14] It is perhaps in Souza's images of women where this conflict is most expressively played out.

If Souza imagines his female figures into representations that seem to both encourage and support gendered and racial assumptions, then Lucian Freud subjects his female subjects to an unrelenting and brutal gaze that produces quieter echoes of the conflict at the heart of Souza's work. His *Girl with a White Dog* 1950–1 (pp.108–9) is the last in a series of portraits of Kitty Garman, the daughter of Kathleen Garman, a prominent figure in artistic circles in the early twentieth century, and the sculptor Jacob Epstein. Freud and Garman met in 1947 and married the following year. She is the *Girl with Roses* 1947–8 (p.53), which was painted when she was already pregnant with their first daughter Annie, and for which she was instructed to sit up with confidence. She recalled that 'I was arranged', and the intensity of the gaze from her large eyes, off to one side, and her delicate though resolute grip on the rose suggest anxiety and tension rather than self-possession.[15] Writing in 1954 in a statement in *Encounter*, Freud claimed that the aim of the artist should be 'to communicate their feelings about the object of their choice', while also retaining a degree of emotional distance; his aim was to 'translate life into art almost literally, as it were' through a process of close scrutiny that would 'eventually reveal the *all*'.[16] This *all* was considered by the art historian Lawrence Gowing, who found in Freud's portraits of Garman 'the state of being bare of defences'. To him, they presented love as 'the condition of being at one another's mercy'.[17]

This is encapsulated by the convergence of gazes in the Kitty portraits, where the close, obsessive, unrelenting scrutiny of Freud the artist meets Kitty's own enduring, though fearful and resigned gaze. Together, they suggest the state of devouring another at the same time as being devoured yourself.

By the time of the completion of *Girl with a White Dog*, Freud and Garman's marriage was nearing its end (they divorced the following year, in 1952). Here, Freud has stepped back slightly. Garman sits on a mattress on the floor of their home at 27 Clifton Hill in St John's Wood in North London. She wears a yellow robe that has been loosened around her shoulders to reveal the upper part of one arm and her breast. She raises this arm to her body in a slightly defensive pose. She supports herself with her other arm, and you can see her wedding ring on her finger. Next to her, resting its chin on her leg, is a white bull terrier, one of a pair that the couple had received as wedding gifts (the other, a black one and Freud's favourite, was run over while he was painting this work). If Freud's earlier portraits of Garman had looked with an intensity and anxiety, this later work seems to suggest a loosening of that tension, which comes with time and the kind of intimate knowledge for which Freud seemed to be striving at this moment. There are hints at a domestic setting – the interior, the mattress, the dog – though it appears bare, makeshift and mournful. To follow Freud's look here is to meet the eyes and the body of a woman who we have seen being loved and consumed across his portraits of her, and it is to find the quiet sadness of mutual knowledge reaching its end.

The heightened, often uncomfortable intimacy of Freud's portraiture continues across his career, but its terms shift in relation to his sitters. In *Sleeping by the Lion Carpet* 1996 (p.157) he painted Sue Tilley, then an official at the Department of Health and Social Security, who was a recurrent subject for him in the 1990s (he came to refer to her as 'Big Sue'). In this painting, Sue is sleeping: being painted by Freud involved a commitment to sit for hours at a time on several days a week for several months, and, with her arm resting on the chair and her head in her hand, she has fallen asleep. The result is an image that contains not the ferocious, almost damaging exchange of looks from his Kitty portraits, but a quieter though no less monumental intimacy and ease. Tilley is vulnerable – she is naked and asleep – and Freud's eye and paintbrush are allowed to roam all over her body, taking in 'the amazing craters and things one's never seen before...the sores and chafes made by weight and heat' as he put it, with a typical combination of detachment and awe.[18] But she is also made powerful, in the representation of Tilley and Freud's mutual ease, and in the careful, prolonged attention he devotes to an overweight body that might otherwise be ignored or derided. The visual comparison with the lion carpet propped up in the background is, perhaps, telling of the shifting of the terms of intimacy and gender here. On the carpet, a lioness stands alert over a sleeping or resting lion; in the studio, it is Freud who takes on the lioness's role, keeping watch over the sleeping Tilley, whose dormant power aligns her, pointedly, with the king of the jungle.

Lucian Freud
Girl with Roses 1947–8
Oil paint on canvas
106 × 75.6
British Council Collection

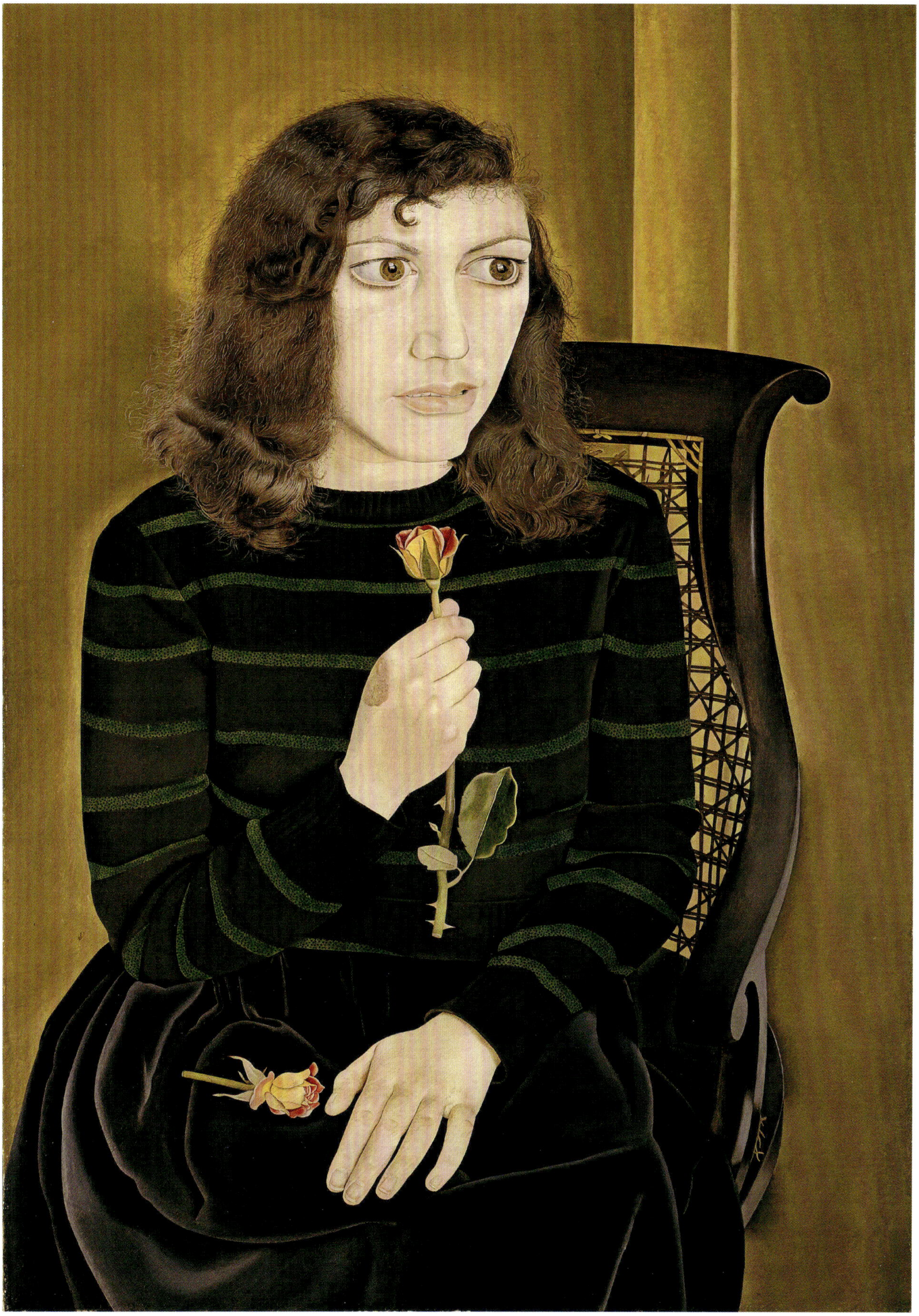

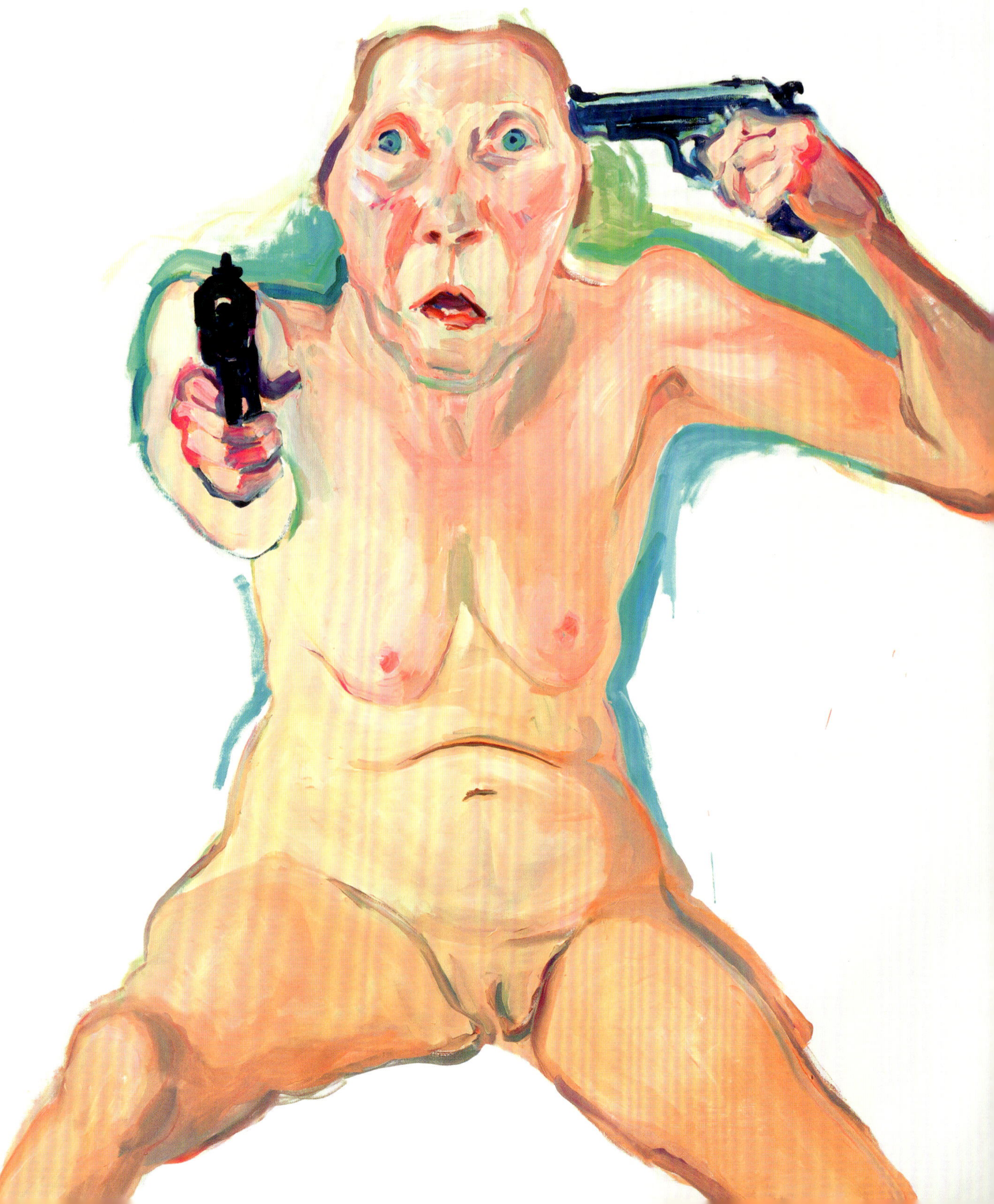

The Skin of the Day
Charlotte Mullins

'What is meant by "reality"?' asks Virginia Woolf in her 1929 essay 'A Room of One's Own'. For Woolf, 'reality' is a slippery, nebulous thing, something hard to pin down, something that can only be glimpsed obliquely. It is 'what remains over when the skin of the day has been cast into the hedge[...]what is left of past time and of our loves and hates'. This will-o'-the-wisp can only be ensnared by great writers, she argues, but when they grasp it and share it with readers, 'one sees more intensely afterwards; the world seems bared of its covering'.[1]

The artists in this exhibition have spent their lives trying to grapple the skin of the day from out of the hedge, to pin down the intensity of a lived moment, of reality. For artists working today painting reality is especially challenging, for it is 4D, 4G, digital and virtual, breathlessly unrelenting and flat-out, day in, day out. Yet, despite the speed of contemporary life – or perhaps because of it – an increasing number of artists now use paint to try and capture their experience of it.

Figurative painting has oscillated in visibility over recent decades. It last came to prominence in Britain in the 1980s, a time when Paula Rego first showed her unsettling domestic scenes such as *Looking Back* 1987. Celia Paul, who graduated from the Slade School of Fine Art in London in 1981, remembers benefiting from this resurgence of interest when she held her first solo show in 1986. However, by the time Cecily Brown graduated from the Slade in 1993, figurative painting had been largely eclipsed by the chutzpah and headlines of the Young British Artists. Brown didn't feel part of this new grouping and chose to move to New York, where the reception for painters was more welcoming. Jenny Saville was part of the YBAs, after she graduated from the Glasgow School of Art in 1992, thanks to significant early support from YBA patron Charles Saatchi. However, she didn't receive her first public solo show in the UK until 2012, at Modern Art Oxford, and she also had to build her career through exhibitions in America.

Over the last decade, contemporary figurative painting has slowly returned to prominence both in Britain and on the international stage. Increasing numbers of exhibitions in commercial galleries and museums and buoyant sales in auction houses suggest that figurative painting has moved beyond needing to prove itself as a valid medium at every turn. Finally it coexists with authority alongside more recent trends in contemporary art, such as performance and photography.

In a revved-up world, figurative painters are not afraid of taking time – a day, a month, a year – to complete a single work; distilling their experiences, compressing lived time, into one image. These paintings can be seen in a single glance but they truly reward slow looking, expanding back over time to reveal new meanings. In this way they are both haiku and epic, a quick hit and a slow burn, offering both surface chimeras and unfathomable depths. Such paintings take us

Maria Lassnig
Du oder Ich (*You or Me*) 2005
(detail)
Oil paint on canvas
203 × 155
Private collection. Courtesy
Hauser & Wirth

beyond words and act directly on our emotions. The youngest artist in *All Too Human*, Lynette Yiadom-Boakye, explains:

> It is the reason why I paint some things and write others. It's all there, thoughts about race, masculinity, femininity, what [it] is to be human and in the world alongside everyone else. But it is complex, joyful, miserable, infuriating and overwhelming – so not easily put into words. That is why it is painted. The marks, the light, the dark, the colour, the composition, the form, the scale: all of these things take on meanings to me, like a language to speak.[2]

The duality of immediate access and slowly revealed layered meaning, a complexity beyond words, is not new. It stretches back to the manifold gazes in Édouard Manet's bars and concert halls; the screaming flesh imprisoned by Francis Bacon. It is found in the dark perversions of Balthus, in the narrative questions that hover inside Walter Richard Sickert's bandstands and bedrooms. Virginia Woolf was entranced by Sickert's paintings, writing of them moving into a 'silent territory' beyond words, connecting with us on an instinctive level.[3] Bacon spoke of wanting his own paintings 'to bring the figurative thing up on to the nervous system more violently and more poignantly', to make the viewing experience an acutely physical one.[4] These artists all painted life as it was lived as well as seen; as it was felt, smelt, touched, desired. A look in the history books would suggest that this approach has been largely the preserve of male artists. The final sections of *All Too Human* reveal that female figurative artists are finally receiving the attention and respect they deserve, and that the books will need to be updated.[5]

An orgy of brushstrokes

The paintings of Cecily Brown offer suggestive glimpses of figures: the curve of a thigh, the twist of a hip, a groping hand, a head thrown back in ecstasy. Bodies rise from beds of fleshy paint in shades of pink and peach, brushstrokes soft as butter and breathily applied. What is that hand reaching for? Are those mounds buttocks or breasts? What is going on in the bushes? In *Teenage Wildlife* 2003 (p.200) a figure in an unbuttoned white shirt fondles a naked girl, who reaches up and hooks her hand over a tree's low-lying branch as if to steady herself. As we spy on them through the bushes the lovers threaten to expose themselves, but the paint dances this way and that and never quite coalesces into solid forms. It is as if Manet's *Le Déjeuner sur l'herbe* 1863 (p.57) has been put through a blender, gobbets of flesh and clothing flung out at the canvas alongside leaves and earth, leaving only the frenzied energy of the paint itself and our own imagination to piece together this new reality.

Brown's figures often appear as if conjured from memory, limbs and gestures remembered with a potency that engages with the viewer on a visceral level. Her

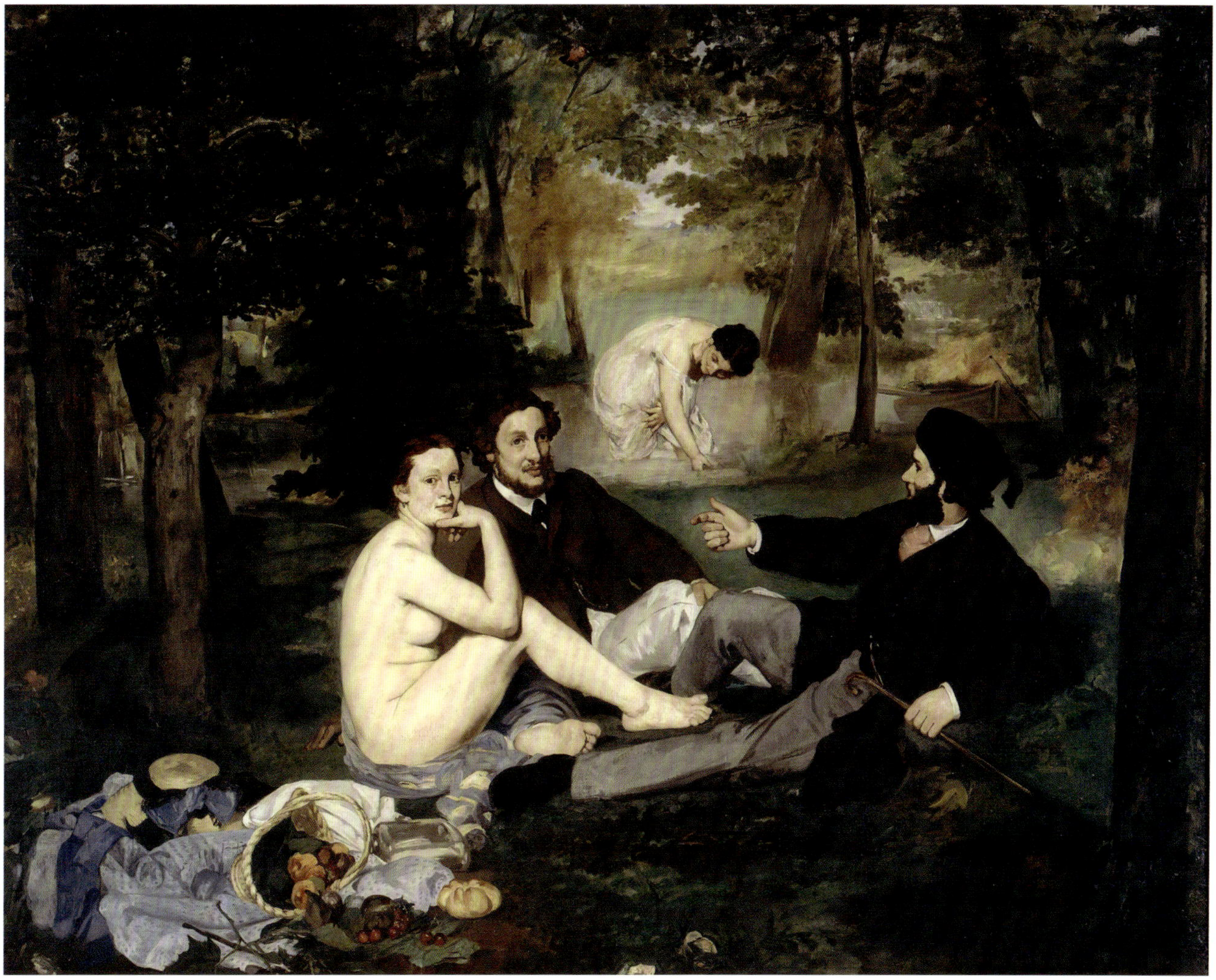

Édouard Manet
Le Déjeuner sur l'herbe 1863
Oil paint on canvas
208 × 264.5
Musée d'Orsay, Paris

paintings are things we actively experience rather than passively see. We absorb the sexual tension, smell the sweat and feel the arousal, the immediacy of bodies coming together through a maelstrom of paint. These paintings speak directly to us, force their way inside us, much like those mutilated forms of Francis Bacon, whom Brown cites as one of her chief inspirations alongside Lucian Freud. Brown also shares an interest in paint as flesh with abstract expressionist Willem de Kooning, and there's something of the raw energy of the Russian-born French painter Chaïm Soutine in her work as well. Ultimately, however, Brown's paintings are more suggestive, less fixed, her figures less defined than those of her male predecessors. 'My whole obsession over the past twenty years has been trying to look at something and hold it,' she says. 'But there's an impossibility to that. There is a slippage inherent in trying to fix an image.'[6]

Instead of trying to pin a subject down – by working from a single model, for example – Brown prefers to work from a wide range of sources. She draws on historical paintings, advertising, porn, anything that speaks to her, working intuitively and across as many as twenty canvases at once. As she works she splices together genres, from plein air and bacchanals to interiors and the history of the nude, creating suggestive scenarios that goad the viewer into taking an active stance. She conjures the sensation of existence, what it is to be a body with

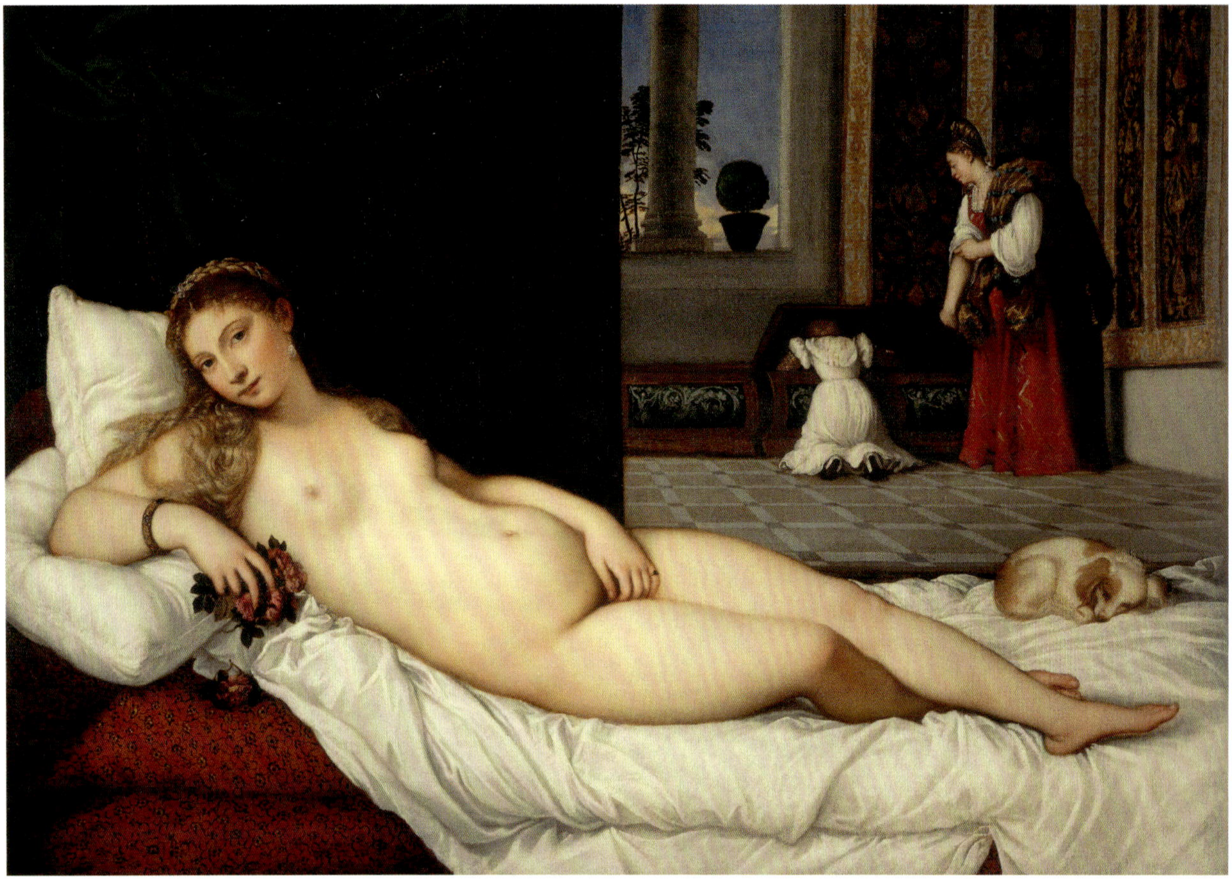

Titian
The Venus of Urbino 1538
Oil on canvas
119 × 165
Uffizi, Florence

all its physical needs and desires, rather than aiming for a skin-deep resemblance of a specific figure. This approach acknowledges that we all exist in a fleeting present, creating our own subjective view of the world from a series of staccato moments that we store as memories. This view constantly twists and shifts and grows around us. There is no such thing as a singular reality, her paintings seem to say. You won't be able to pin such a thing down, because a clean-cut one-size-fits-all version simply doesn't exist.

Body as battleground

The postwar period in Britain was dominated by men looking at the figure: not just Bacon, Freud and the artists in this exhibition, but also David Hockney, Allen Jones, and Gilbert and George, and sculptors Henry Moore and Antony Gormley. However, the twenty-first century is more expansive, and embraces new perspectives, new voices. An increasing number of female figurative artists are now supported by commercial galleries and institutions, which garners a global audience for their work. The figure, particularly the female figure, has been reappropriated and put to work to question underlying systems that still shape how women are perceived and how they perceive themselves. Historically, paintings such as Titian's (1490–1576) *The Venus of Urbino* 1538 (above) or Velázquez's *The Toilet of Venus* 1647–51 were sites of male activation based on female passivity (the female nude as an object to be admired by the male viewer). By contrast, Brown's orgiastic explosions of nudity, Lisa Yuskavage's (b.1962)

Marlene Dumas
Stern 2004
Oil paint on canvas
110.1 × 130.2 × 2.4
Tate. Purchased with assistance from Foundation Dutch Artworks and Bank Giro Loterij 2007

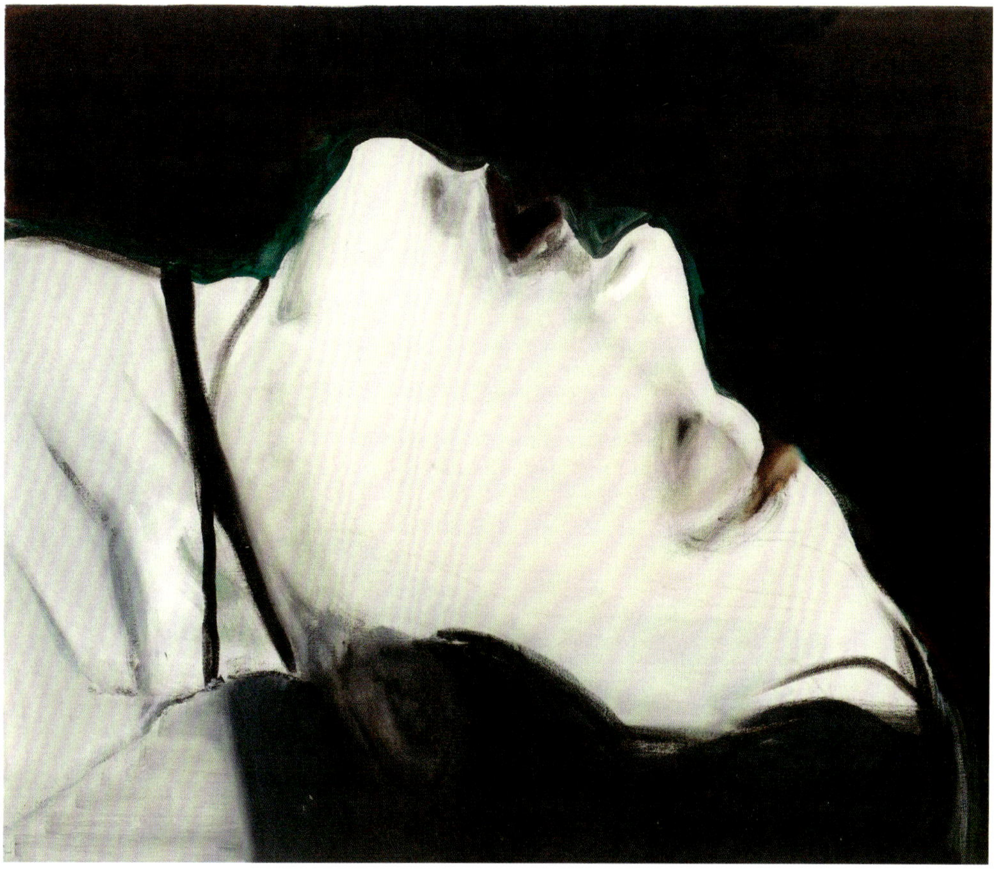

Lisa Yuskavage
Brood 2005–6
Oil paint on linen
195.6 × 175.3
Jeffrey A. Altman collection: David Zwirner Gallery

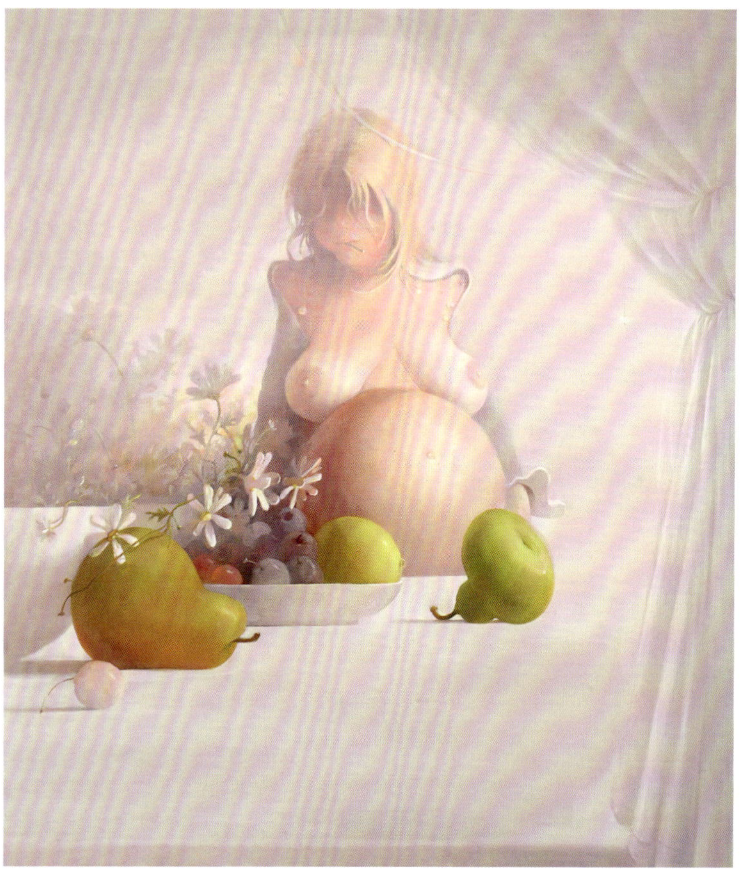

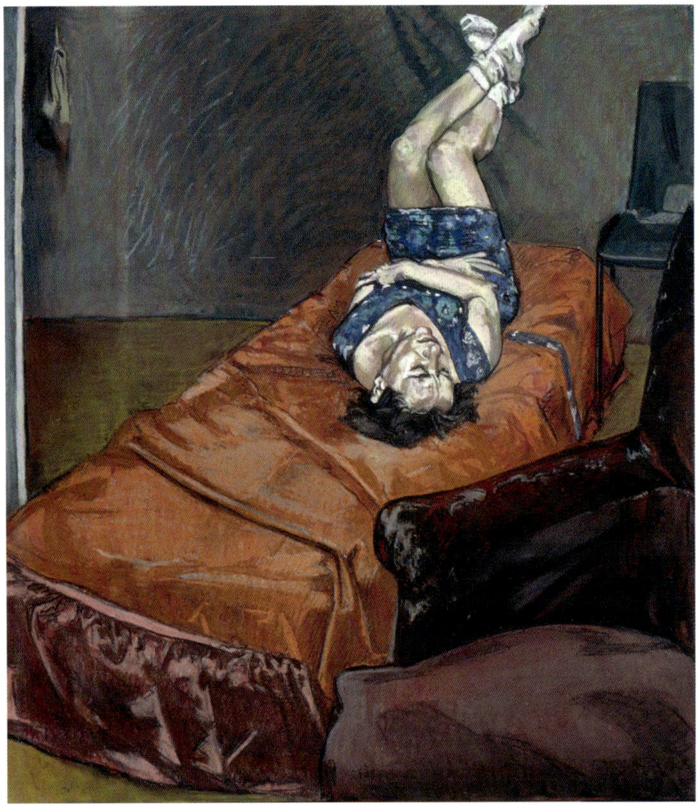

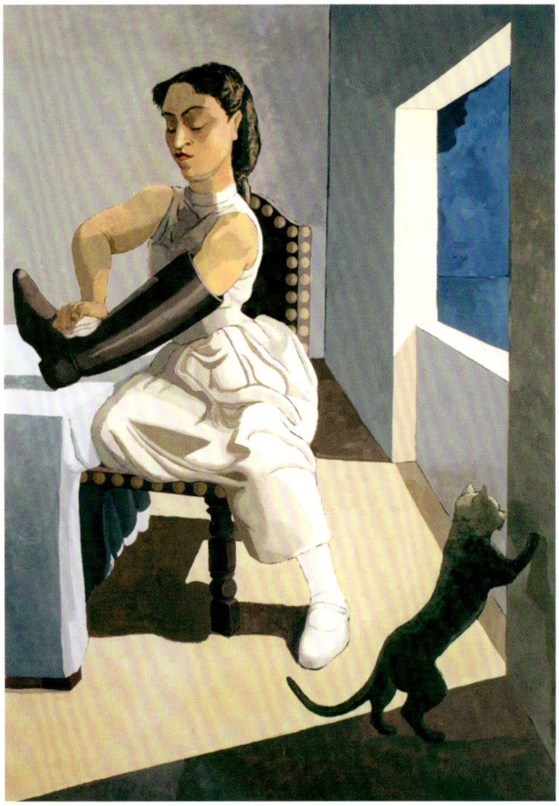

Paula Rego
Untitled No. 7 1999
Pastel on paper mounted on aluminium
110 × 100
Private collection

Paula Rego
The Policeman's Daughter 1987
Oil paint on canvas
213 × 152
Casa das Historias Paula Rego

fecund models (p.59), Maria Lassnig's (1919–2014) confrontation of ageing (p.54), Marlene Dumas's (b.1953) evocations of death (p.59) and Jenny Saville's body as battleground (pp.198–9) all force us to confront and question the (male) history of the female nude.

Paula Rego's strident paintings from the 1980s and 1990s now appear as an early clarion call for this reclaiming of the figure by female artists. The women she paints reveal raw, human instincts in her 'Dog Women' series (such as *Dog Woman – Moth* and *Bride* 1994, pp.26 and 190). They are presented with unflinching realism, even when subjected to real-life travesties such as illegal abortions, as in *Untitled No. 7* 1999 (above). (Compare this woman to the one laying on Sickert's single bed in *Nuit d'Été* c.1906, p.66.) Men often appear submissive, as in *The Company of Women* 1997 (p.186), or physically absent, as in *The Policeman's Daughter* 1987 (above). Despite this, their status in society often shapes the lives played out in Rego's dark, claustrophobic tales, where strong and active women act out each unsettling scene.

In 'A Room of One's Own', Woolf advocated the need for a woman to be a woman and not to try and pretend to be a man to succeed as a writer.[7] Rego's paintings embody this idea that a woman's voice should be authentic, distinct from and not deferential to the male voice. Fifty years after Woolf's essay was published, at a time when Rego was developing her mature voice, French feminist Luce Irigaray clearly felt progress was yet to be made. She wrote: 'If we continue to speak this sameness, if we speak to each other as men have spoken for centuries, as they taught us to speak, we will fail each other. Again.'[8] Both Woolf and Irigaray argued that for women's voices to be heard and respected they need to be their own, and not the echoes of men's. Their voices have an equal right to be heard, whether soft or strident, melancholy or celebratory.

Jenny Saville
Propped 1992
Oil paint on canvas
213.5 × 183
Gagosian

Michael Andrews
Laughter Uluru (Ayers Rock), The Cathedral I 1985
Acrylic paint on canvas
243.9 × 274.3
Tate. Purchased with assistance from the Friends of the Tate Gallery 1993

Jenny Saville incised the above lines by Irigaray into the exaggerated curves of her own flesh in *Propped* 1992 (below). The quote was written backwards across the width of the canvas, which was displayed opposite a mirror. The viewer had to study the painting using the mirror in order to decode the words. The viewer therefore became complicit in the objectification of women by looking into the mirror to study her naked form, reinforcing the notion of woman as image. Saville often uses reflection and mirroring in her paintings, as in *Reverse* 2002–3 (pp.198–9). In this work an oversized head lies prone, awkwardly twisted above a naked shoulder, resting on a mirrored slab. There's a whiff of the mortuary and yet the woman is definitively alive, her skin livid with blood pulsing beneath the surface. Gravity works on her mouth, her cheek, her nostrils, pulling her face down to meet its own reflection. This head is vastly oversized, two and a half metres long and two metres tall. Yet up close it disintegrates as an image, gestural brushstrokes criss-crossing the surface in assertive swathes.

The model for *Reverse* is Saville herself. She often works from photographs of her own body as well as images she collates in scrapbooks. She is particularly fascinated by mouths, as Bacon was. They are an essential part of the body, used for eating, drinking and speaking, but they also have their own latent sexuality. Despite the morbid presentation of the body in *Reverse*, the head's giant lips still glisten suggestively. They have been placed at the centre of the composition, upended, reimagined. The mouth is reminiscent of the geographical slash in Andrews's *Laughter Uluru (Ayers Rock), The Cathedral I* 1985 (below). Both rupture the surface in unexpected ways, suggesting a break in the skin, a depth to plumb, a visual violation.

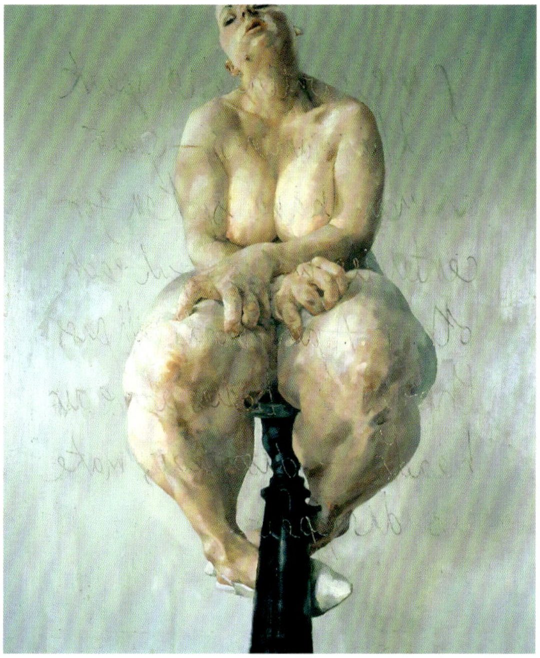

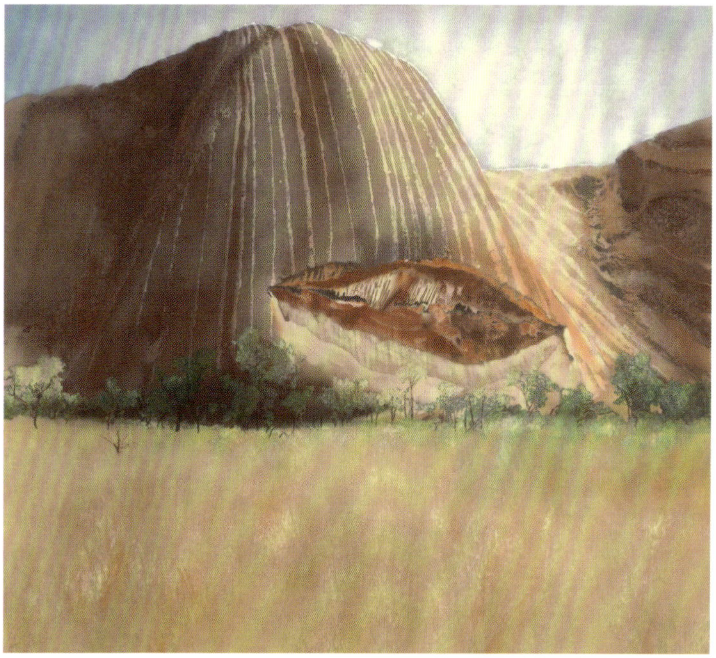

Saville's work continues to question what it is to inhabit a body subjected to societal expectations. As she says, 'The history of art has been dominated by men, living in ivory towers, seeing women as sexual objects. I paint women as most women see themselves. I try to catch their identity, their skin, their hair, their heat, their leakiness.'[9] The body, its display and objectification, is always political in her work, but her paintings are also an investigation into what it is to paint flesh, to create flesh as paint. Much of her work's strength lies in the tension between the represented form and the skin, the surface, of the painting.

The fictions of life

Lynette Yiadom-Boakye displays a similarly deft touch for the formal qualities of oil paint – how it creates light and shade, tonal depth and surface highlights; how colours can convey emotion. As she says, 'I love the fact that the act of mark-making and the materials themselves become the meaning.'[10] Single figures or small groups emerge from dark grounds in her paintings, caught up in their own lives. A man holds an eagle; a woman balances on a rock; a dancer pulls his body into the shape of a star. Their clothes are nondescript and her figures don't wear shoes, so there is little to place them in time or space. They exist outside of our world, outside of time. In *Coterie of Questions* 2015 (p.204) a man sits, head tilted away from us, eyes closed as if towards the sun, hands brought together to form an oval. The purpose of this oval is kept from us. Is he deep in thought? What is he doing? Who is he? Why has he been painted like this? What question is he trying to answer? Yiadom-Boakye paints fast, wet on wet, letting the paint dictate the form as it moves and grows like a skin over the surface. Each work lives or dies in a day, and she finishes each one in a single eight-hour session. This daily deadline gives her work a jolt of energy, an adrenalin shot that keeps it fresh, even purposely sketchy.

Yiadom-Boakye was a voracious reader as a child, reading the pictures in encyclopedias before she could read the words, and she continues to enjoy reading images, visiting museums regularly and drawing inspiration from the works she sees there – paintings by Diego Velázquez, Francisco Goya, John Singer Sargent, Edgar Degas, Édouard Manet and Walter Richard Sickert. She has compiled endless scrapbooks of poses from paintings, photographs, magazines and drawings: how bodies stand and sit and jump and lie. All these sources coalesce in her mind and contribute to the characters she paints, but essentially the characters are fictions of her imagination that are brought to life by her paintbrush. 'The subject's existence is tied to the fact that they're all constructs, they're paintings,' she says, 'and the possibilities are, in some ways, limitless because of that.'[11]

Woolf's observation about Sickert's paintings, that 'it is difficult to look at them and not to invent a plot, to hear what they are saying', could well have been written about Yiadom-Boakye's own work.[12] Yiadom-Boakye imbues her characters with credibility – they have weight in their limbs, backstory in their poses, faces shaped by layers of emotion. She brings her series of figures to life as a playwright might conjure a dramatis personae, editing shows to ensure individual works 'talk' to each other; hanging them low so the viewer can engage with them, stride right up, look them in the eye, as if to strike up a conversation.

The figures in Yiadom-Boakye's paintings are always black, just as Brown's fleshy bodies and Saville's naked women are largely white. Each artist paints from a position of self-knowledge, but Yiadom-Boakye is resigned to critics focusing on the blackness of her growing lexicon of characters. The lack of visibility of black figures in art history is being addressed by a generation of artists including Kerry James Marshall, Mickalene Thomas and Kehinde Wiley. However Yiadom-Boakye feels more affinity with Chris Ofili and Isaac Julien, artists who normalise the black human experience (as does Njideka Akunyili Crosby). 'People are tempted to politicise the fact that I paint black figures, and the complexity of this is an essential part of the work,' she says. 'But my starting point is always the language of painting itself and how that relates to the subject matter.'[13]

Painter and model

Today the ease of access to museums and galleries around the world, coupled with the availability of cheap travel, high-quality digital reproduction and the Internet, means that artists have unprecedented access to historical works of art. Yiadom-Boakye learned to paint figures by studying first-hand the works of old and modern masters (despite graduating in 2003 from the Royal Academy Schools in London, the only British institution of its kind to maintain a dedicated life-drawing room). Saville has spoken of her interest in Peter Paul Rubens, Velázquez, Sargent and de Kooning, all gestural painters who transformed paint into flesh. Celia Paul feels a certain affinity with Dutch artists of the Golden Age, in particular Rembrandt, as well as Sickert, Gwen John and Lucian Freud. Brown has spoken of artists having 'a natural conversation with the old masters', and her own studio is teeming with reproductions of paintings by Hieronymus Bosch, Pieter Breugel the Elder, Titian and Eugène Delacroix.[14]

As if acknowledging the long reach of painting's history within present-day practice, Saville, Paul, Yiadom-Boakye and Brown maintain a constant dialogue with their predecessors. Brown's 2015 painting *Boy with a Cat* (p.201), for example, could be seen to converse with Pierre-Auguste Renoir's (1841–1919) tender *The Boy with the Cat* 1868 (p.64), while transforming the boy into a full-frontal legs-akimbo reclining male nude. Alternatively this painting could be seen to be a riposte to Titian's sexually alluring *The Venus of Urbino*, her dowry ripening behind her. Or is it in part a homage to Freud, whose famed pile of studio rags the porn-star nude now appears to be lying on?

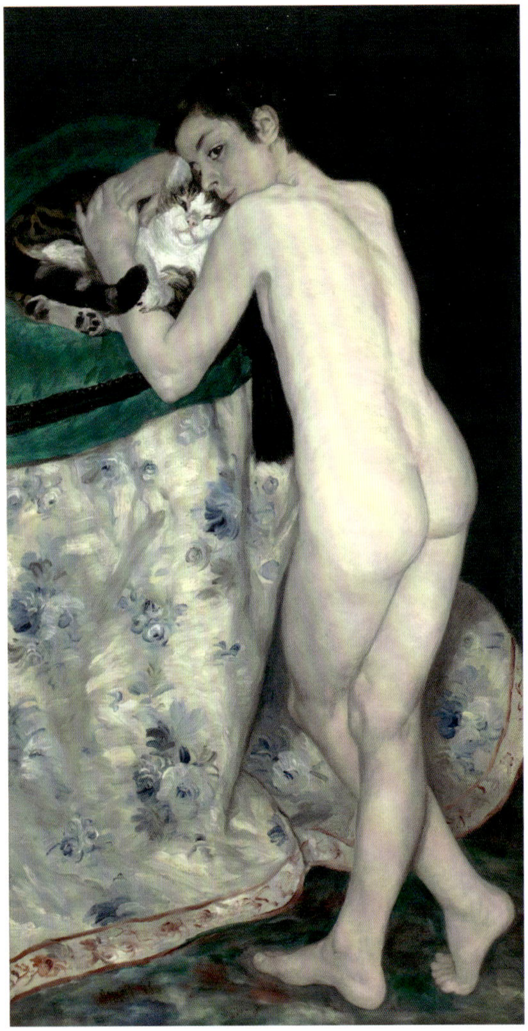

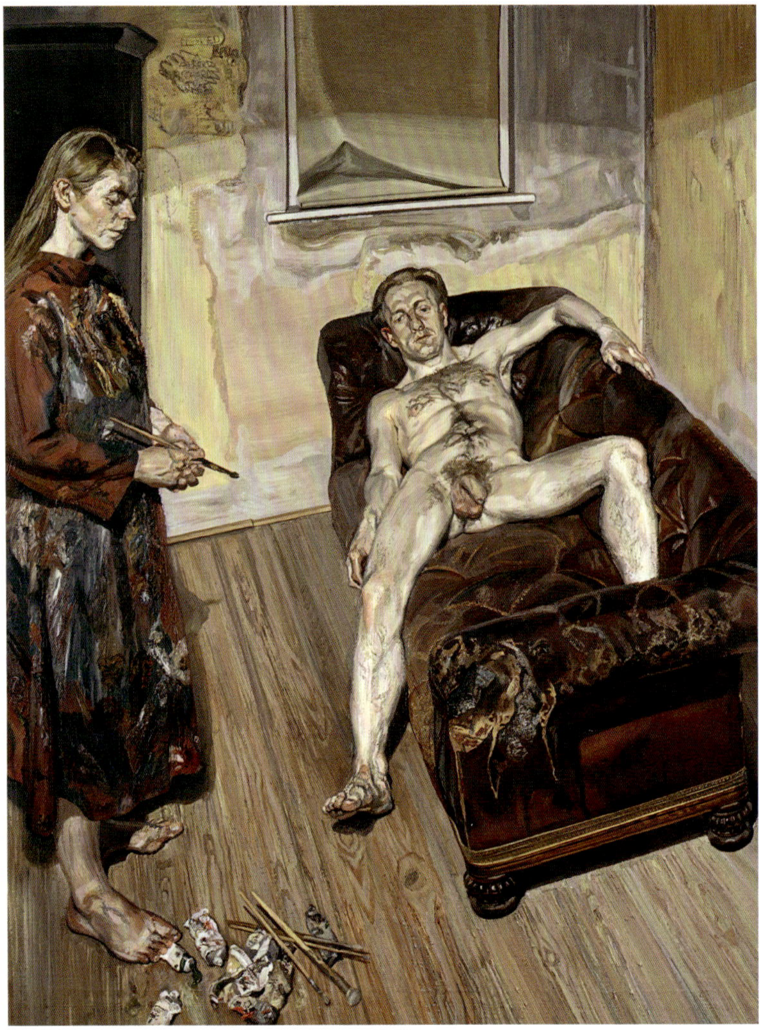

In the paintings of Brown, Saville and Yiadom-Boakye, Freud's legacy as a supreme conjurer of human flesh can be intuited to varying degrees. However, it is in Paul's work that we feel the strongest influence of Freud's palette. Her muted tones seem to be a measured response to the brutal honesty Freud brought to bear on her own flesh and the bodies of his other regular sitters. Paul's first encounter with Lucian Freud was at the Slade School of Fine Art in 1978. She was eighteen, a student, and he was a visiting tutor. She had seen a recent exhibition of his perspicacious portraits of his mother and felt an instant connection. She was drawn by the shared subject matter (her mother would remain her chief subject for thirty years) and the knowledge that Freud only worked from sitters he knew very well, as she did. She felt his palette was honest, reflecting the greys and browns of London, and she has continued to use a similar palette throughout her own career.

Freud and Paul entered into a relationship that would last ten years and would lead to some of his most tender portraits, including *Girl in a Striped Nightshirt* 1983–5 (p.155) and *Painter and Model* 1986–7 (above). In *Painter and Model* she is the painter depicted, not Freud. She wears her painter's smock and open tubes of paint ooze around her bare feet. However, Freud painted her with no canvas to work on, and her eyes are downcast, her gaze passive. It is the naked male model who asserts himself in the scene, looking straight out at the viewer from his supine

Pierre-Auguste Renoir
The Boy with the Cat 1868
Oil paint on canvas
126 × 66
Musée d'Orsay, Paris

Lucian Freud
Painter and Model 1986–7
Oil paint on canvas
159.6 × 120
Private collection

position on Freud's tattered couch. Despite appearing as an artist in the painting, Paul primarily functions as Freud's sitter, and through his composition Freud makes sure we know this. Now consider Paul's own version of *Painter and Model*, completed twenty-five years later (p.194). In it Paul is seated and alone. She is barefoot and dressed in her long paint-encrusted smock, and once again tubes of paint litter the floor. However, in this painting she looks out at the viewer as both sitter and active artist, a position of quiet authority that resonates throughout her practice. Her canvas is present – it supports the whole picture – and now she is embedded centrally within it.

Paul began painting self-portraits when her mother, her primary model, became too old to climb the stairs to her Bloomsbury flat. Paul has only ever painted a small circle of sitters, chiefly her family, building slow meditative portraits in muted greys and soft squirrel browns, with deft touches of lavender, lemon and taupe adding shadows and highlights. She is intensely private and her works have a melancholy stillness that seems to transcend the real world, offering a distillation of the lived experience that she feels or witnesses in others. 'My work is autobiographical,' she explains. 'I can only work from people and places that I know and love. This is my purpose. I need to be aware of where I am in my life and to consider what is most important and relevant to me at this present moment. I need to take time to think and plan and to be alone.'[15]

Despite her repeated use of the same sitters and the sparse settings she chooses for her portraits (an empty corner of her studio) she hopes her work resonates with the viewer, communicates with them directly. She wants her paintings to connect in the way she feels Sickert's do: 'I too wanted to do paintings that were about something, in the way that a poem or a story is.'[16]

A shared sense of storytelling, of narratives and fictions, and a love of the medium of oil paint, ultimately unites these four disparate artists. They represent the latest developments for this strand of figuration; an experiential, emotive, sensual, at times numinous representation of the figure. They prefer to draw on a broad range of sources rather than working from singular sketches, as if to acknowledge the breadth of ways the world can be seen and represented. They tease out the complexity of what it is to live in the world, allowing room for the viewer to draw their own conclusions. The smiles they paint can be both open and inscrutable, gestures can be emphatic and mysterious, eyes can be brimful of emotion and, simultaneously, flicks of paint on the surface. The bodies they paint have an authenticity to them, whether dragged half-formed from memories, breathed into life in the studio or wholly imagined. Their representations of the body, of lives lived within it, are not priapic or monolithic, possessive or predatory. Instead they are polyvalent, fragmentary, questioning, exploratory. They demand our attention in a variety of ways – softly, imaginatively, politically, suggestively – and connect to a broader international network of artists who employ the figure as a vehicle to question what makes us human, and what it means to live in the twenty-first century.

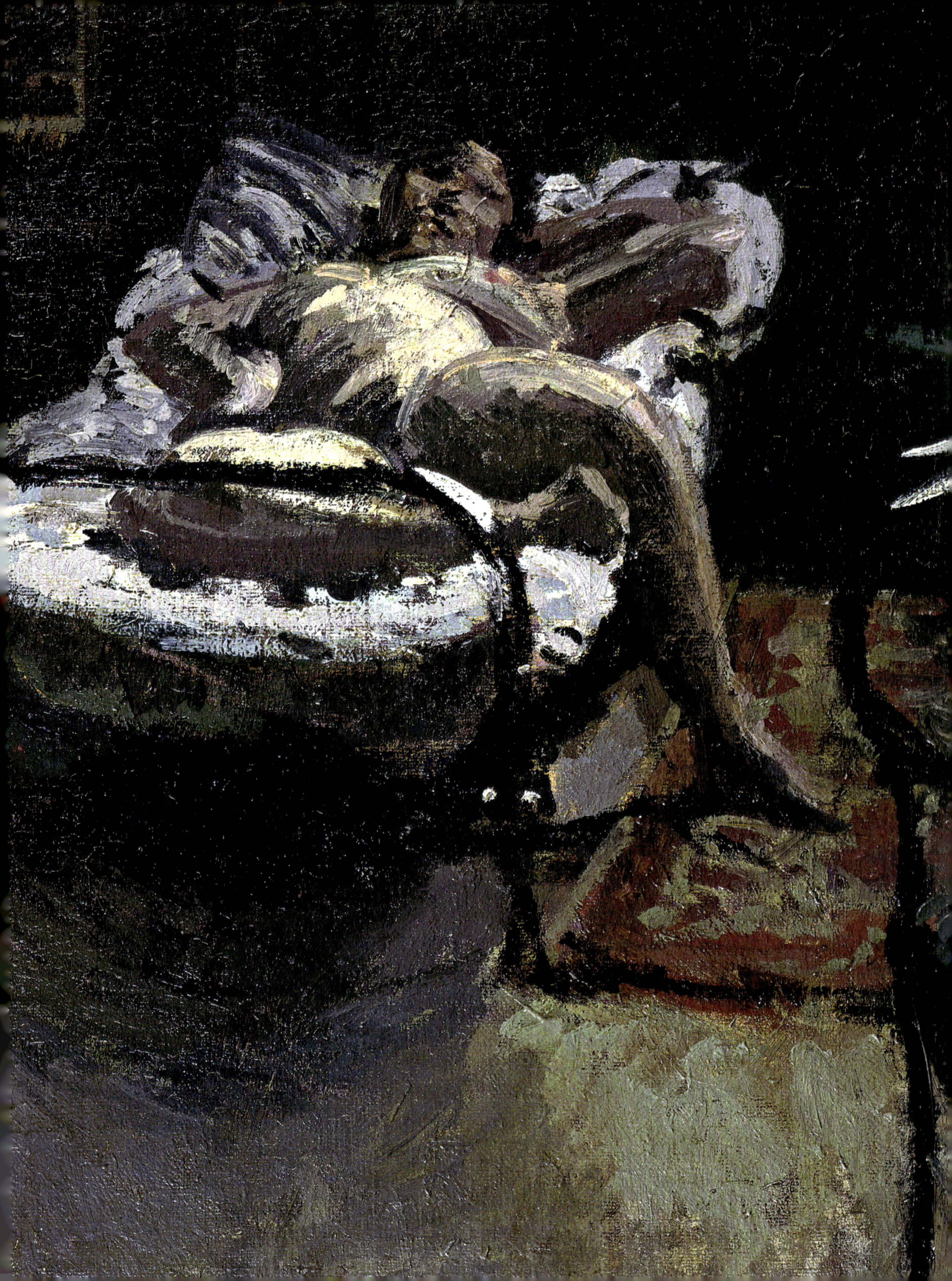

The Raw Facts of Life

Elena Crippa

A number of painters working or exhibiting in Britain in the first half of the twentieth century proved particularly influential in relation to the subjects they chose, and the way in which they handled paint, constructed their compositions and structured gaze within the picture and beyond the picture plane, in relation to an imaginary spectator. Among them are David Bomberg, Walter Richard Sickert, Chaïm Soutine and Stanley Spencer, who set new paths in the representation of an intimate and sensuous reality, focusing on the portrayal of individuals and places that were close and dear to them, and offering the vivid sensation of an intensely experienced visual and haptic encounter. In different ways, their work marked an engagement with forms of realism indebted to developments that had been taking place across the Channel.

Walter Richard Sickert was born in Munich, moved to London with his family as a child in 1868 and trained at the Slade School of Fine Art and as assistant to James Abbott McNeill Whistler. After years spent in Paris, Dieppe and Venice, Sickert returned to London in 1905, where he was unimpressed with the lack of radicalism in the British art scene. Over the following years, he sought with renewed energy a radical way of engaging with modern painting, offering a realist account of contemporary urban life. Sickert's pictures of nudes in intimate settings and representations of spectatorship remain influential over a century after first being exhibited. His nudes connect back to Edgar Degas's and Pierre Bonnard's intimate scenes in which naked bodies, rather than academic nudes, are represented and unconventional poses are explored.[1] With Degas, Sickert also shares the tight construction of compositions that stage theatrical scenes and create a sense of mystery and unresolved narrative. In his representations of the eager, embodied gaze of music-hall audiences as much as in those of nudes in modest interiors, his paintings represent the experience of partaking in the modern world as shaped by the intersection of desiring, voyeuristic or surveilling gazes.

Originally from Russia, Chaïm Soutine moved to Paris in 1913 as a young man. For a few years he was based at La Ruche, near a slaughterhouse. Game, fish and the hanging carcasses of animals and their flesh became recurrent subjects, their unmoving material enlivened and set in motion by the thick impasto, gestural brushwork and animated forms. Soutine could only paint in the presence of his subject, and sitting for him was a demanding task. His models were to remain in stationary positions for hours, so that an intense sense of endurance, as much as their features, is ultimately the subject of his portraits. Between 1919 and 1922 Soutine spent most of his time in Céret, southern France, where he painted numerous landscapes of groups of houses on hilltops. His work was exhibited widely in London in the 1930s and again in the 1950s and 1960s. Between 1953 and 1964 *Landscape at Céret* c.1920–1 (p.73) was shown at least ten times, in a number of exhibitions at the Redfern Gallery, in a group exhibition at the ICA and at his 1963 retrospective at the Tate Gallery. The painting exerted a particular influence on Francis Bacon.[2] Bacon certainly shared with Soutine an excitement about the colour of meat; the working of oil paint as a living substance, capable

Walter Richard Sickert
Nuit d'Été c.1906 (detail)

of conveying a sense of the raw quality of reality; and the distortion of forms, as if animated from within. For his part David Bomberg, who had referred to Soutine as 'our colleague', shared with him an engagement with the representation of masses and the conveyance of tactile experiences.[3]

Bomberg was born in Birmingham and moved to London at the age of five. He attended Sickert's evening art classes before enrolling at the Slade School of Fine Art in 1911. During his early career Bomberg experimented with many avant-garde movements and exhibited with the London Group and the Vorticists. The onset of the First World War interrupted his work and had a profound effect on him. After the war, he realised the threat of mechanisation on humanity and moved away from the verve of his earlier geometric forms. He decided instead to attend to the natural world, favouring a more organic style of painting. Important expeditions and prolonged stays abroad, particularly in Palestine and Spain, proved key in the development of his work and his engagement with landscape. He reasserted the importance of the formal strength of his work, while dedicating himself to the representation of views in which the dominant presence of the masses of mountains and hilltops is combined with the structured fabric of buildings. Bomberg struggled to see his mature work recognised, and suffered neglect. In *Self-Portrait* 1931 (p.76), wearing a large, bucket-shaped hat and intensely returning the viewer's gaze, he is posing as a dandy, with a demeanour of defiant resilience.

Stanley Spencer was a fellow student of Bomberg's at the Slade. Soon after completing his studies he became known for painting biblical scenes. Often set in his native Cookham, a small village beside the River Thames where he lived most of his life, these scenes were populated with portraits of friends and lovers as well as self-portraits. During the 1930s, when he became more isolated from his circle of artist friends, he nearly exclusively painted those who were more immediately involved in his personal life, particularly his second wife, the artist Patricia Preece. In her numerous portraits, including six erotic nudes, Preece's features are accentuated rather than idealised, while the atmosphere is often of sexual tension. These pictures are indebted to a key modernist redefinition of realism which encompasses the work of Degas and George Grosz, and which the art historian David Alan Mellor has defined as 'an abrasive, anti-sentimentalising objectivity'.[4] In Spencer's portraits the sharpness of the scrutinising gaze is combined with an intensity of feeling that seems to bubble under the skin of the figures, offering a sense of tense presentness, enlivened by desire. As the artist and art critic D. S. MacColl wrote in 1935, Spencer is a 'Super Realist, a visionary who sees violently and strangely, transforming, swelling or deflating forms'.[5]

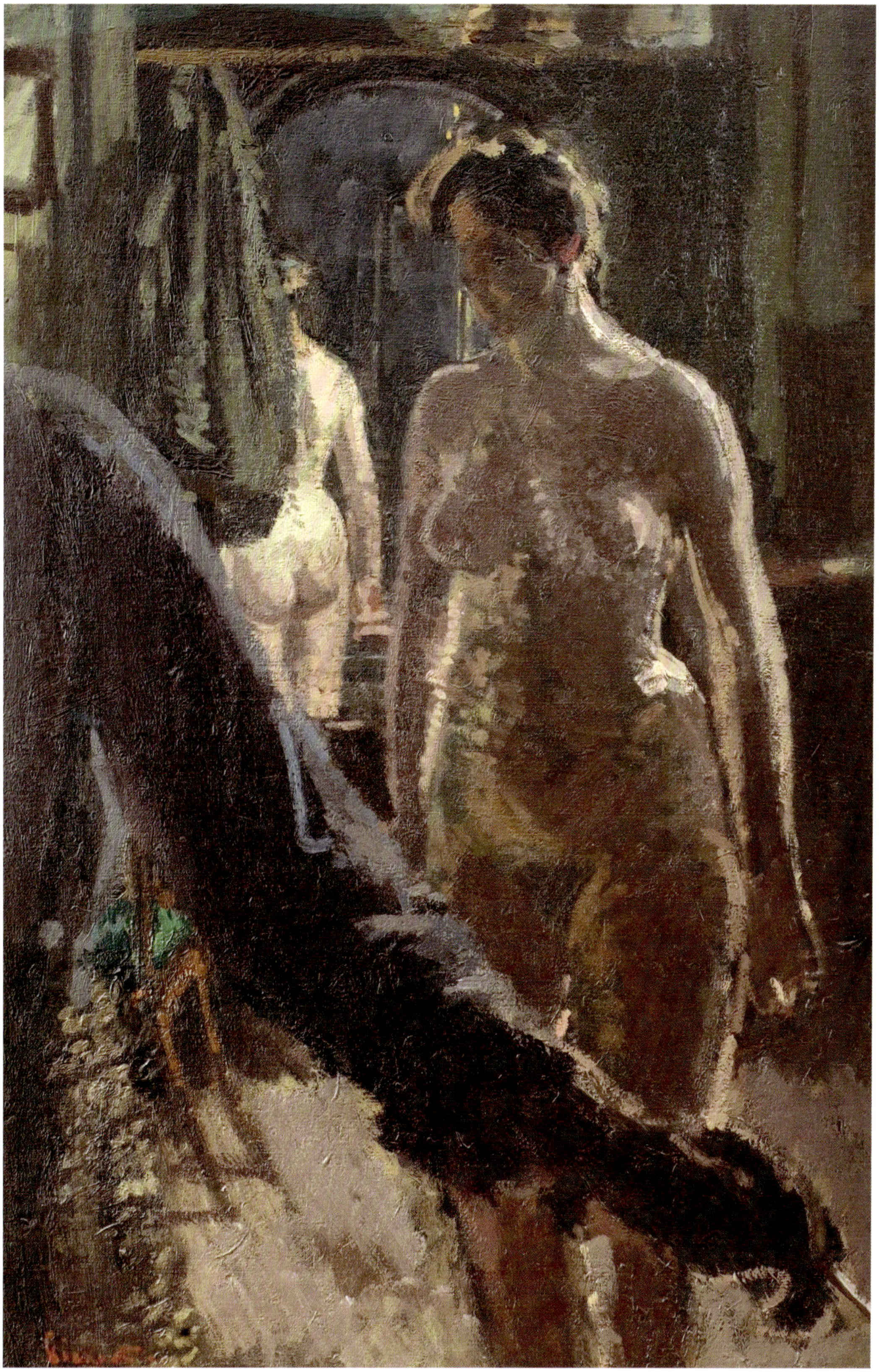

Walter Richard Sickert
The Studio: The Painting of a Nude 1906 (also dated 1911–12)

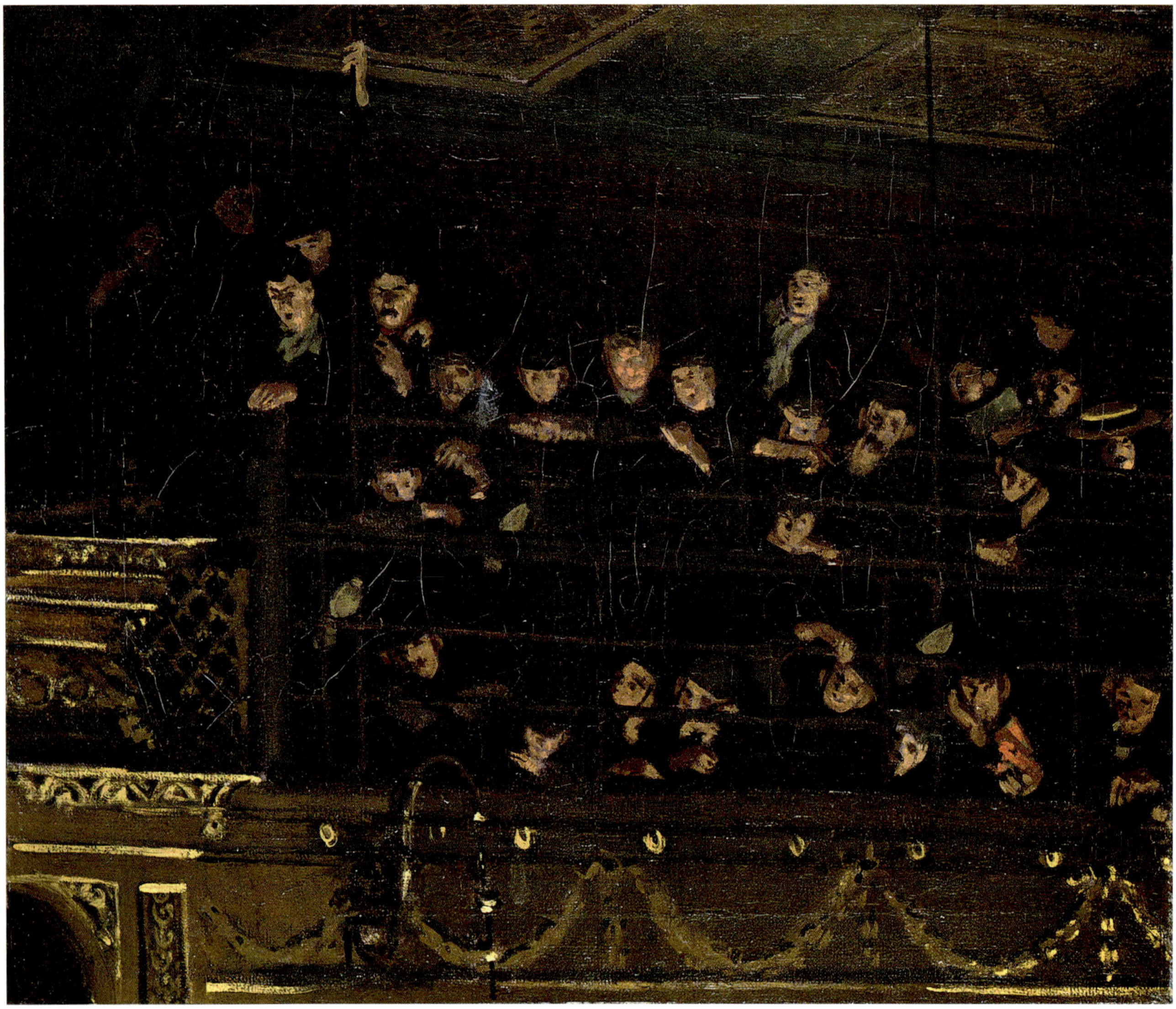

Walter Richard Sickert
Noctes Ambrosianae 1906

Chaïm Soutine
The Butcher Stall c.1919

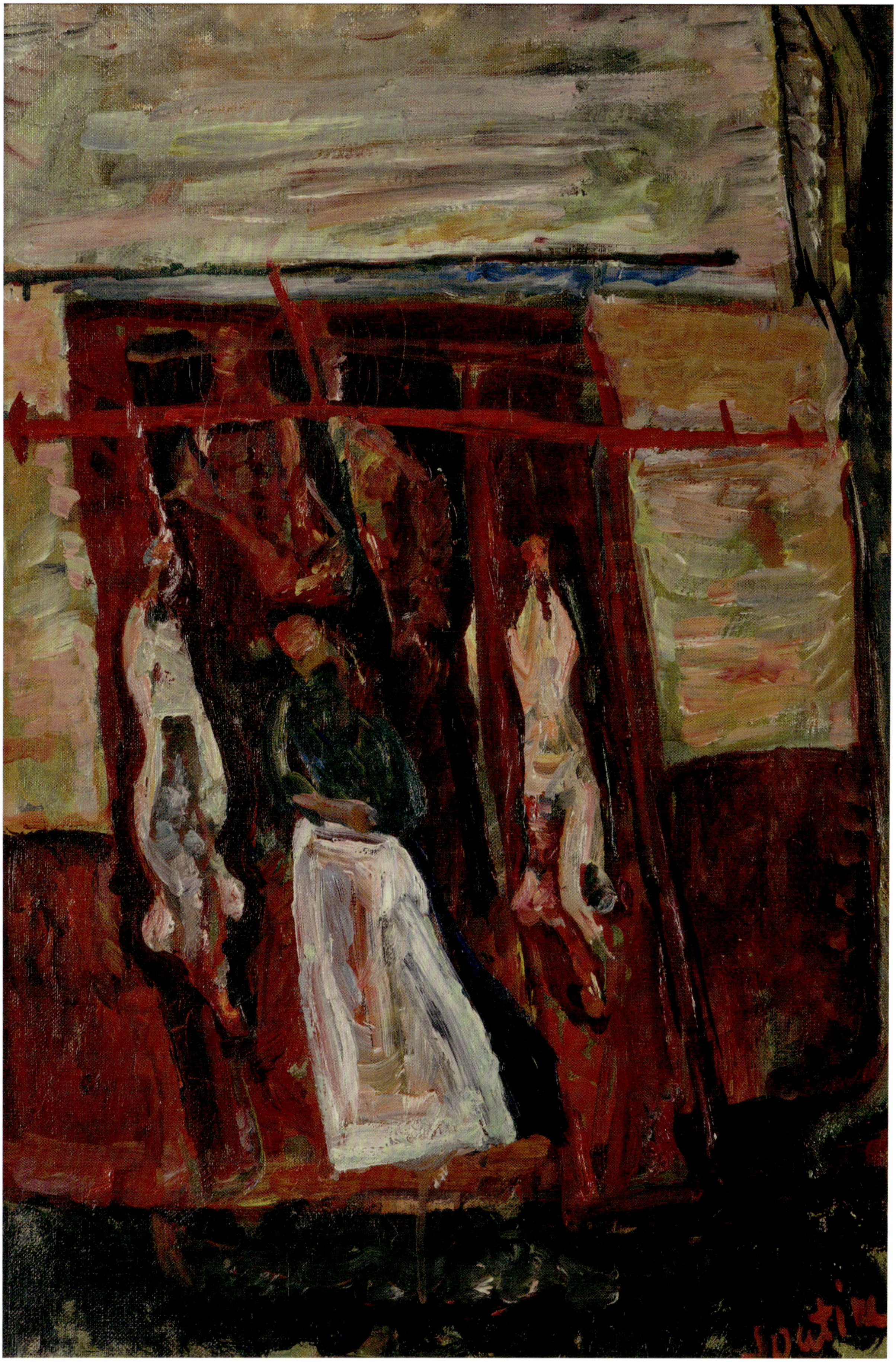

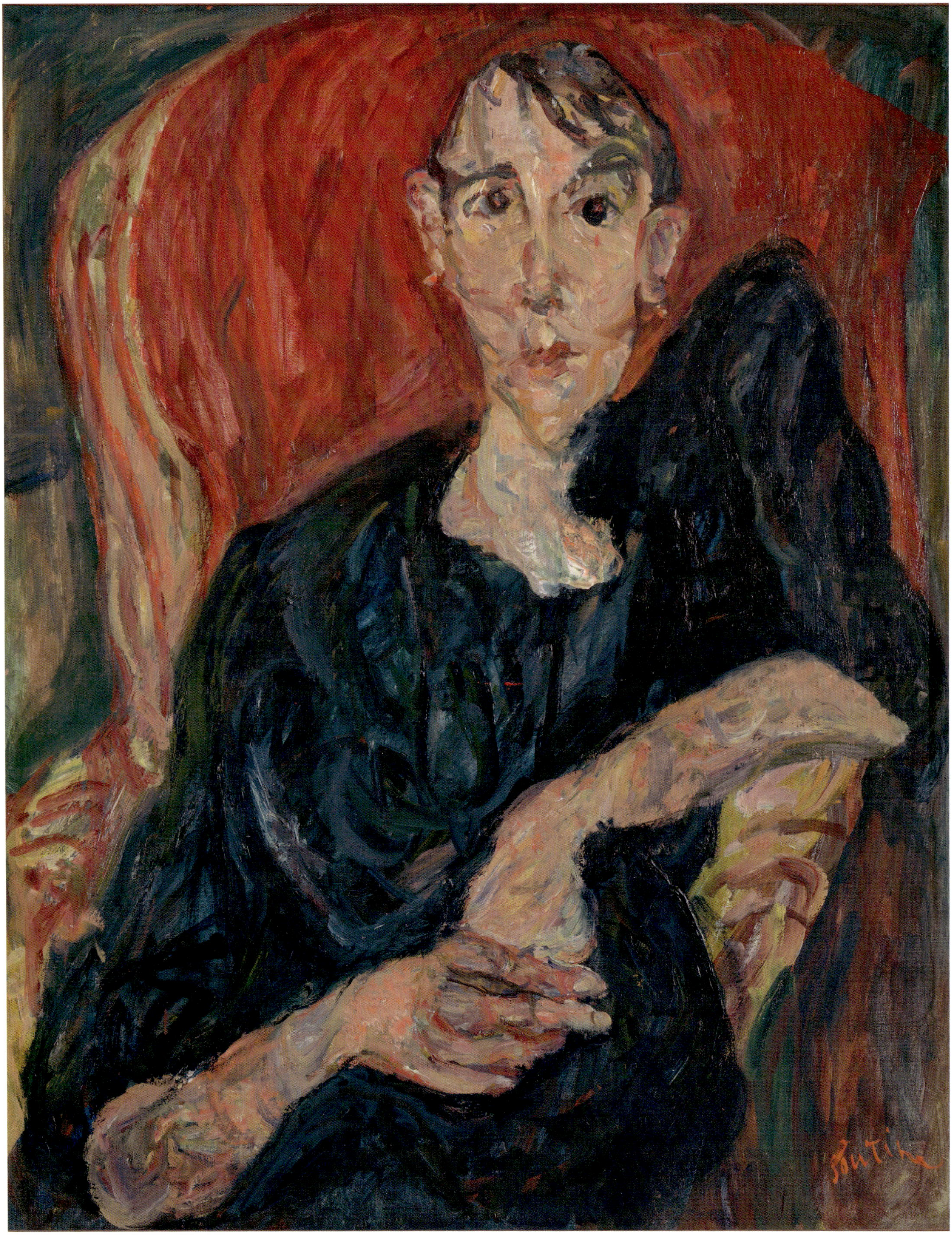

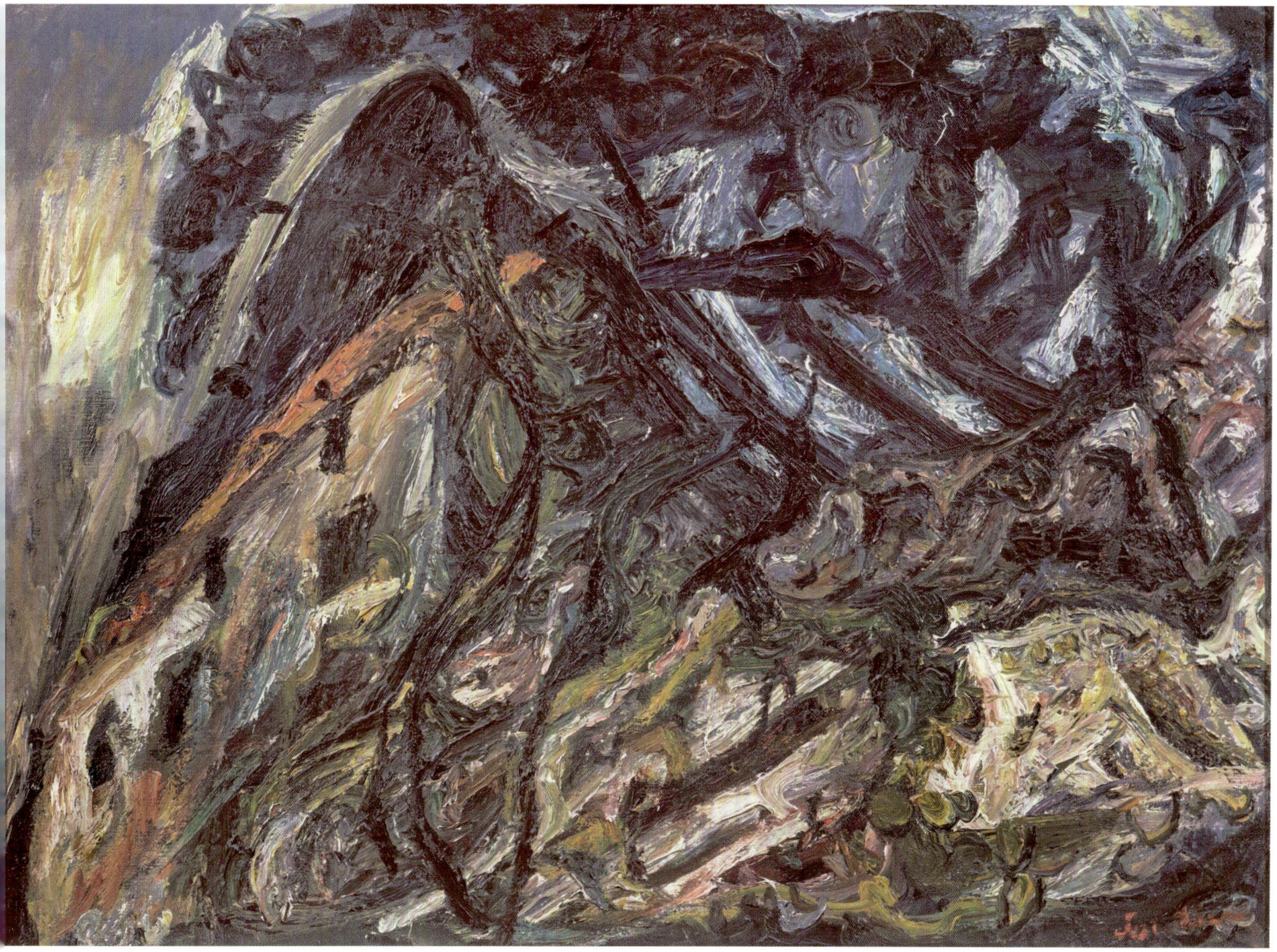

Chaïm Soutine
Polish Woman c.1922

Chaïm Soutine
Landscape at Céret c.1920–1

David Bomberg
Toledo from the Alcazar 1929

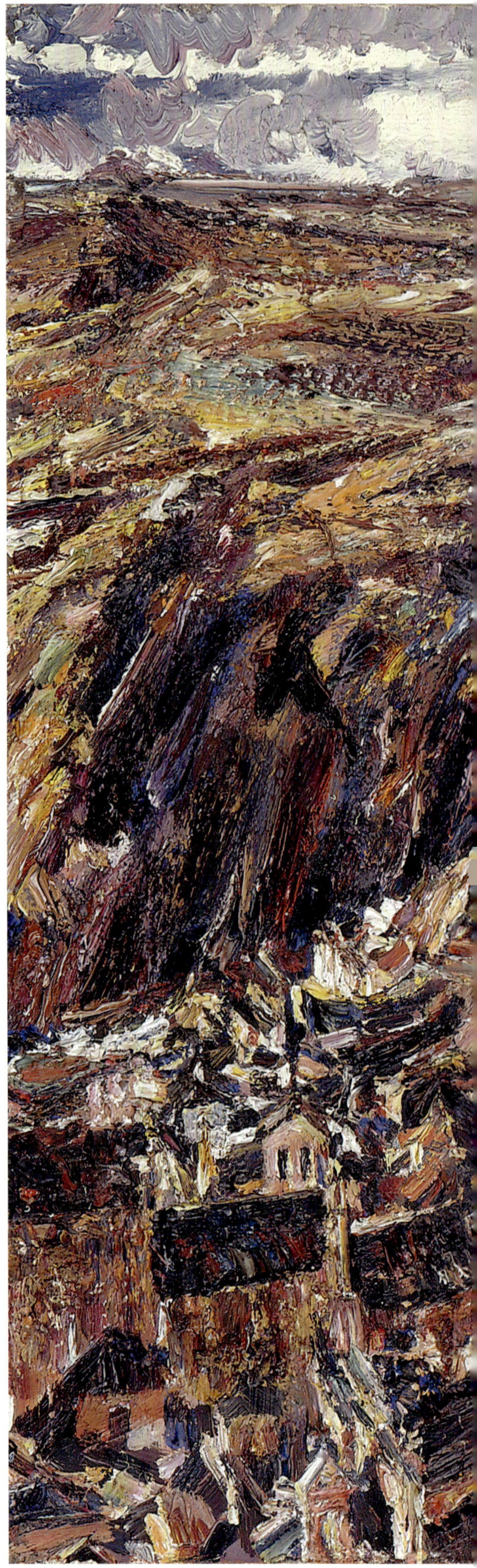

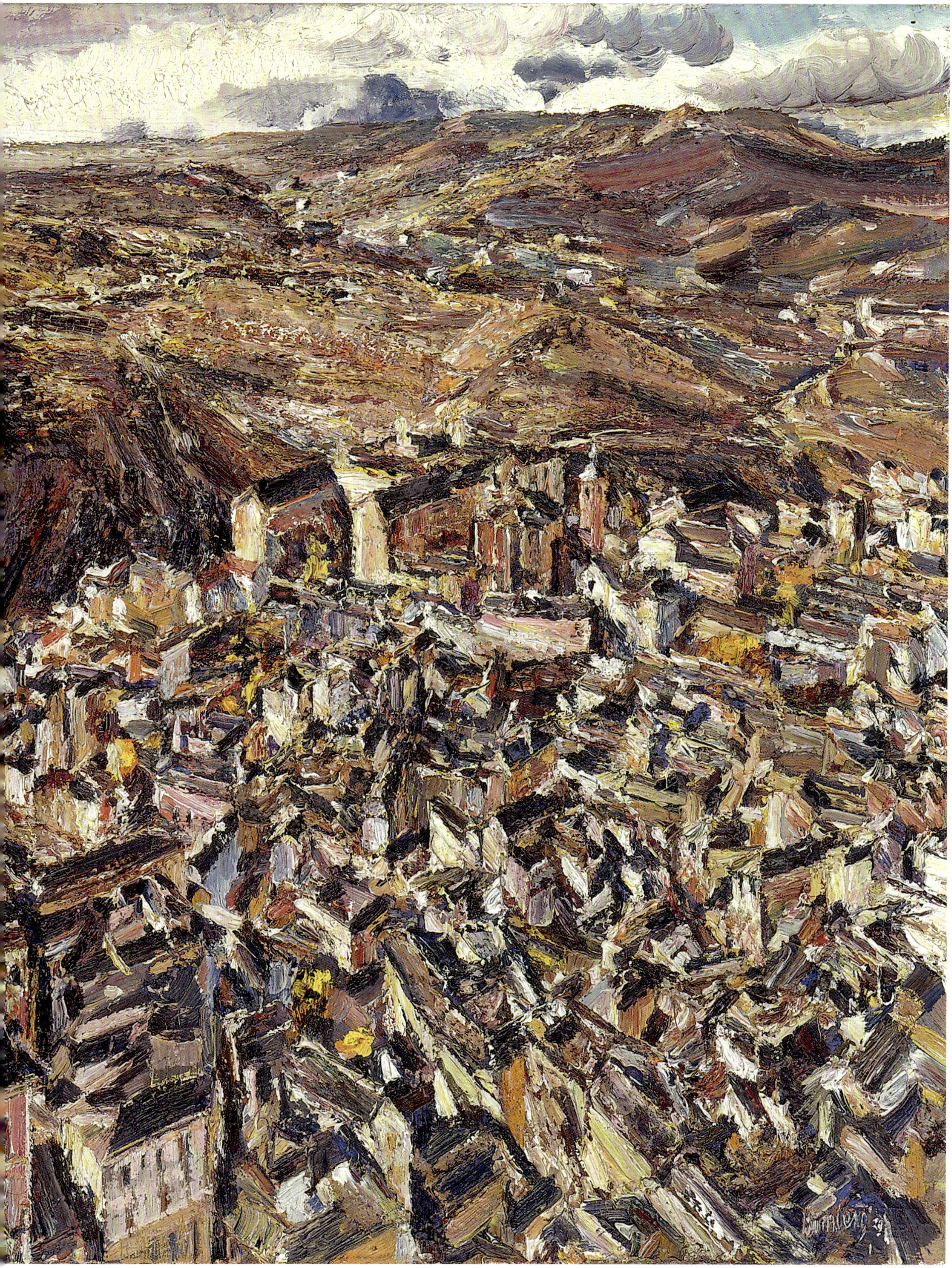

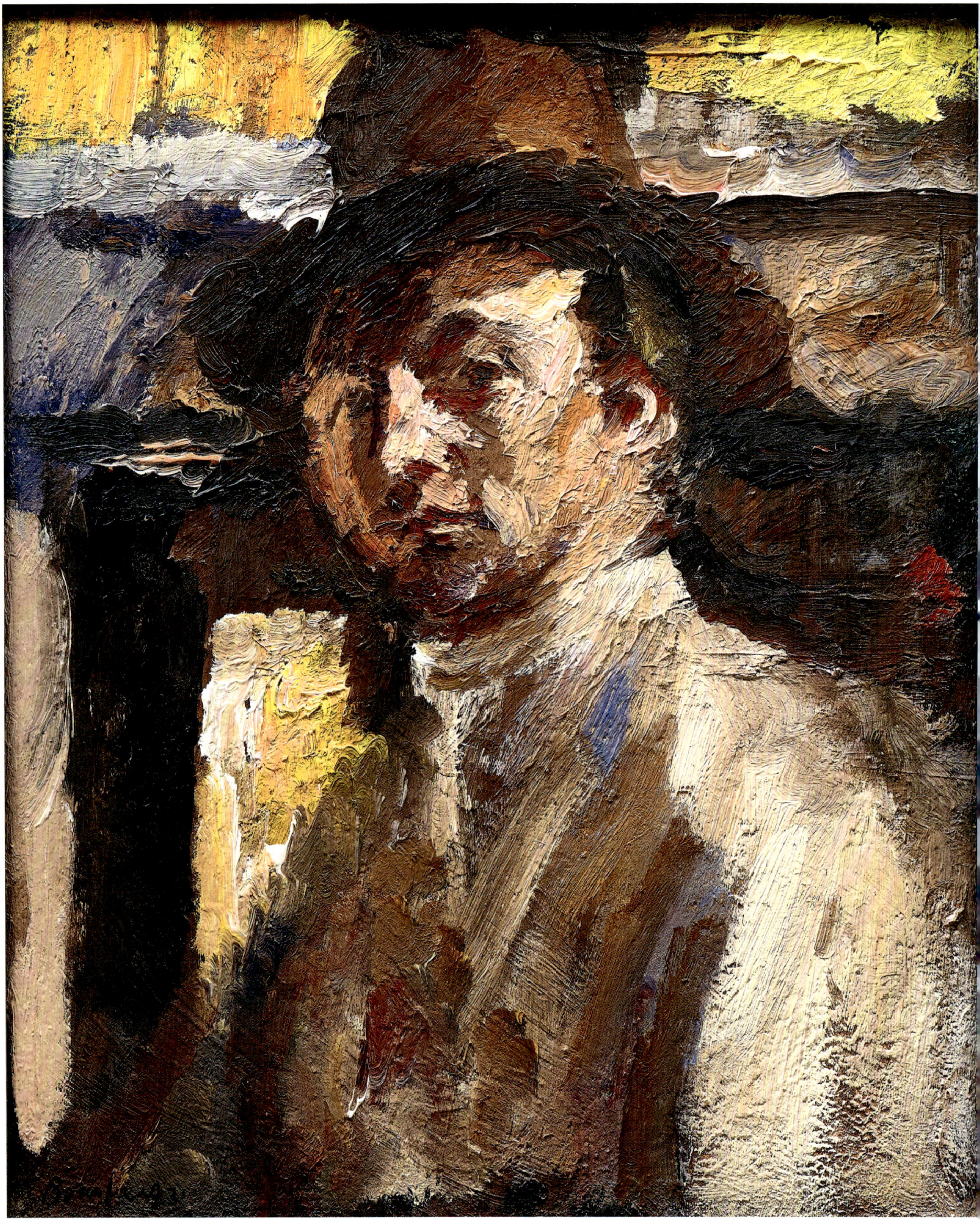

David Bomberg
Self-Portrait 1931

David Bomberg
The Bridge and the River Tajo, Ronda 1935

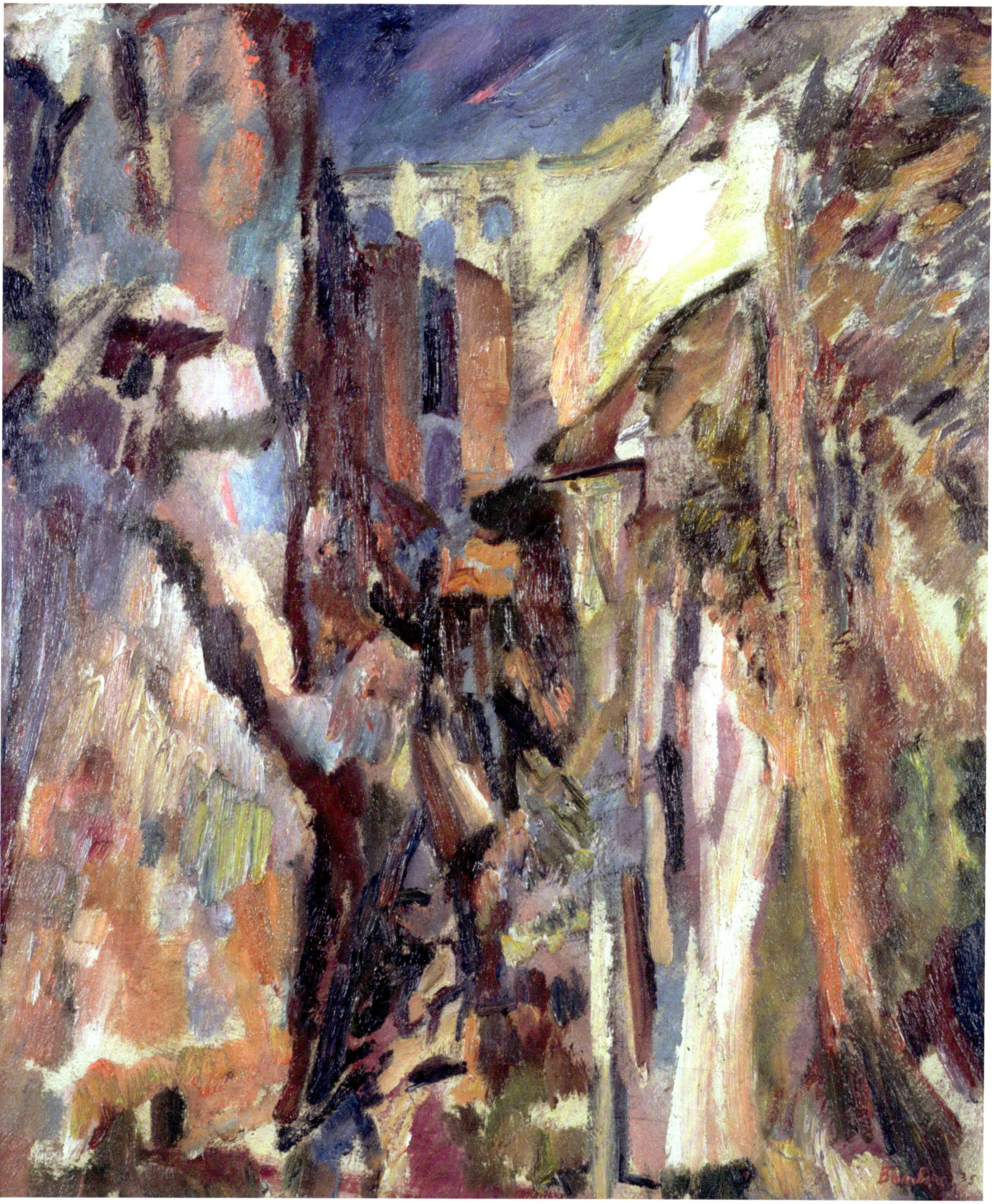

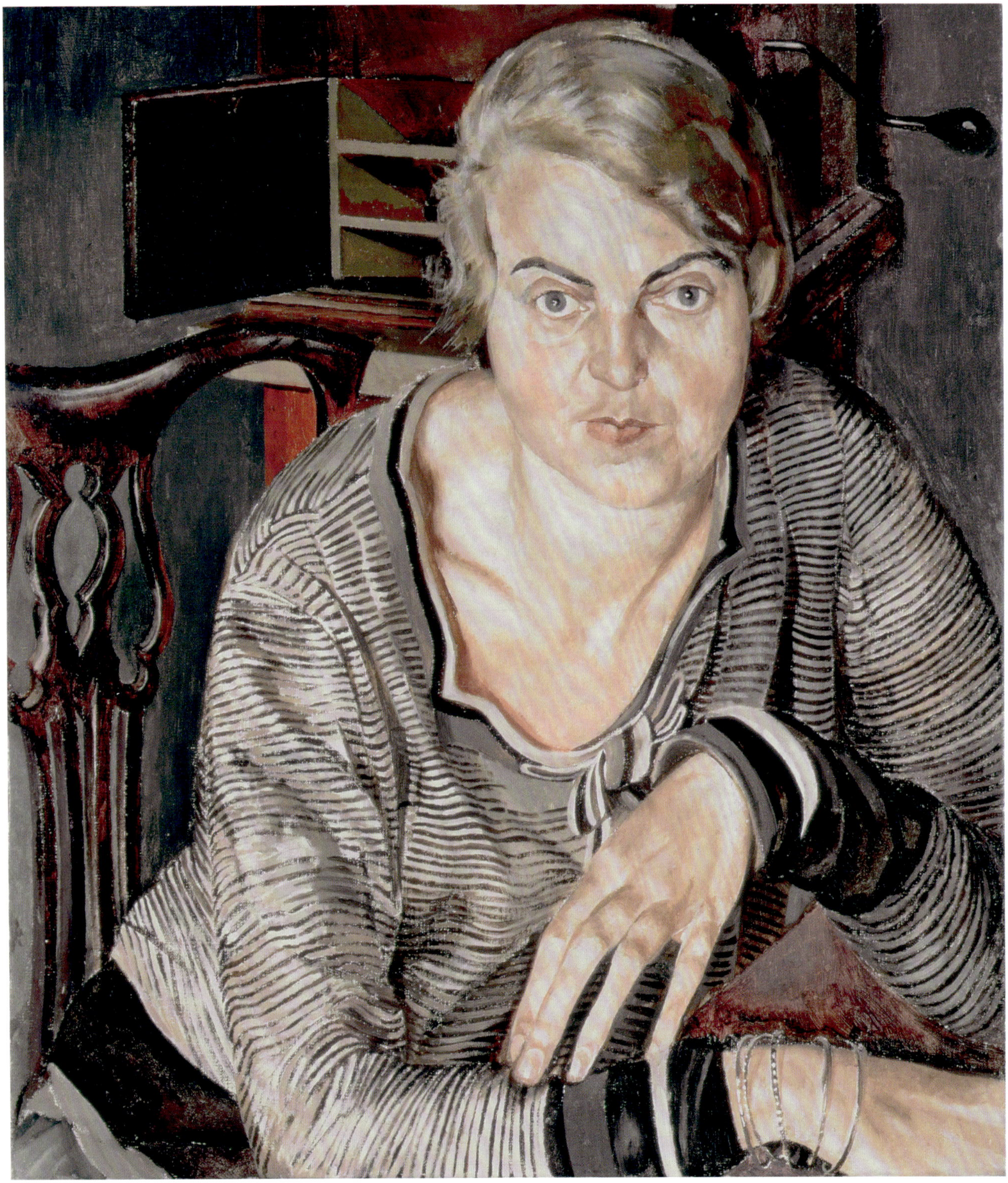

Sir Stanley Spencer
Patricia Preece 1933

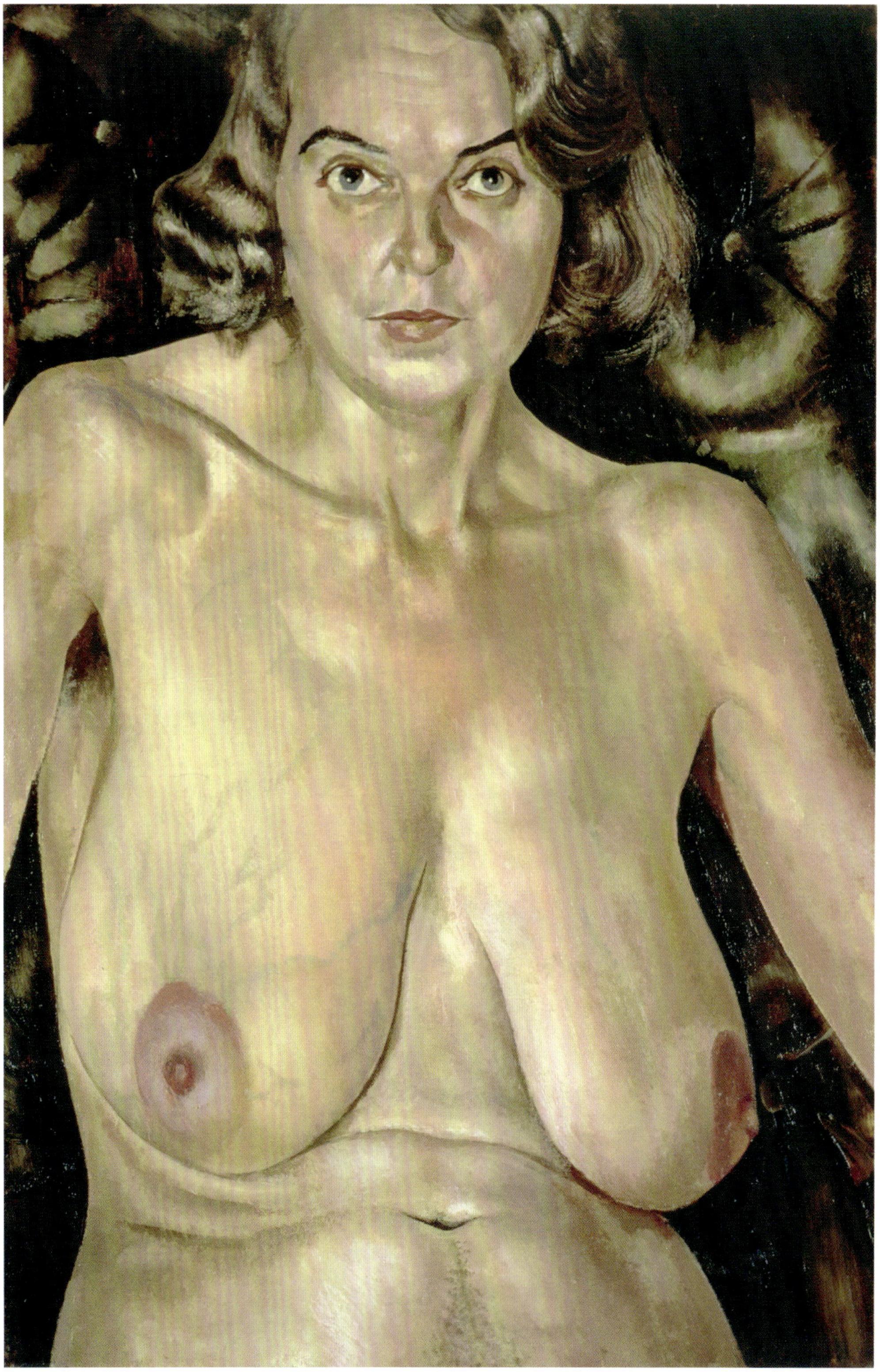

Sir Stanley Spencer
Nude Portrait of Patricia Preece
1935

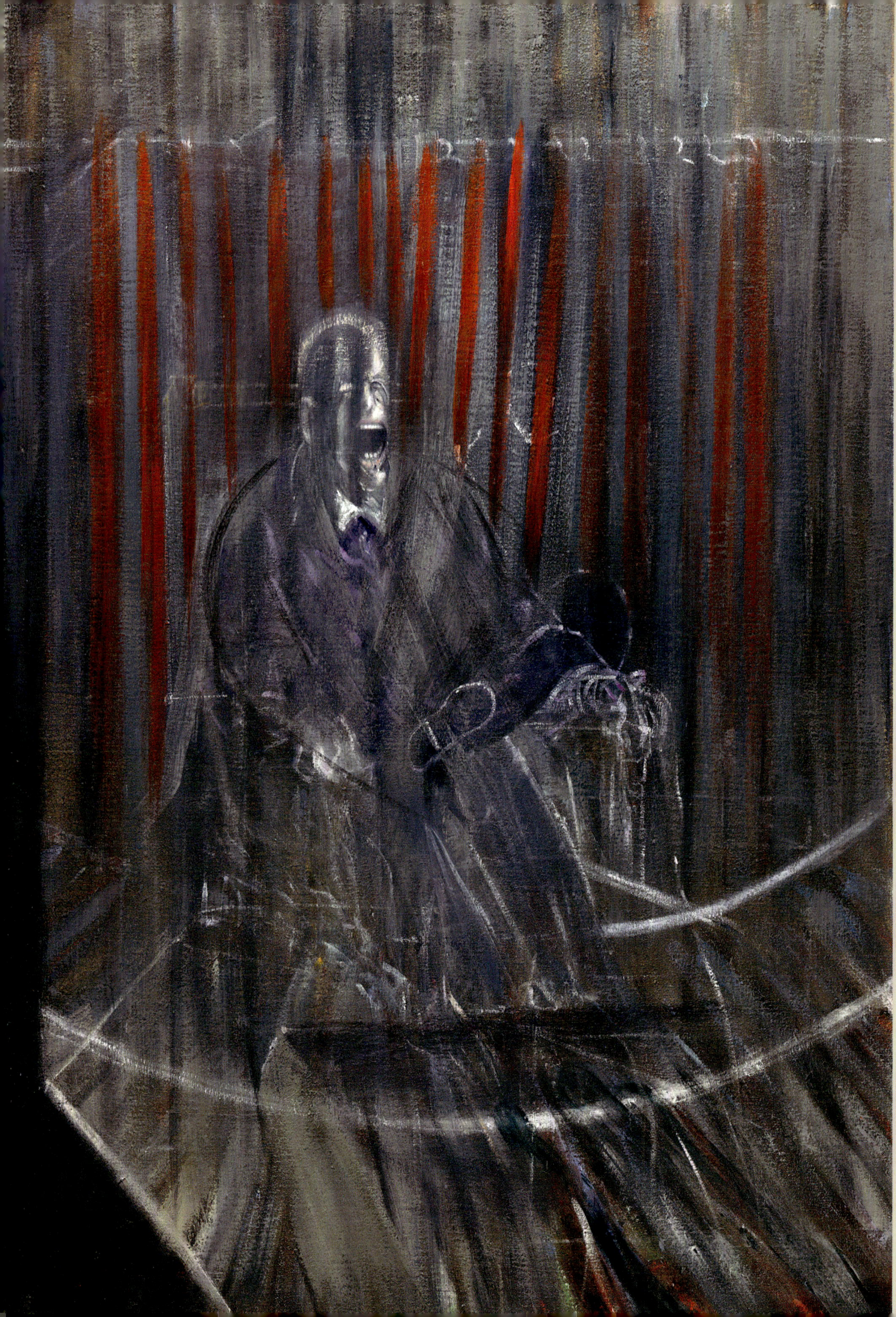

Francis Bacon and Alberto Giacometti

Elena Crippa

In the 1950s, the art critic David Sylvester promoted a type of realism that conveyed an experience of reality without veering towards what he viewed as the illustrational concerns of social realism.[1] In a 1950 lecture titled 'Towards a New Realism', Sylvester championed the return of the centrality of the observable world as the subject of modern art, but in a way that reflected a contemporary position. For Sylvester, modern man 'conceives of reality as the series of sensations and ideas that occur in the consciousness of each individual'.[2] The resulting works were not representations of objects, but of a subjective experience of those objects; they were not scenes taking place independently from an observer, but images in which the observer participated. As paradigms of this new art, Sylvester showed images of work of Francis Bacon and Alberto Giacometti. Sylvester's analysis of the pillars of a modern form of realism – as a record of the personal experience of the artist and trigger of the embodied experience of the observer – was indebted to the popularisation of existentialism through the writing of Jean-Paul Sartre. In particular, Sartre's text on Giacometti, published for the catalogue of an exhibition he held in 1948 in New York, was hugely influential among British artists and intellectuals, with Sylvester referring to it as a 'talisman'.[3]

Popularised at a time marked by the anxiety that followed the war, full realisation of the systematic extermination of the concentration camps and the threat of atomic weapons, existentialism came to be widely seen as the intellectual expression of an epoch that demanded concrete solutions. Its philosophy promoted a responsible freedom in an absurd world into which humans had been unwillingly hurled. Human reality was situated in the world primarily via practical concerns and authentic experiences rather than epistemic relationships. It may not come as a surprise that, if existentialism greatly contributed to discussions of figurative art in the postwar period, it played a particularly important role in shaping the responses to the work of Bacon and Giacometti. Their isolated figures from the late 1940s and 1950s, angst-ridden and with a sense of stoic endurance, seemed to encapsulate the position of the individual mapped by existentialism. Additionally, the work of both artists was defined by its process of making, the image unravelling or the object forming through the artist's engagement with their materials. The imprint or mark of the artist's hand was crucial in creating portraits redolent of an intense and subjective experience.

The subjects that dominated the two artists' work, frozen postures and gestures, gave their figures a sense of enduring presence. If some of Giacometti's recurring tropes in the 1950s were the pointing man and the standing woman, Bacon elected grimacing mouths as his trademark. The philosopher Giorgio

Francis Bacon
'Study after Velázquez' 1950
(detail)

Agamben wrote that: 'What characterises gesture is that in it nothing is being produced or acted, but rather something is being sustained and endured.'[4] For Agamben, differently from an action carried out exclusively to reach a specific objective, but also differently from acting out a role or performing a choreographed dance, gesture is neither the means towards an objective, nor an objective in itself. Instead, it is the exhibition of humans' capacity and struggle to communicate – it is the expression of means without ends, suspended between desire and fulfilment. It is being in its pure presence. Such essential quality of gesture, visible in the work of both Bacon and Giacometti, sets their figures in a continuous present: on one side as still embodiment of stoic endurance; on the other side as pure gesticulating presence, unaware of itself and its meaning.

Bacon and Giacometti's relation to the history of figurative art has also been discussed as being alike. Writing in 1963, the art critic and curator Lawrence Alloway built on the established pairing of Bacon and Giacometti's work but, rather than pursuing an existentialist reading, addressed what he saw as their similar way of engaging with the iconography of official and monumental portraiture.[5] In Alloway's view, both artists borrowed the subjects and monumentality of the 'Grand Manner', continuing the past tradition only in order to create a sense of ambiguity or disruption, by virtue of infringing on the orderly status of such paradigms and turning monumental sculpture or official portraiture into the avatars through which a more disquieting vitality and restless sensibility emerge. This is undoubtedly the case in Bacon's adoption of Velázquez's Pope or the Crucifixion – two tropes he returned to many times, not just in the 1950s but also in the following decades; and of Giacometti's caryatid-like figures and his appropriation of the traditional format of the portrait bust.

Bacon and Giacometti's search for a new human image, representative of one's time and experience of life, was shared by many other artists across Europe and beyond. Numerous British artists and intellectuals revolved around Giacometti at the time, having visited him in Paris or being influenced by the work that they began seeing through reproductions in the late 1940s, and in the flesh in London galleries in the 1950s and 1960s. They were also deeply affected by the artist's rigorous discipline of trial and error, and by his capacity to create great art with modest means in a small room. As Frank Auerbach reflected, in the 1950s: 'an artist like Giacometti offered hope, to continue to give everything for a truthful art without any compromises'.[6]

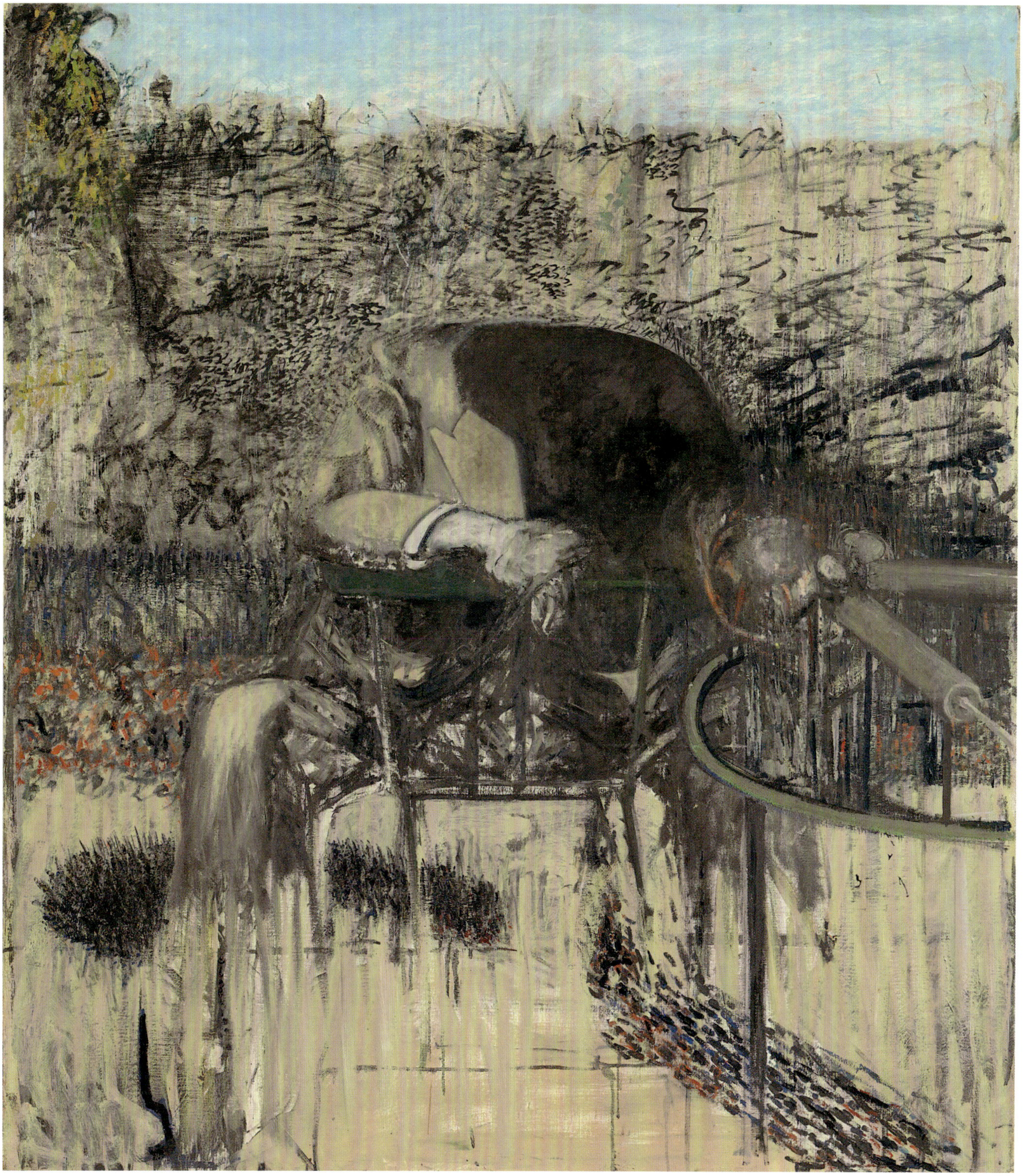

Francis Bacon
Figure in a Landscape 1945

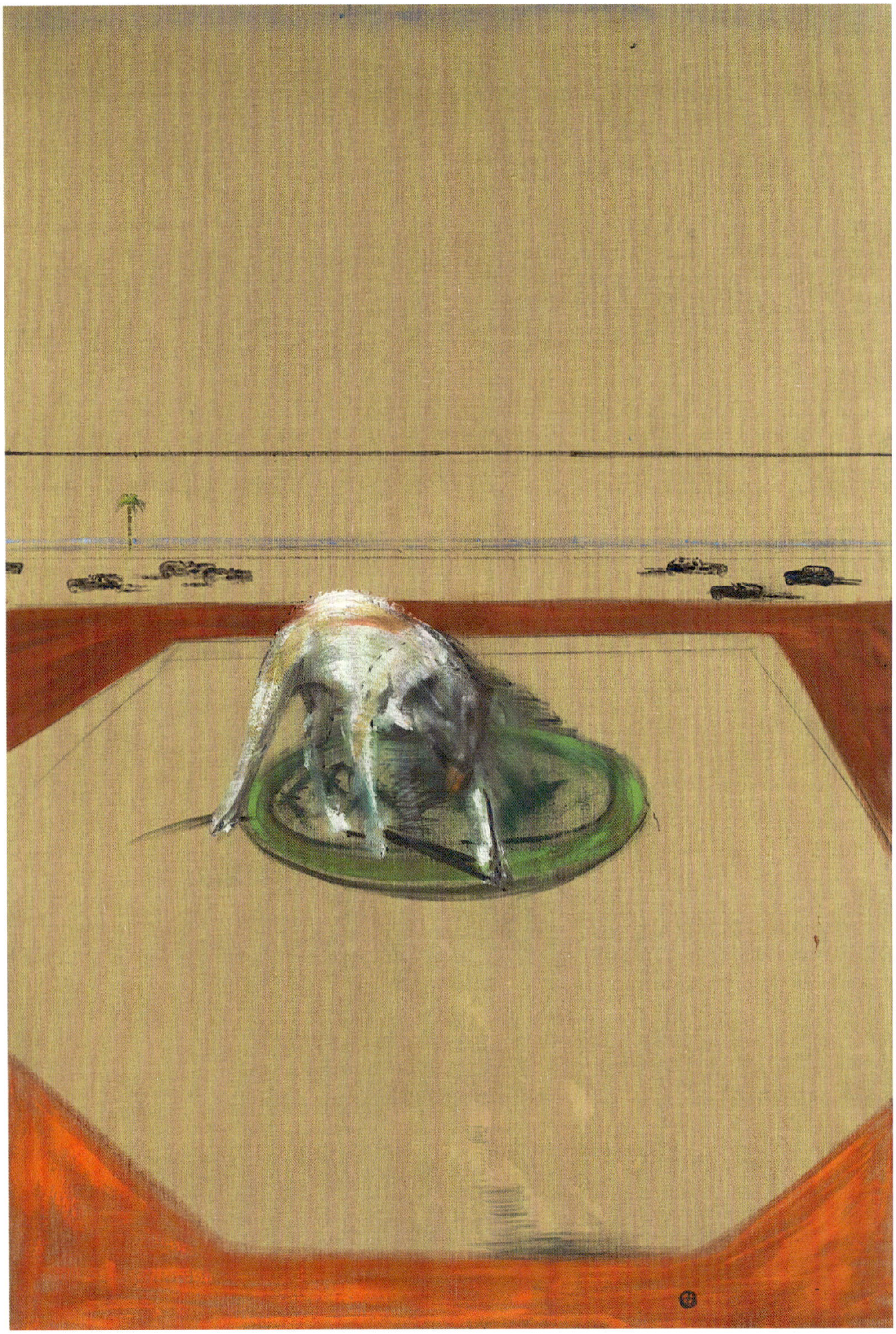

Francis Bacon
Dog 1952

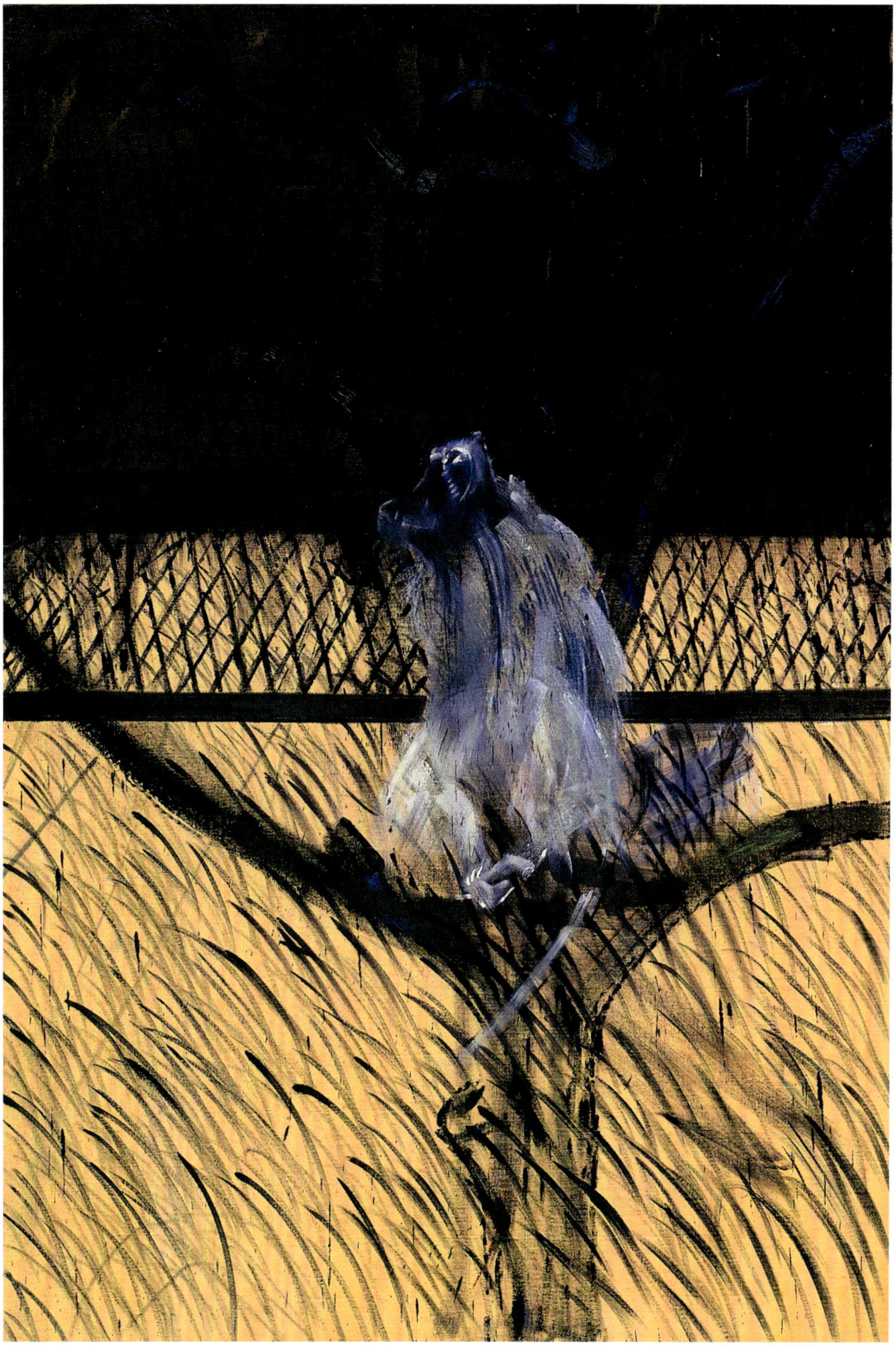

Francis Bacon
Study of a Baboon 1953

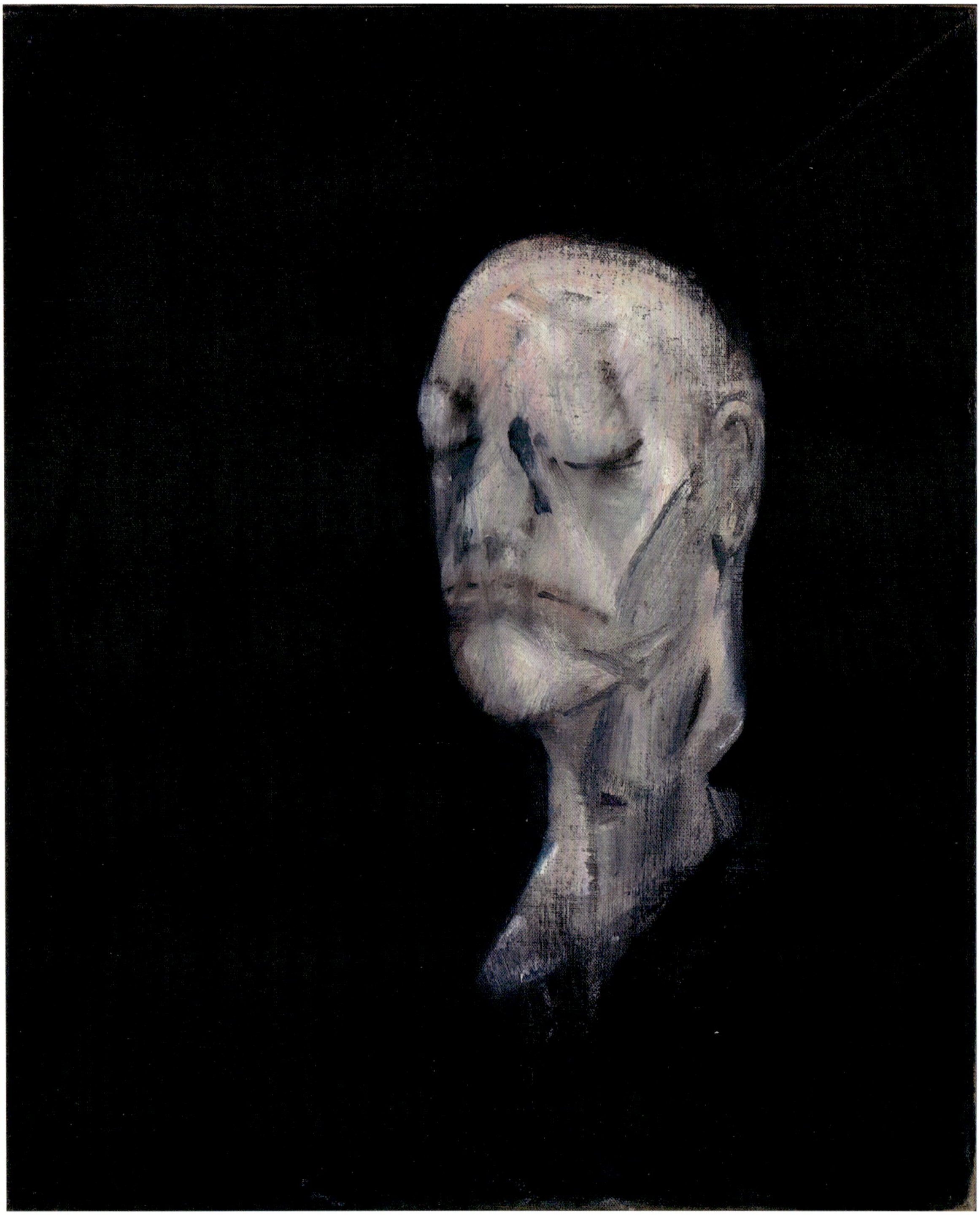

Francis Bacon
Study for Portrait II (after the Life Mask of William Blake)
1955

Francis Bacon
Study for Figure VI 1956–7

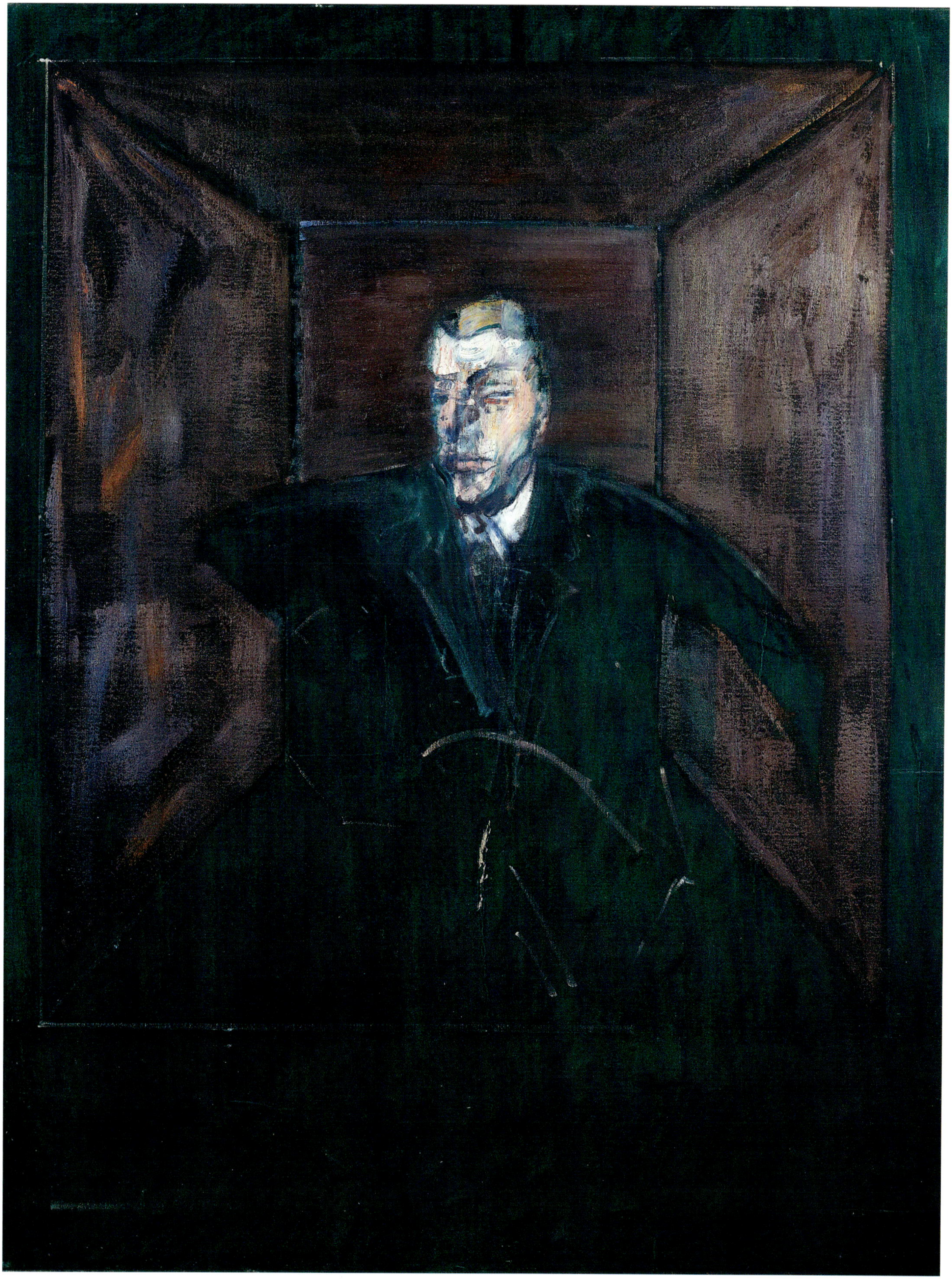

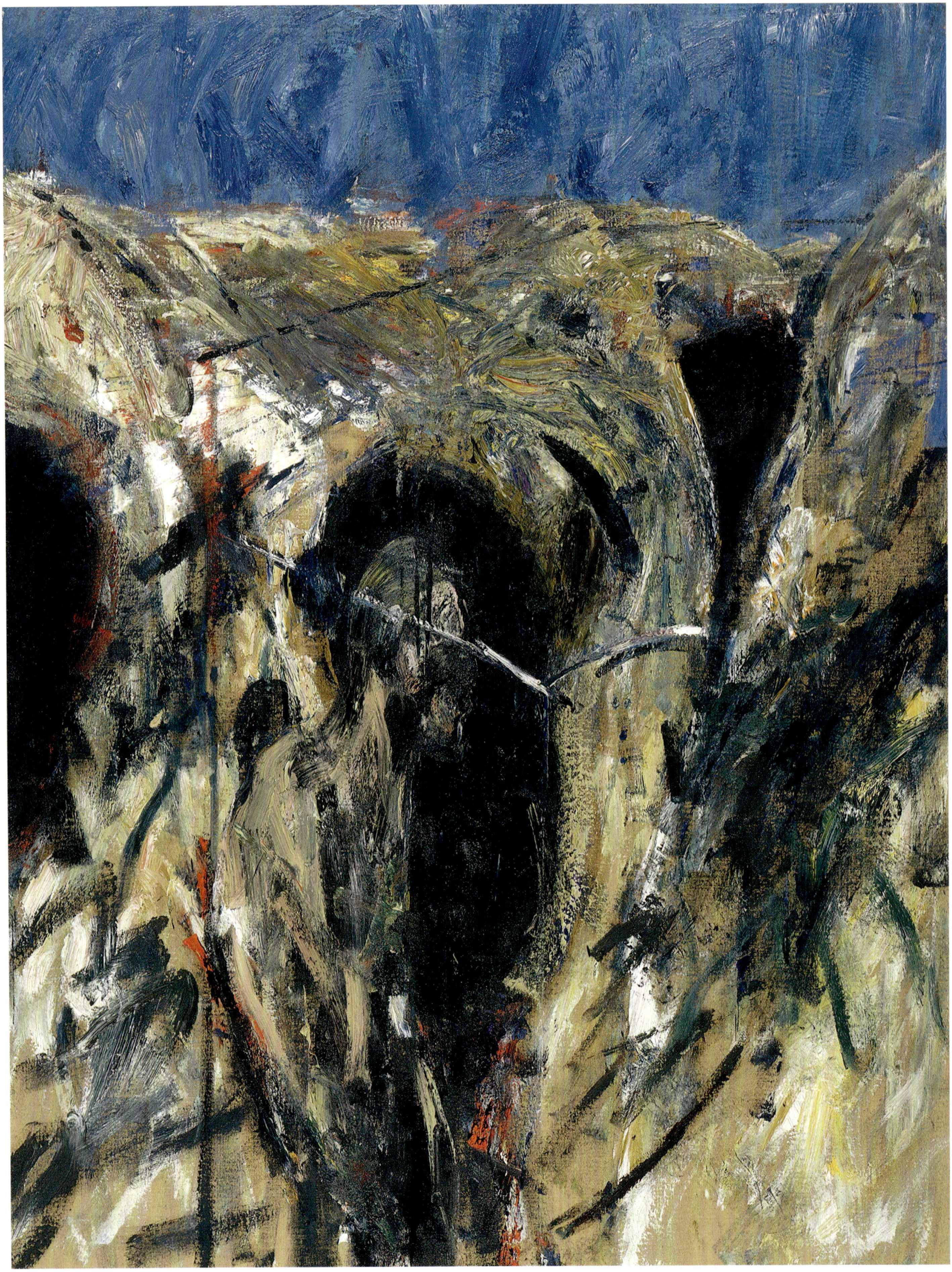

Francis Bacon
Figure in Mountain Landscape
1956

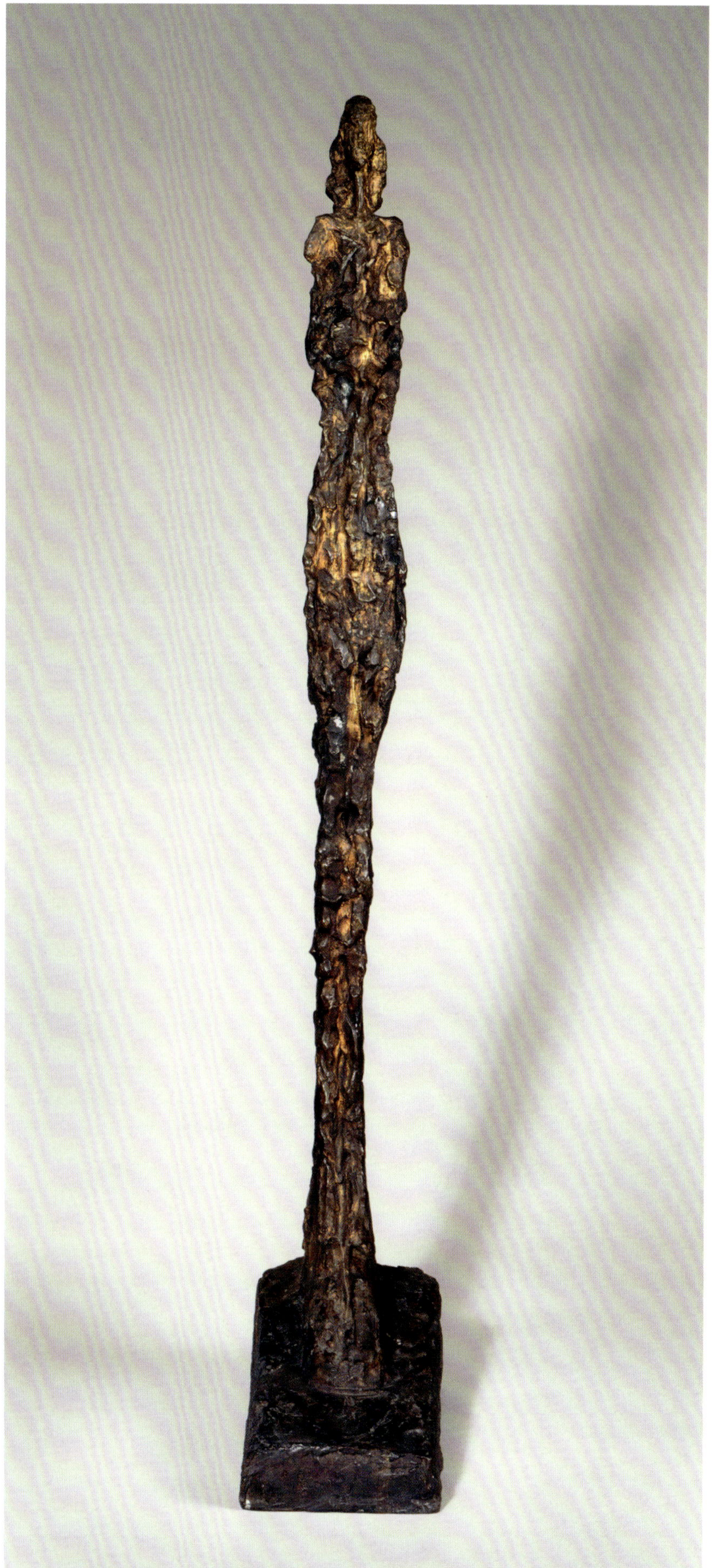

Alberto Giacometti
Woman of Venice IX 1956

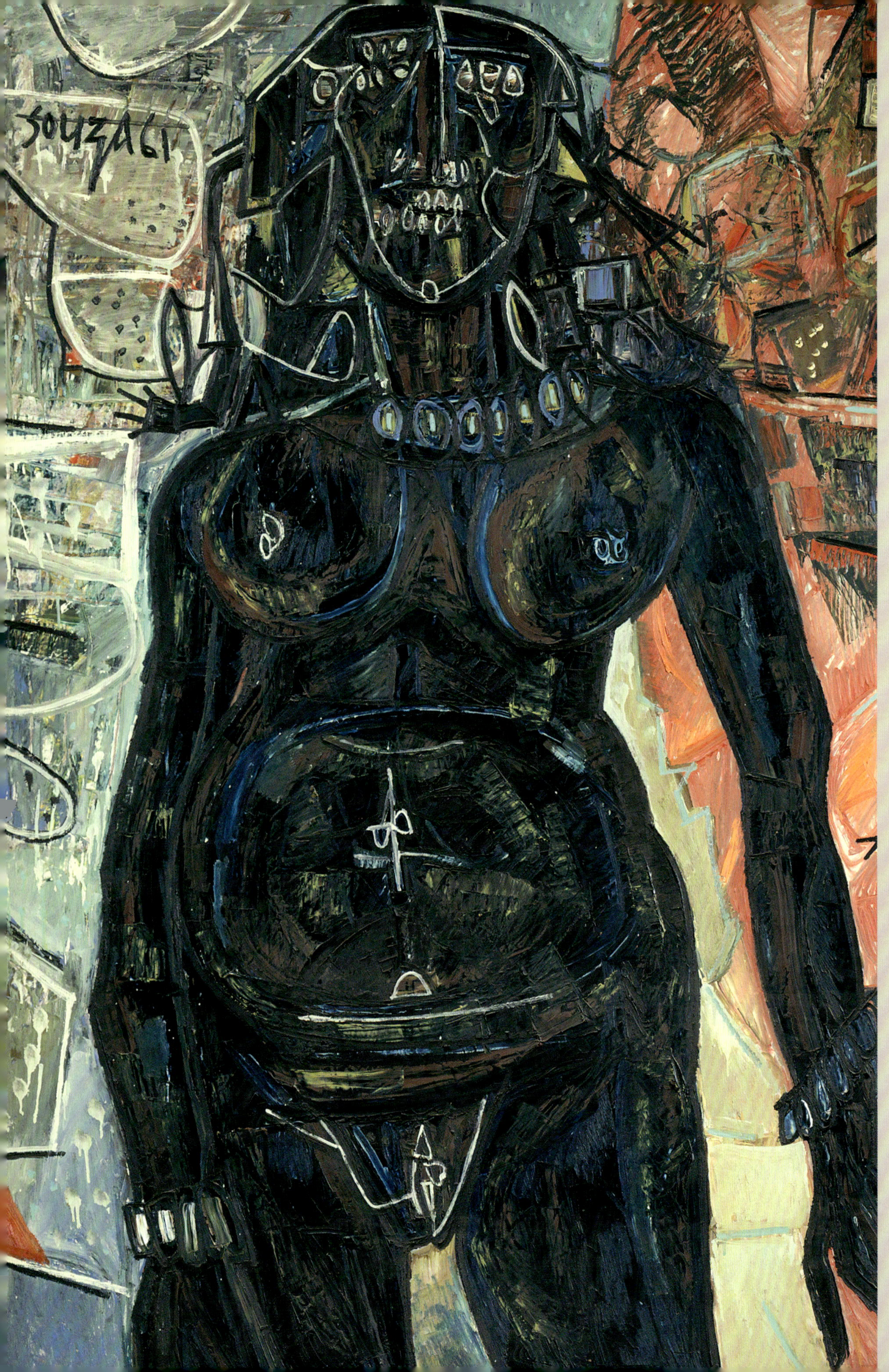
SOUZA 61

Francis Newton Souza

Priyesh Mistry

Francis Newton Souza painted *Mr Sebastian* (p.19) in 1955, six years after his arrival in London from Bombay. It is a portrait of St Sebastian, and Souza presents the martyr in modern dress, reducing his status to a common man and subverting the spiritual reverence bestowed on previous depictions of the subject. Arrows instead puncture the awkward and angular features of the saint's face, as opposed to his suited body. Here Souza combines the sacred with the profane, an act that belies more than a simple act of direct translation. This subversive approach recurs across the multiple genres of painting that Souza engaged throughout his career, an act that asserts his intersecting identities across European traditions of painting. As George Butcher, a long-standing advocate since Souza's time in London, suggests: 'his life and work are now in the deliberate vibration between the old and the new and between the East and the West';[1] the result of his position as a modernist artist from post-Independence India, working with the idiom of expressionism in postwar Britain.

Born in 1924 in the Portuguese enclave of Goa in India to devout Christian parents and sent to a Jesuit school, Souza's relationship to his Christian upbringing became strained as he developed his secular understanding of life and suffering. Much like the revolution in his depiction of St Sebastian, his celebrated *Crucifixion* 1959 (p.97) presents Christ as a masked monstrosity; a primal, skeletal figure in dense black, his limbs pinned to the outer edges of the frame to become the cross itself. Instead of arousing compassion for the saviour, his redeemer confronts the viewer in malice and provocation, delivering a post-colonial dilemma; the contradiction of inherited faith alongside the deconstructed form of Modern European painting.

Souza later began his art education at the Sir J.J. School of Art in Bombay, which was dominated by the strict aesthetics of British colonial art school teaching. Rebelling against this instruction and following a brief participation in the Communist Party, Souza formed the Progressive Arts Group in 1947 with five other Indian painters of diverse backgrounds, including S.H. Raza and M.F. Husain. Taking inspiration from modernist practices from Europe through the books and collections of European expats, the group labelled themselves as the pioneers of an innovative art form for a newly independent India. Souza developed his form of figuration using quick and fervent strokes of thick paint on the canvas, and gained some critical success and prominence during the two years in which the group was active. Yet he decided to leave India, becoming increasingly resentful at what he felt was a lack of true recognition of his art.

However, when Souza arrived in London from Bombay in 1949, he found himself again disappointed at what he perceived as a general apathy for contemporary arts and culture. He chose to travel to the UK as he considered it the 'most civilised country in the world',[2] but found no opportunities for unknown artists in the small gallery scene that focused on a few big names, and even fewer for a foreign modernist painter from a decolonised country. His initial years in London were subject to much hardship and he was supported by his wife, having refused to take up a job and committing

Francis Newton Souza
Black Nude 1961 (detail)

instead to painting, drawing and writing short pieces of journalism. Souza's fortunes soon changed in what proved to be a prolific period. Following the success of his published writing and the exhibition of his work in Paris, Victor Musgrave at Gallery One came to represent Souza, holding annual exhibitions of his work from 1955 into the early 1960s.

It was at the first of these exhibitions that the critic John Berger reviewed Souza's paintings: 'I find it quite impossible to assess his work comparatively. Because he straddles several traditions but serves none.'[3] Positioning Souza as an Indian artist, Berger refers to the many artistic traditions with which Souza draws parallels in Europe and also reveals the extent of Souza's dilemma with the reception of his work in the West. Unable to situate the artist, Berger distances any dialogue with the Western canon. Indeed comparisons can be made with Picasso, Chaïm Soutine, Georges Rouault, and his contemporary and namesake Francis Bacon; however, it is only in the synthesis of these styles with the candid and subversive approach to his subjects that Souza's unique vision has been recognised.

As Souza directs his figurative works to the viewer, he continues to pass on his challenge. This act of confrontation is forthright in *Black Nude* 1961 (p.92), which Butcher once described as the 'devouring Indian goddess of evil, Kali, transformed into a nuclear symbol'.[4] Akin to the deviant eroticism with which Souza treats his female nudes, he portrays a gargantuan woman that he both worships and derides. His earlier painting, *Nude Holding Breasts* 1960 (p.100), offers the viewer an alternate proposal of exoticism. Classically posed at an angle with draped textile over her lower body, reminiscent of Renaissance masterpieces, the three-quarter portrait is painted with more generosity than the haste of the monstrous *Black Nude*. Here, Souza's dark-haired olive-skinned nude Mona Lisa holds more assurance, an agency of her own sensuality through her oval-eyed gaze.

Despite the success he earned in the UK, Souza moved away from London to New York in 1967, where he resided for the rest of his life and continued to make work in a modern idiom. In this fostered language, Souza nurtures a personal and distinctive art form that fluctuates between his need to communicate and the urgency of his making: 'I don't believe that a true artist paints for coteries or for the proletariat. I believe with all my soul that he paints solely for himself.'[5]

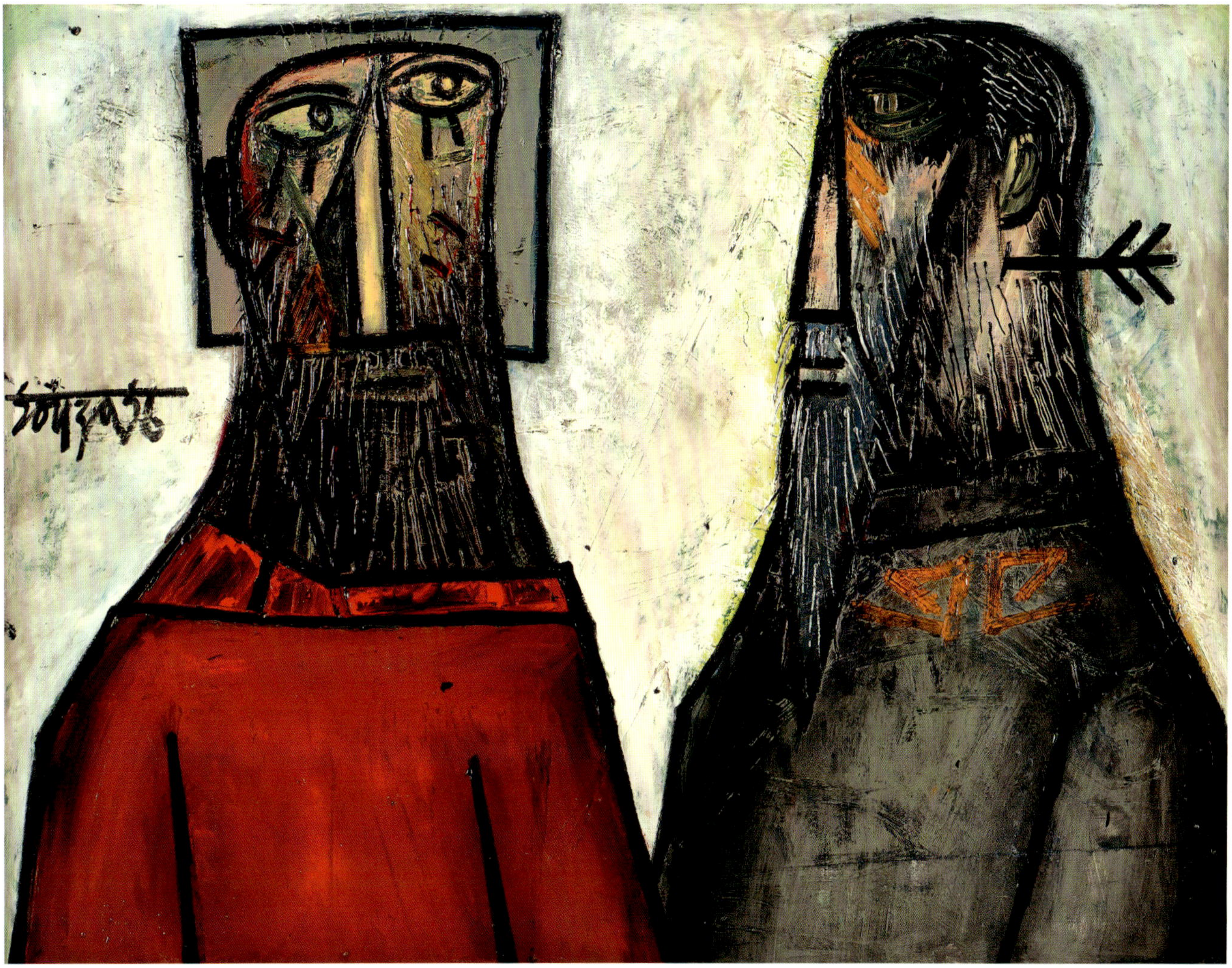

Francis Newton Souza
Jesus and Pilatus c.1955–6

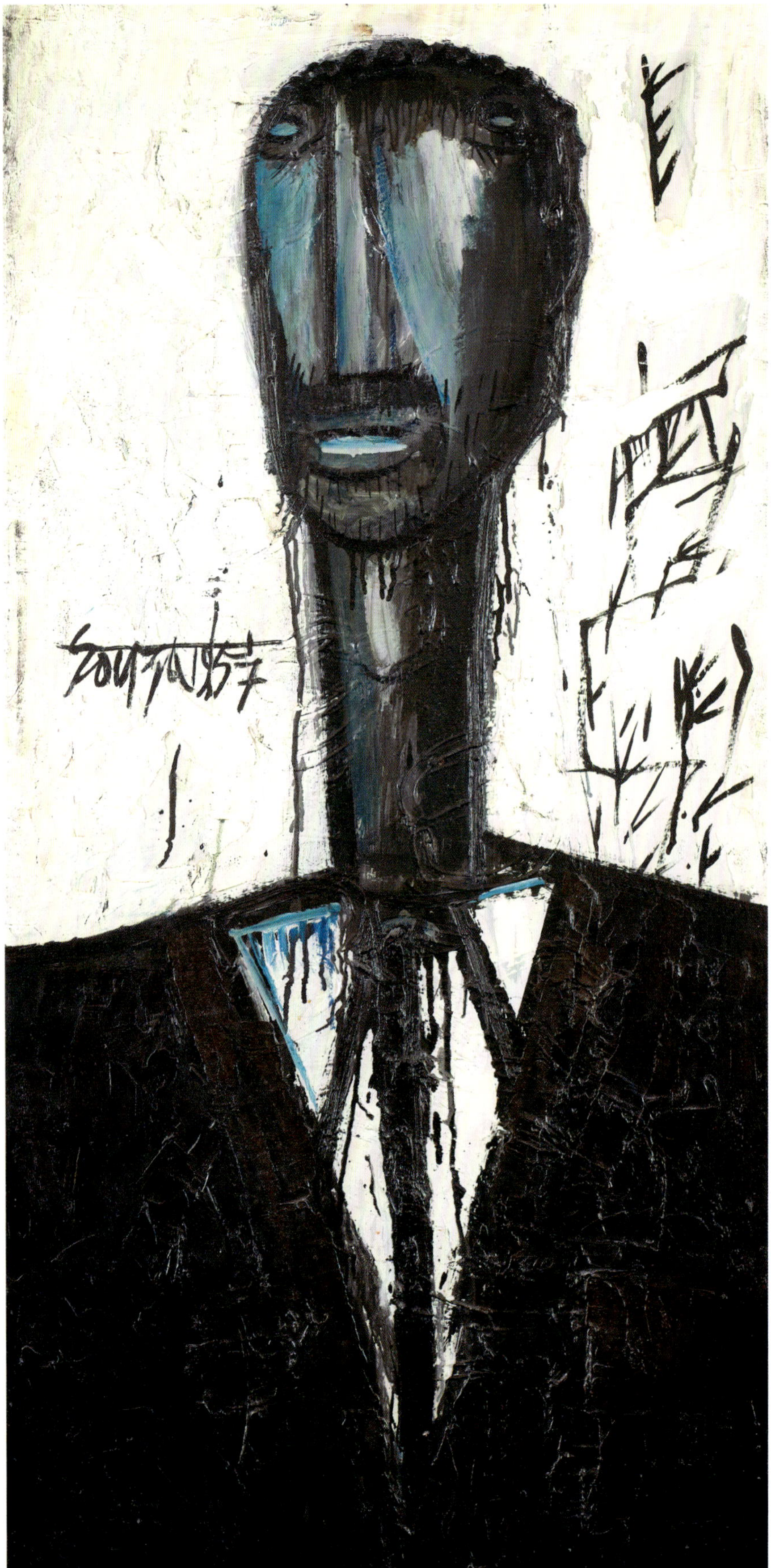

Francis Newton Souza
Negro in Mourning 1957

Francis Newton Souza
Crucifixion 1959

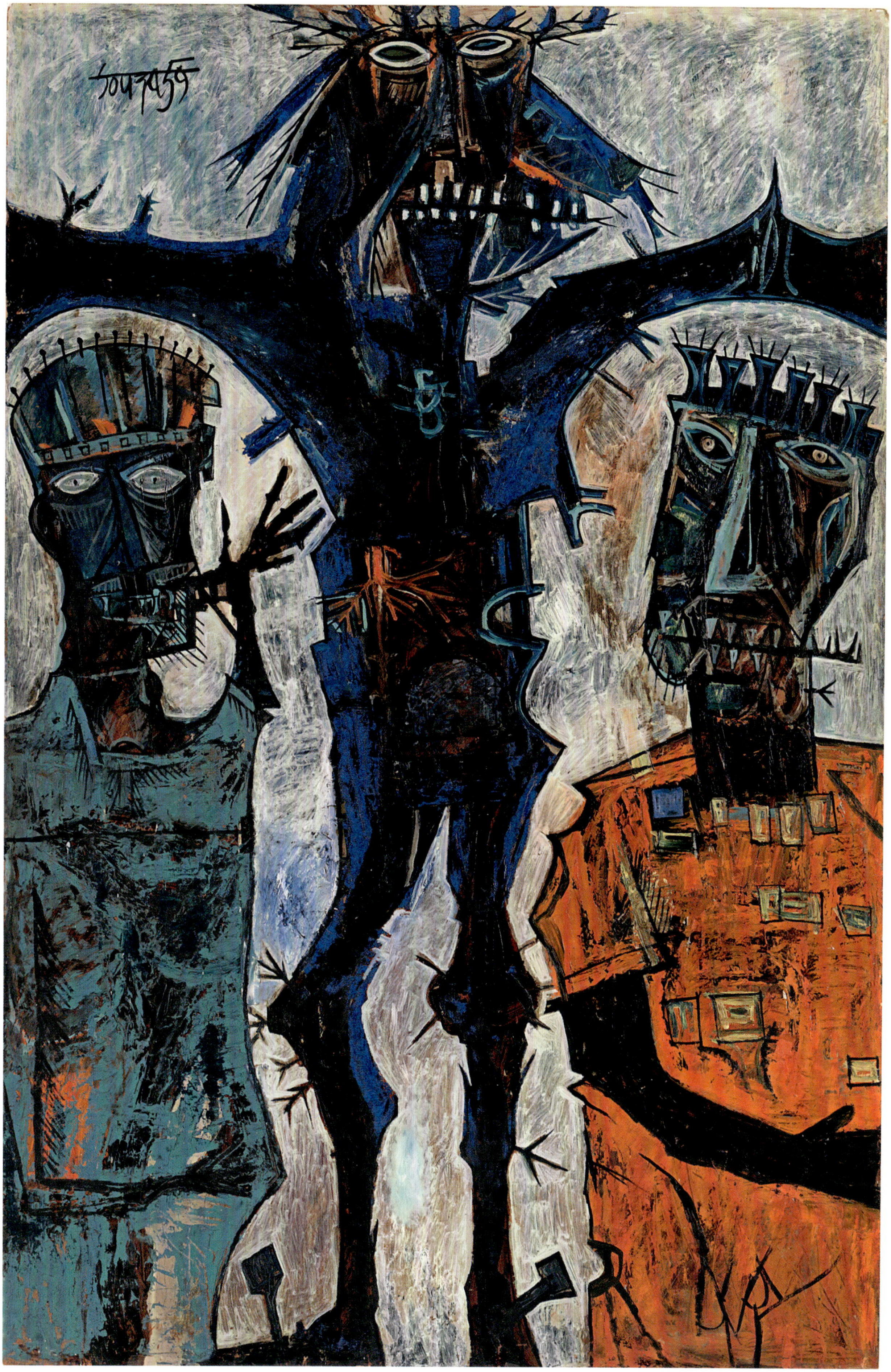

Francis Newton Souza
Red Sun 1960

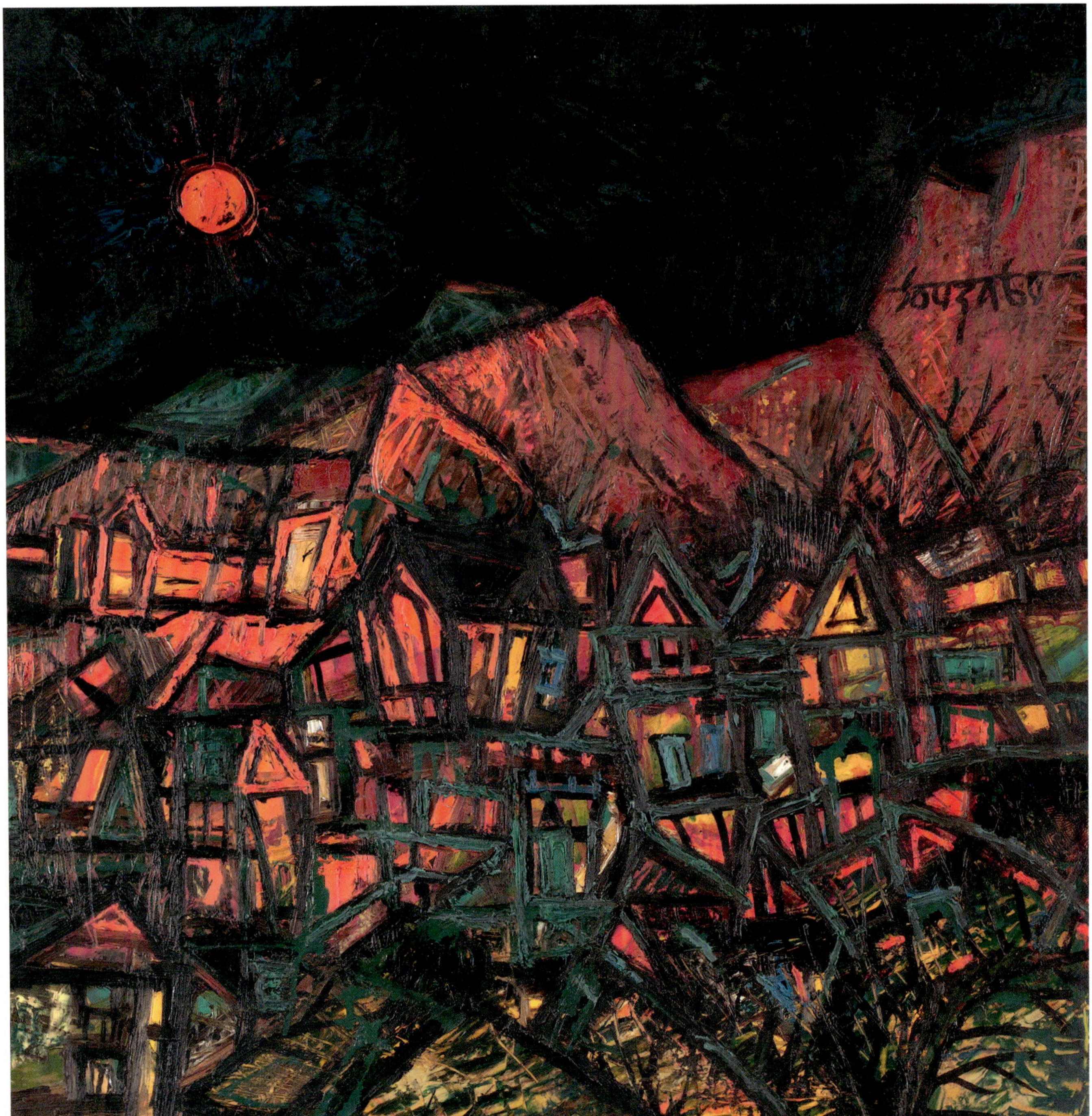

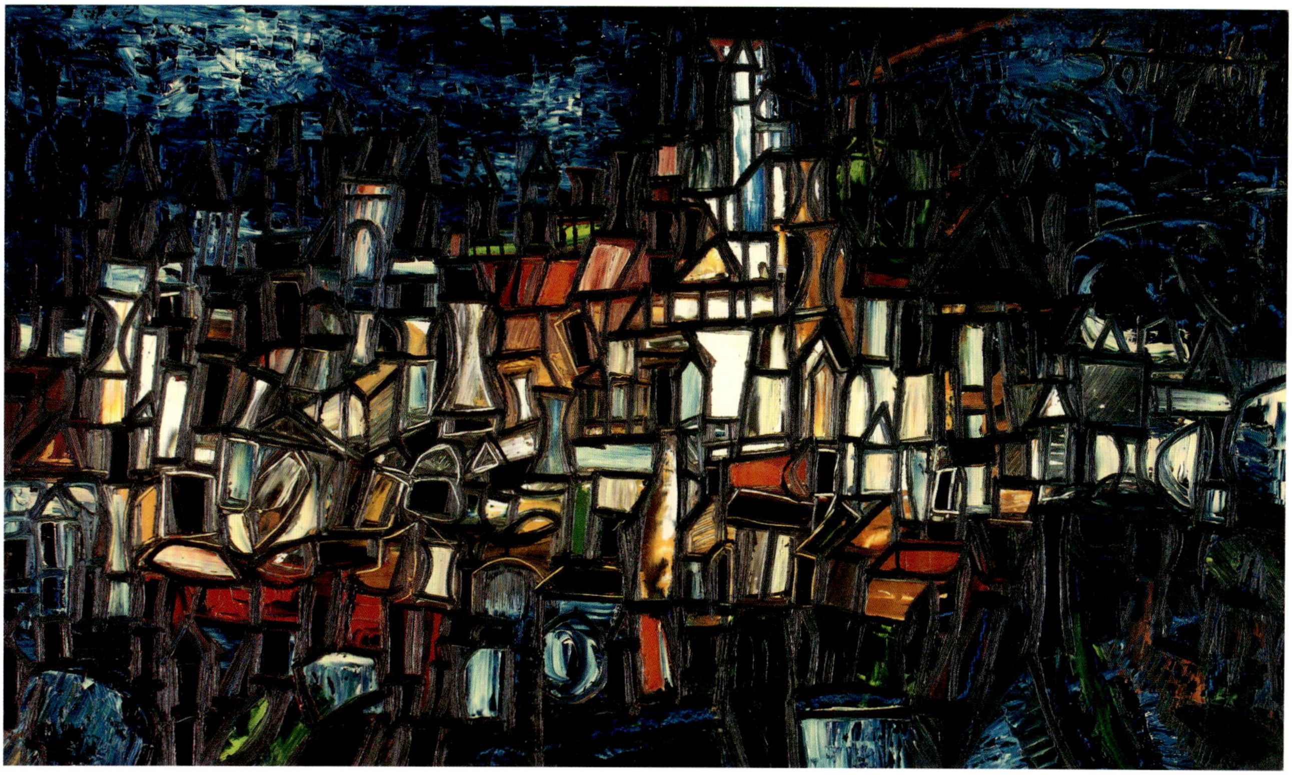

Francis Newton Souza
Citadel 1961

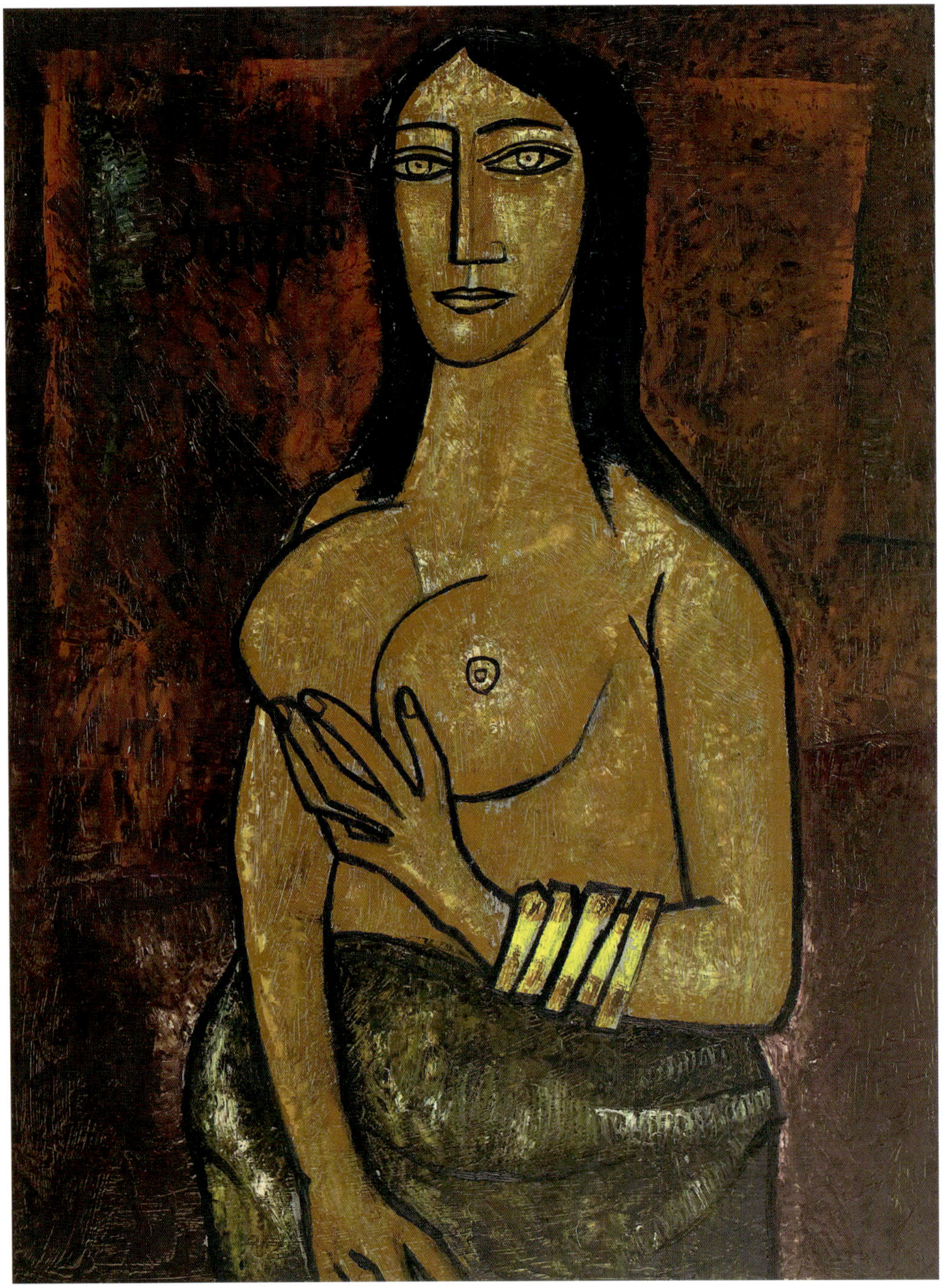

Francis Newton Souza
Nude Holding Breasts 1960

Francis Newton Souza
Two Saints in a Landscape 1961

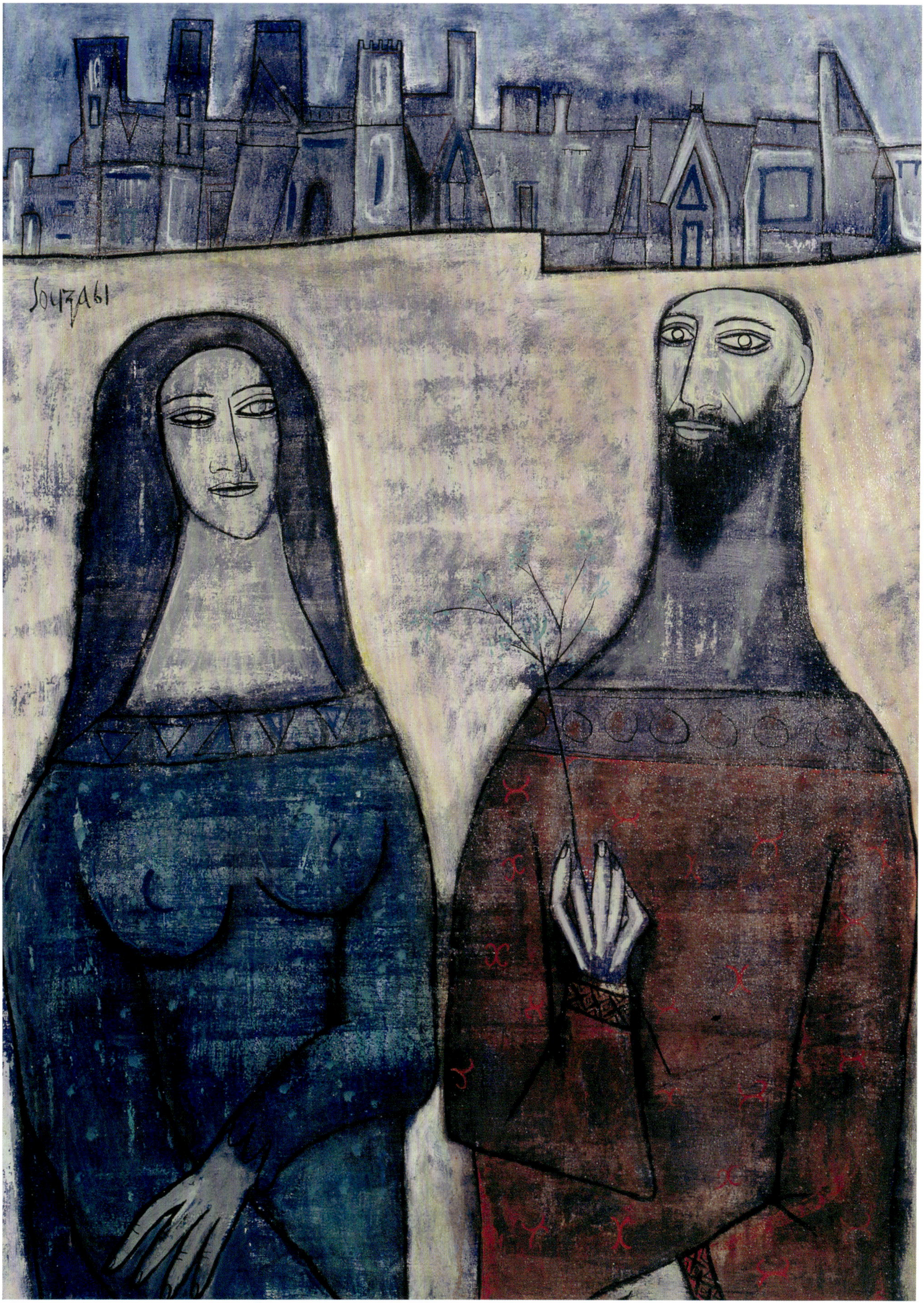
SOUZA 61

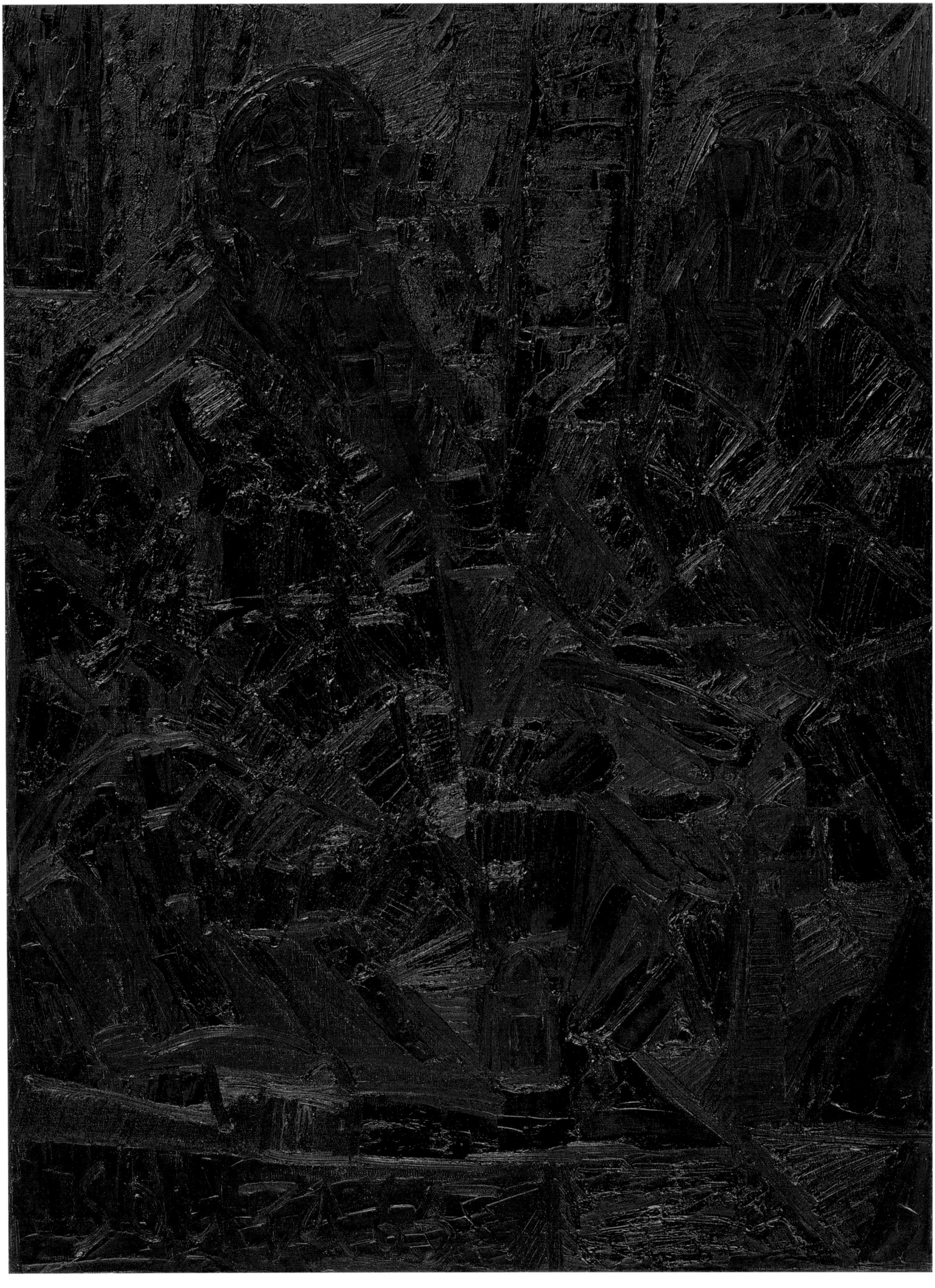

Francis Newton Souza
Two Saints (After El Greco)
1965

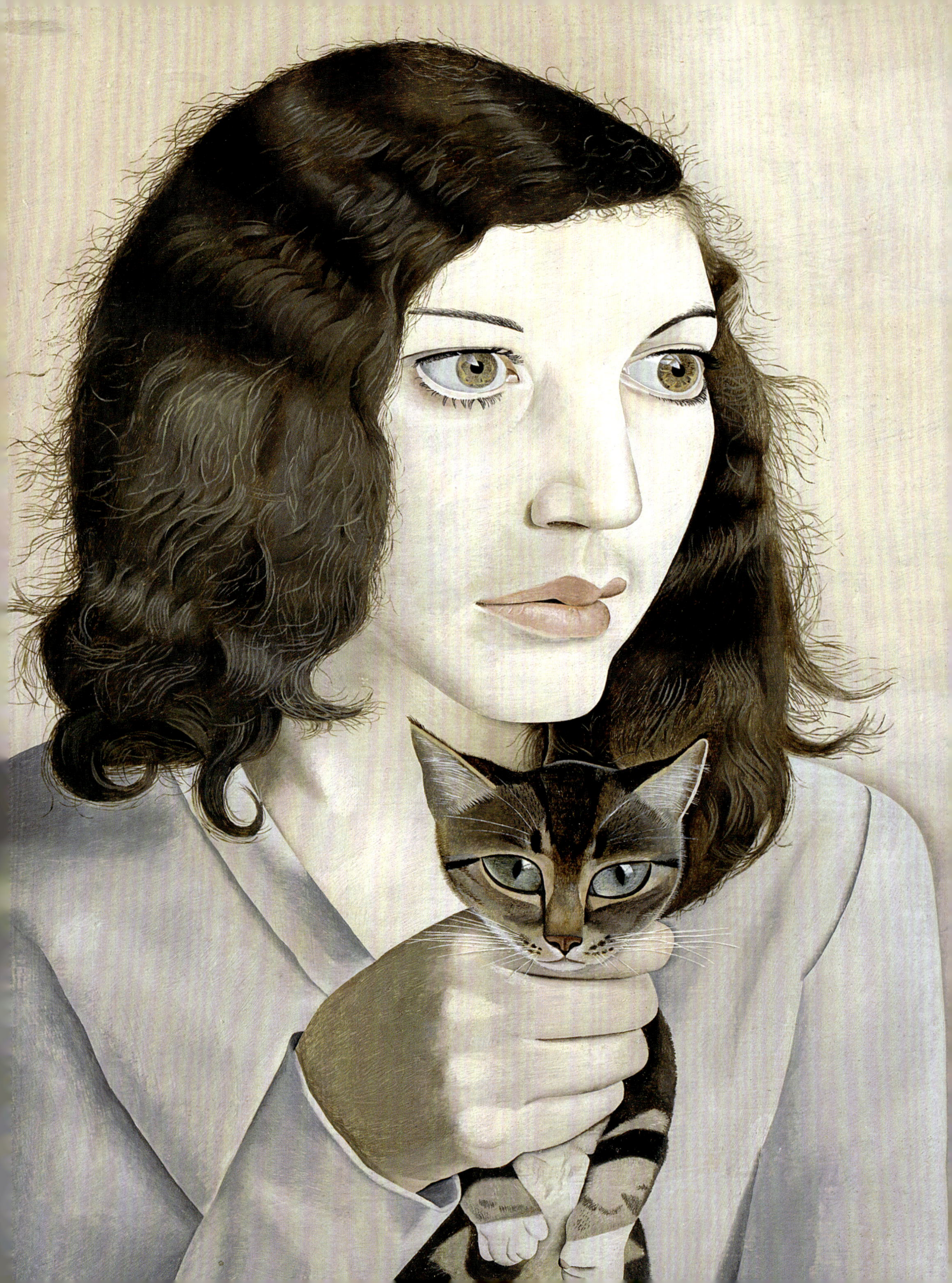

William Coldstream and the Slade

Emma Chambers

William Coldstream, Lucian Freud and Euan Uglow strove to fix the visible world on canvas through intense observation and long hours spent painting directly from the model. Coldstream spent much of his working life in art schools, and his teaching influenced a generation of British artists including Uglow and Michael Andrews, who both trained at the Slade School of Fine Art in the 1950s when Coldstream was Slade Professor of Fine Art and Lucian Freud was a visiting tutor at the school.

For Coldstream painting was above all a process of perception, in which the artist approached their subject without preconception and tried to represent exactly what they saw, rather than using compositional devices to simulate its appearance. He attempted to fix observed reality through measurement, establishing the position of objects in space by marking the relative locations of key features on the canvas with horizontal and vertical lines. Rather than beginning with key areas of the subject, Coldstream built up a work in balance across the whole canvas, and the image only gradually emerged from his network of measuring marks.[1]

Coldstream stated: 'Once I have started painting ...I am occupied ...mainly with putting things in the right place... I never consciously try to make things fit into any preconceived plan or form and I find I lose interest unless I let myself be ruled by what I see.'[2] Coldstream allowed his models to find a position that was comfortable to decrease his intervention in the composition of the image.[3] *Seated Nude* 1952–3 (p.110) was painted over thirty sittings of about two hours from a fixed position eight or nine feet away.[4] The painting appears in the background of *Orange Tree I* 1974–5 (p.111). Coldstream often included incidental background objects in his paintings, and rather than arranging them to create a pleasing visual effect he addressed their existing relationships in space as a problem to be solved. Discussing *Seated Nude* 1973–4 (p.112), Coldstream remarked that he had deliberately not moved the radiogram behind the model as the interest for him was in addressing a predetermined situation.[5]

Euan Uglow developed a painting practice based on Coldstream's ethos of rigorous observation and measurement. Like Coldstream, Uglow worked from a fixed point, making a series of measurement marks, then incrementally defining the form of the model rather than making a preparatory drawing outlining the form. In *Woman with White Skirt* 1953–4 (p.113), the verticals and horizontals of the screen in the studio are used as coordinates to establish the model's position in relation to a fixed point. The interest in Renaissance mathematics and perspective of another teacher at the Slade, Sam Carter, was also influential on Uglow, who developed a conceptual approach in which models were often positioned in highly constructed poses to investigate mathematical problems or to explore the relationship between vision and proportion.[6] Uglow used a series of precise technical procedures to structure his still-life paintings – purpose-built structures that he called

Lucian Freud
Girl with a Kitten 1947 (detail)

'set-ups' and used to frame the process of viewing, controlling light and shadow and the placement of objects.[7] His portraits were also highly controlled. When he painted Georgia Georgallas (pp.116–17) he designed every aspect of the painting's composition, dressing her in a football shirt and shiny pink tights against a patterned cloth and insisting that her long hair was cut to shoulder length.[8] While Coldstream considered the measuring marks in his paintings to be incidental to the image, Uglow referred to these marks as 'statements' which charted the evolution of the painting through time and were 'to do with what happened today, yesterday and the month before'.[9] The artist's presence in front of the model and the accumulation of hours of observation and painting in the studio are visible on the surface of the work, and inform its artistic meaning.

Uglow famously said to his model 'nobody has ever looked at you as intensively as I have',[10] and the act of intense visual scrutiny was also at the heart of Lucian Freud's work, although his way of registering this process of observation on canvas was completely different. Freud would sketch the basic structure of the image in charcoal and then work outwards from the centre of the face to the edges of the canvas. His early works were painted with very fine sable-hair brushes to achieve a smooth, minutely detailed surface. Freud has described how his early portraits emerged from his 'visual aggression' with sitters, stating: 'I would sit very close and stare. It could be uncomfortable for both of us.'[11] This close-up method also produced a compression of space in the portrait and a very intense engagement with the model, which gives his portraits a distinct psychological charge. The use of props such as drapery and animals also suggests an implicit narrative to the viewer, which belies Freud's statement that 'everything is what it is and not another thing'.[12]

The composition of *Girl with a Kitten* 1947 (p.104), a portrait of Freud's first wife Kitty Garman, is structured by a series of looks: the pensive gaze of the sitter into the distance is countered by the direct stare of the kitten that she holds, which matches the 'visual aggression' of the artist and engages directly with the viewer. The portrait exudes an atmosphere of tension and anxiety as Kitty holds the kitten tightly by the neck, both sitter and animal seeming trapped by the artist's vision. In the semi-nude portrait of Kitty, *Girl with a White Dog* 1950–1 (pp.108–9), Freud's focus is on the contrasting textures of skin, fabric and fur, giving the painting a tactile quality. Freud has written of his later work of wanting the likeness of the portrait to come from the body rather than the head.[13] Here the rendering of the delicate veined skin of Kitty's exposed breast is given equal attention and is as expressive of identity as her face.[14]

Freud was described by art historian Herbert Read as 'the Ingres of existentialism', referring to the smooth paint surface and intense linear realism that he shared with the French eighteenth-century painter, and the focus on the loneliness and vulnerability of human existence through the depiction of a single isolated figure.[15] Existentialist ideas also underpin Coldstream's and Uglow's work: the critic David Sylvester suggested that Coldstream's process of measuring to establish the exact position of the model in relation to the painter was governed by existentialist ideas of 'apartness' and an 'unremitting insistence on the otherness of other beings and things'.[16] Uglow's repetitive subject matter of the single model in a studio setting has also been linked to the artist's interest in a character from Albert Camus's *The Plague*, who wrote and rewrote a single line in a book that he was trying to complete.[17] This obsessive and repetitive practice in the search for an objective truth governs the analytical gaze of all three artists.

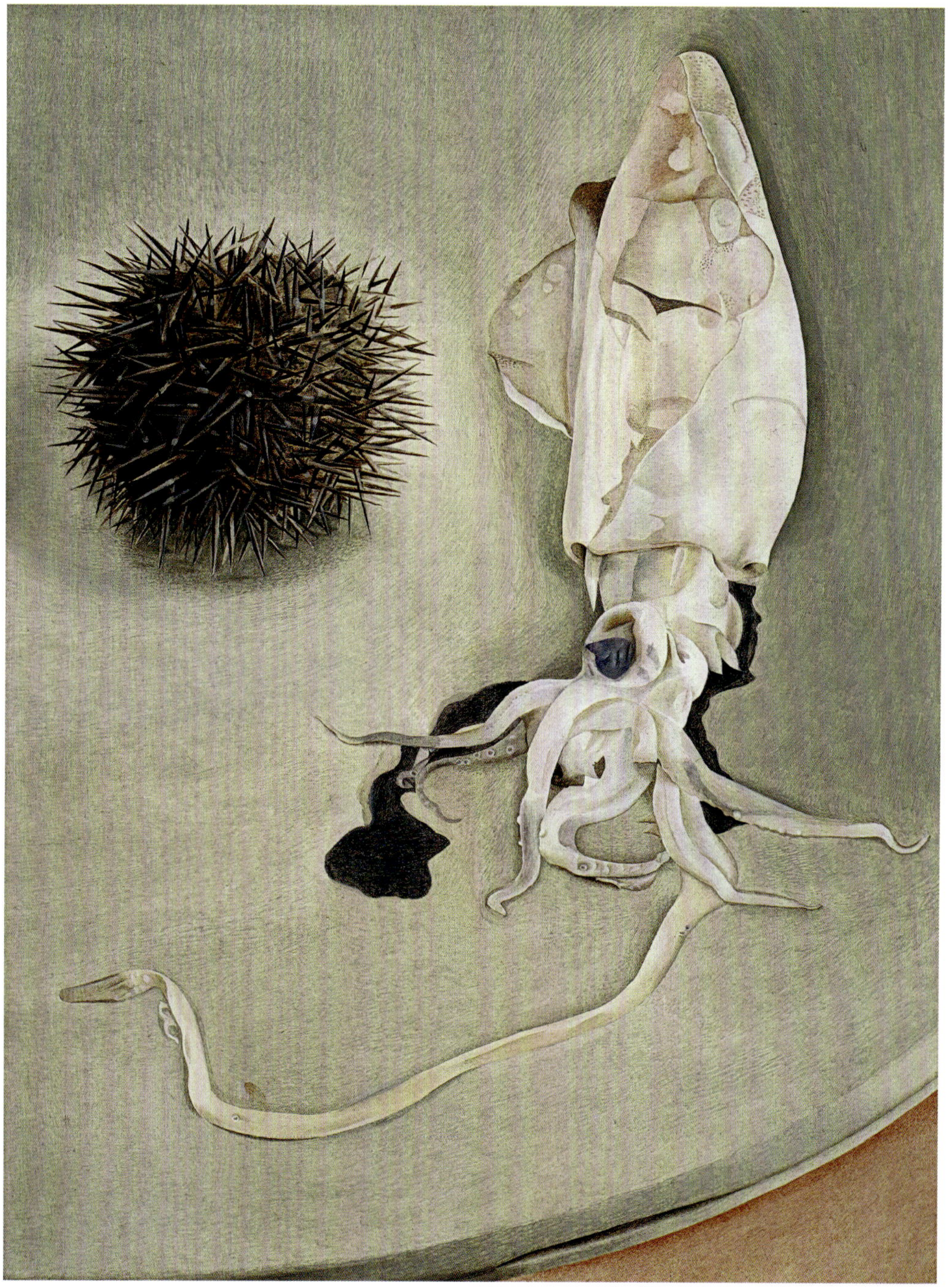

Lucian Freud
Still Life with Squid and Sea Urchin 1949

Lucian Freud
Girl with a White Dog 1950–1

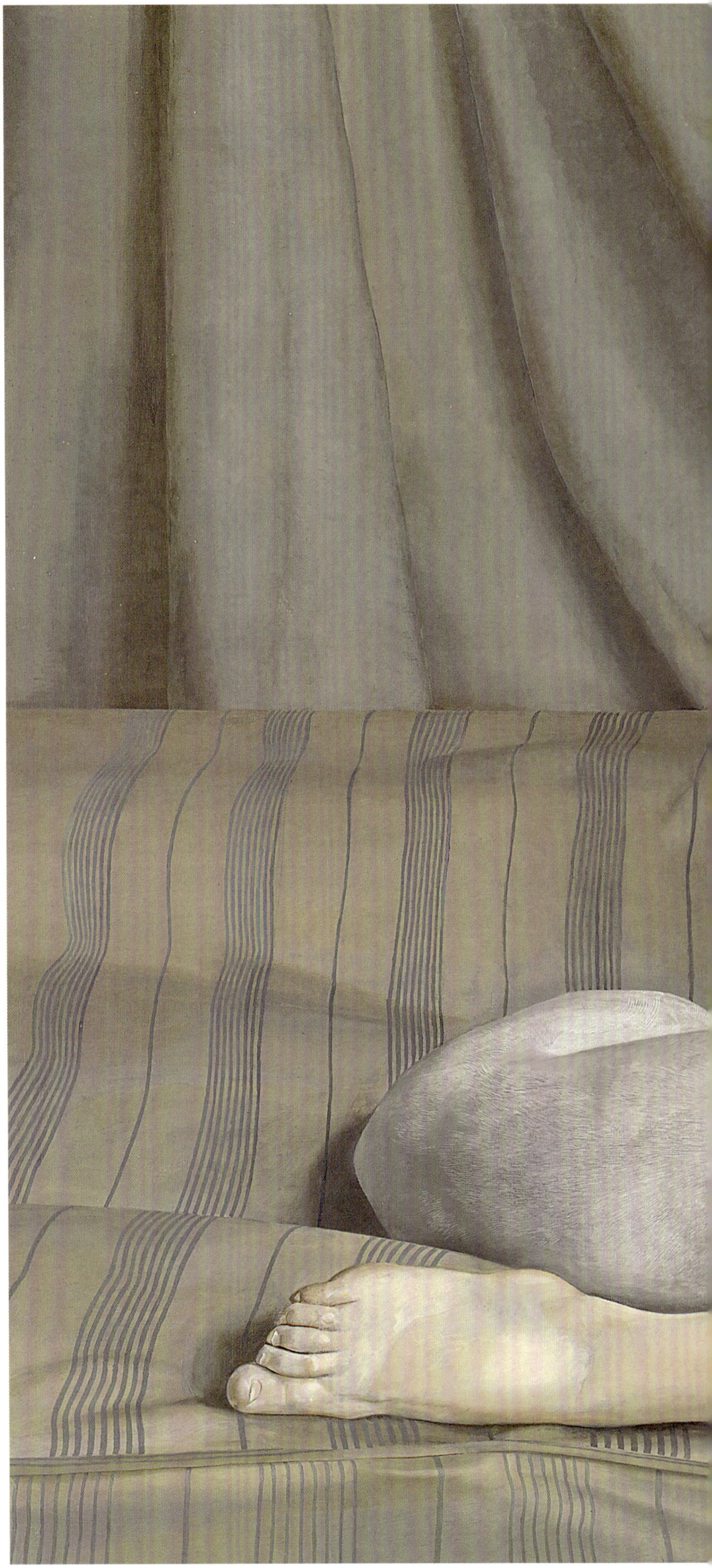

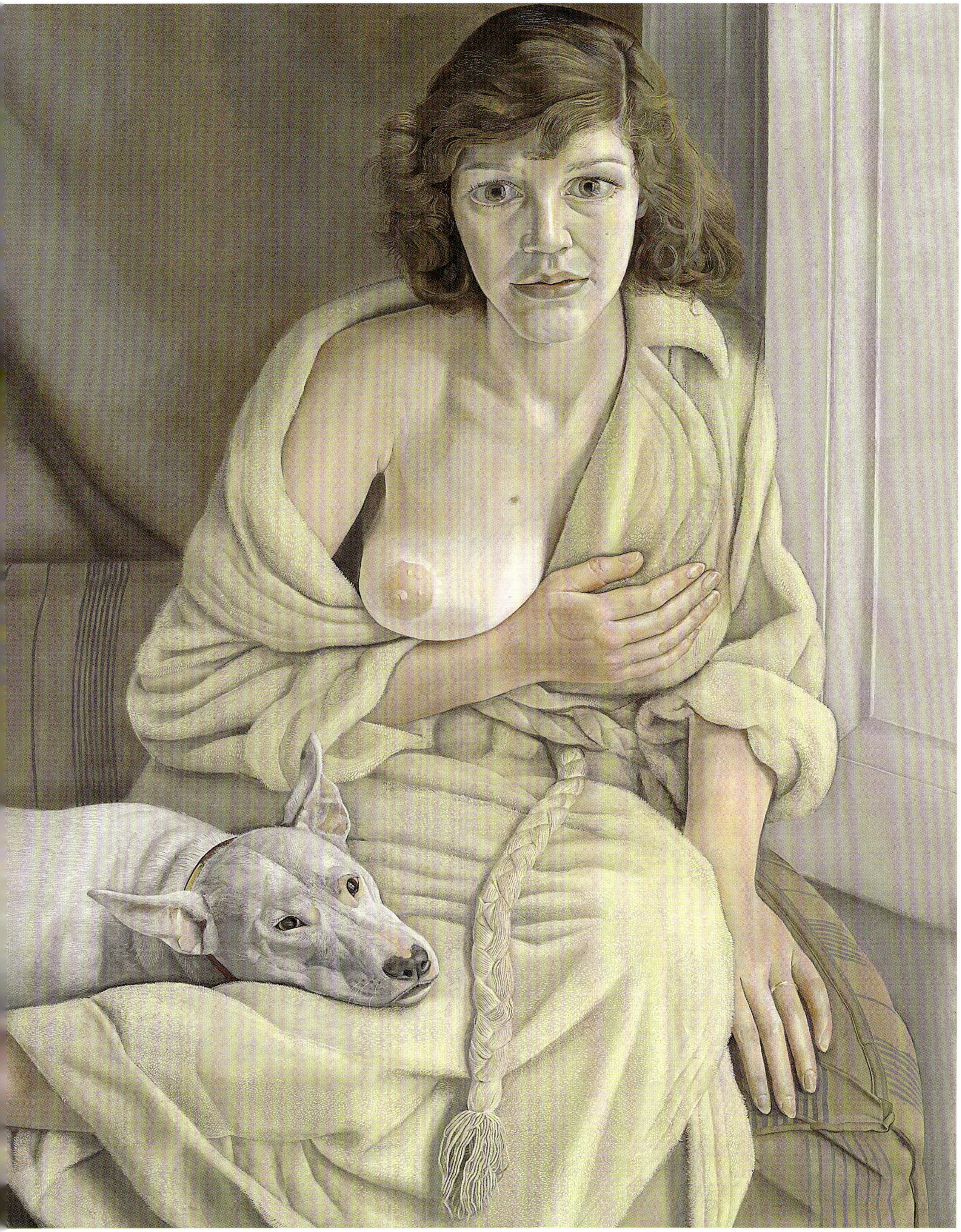

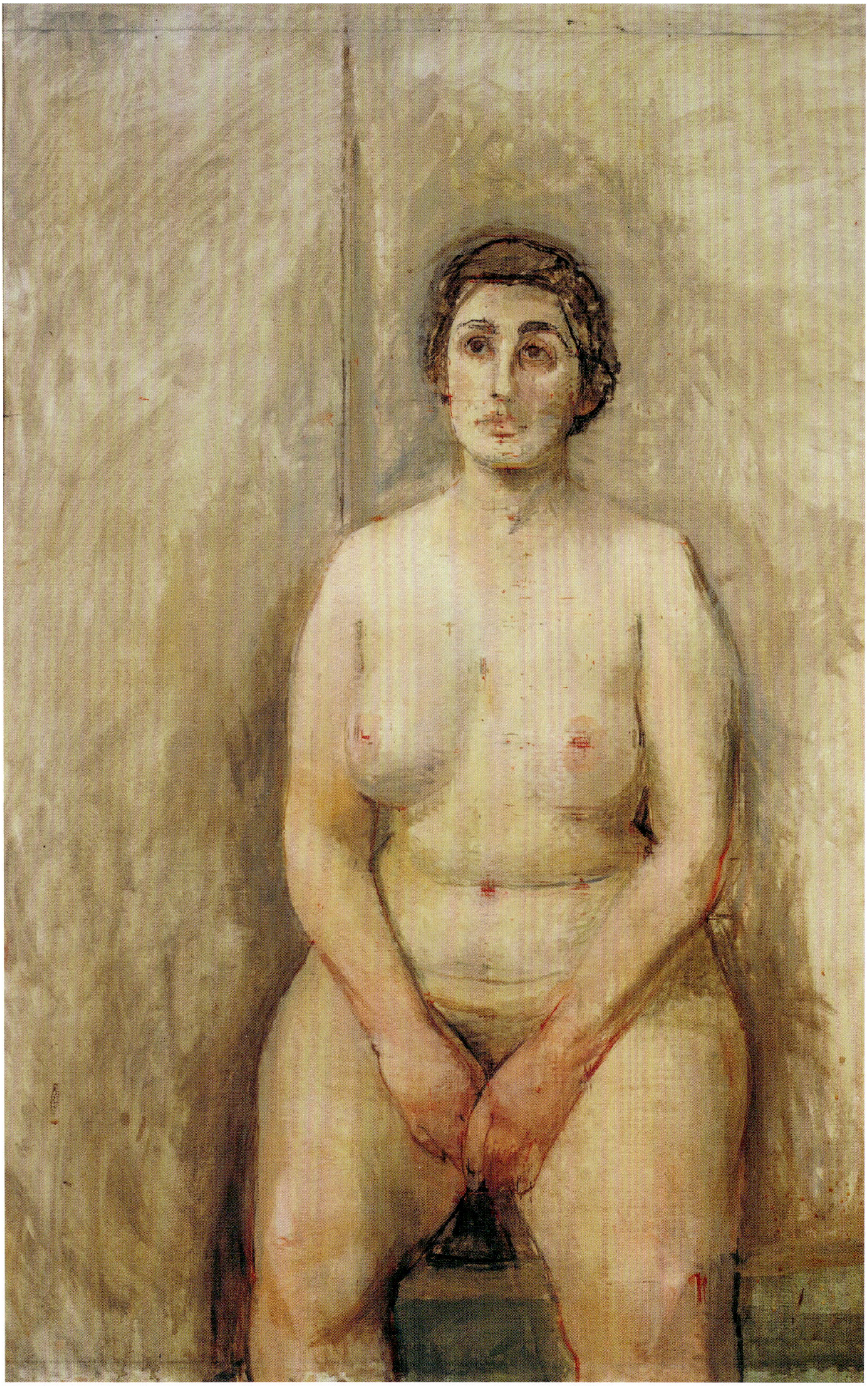

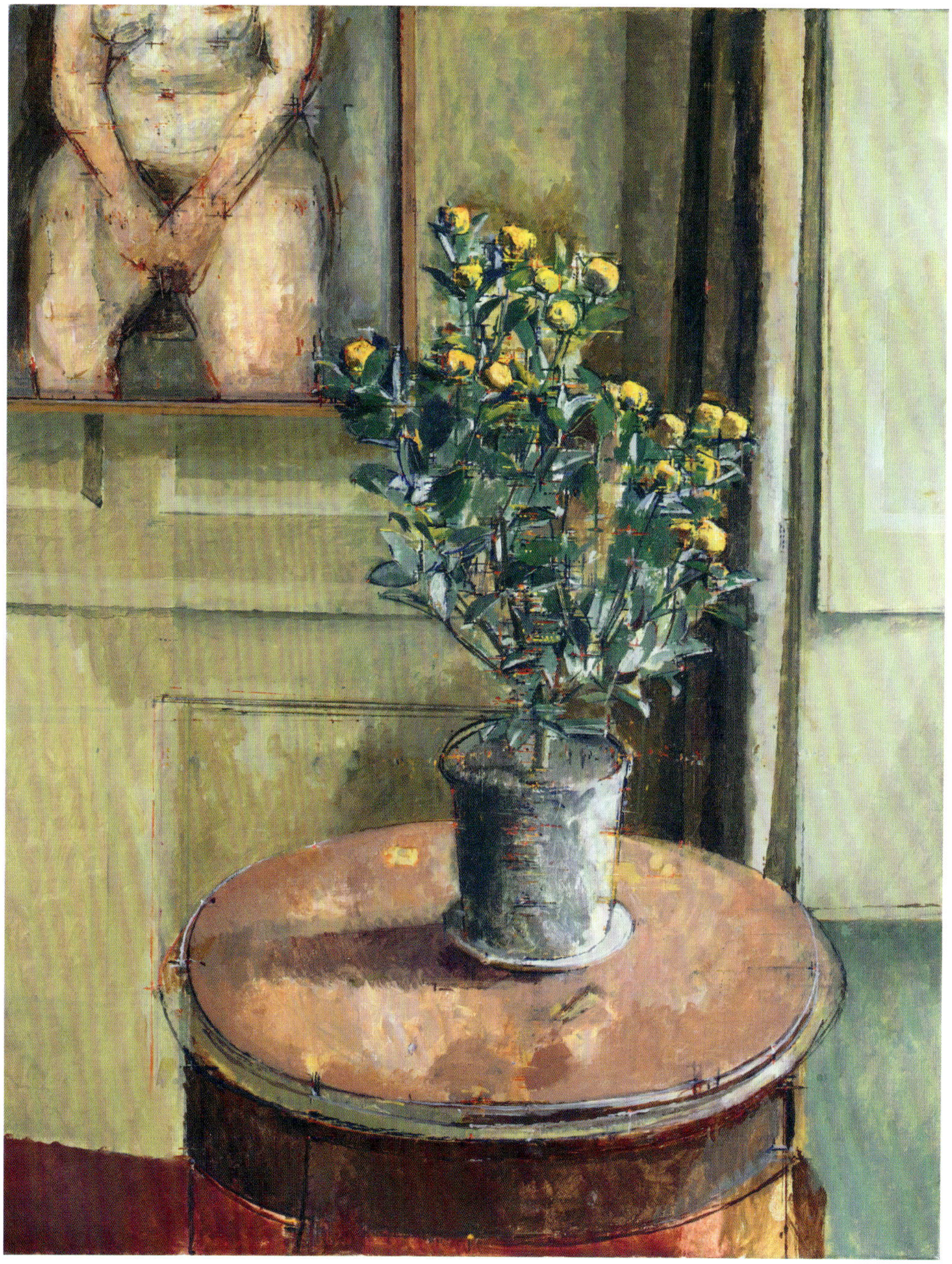

William Coldstream
Orange Tree I 1974–5

William Coldstream
Seated Nude 1952–3

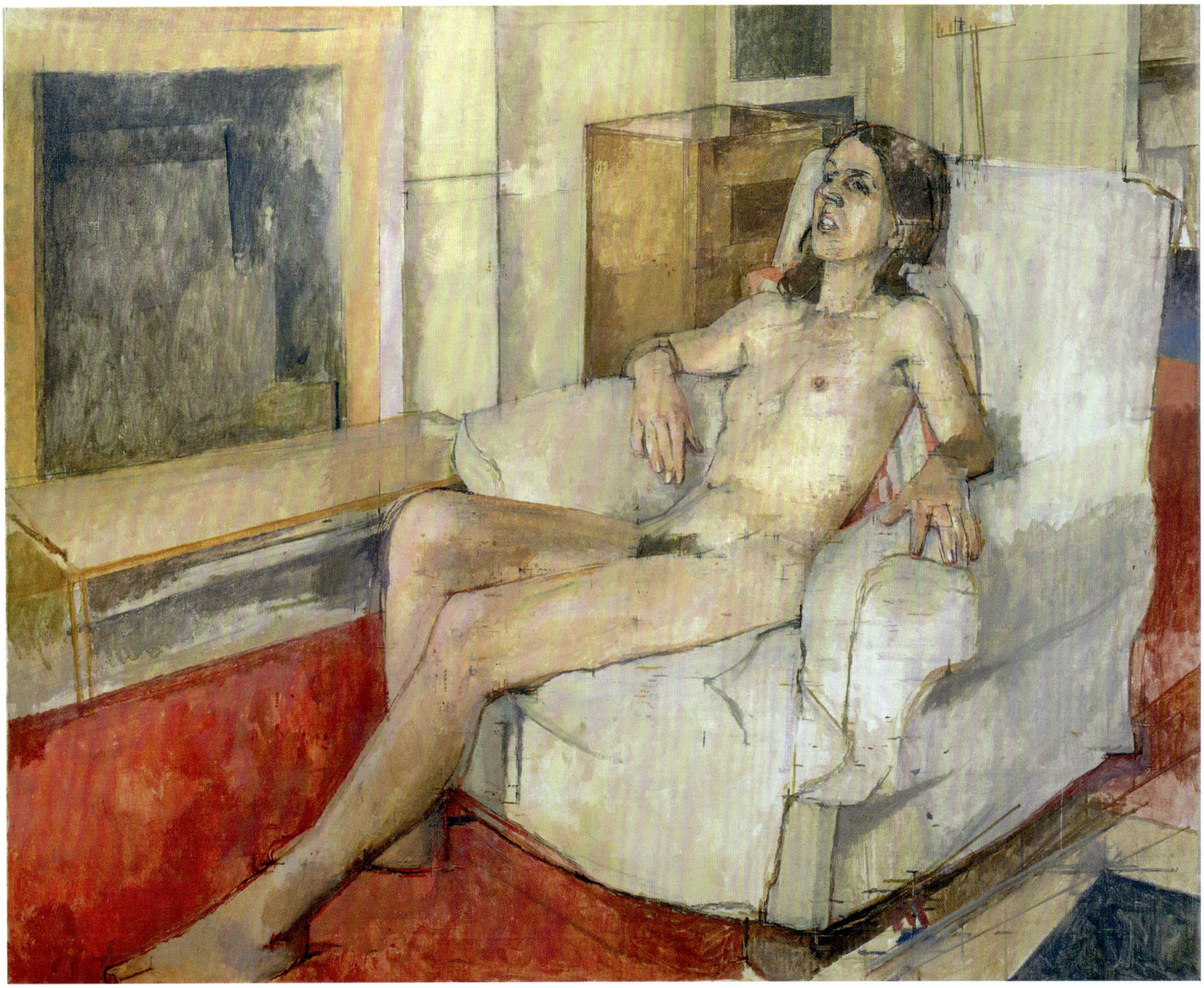

William Coldstream
Seated Nude 1973–4

Euan Uglow
Woman with White Skirt
1953–4

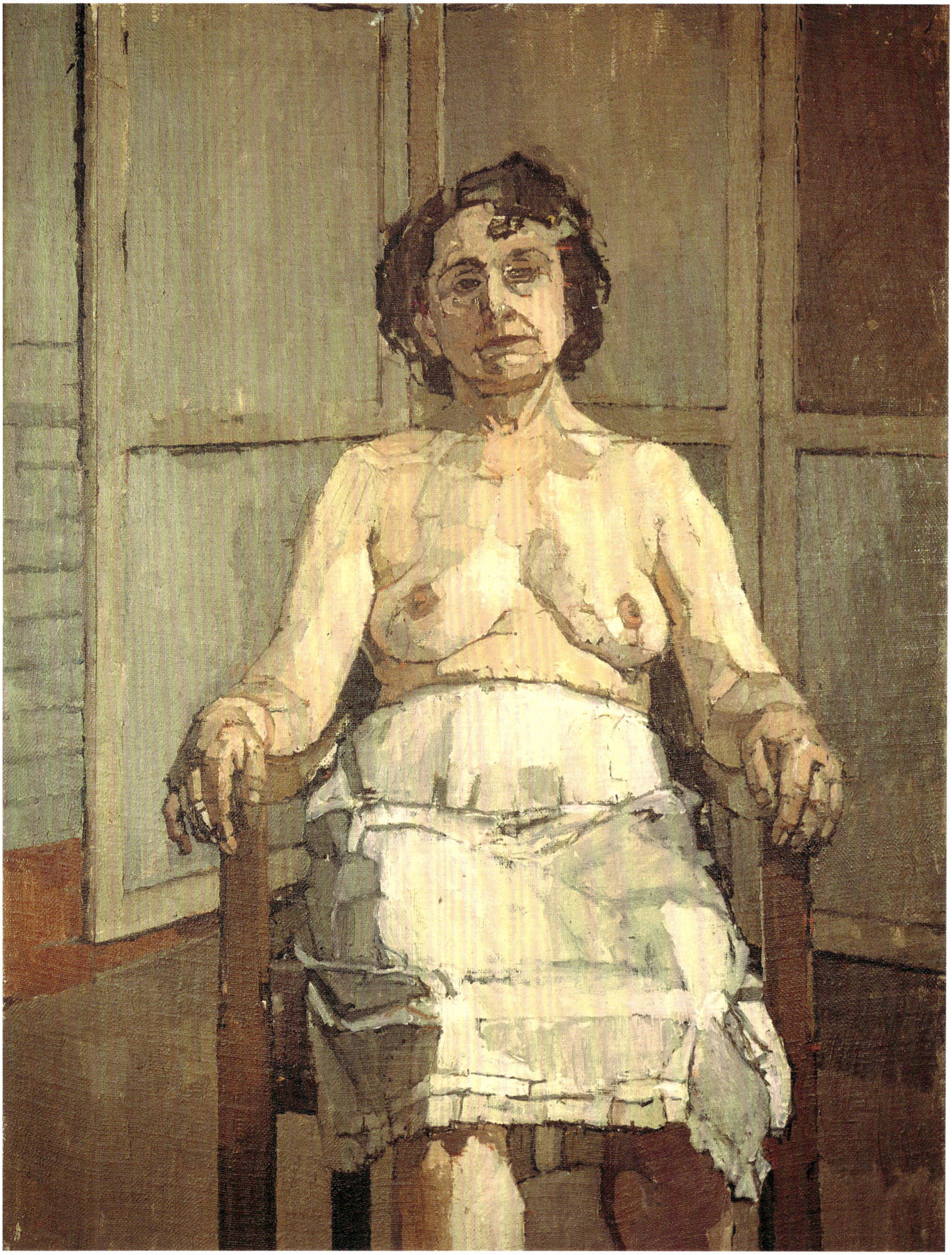

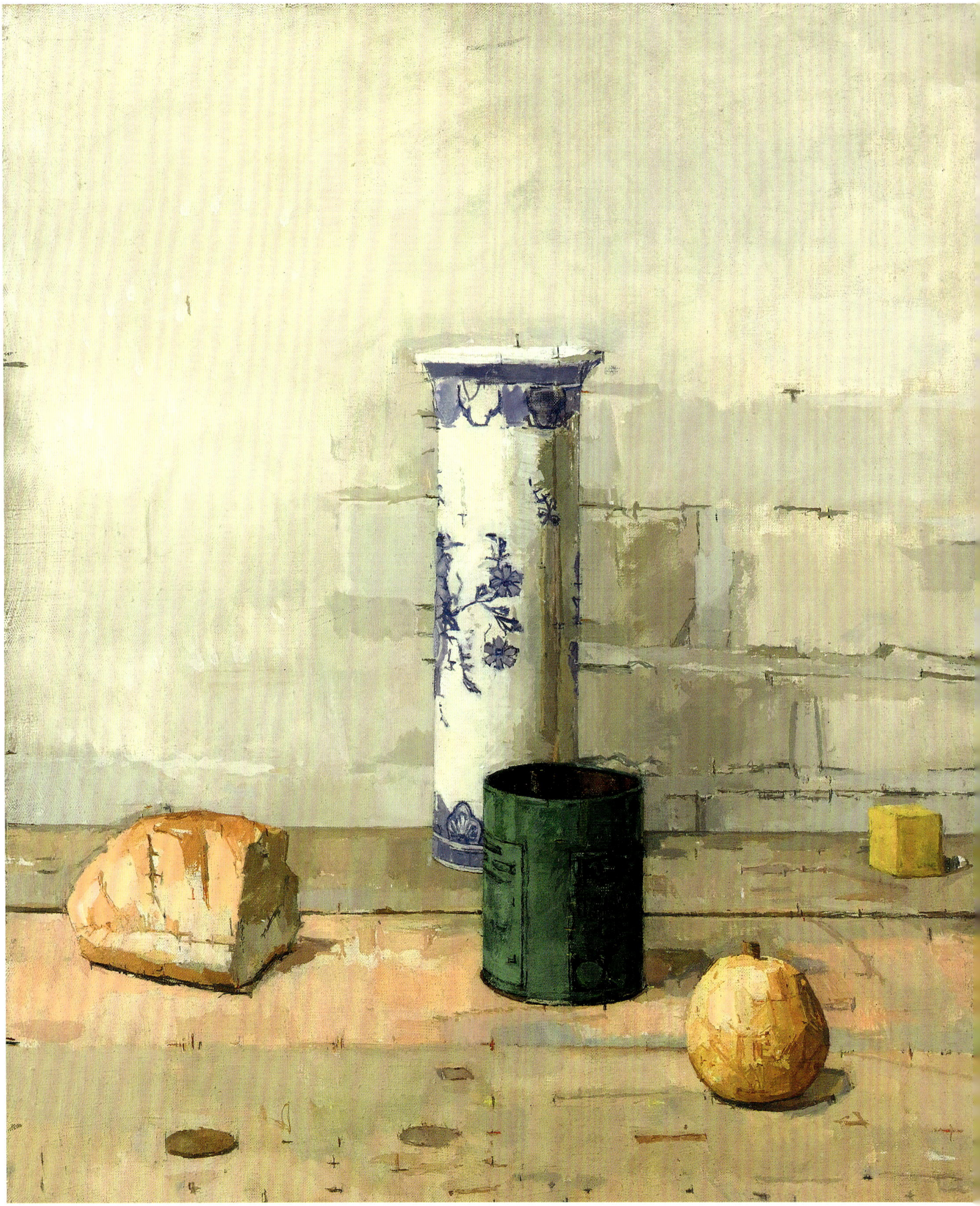

Euan Uglow
Still Life with Delft Vase 1959

Euan Uglow
Georgia 1973

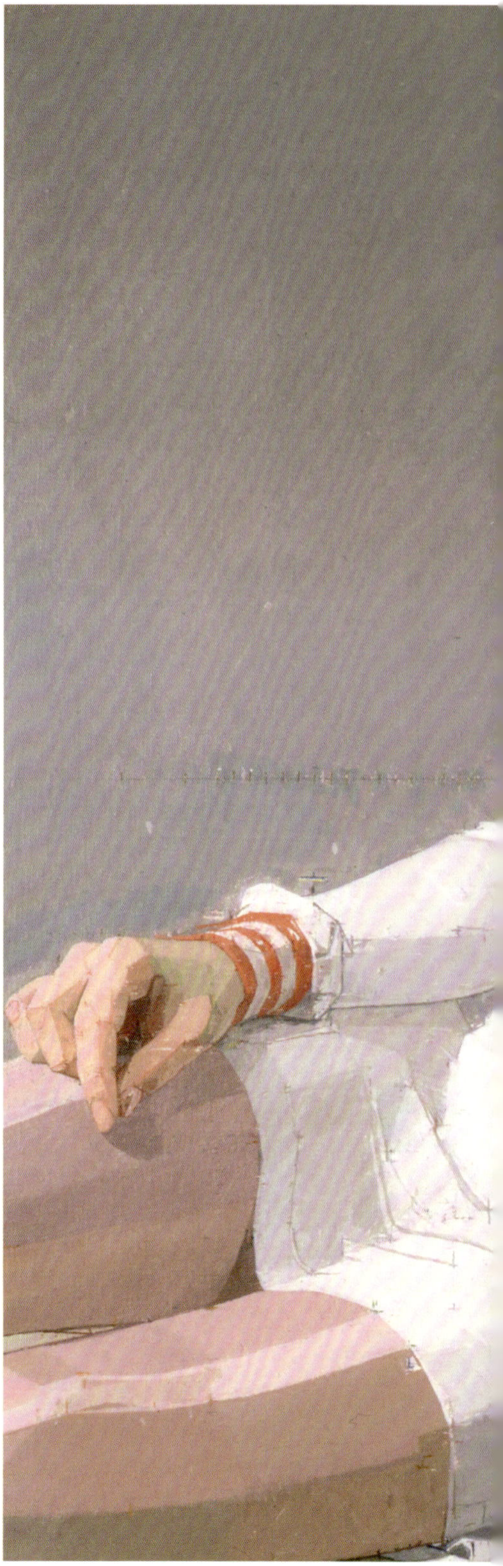

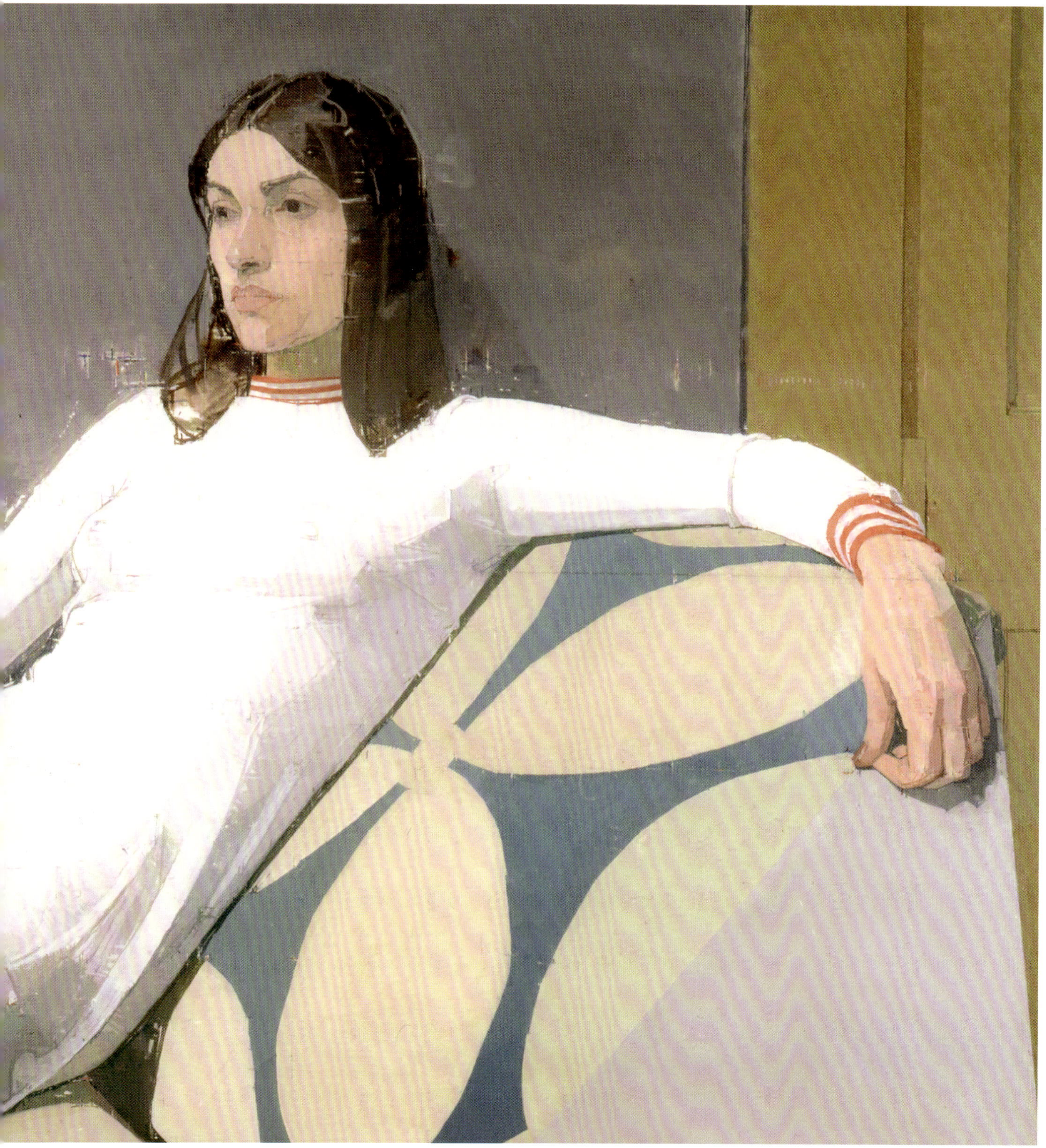

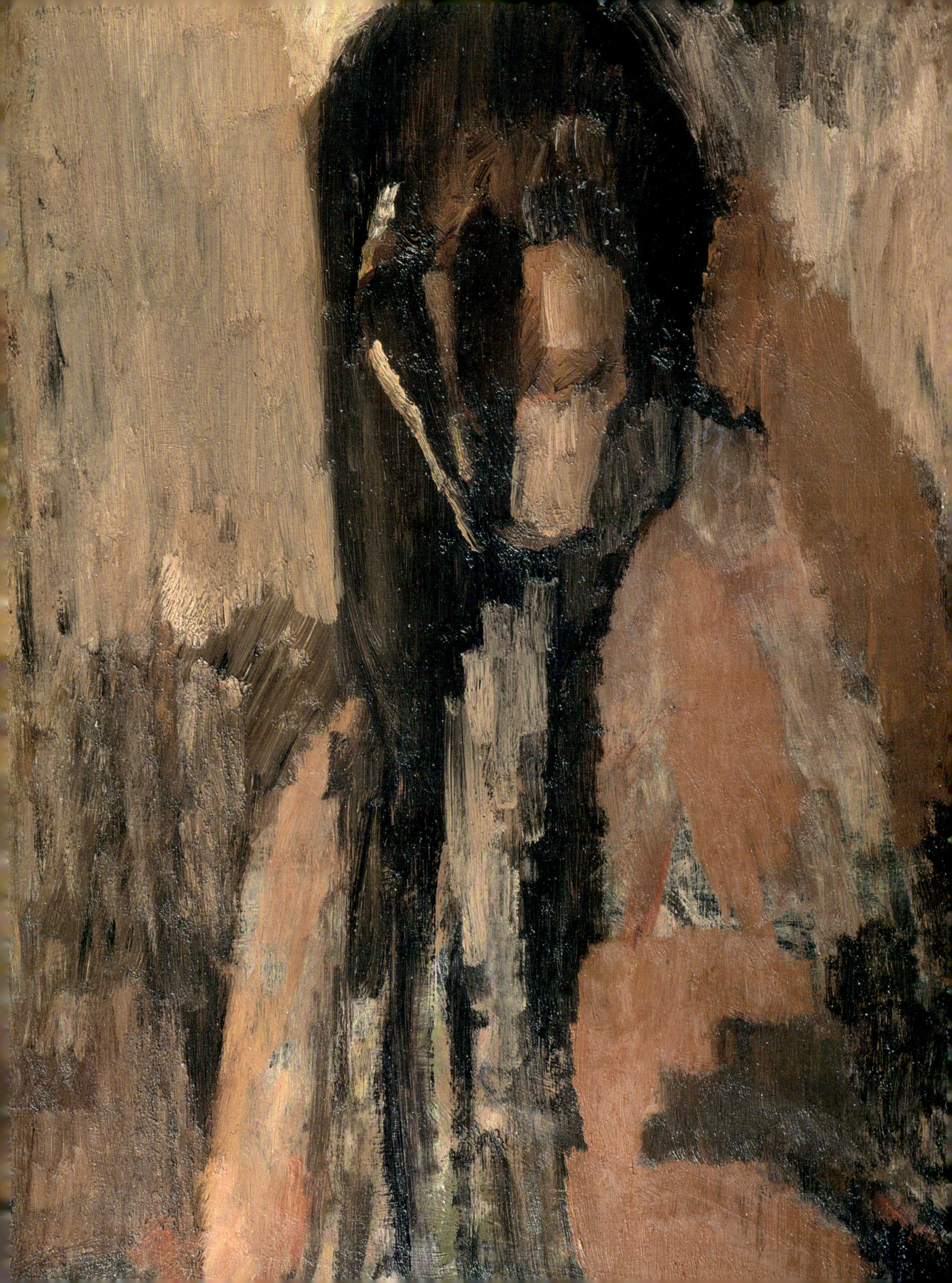

David Bomberg and the Borough Polytechnic

Elena Crippa

During his stay in Palestine in the 1920s, David Bomberg developed an interest in architectural forms, which he continued to pursue during prolonged stays and painting expeditions in Petra, Toledo and Ronda over the following decades. Between 1944 and 1946, he made numerous close-up drawings of St Paul's Cathedral, by then a symbol of the British resistance among the ruins of the bombed cityscape. His only painting of the blitzed scene, *Evening in the City of London* 1944 (p.121), has a strong formal discipline that highlights the architectural scaffolding of the city and yet is ethereal, permeated with a haze of colour that softens the substance of the buildings. This painting exemplifies Bomberg's approach to the drawing and painting of the formal and structural qualities of cityscapes and landscapes, which he brought to his teaching. Despite his desire to teach, which went back at least to the mid-1930s, he only had temporary jobs in minor institutions. From 1945 to 1953 he finally found a stable post teaching day and evening classes at Borough Polytechnic.[1]

If William Coldstream, as Slade Professor of Fine Art and chair of many committees and trustee of national art institutions, was part of the art establishment, David Bomberg was unquestionably an outsider. He was critical of the technical training imparted in art schools and of the strict adherence to traditional canons of representation, which he referred to as the '"hand and eye" disease'.[2] For Bomberg, drawing pertained to the representation of one's feeling of form, rather than to the appearance of form. As he wrote in 1937, in a syllabus for a proposed series of lectures that anticipated his approach in the postwar period, impression by sight is two-dimensional, while 'the sense of touch and the associations of touch produce on sight the illusion of the third dimension'.[3] Key was a direct and personal experience of reality, so that life drawing with malleable and sensuous media, charcoal and oil, was central to his teaching. He also encouraged students to draw outdoors, as he himself had done and continued, intermittently, to do. His insistence on the rendering of a haptic and not only optic experience of forms, and the organic character of mass, organising and simplifying the order underlining one's personal vision, was to prove influential among many of his students.

In 1946, a number of Bomberg's students went on to form the Borough Group, a closely integrated unit that aimed to further knowledge of Bomberg's and their own work and ideas and collectively show their work by organising annual exhibitions. Among members of the group, disbanded in 1950, were Dennis Creffield, Cliff Holden, Edna Mann, Leslie Marr, Dorothy Mead and Miles Richmond. Many of these painters were close friends and progressed by working alongside one another. For example, Dorothy Mead and Dennis Creffield regularly worked together, sketching outdoors. Despite initially disapproving of Bomberg's teaching methods when she was first taught by him as a sixteen-year-old at the South-East Essex School of Art in 1944, Mead

David Bomberg
Vigilante 1955 (detail)

was ultimately won over by Bomberg's approach and followed him as a student at the Borough Polytechnic in 1945, where she remained until 1951. With Bomberg's support, she went on to attend the Slade School of Fine Art from 1956 to 1959. In spite of winning the Figure Painting Prize and the Steer Prize for landscape in 1958, she was to leave the school without securing a diploma, as she refused to sit the compulsory exam on perspective. As Mead stated in a letter to Coldstream, 'perspective is completely alien to me in my work as a painter', as she felt that 'scientific method, academic attitude and scholarship are activities antithetic to creation' because 'as a painter I cannot profess to know – I can only search for meaning'.[4] This episode highlights how dramatically different was the curriculum underpinning the teaching in an art school such as the Slade, bound to the criteria and examination procedures set nationally for obtaining the National Diploma in Design, from the freer approach in Bomberg's classes, which did not prepare students for examination.

Other students such as Frank Auerbach, Leon Kossoff and Gustav Metzger never joined the Borough Group, but attended Bomberg's classes. In particular, Auerbach proved an exceptionally dedicated pupil: he studied under Bomberg from January 1947, while awaiting the start of the academic year at Saint Martin's School of Art, to 1953, when Bomberg's contract was terminated and after he had begun his advanced studies at the Royal College of Art. Auerbach has described Bomberg's teaching as an 'experimental journey', which did not prepare pupils to pass the exams at the time set in art schools, but 'had this sort of idiom that allowed one to go for the essence at the very beginning'.[5] Both Auerbach and Kossoff, fellow students at Saint Martin's School of Art and at the Royal College of Art as well as at Borough Polytechnic, took on Bomberg's example and encouragement to work from the model and from the view in front of them. They built on Bomberg's emphasis on structure and mass, going on to develop personal approaches. Bomberg had drawn and painted buildings and scenes in London but his marked preference was for landscape over cityscape. Conversely, Auerbach and Kossoff developed an early fascination for the dramatic and changing materiality of the cityscape of London. For around a decade, beginning in the early 1950s, they elected building sites around the bomb-scarred capital as one of their major subjects. As Auerbach remarked, London after the war did not just speak of ruin but 'was a marvellous landscape with precipice and mountain and crags, full of drama formally'.[6]

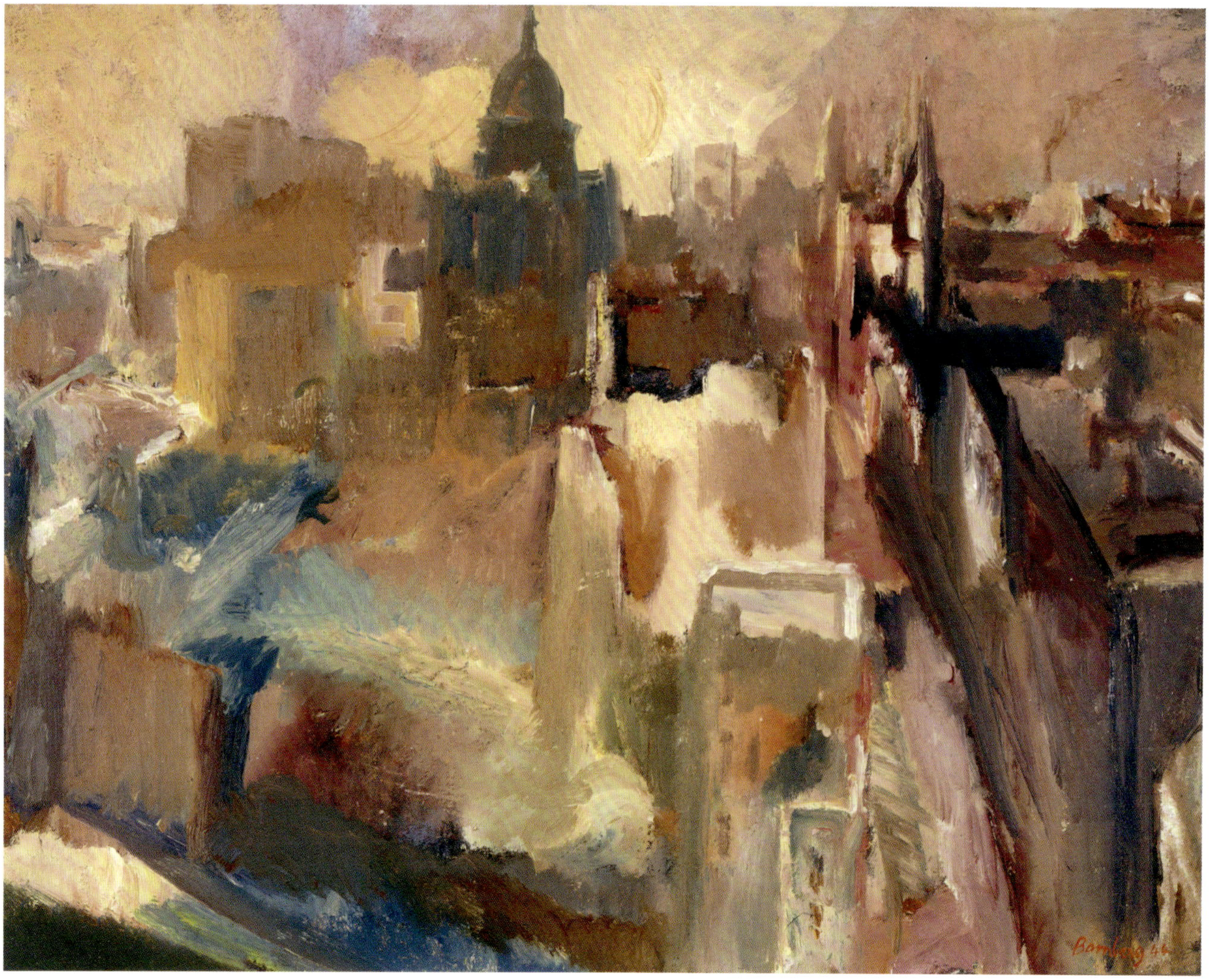

David Bomberg
Evening in the City of London
1944

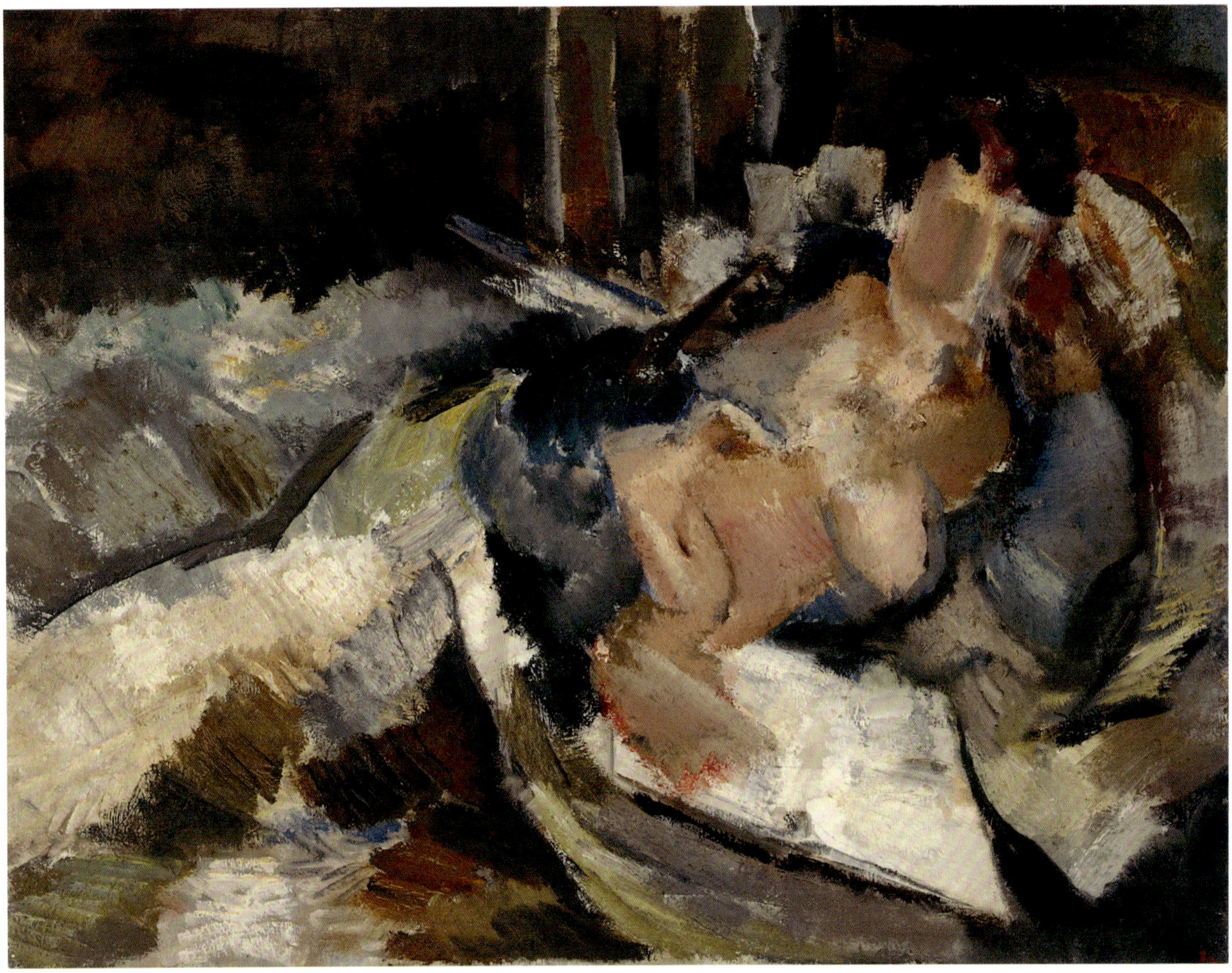

Dorothy Mead
Reclining Figure c.1954

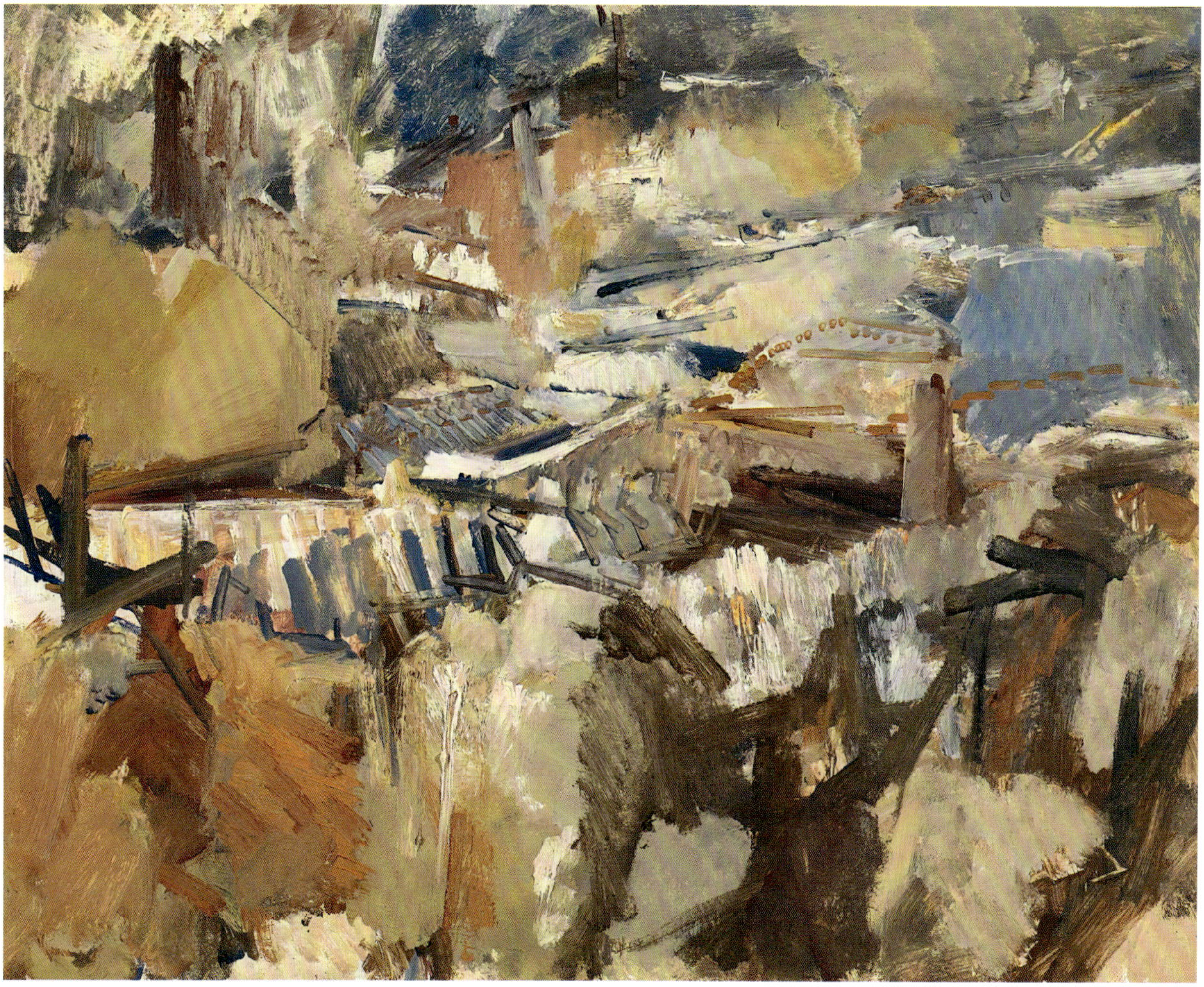

Dennis Creffield
Isle of Dogs from Greenwich Observatory 1959

Frank Auerbach
Rebuilding the Empire Cinema, Leicester Square 1962

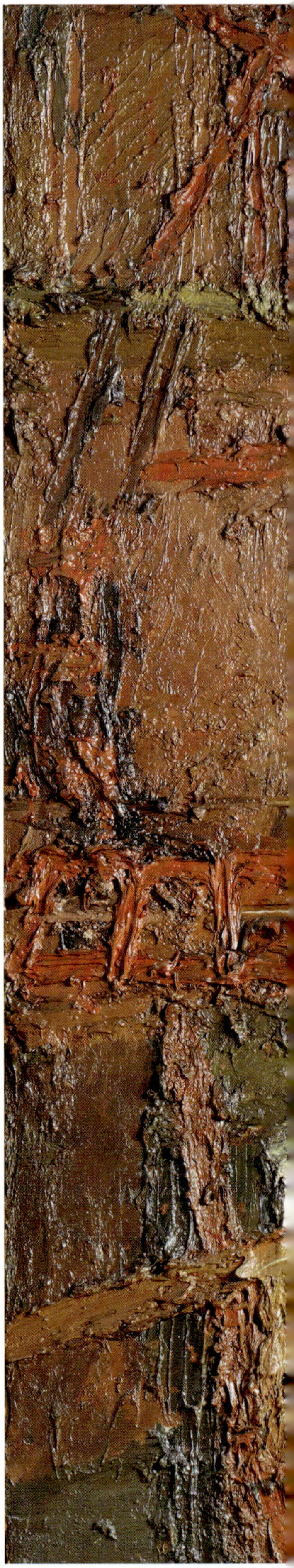

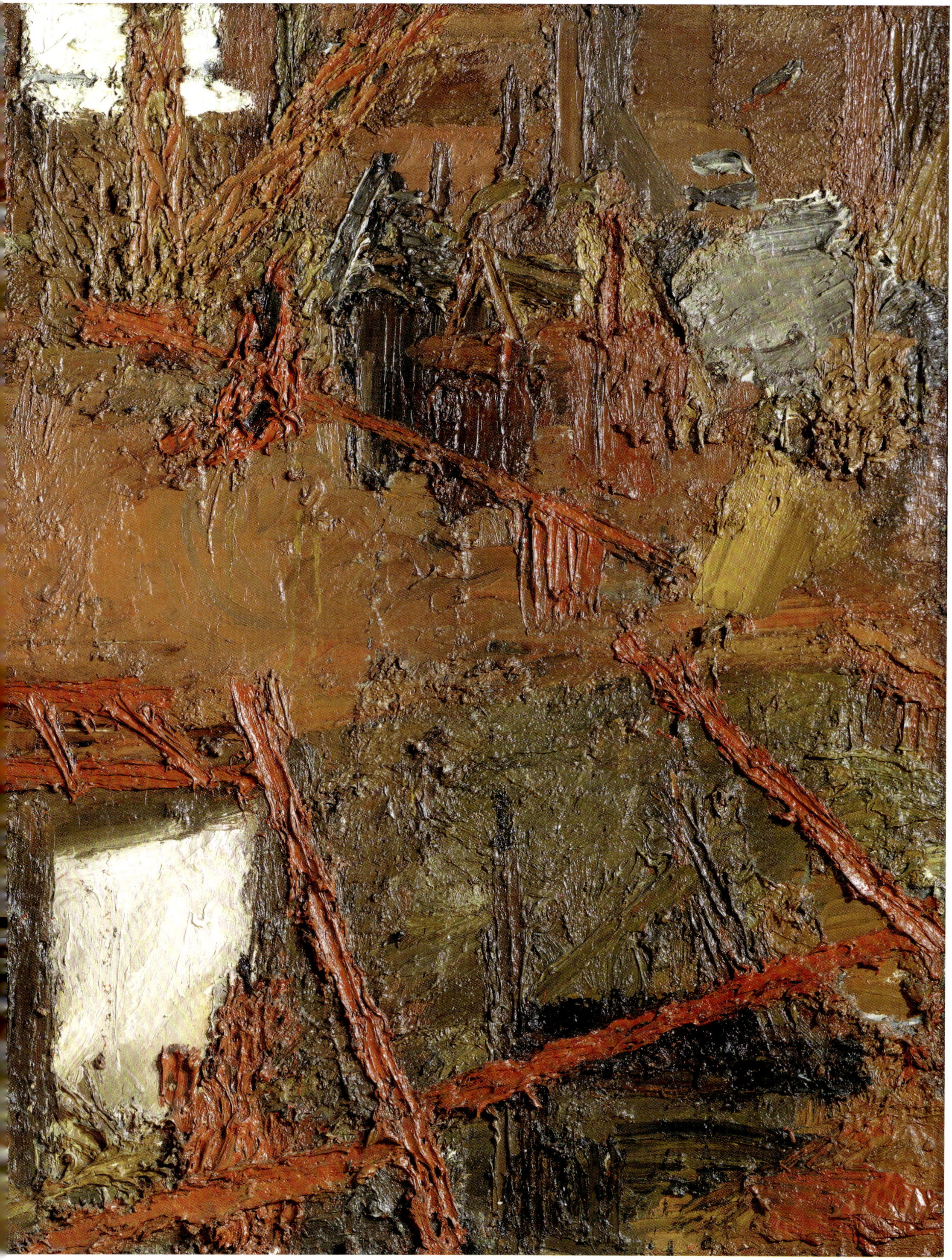

Frank Auerbach
Head of E. O. W. I 1960

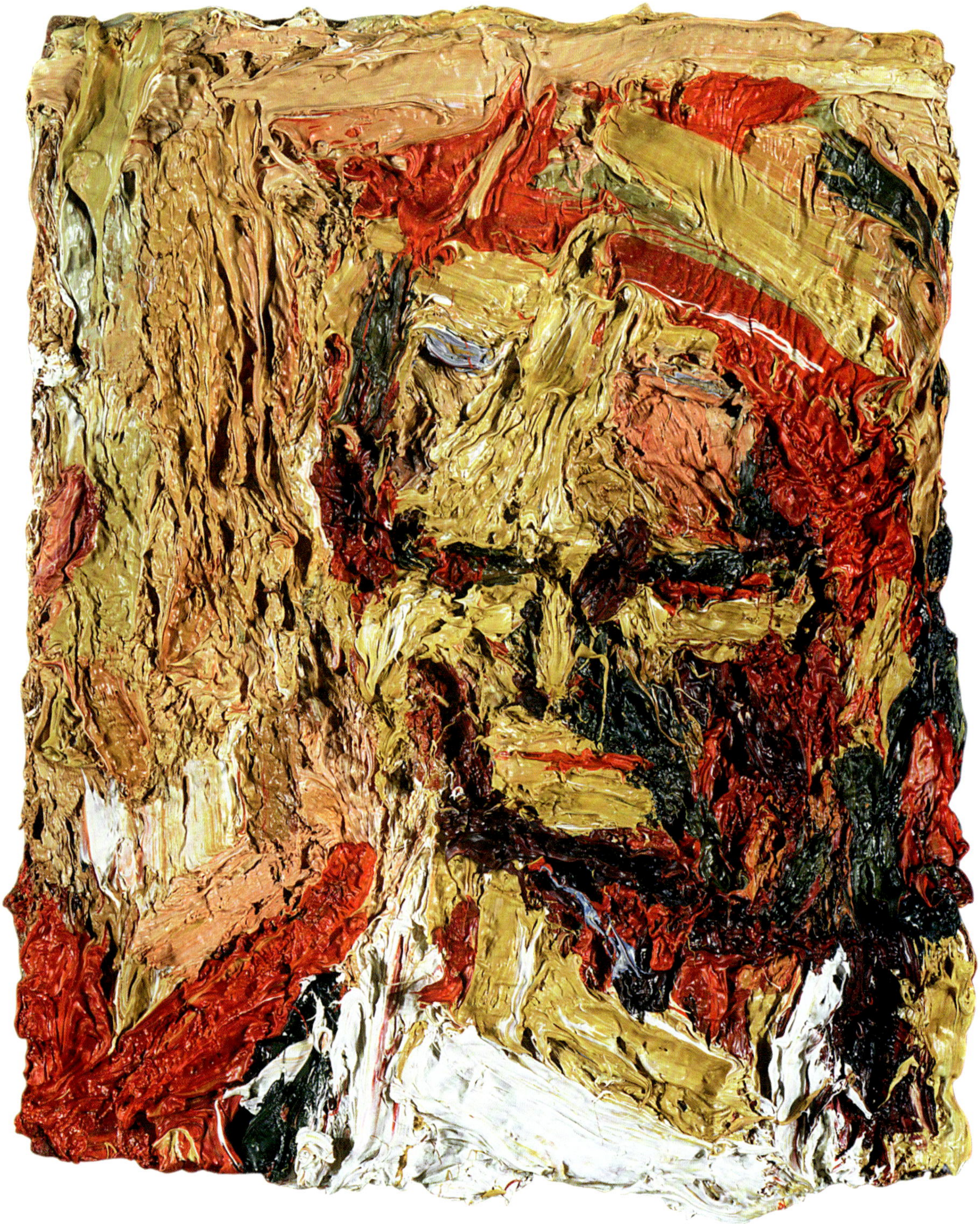

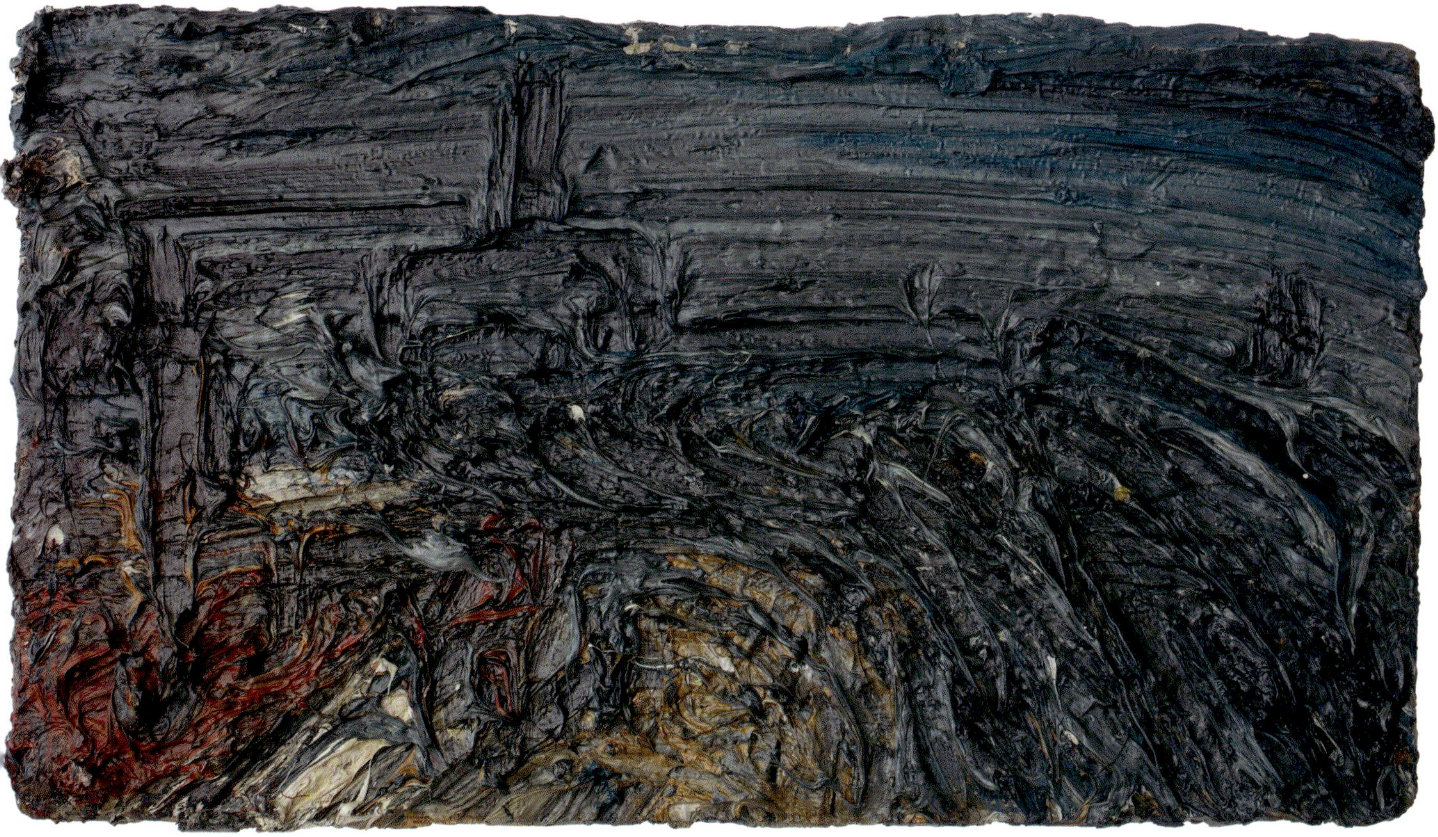

Leon Kossoff
Early Morning Willesden Junction 1962

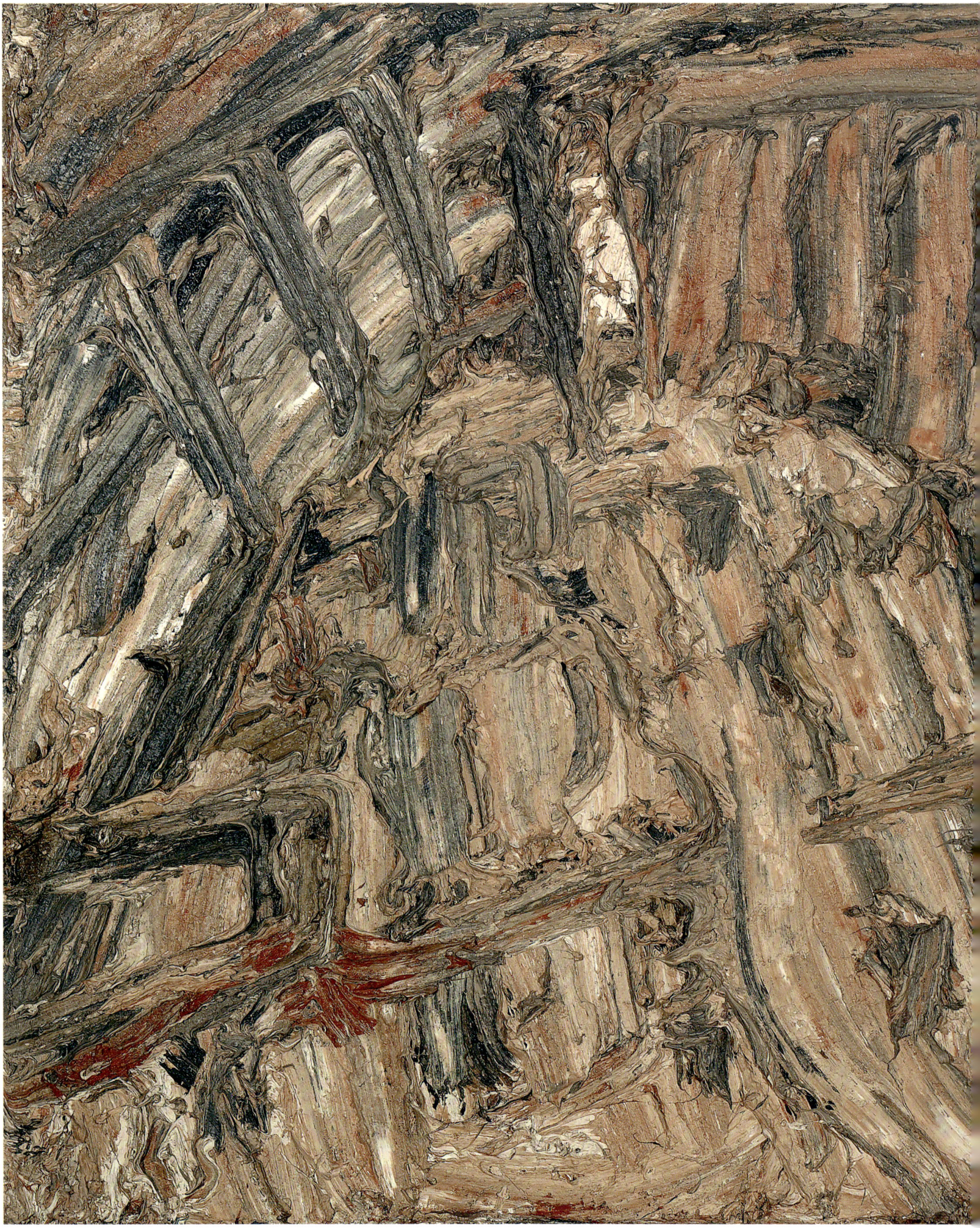

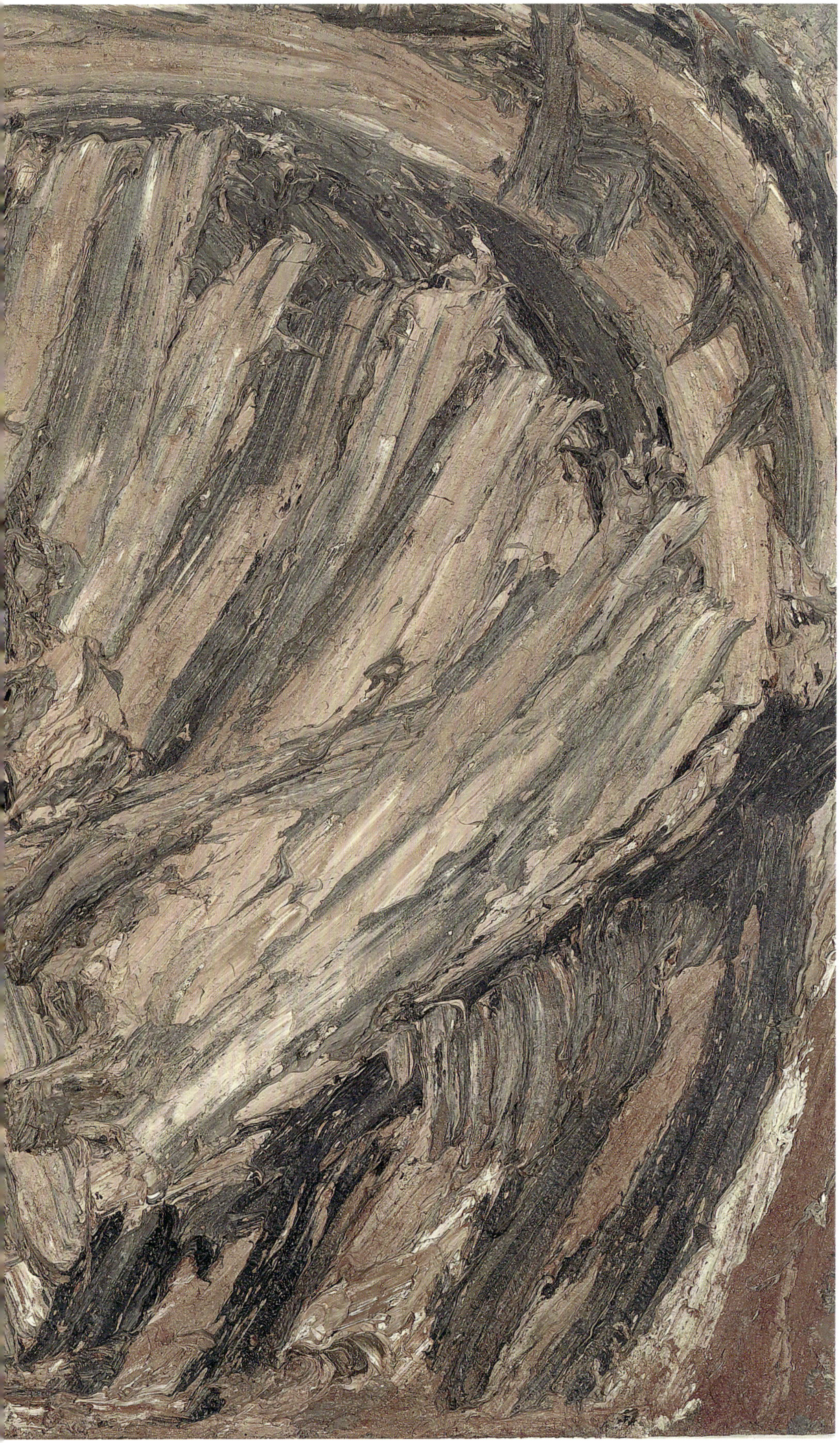

Leon Kossoff
Building Site, Victoria Street
1961

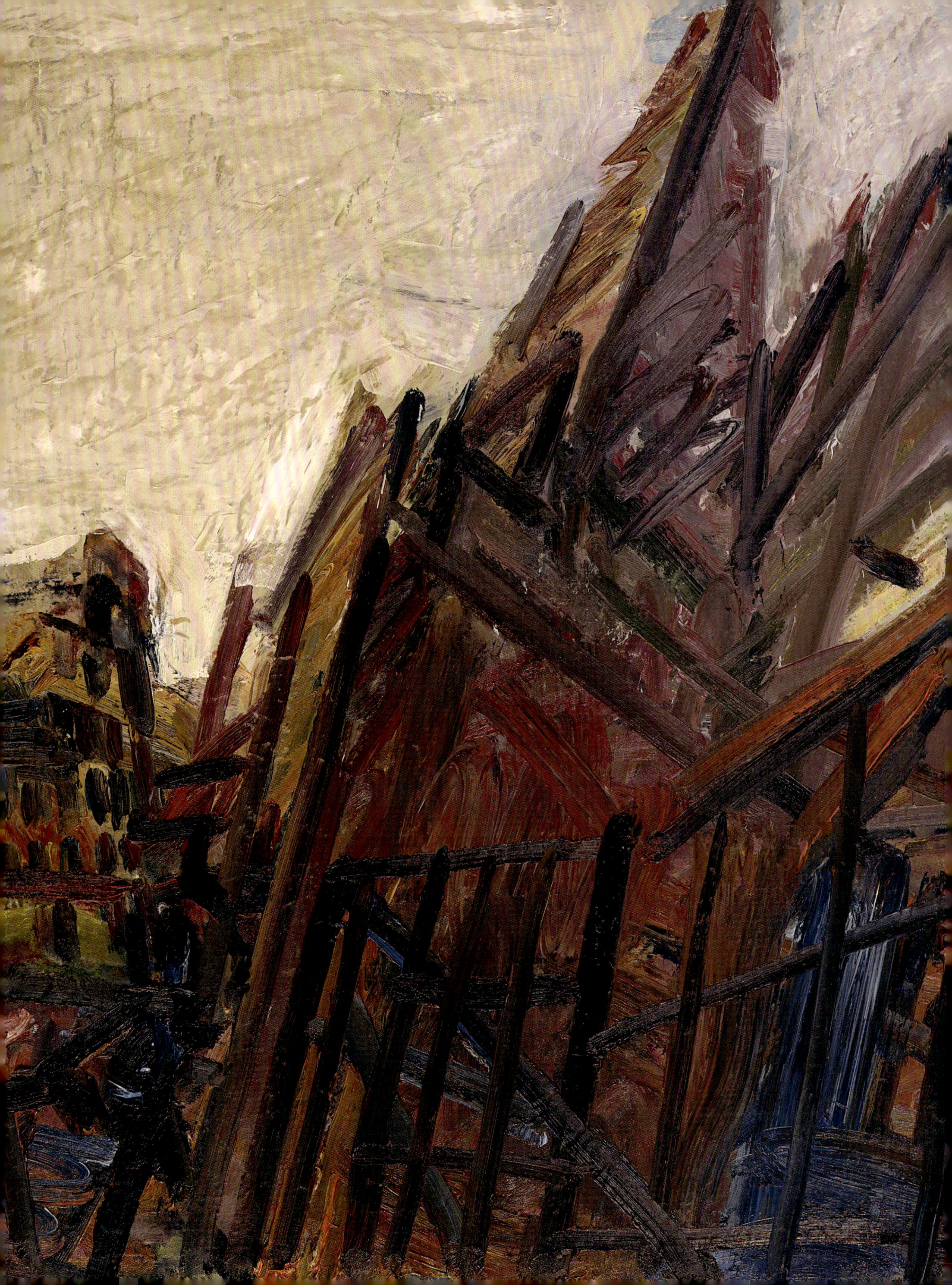

Frank Auerbach and Leon Kossoff

Elena Crippa

In the first half of the 1950s Frank Auerbach and Leon Kossoff not only studied in the same art schools and with Bomberg, they were also close friends and often sat for each other. They had long and sustained careers, and both painters continue to live and work in London. Despite the great differences in their work, their attachment and continual return over six decades to the sites of London close and dear to them is particular to their parallel pursuit. While the painting of figures from life remained an equally important endeavour, the two painters shared an enduring fascination with the dramatic and changing materiality of the British capital.

A recurring subject of Auerbach's work since the 1950s is Primrose Hill, adjacent to Regent's Park, not far from the artist's North London studio where he has lived and worked since 1954. By the time of the execution of *Primrose Hill* 1967–8 (p.22), he had begun scraping down the surfaces of his paintings before the next session, when he would start anew, the support becoming thinner and the brushstrokes more fluid.[1] As the eye wanders over the surface of *Primrose Hill*, exploring the changing relationships between shapes and colours, the brushstrokes offer a clear sense of movement and directionality. The coming together of these conflicting elements seems to reflect the experience of perceiving life, whereby a constantly changing set of relationships between viewer, object and light means that what we are looking at is never static, never the same.

Another recurrent subject in Auerbach's work is the streets of his neighbourhood, around Mornington Crescent. These streets, possibly more than any of the other subjects elected by the painter, are representative of the unplanned, at times chaotic and often bitty cityscape of London that has kept him intrigued. In Auerbach's words: 'I feel London is this raw thing [...] This extraordinary, marvellous unplanned city where whenever somebody tries to get something going they stop halfway through, and next to it something incongruous occurs.'[2] It is indeed this constant state of movement, change and alteration of the city, matched by the artist's own changes in mood and intent, that can be experienced in different pictures of the same subject executed over time.

In *Chimney in Mornington Crescent – Winter Morning* 1991 (opposite), the tall and iconic chimney at the back of the Carreras Cigarette Factory dominates the picture. In the many paintings in which it appears, its top part just fits into or exceeds the limits of the canvas. Indeed, it is impossible to apprehend it entirely when standing in its proximity, and Auerbach's paintings are always the results of drawings made in and as part of a particular location, rather than by apprehending a scene in a remote and

Frank Auerbach
Chimney in Mornington Crescent – Winter Morning
1991 (detail)

detached way. The great dynamism of the picture is engendered by both the energetic, large brush marks and by the vertiginous effect caused by the steep angle of the building flanking the road, particularly the chimney, which seems to project outward. If this sense of dynamism is reminiscent of Chaïm Soutine's animated landscapes, Auerbach's pictures always preserve a clear sense of structure. As Freud wrote: 'The mastery of these compositions is such that in spite of their often precarious balance, like a waiter pretending to slip while carrying a huge pile of plates, the structure never falters. It is the viewer who has to hold tight.'[3]

Like Auerbach's compositions, Kossoff's paintings ultimately emerge through observations and drawings made in situ, with the artist often returning to the same sites over years if not decades, and the pictures are painted and scraped down over and over again, until finally something convincing and exciting appears. While Auerbach's landscapes are populated mostly by simply rendered figures, anonymous inhabitants of the cityscape, in those of Kossoff men and women are often the protagonists of densely populated scenes set in the public spaces of the metropolis. Kossoff's intense and moving portrayal of human presence developed alongside a continuous engagement with specific sites of London – the city where he was born and has lived all his adult life. He depicts locations that he knows intimately, and this intimacy is apparent in the way they are rendered, intensely and yet seemingly unhurriedly, a testament to the passing of time. *Children's Swimming Pool, Autumn Afternoon* 1971 (pp.134–5) is one of five large paintings of swimming pools that Kossoff completed between 1969 and 1972. They represent an important transition in his work. The paint is relatively thinly applied and the scene rendered in a general atmosphere of movement, enhanced by the flickering reflections of the water in the crowded pool. While figures were little defined in his drawings, in his paintings each person became someone particular, known and often dear to the artist.[4] As a result these paintings are filled with a humanity that is never anonymous, the result of intimate observation and knowledge of others.

There are other London sites to which Kossoff has often returned. Christ Church is an imposing Anglican church built in the first half of the eighteenth century, one of many designed by the architect Nicholas Hawksmoor in the Baroque style. A prominent landmark in Kossoff's native district of Shoreditch, in the East End, the church has stood mostly unaltered through the area's many changes and recent gentrification. Kossoff first drew it in the 1950s, when it was semi-derelict, and began painting it in the 1980s, returning to the subject in the 1990s (p.137). In these paintings, as the art historian Andrea Rose has observed, 'Kossoff orchestrates the intensity of his childhood feelings with the look of the building now',[5] combining the unshakable quality of the building with the dreamy quality of the light that seems to emanate from within and envelop the entire scene.

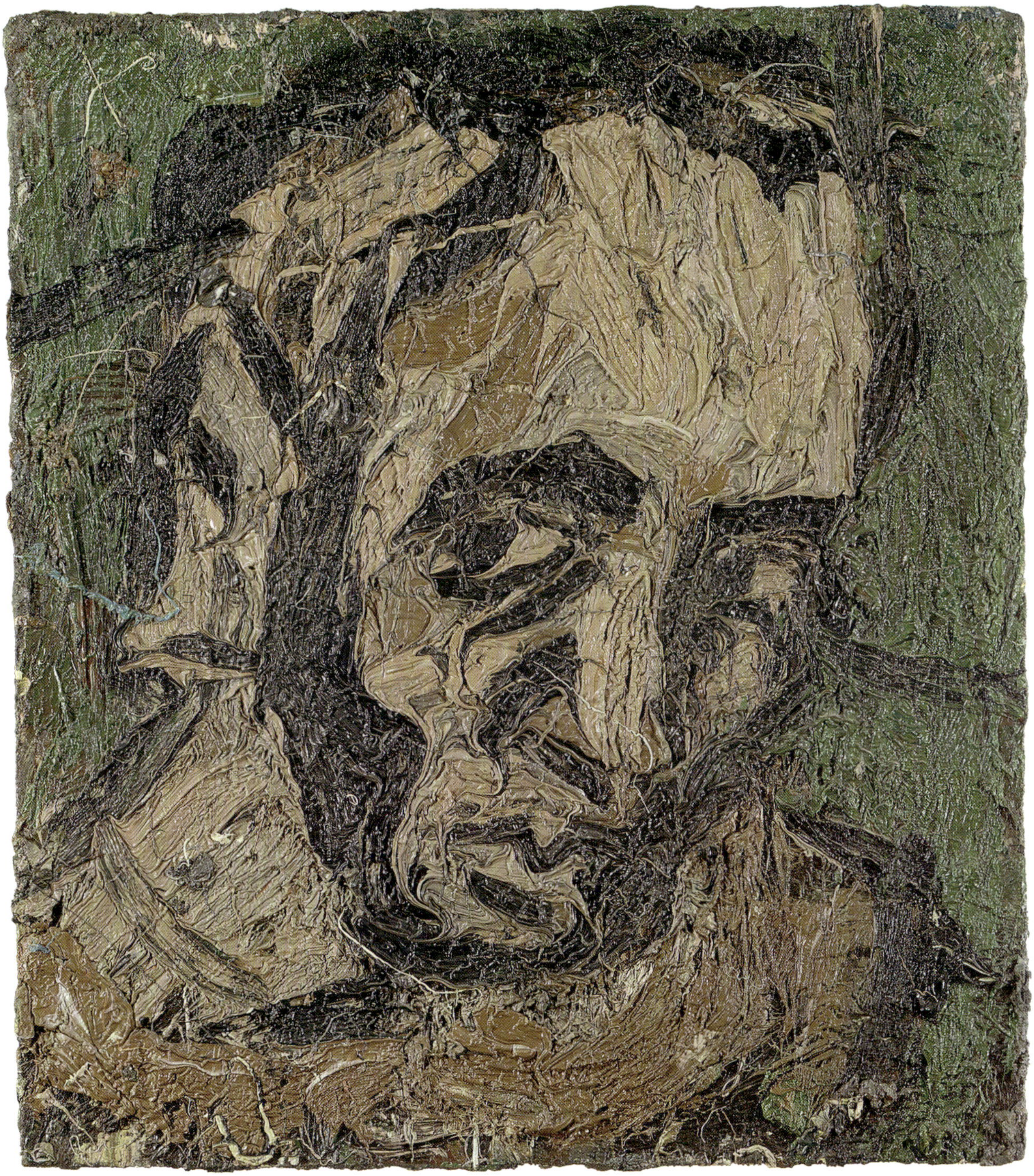

Leon Kossoff
Self Portrait II 1972

Leon Kossoff
Children's Swimming Pool,
Autumn Afternoon 1971

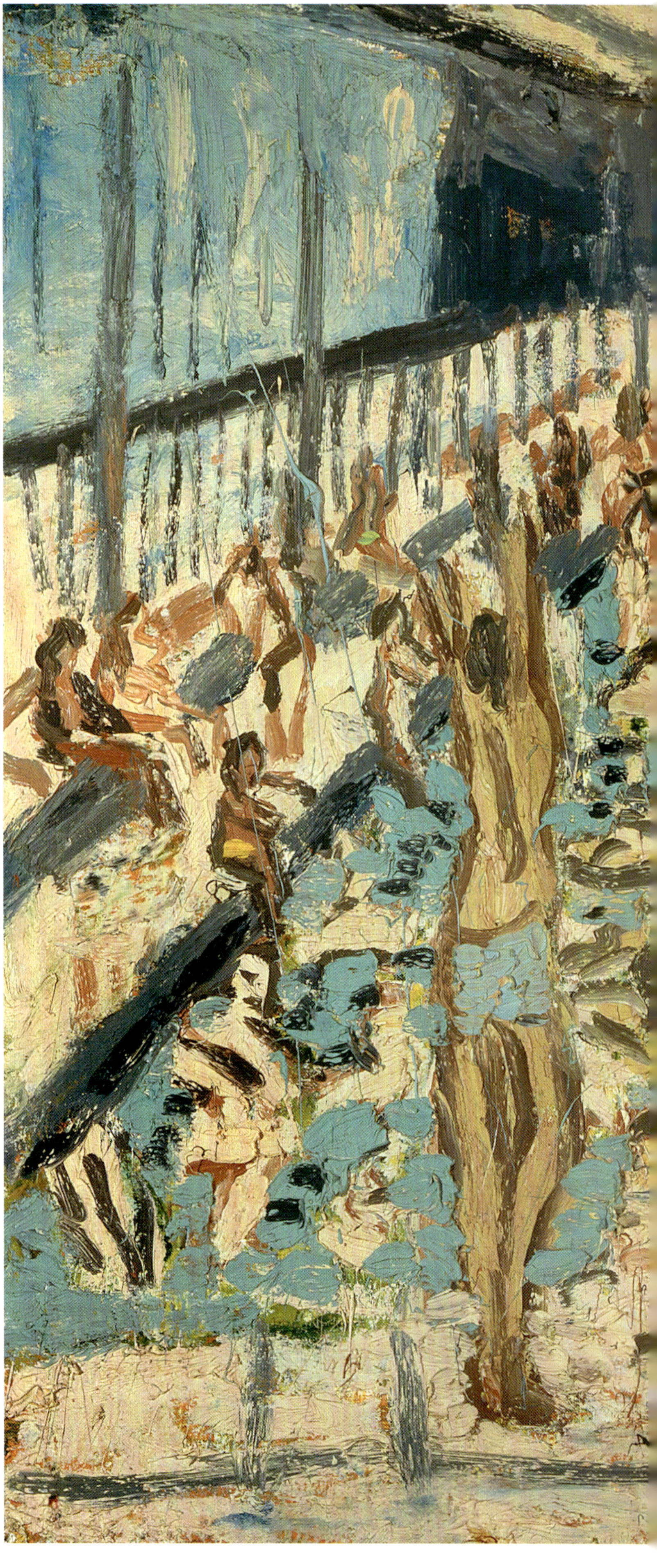

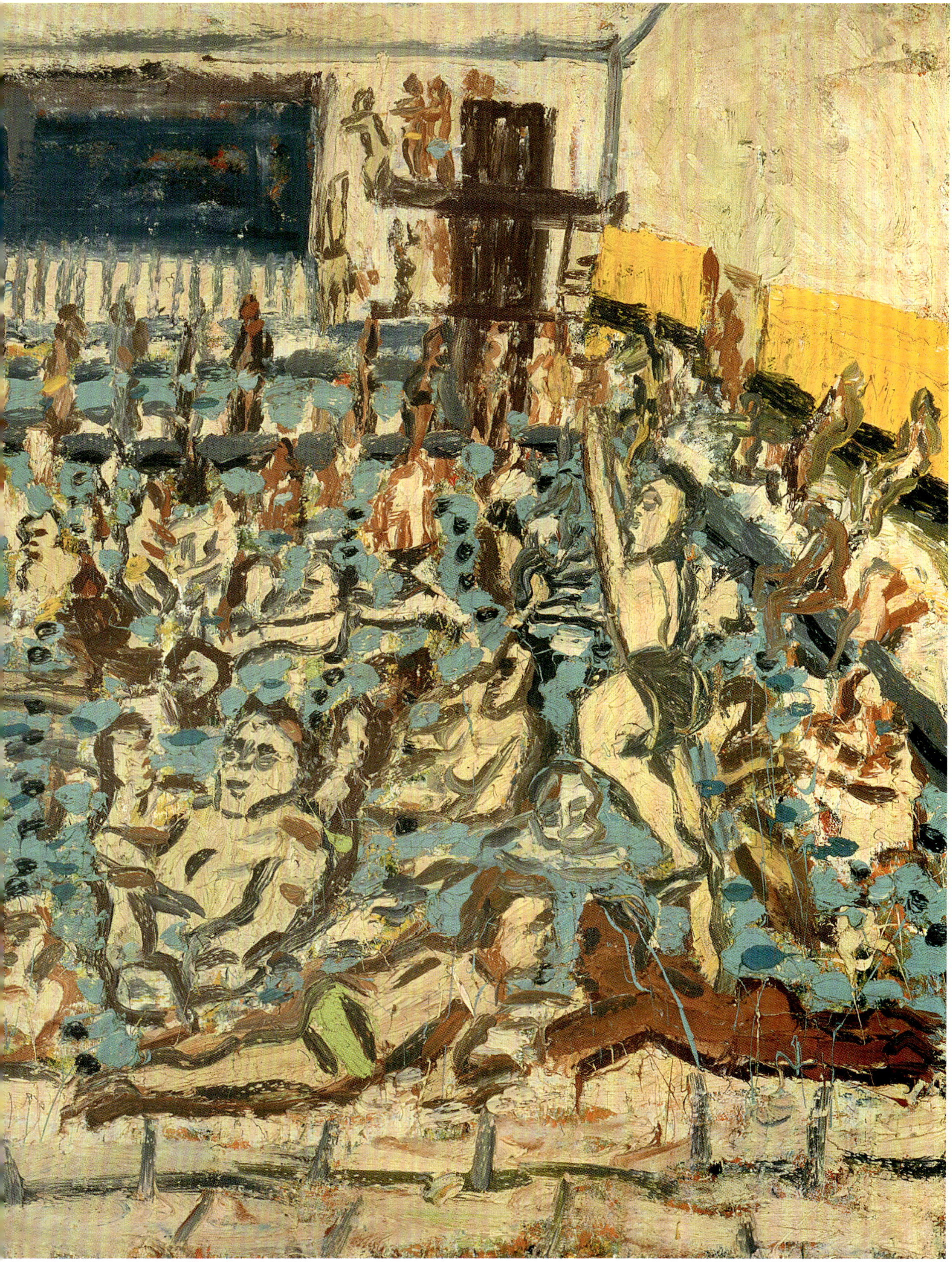

Leon Kossoff
Demolition of the Old House,
Dalston Junction, Summer 1974
1974

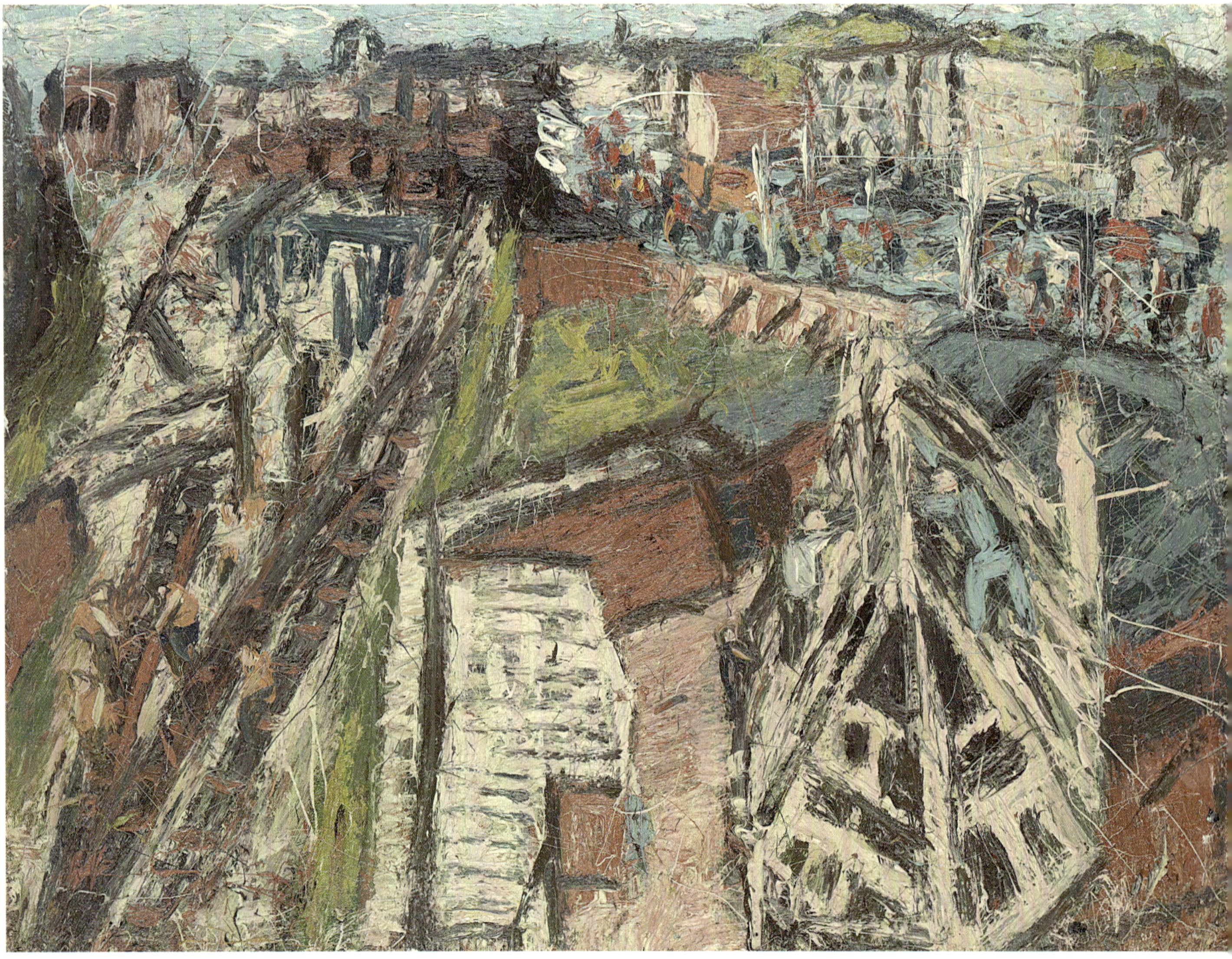

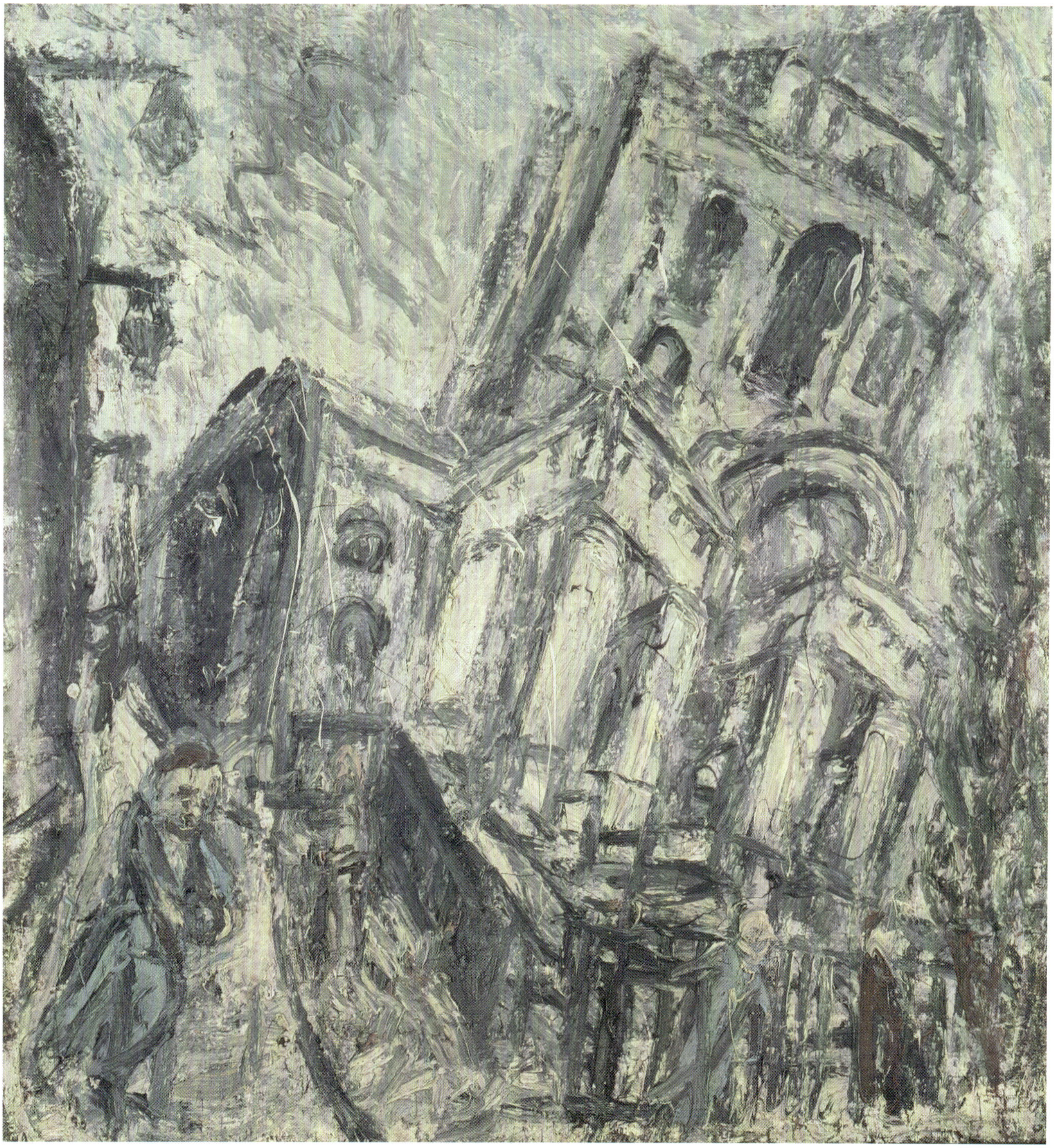

Leon Kossoff
Christ Church, Spitalfields, Morning 1990

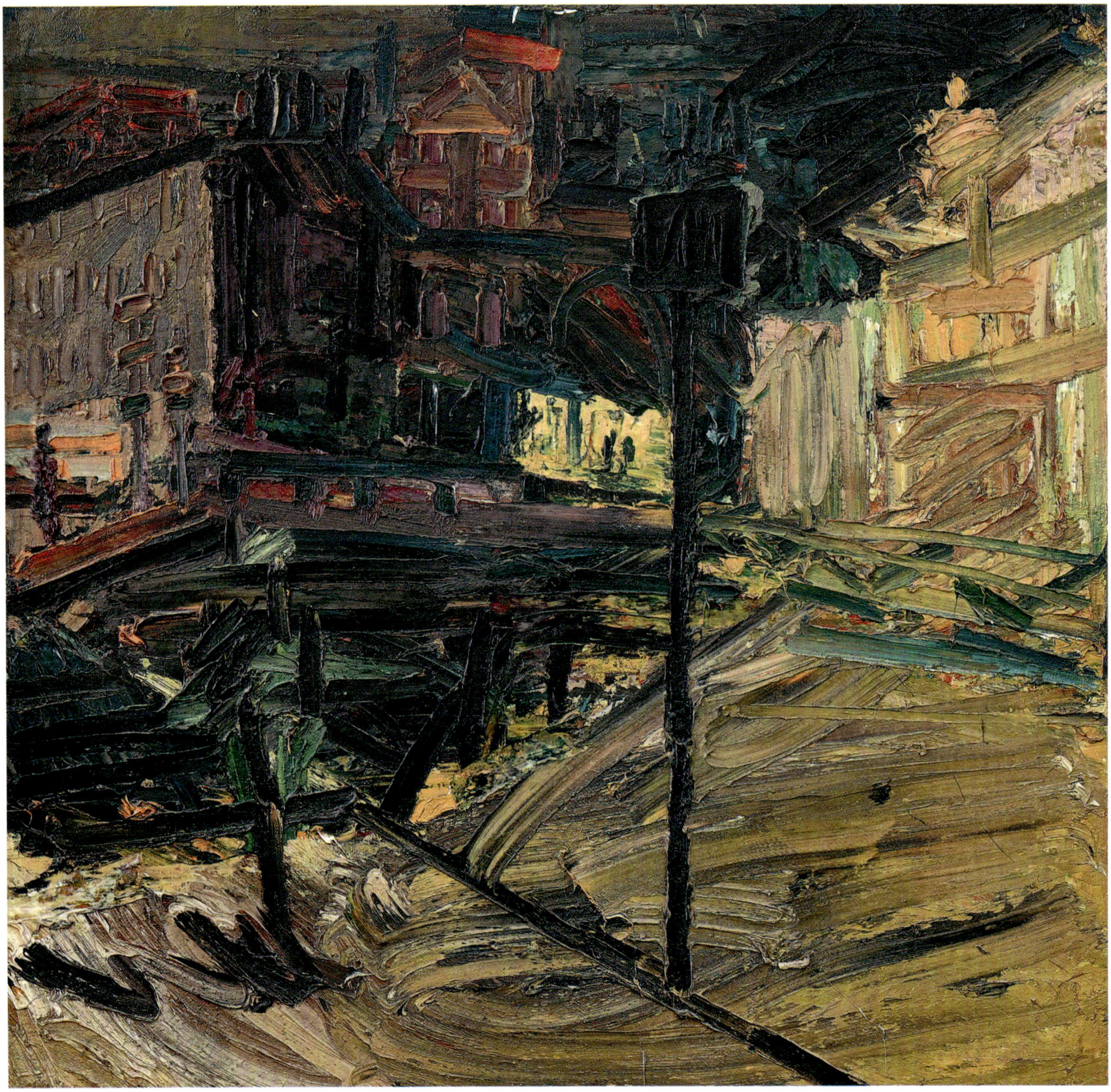

Frank Auerbach
Looking Towards Mornington Crescent Station, Night 1972–3

Frank Auerbach
St Pancras Steps 1978–9

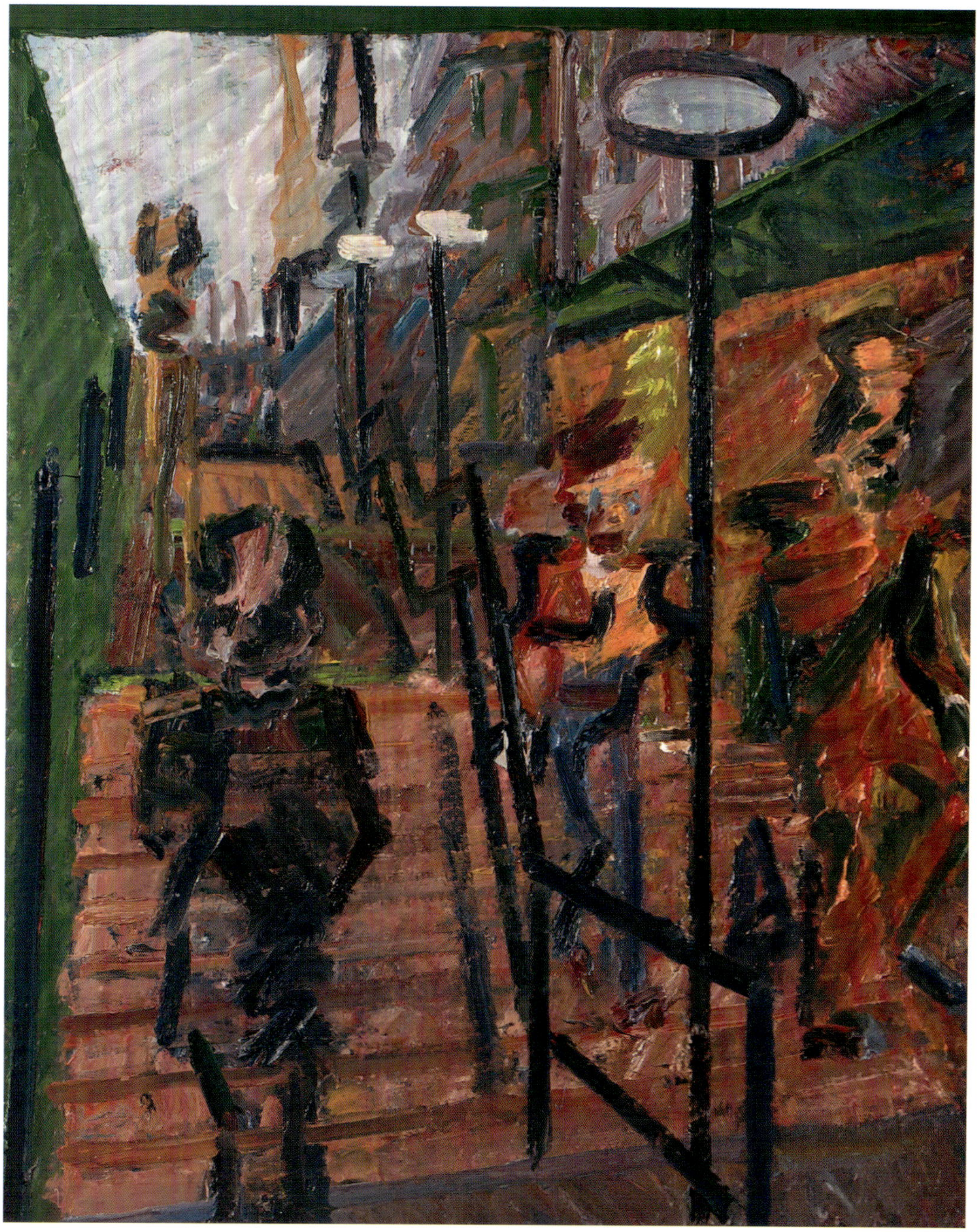

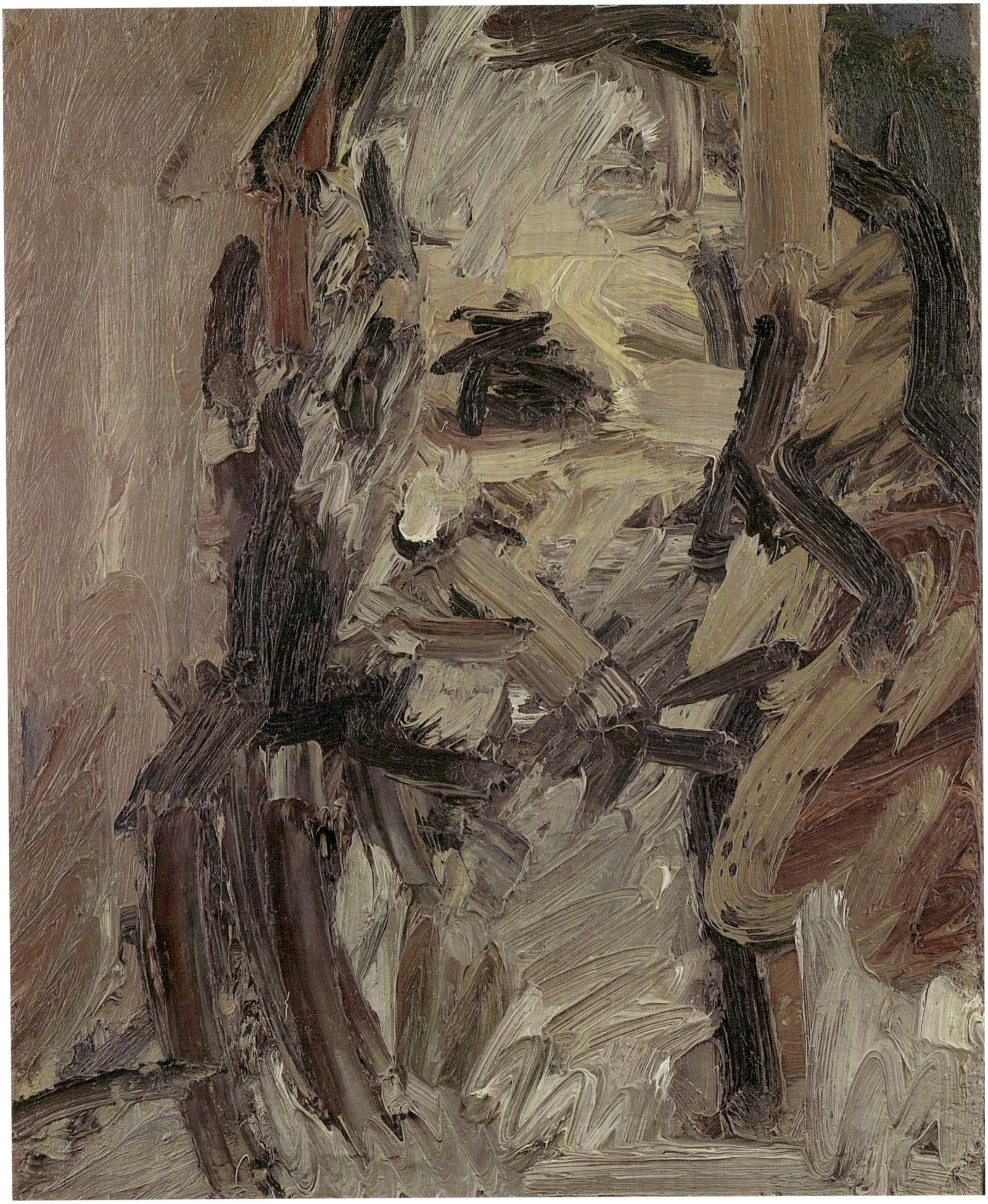

Frank Auerbach
Head of Jake 1997

Frank Auerbach
Park Village East – Winter
1998–9

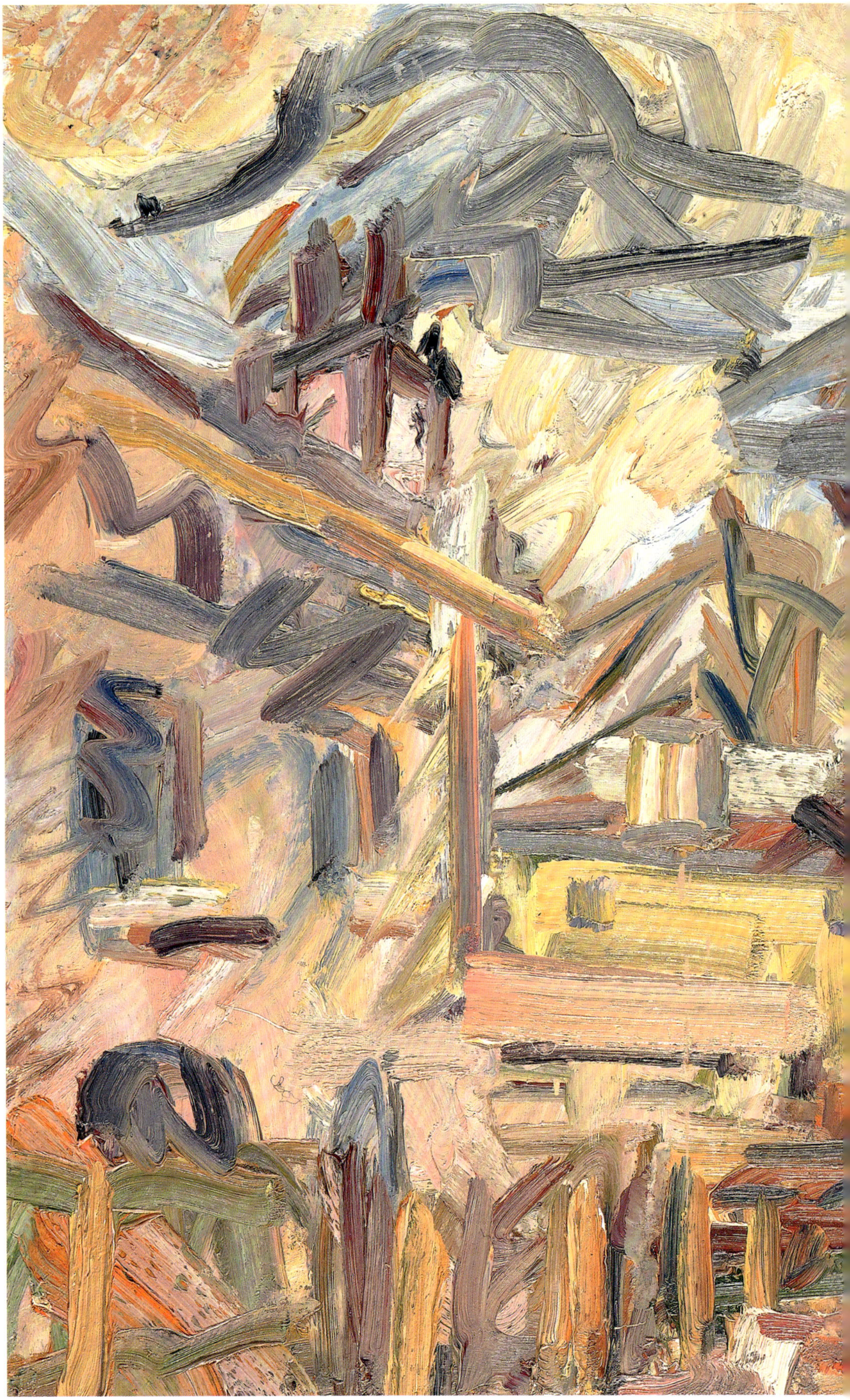

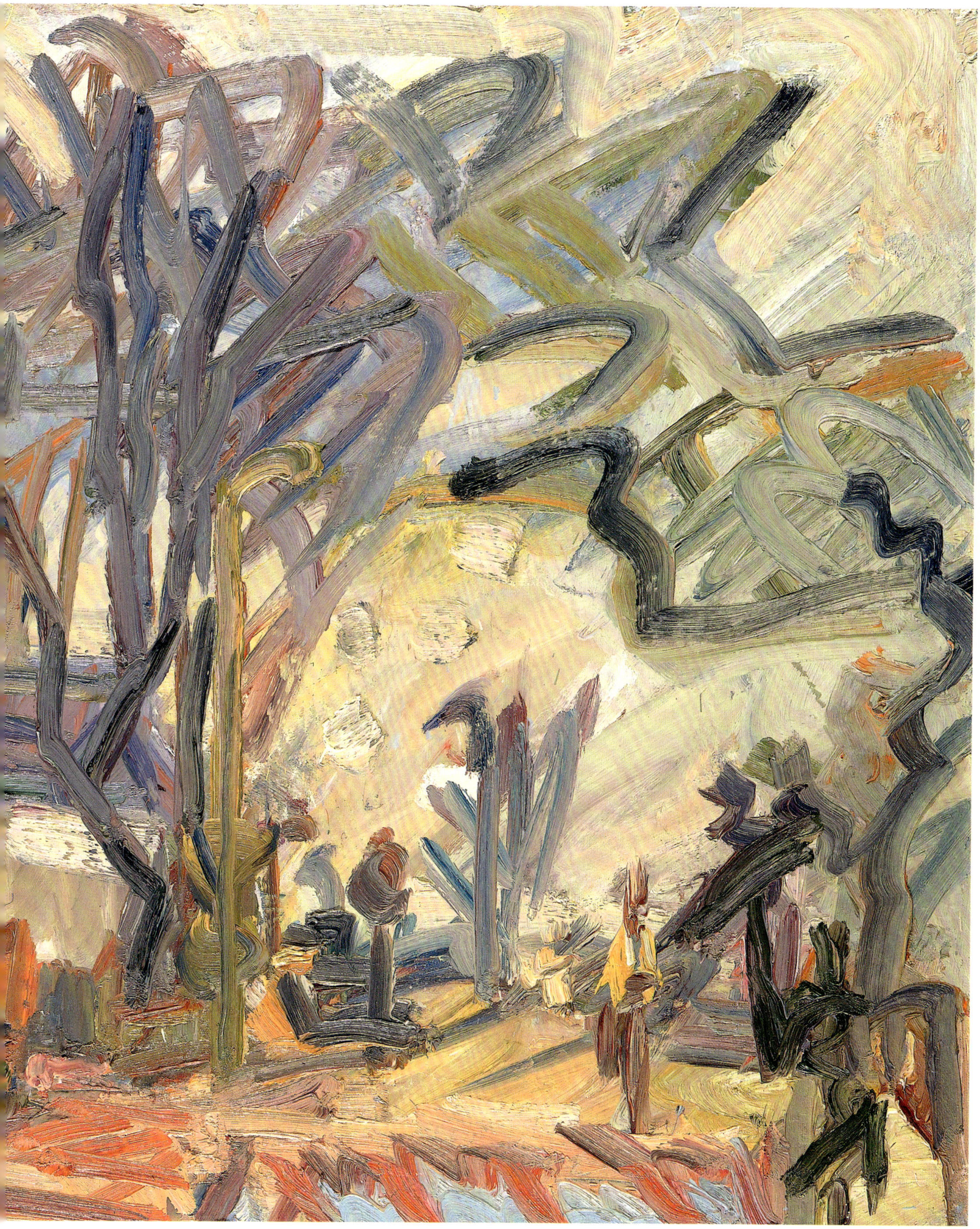

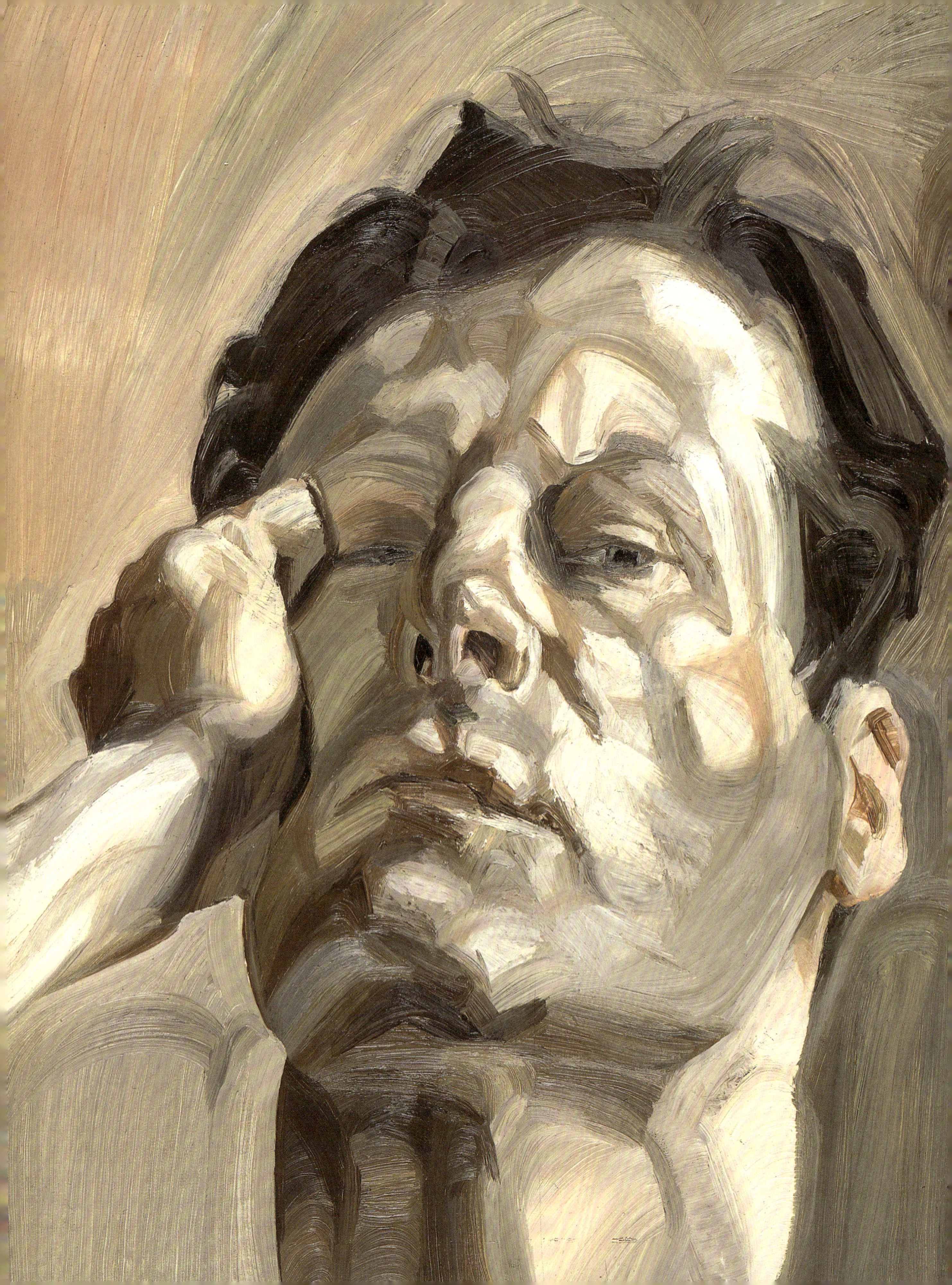

Lucian Freud

Laura Castagnini

While Lucian Freud's early work was based on precise draughtsmanship, a dramatic stylistic shift occurred in the late 1950s. Freud began using thick hog's hair paintbrushes instead of thin sable brushes, and started standing up at the easel rather than working from a seated position. This modification allowed him to paint freely using thick brushstrokes and fluid swabs of muted colour, encouraging a dynamic approach that he maintained for the next five decades. In particular, lead white pigment was an important feature of Freud's palette from the mid-1970s: its grainy texture and brilliant hue enabled him to create his signature pale skin tones and construct the depth of muscles. It is through this manner of working that Freud became widely recognised for his ability to render paint as flesh.

Freud's sculptural and visceral approach to paint is evident in the vertiginous portrait *Frank Auerbach* 1975–6 (p.151). Painted from above, Auerbach's strained forehead is transformed into a mountainous landscape, its wrinkles creasing like rivers around the bulging frontal lobe. Like Stanley Spencer, Freud rejected sentimentality in portraiture, and his unflinchingly honest representations of his subjects are often described as brutal or unflattering. However, Freud described his approach as an attempt to depict the truest possible image of his subjects: 'I'm not trying to make a copy of the person. I'm trying to relay something of who they are as a physical and emotional presence. I want the paint to work as flesh does.'[1] Towards this aim, Freud's models were usually drawn from his personal life. His daughter Bella, for example, returned to the studio for over a dozen portraits throughout her life, appearing first as a writhing baby in *Baby on a Green Sofa* 1961 (p.147). Jacquetta Eliot, a girlfriend of Freud's in the 1970s, is represented in the painting *Naked Portrait* 1972–3 (p.149) as an angular woman laid awkwardly on a smooth bed, her rounded leg splayed towards the ground as if it were made of rubber. Her watery blue eyes gaze vacantly past the viewer, enveloping the entire image in sadness.

From the 1980s onwards Freud embarked on a trajectory of large nudes. Many of these figure paintings utilised props to create theatrical mise en scènes with ambiguous narratives. *Sleeping by the Lion Carpet* 1996 (p.157) features Sue Tilley, an overweight benefits supervisor also known as 'Big Sue', asleep on an armchair. Behind her is placed a pictorial lion rug, its feline protagonists looming menacingly over their unsuspecting prey. Sue Tilley was introduced to Freud by the drag performance artist Leigh Bowery, who was a frequent muse during this period until he died of AIDS-related complications in 1994.[2] In *Leigh Bowery* 1991 (p.156), Freud's second portrait of Bowery, the artist's large bald head is depicted sleeping peacefully on his shoulder. Although the painting captures Bowery without characteristic make-up or outlandish costumes, it does emphasise the recognisable 'knots' in the dimples on Bowery's cheeks: these piercing holes, held open permanently by catgut, were used to secure the plastic mouth coverings that often formed the centrepiece of Bowery's outrageous looks.

Throughout his life, Freud worked exclusively from life in the seclusion of his sparse London studio. The famously paint-splattered walls and bare floorboards reappear throughout his oeuvre, with

Lucian Freud
Man's Head (Self-Portrait I)
1963 (detail)

many recurring furniture items becoming almost as recognisable as the sitters themselves. Different versions of a battered leather brown armchair, for example, appear in numerous paintings such as *Annabel* 1967 (p.148), *The Big Man* 1976–7 (pp.152–3), *Bella* 1996 (p.160) and *Sleeping by the Lion Carpet* 1996 (p.157). Indeed, Freud considered the human and non-human aspects of his paintings to be intrinsically linked, stipulating that the model must pose even while he painted the surrounding objects. The presence of the sitter, he claimed, affected his perception of the studio. Freud's obsessive interest in his physical environment is demonstrated by the painting *Two Plants* 1977–80 (p.154), the result of Freud's moving studios from Paddington to Holland Park in the late 1970s, after which he spent three years acutely observing one corner of the room in order to acclimatise himself to the light of the new space.

Freud was known to paint excruciatingly slowly, observing his subjects intensely over numerous sittings that took months and occasionally years to complete. Freud's son Frank Paul describes his experience of watching his father work while modelling for him: 'The paint is applied slowly; each meeting between the brush and canvas is followed by a long period of vigorous scrutiny of the picture.'[3] The duration of this process often caused his models to adopt an anonymous deathly pallor, their facial muscles drooping with sleep or their eyes glazing over in exhaustion. Somewhat perversely, Freud's studio is at times animated while his human forms stiffen in lifelessness. Familiar objects, such as the studio bed, are anthropomorphised. In *Two Women* 1992 (pp.158–9), Freud places the bed in the centre of the room like a stage, upon which two naked female figures lie together. One woman appears asleep on her back, her hand resting peacefully above her head. Her companion lies awake, a relaxed gaze looking towards an arm expanded absent-mindedly off the bed. They lie in close physical proximity but appear to occupy emotionally distant spaces; their feet touch like lovers. The rumpled bedsheets are skin-toned and appear to be writhing with movement, as if rippling from the effects of an earlier sexual encounter. In Freud's hands, the studio and the body dissolve into one another. As the art historian Richard Shiff has written: 'Materially, body and space become a single tactile plane of paint. Just as the model is flesh, the floorboards and bed sheets are "flesh"'.[4]

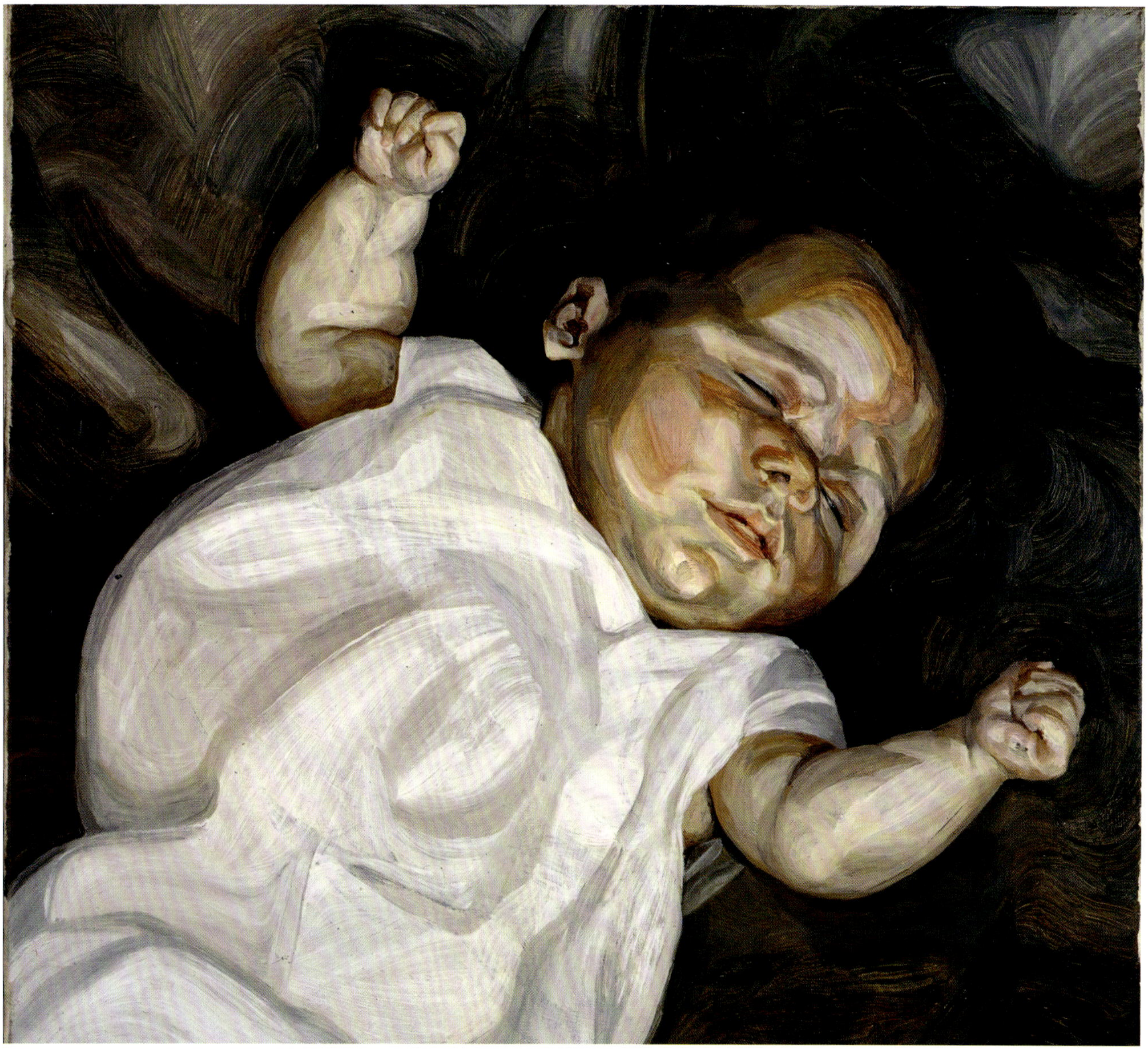

Lucian Freud
Baby on a Green Sofa 1961

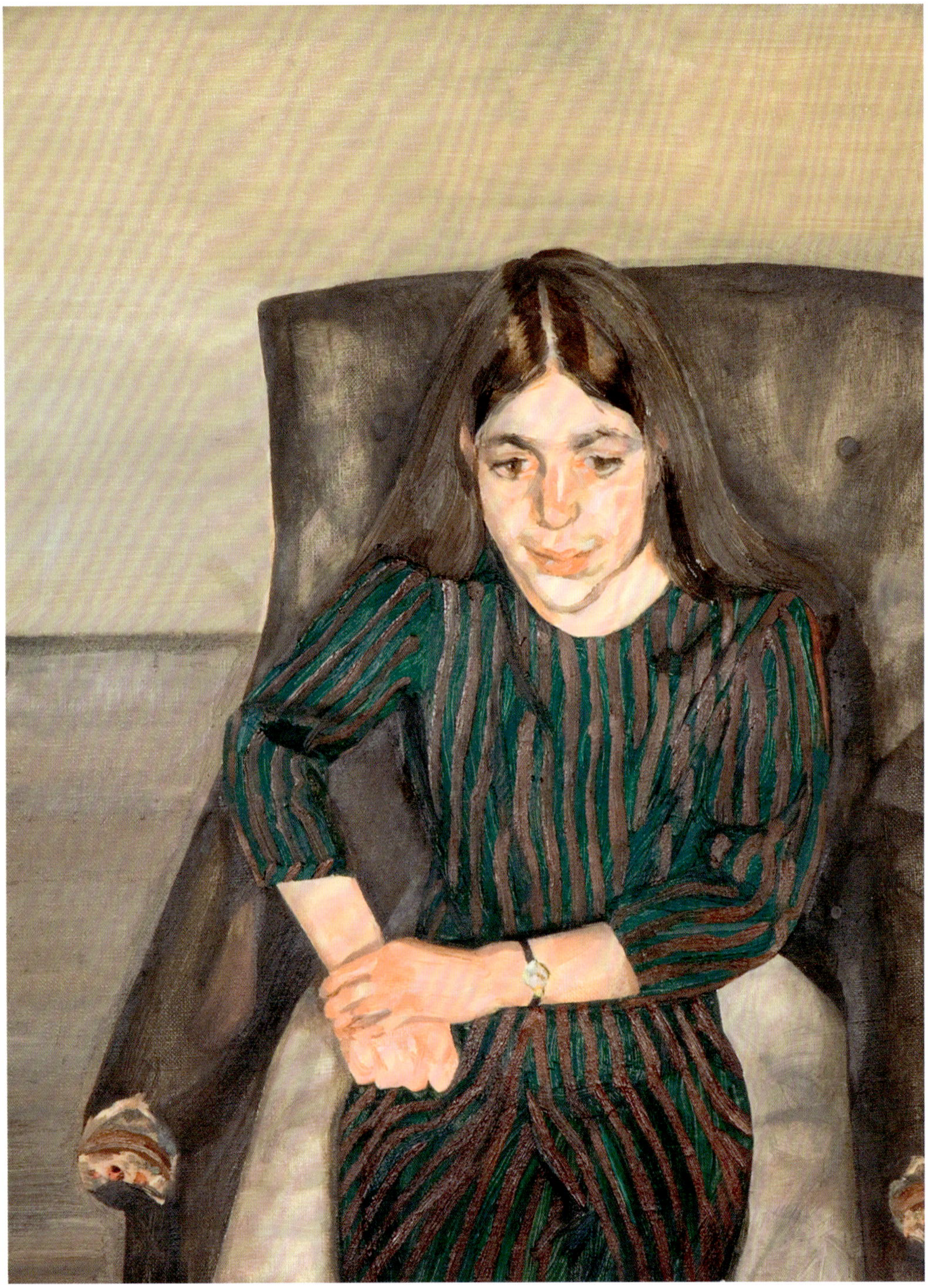

Lucian Freud
Annabel 1967

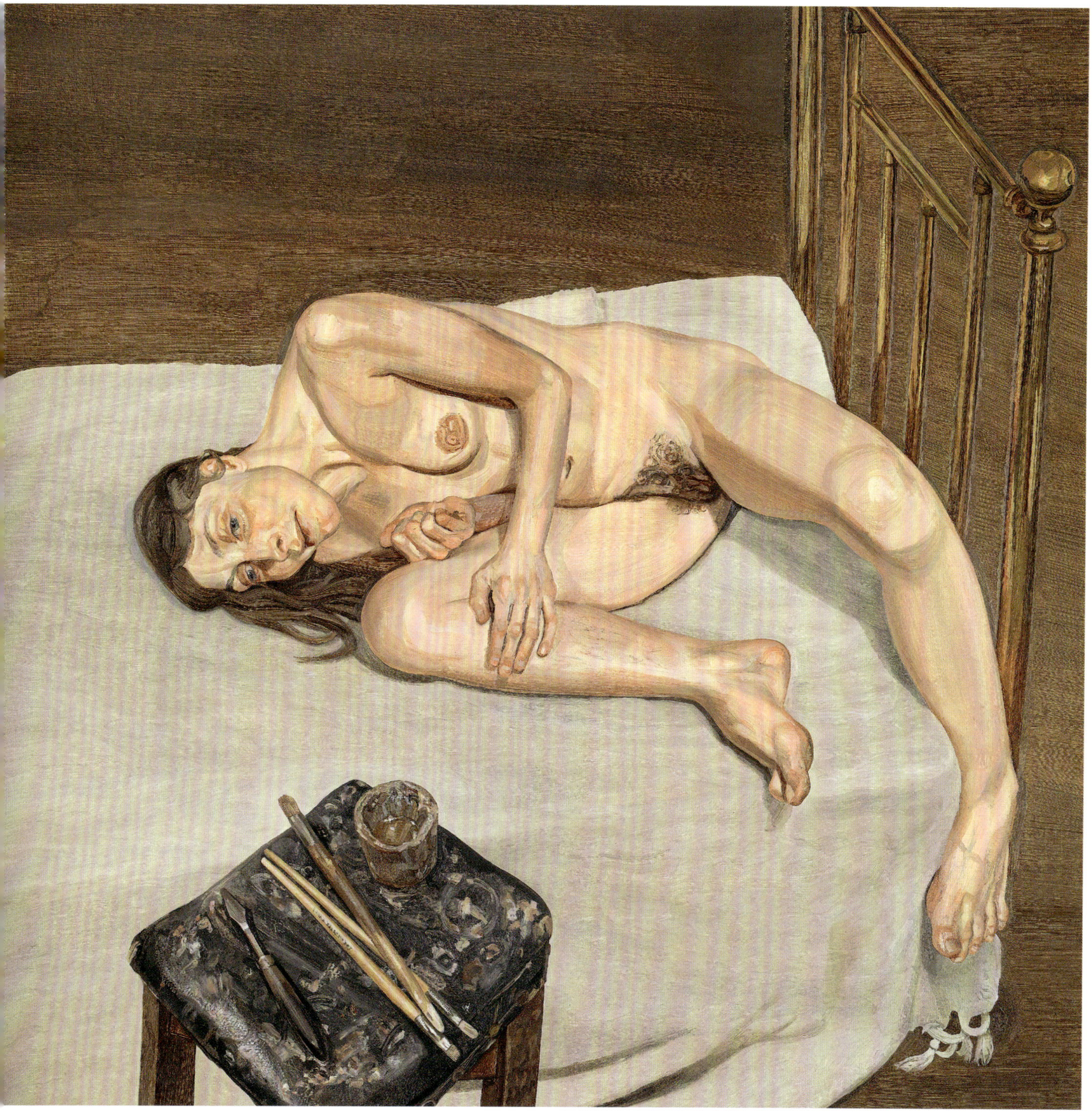

Lucian Freud
Naked Portrait 1972–3

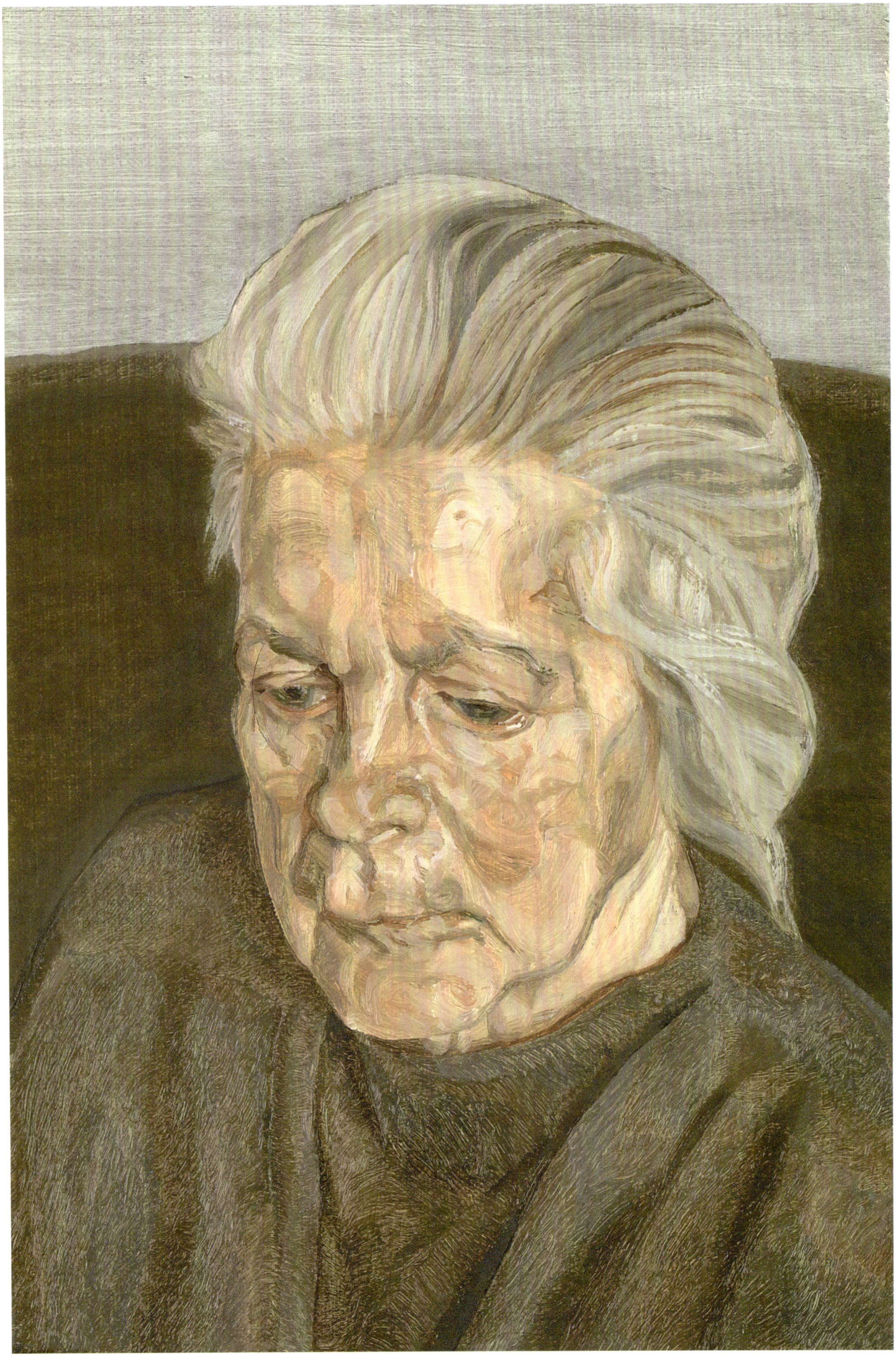

Lucian Freud
The Painter's Mother IV 1973

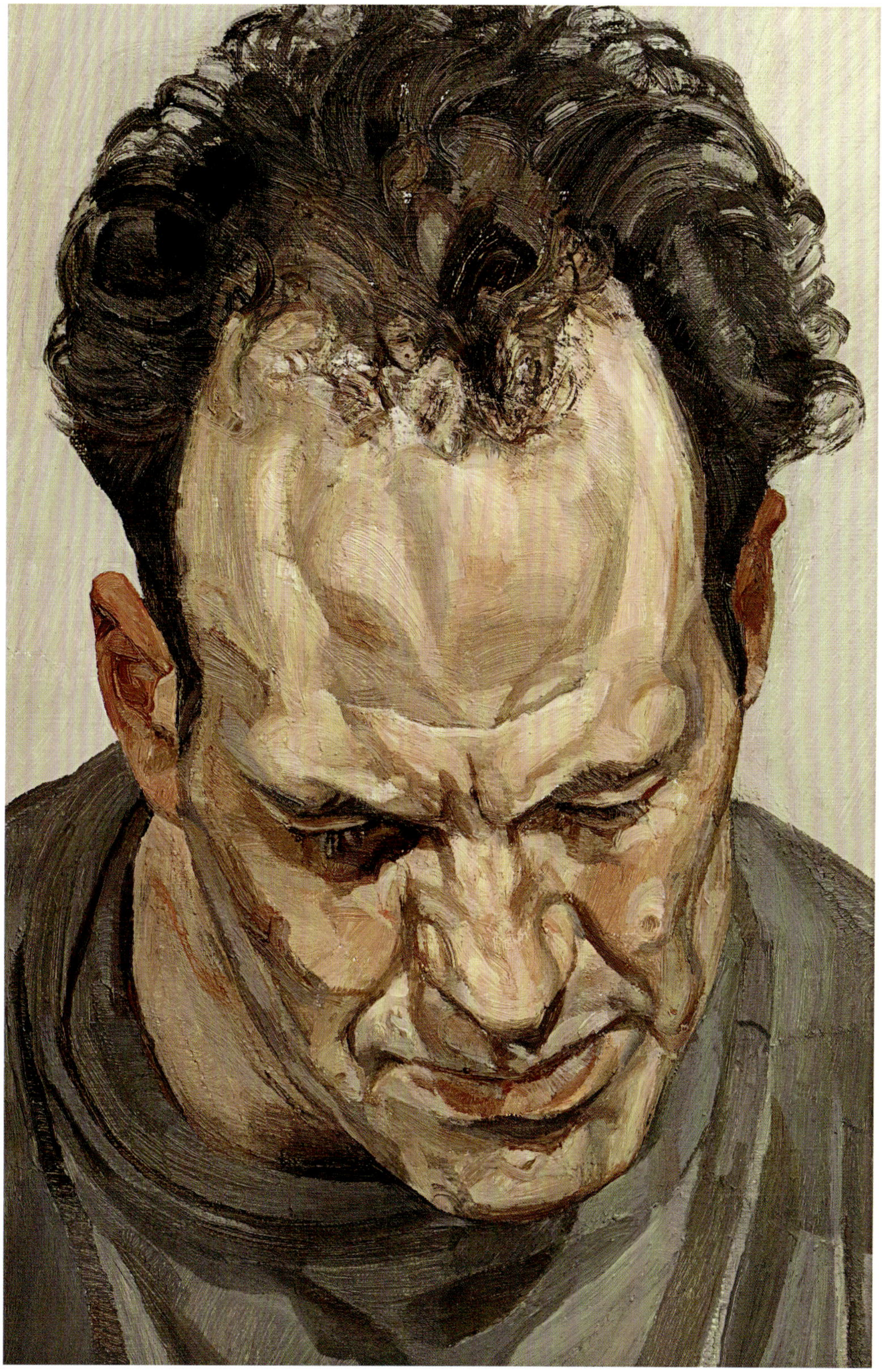

Lucian Freud
Frank Auerbach 1975–6

Lucian Freud
The Big Man 1976–7

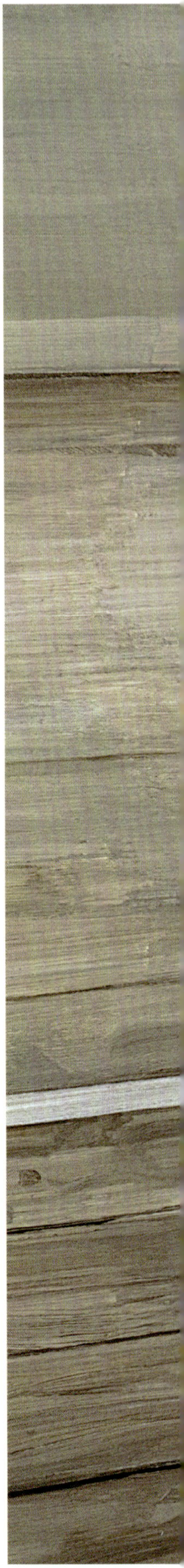

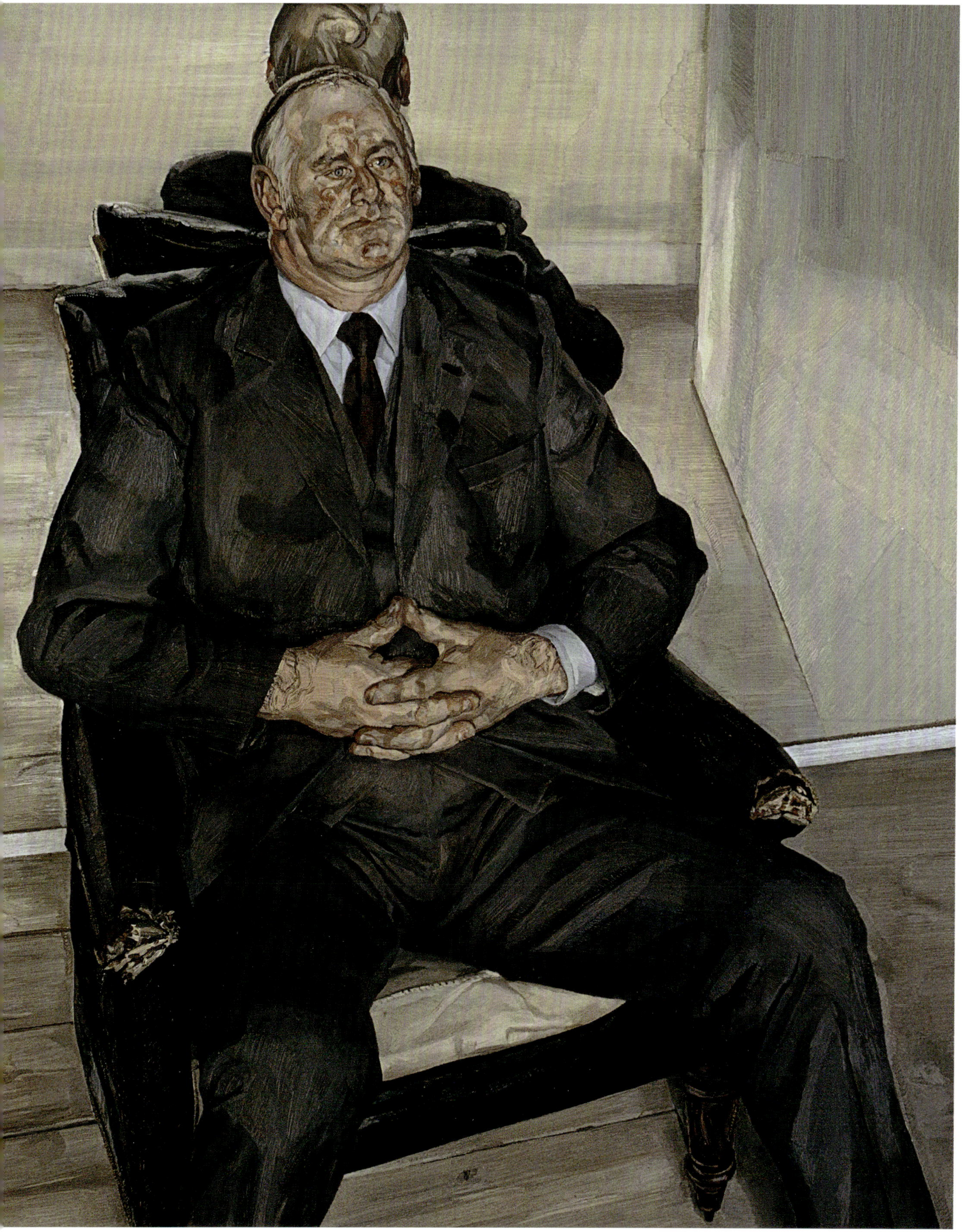

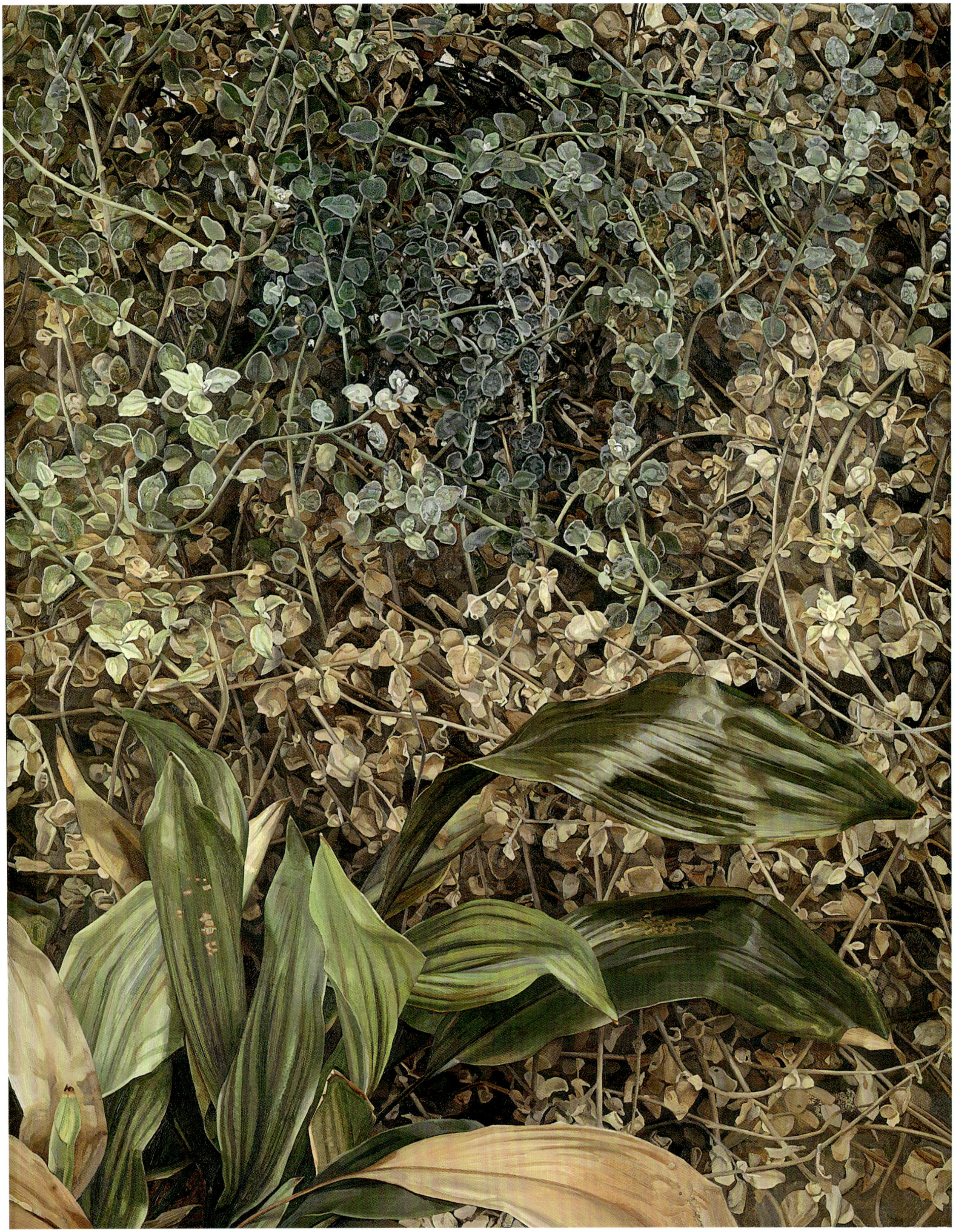

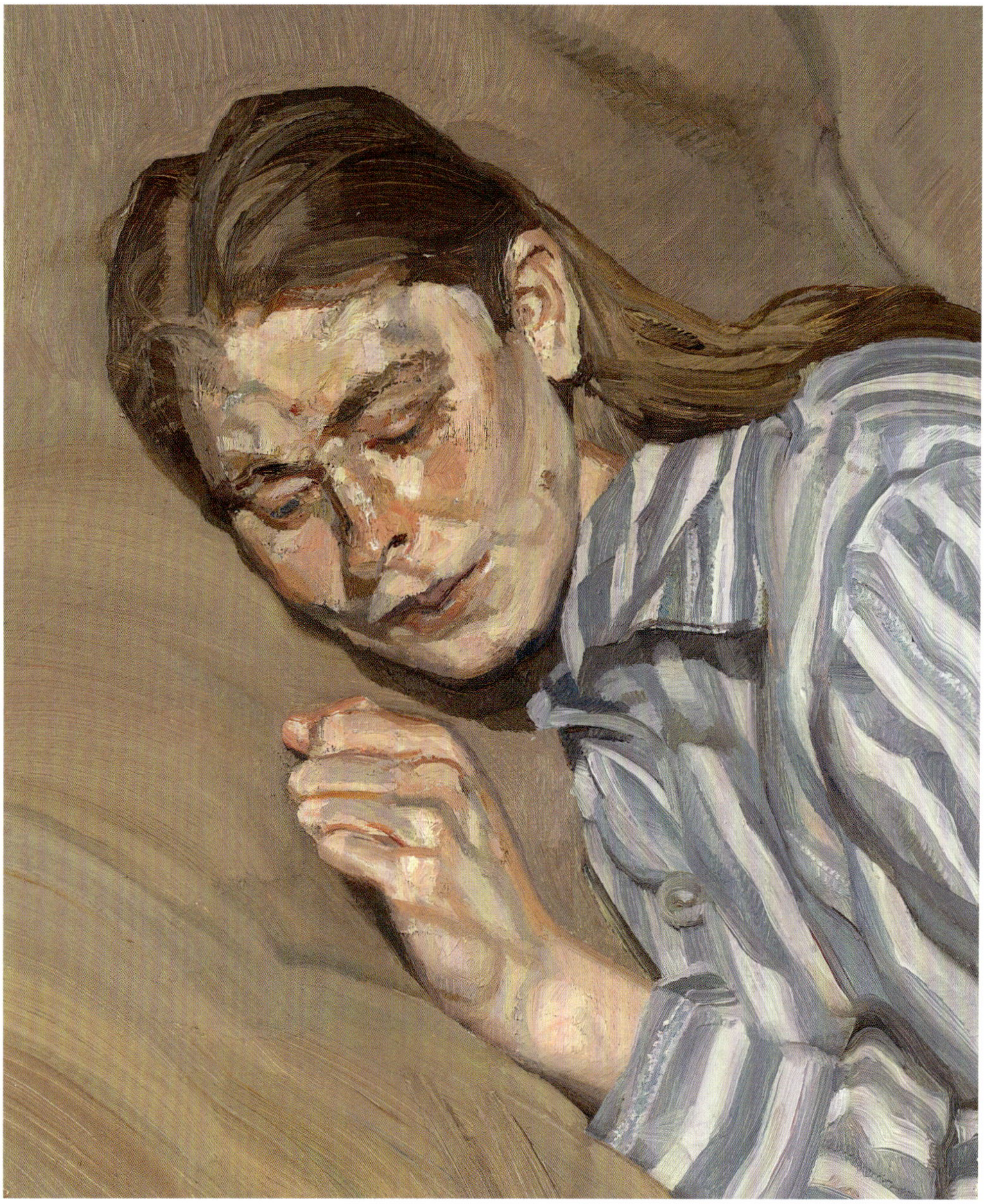

Lucian Freud
Girl in a Striped Nightshirt
1983–5

Lucian Freud
Two Plants 1977–80

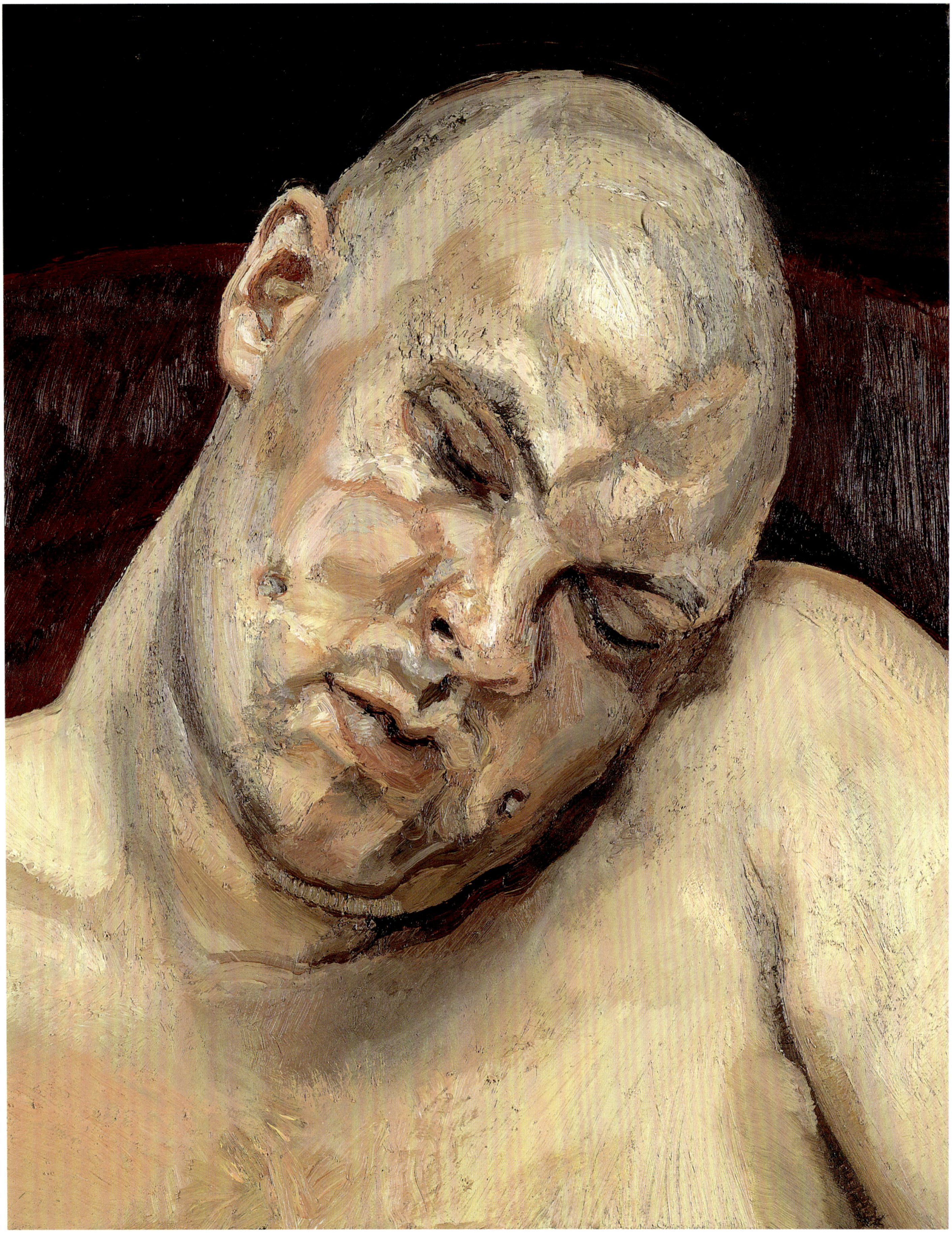

Lucian Freud
Leigh Bowery 1991

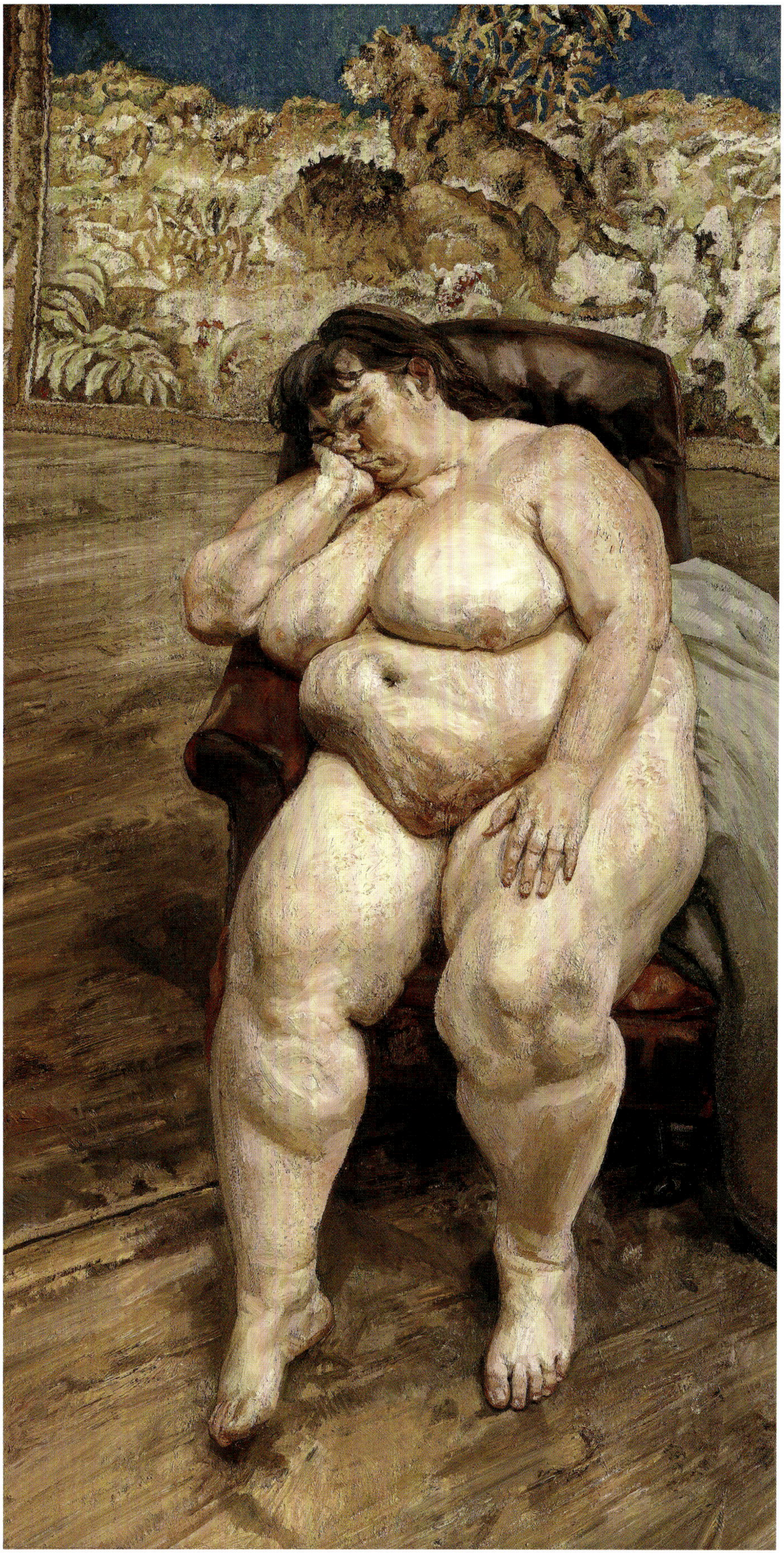

Lucian Freud
Sleeping by the Lion Carpet
1996

Lucian Freud
Two Women 1992

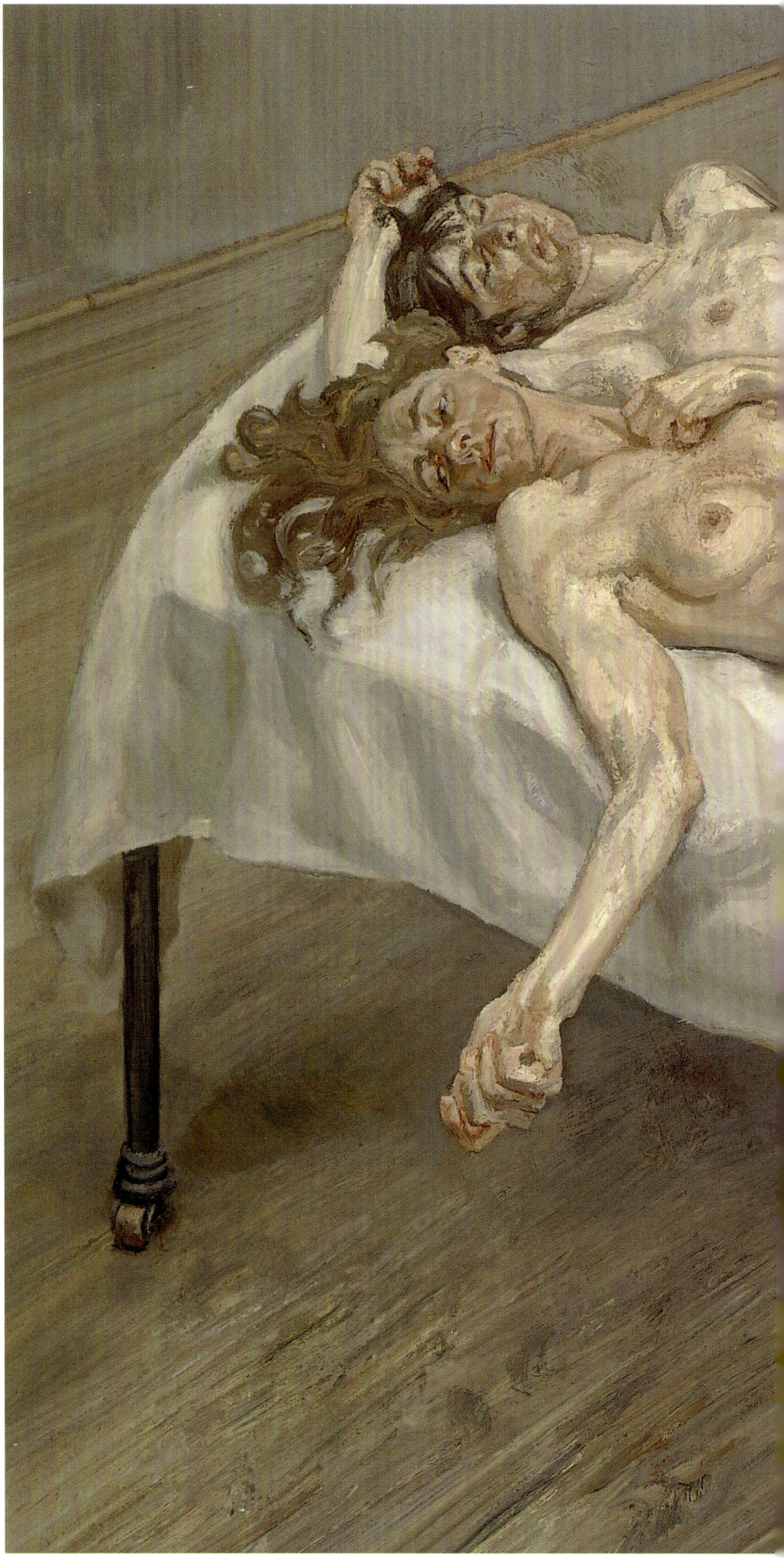

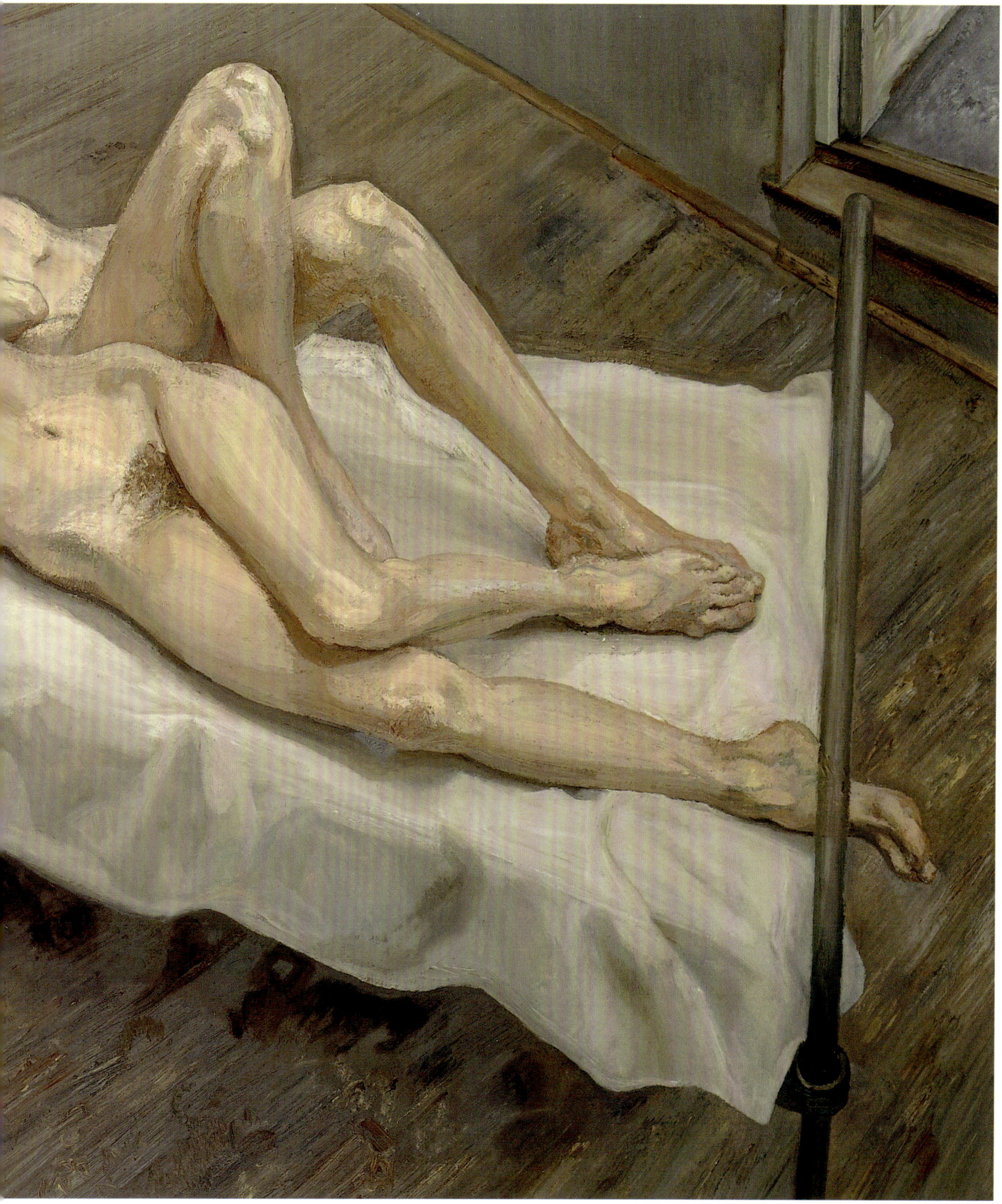

Lucian Freud
Bella 1996

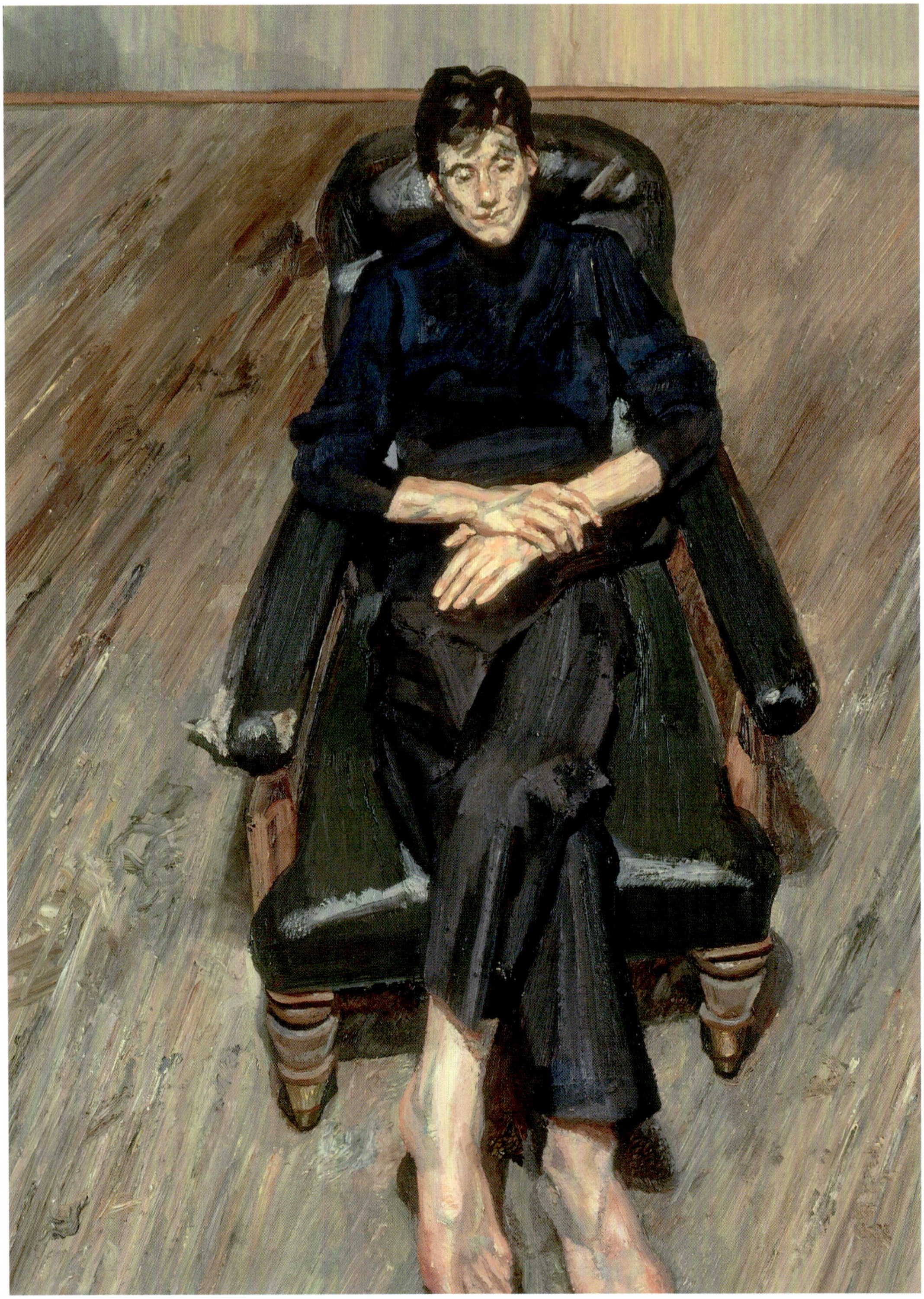

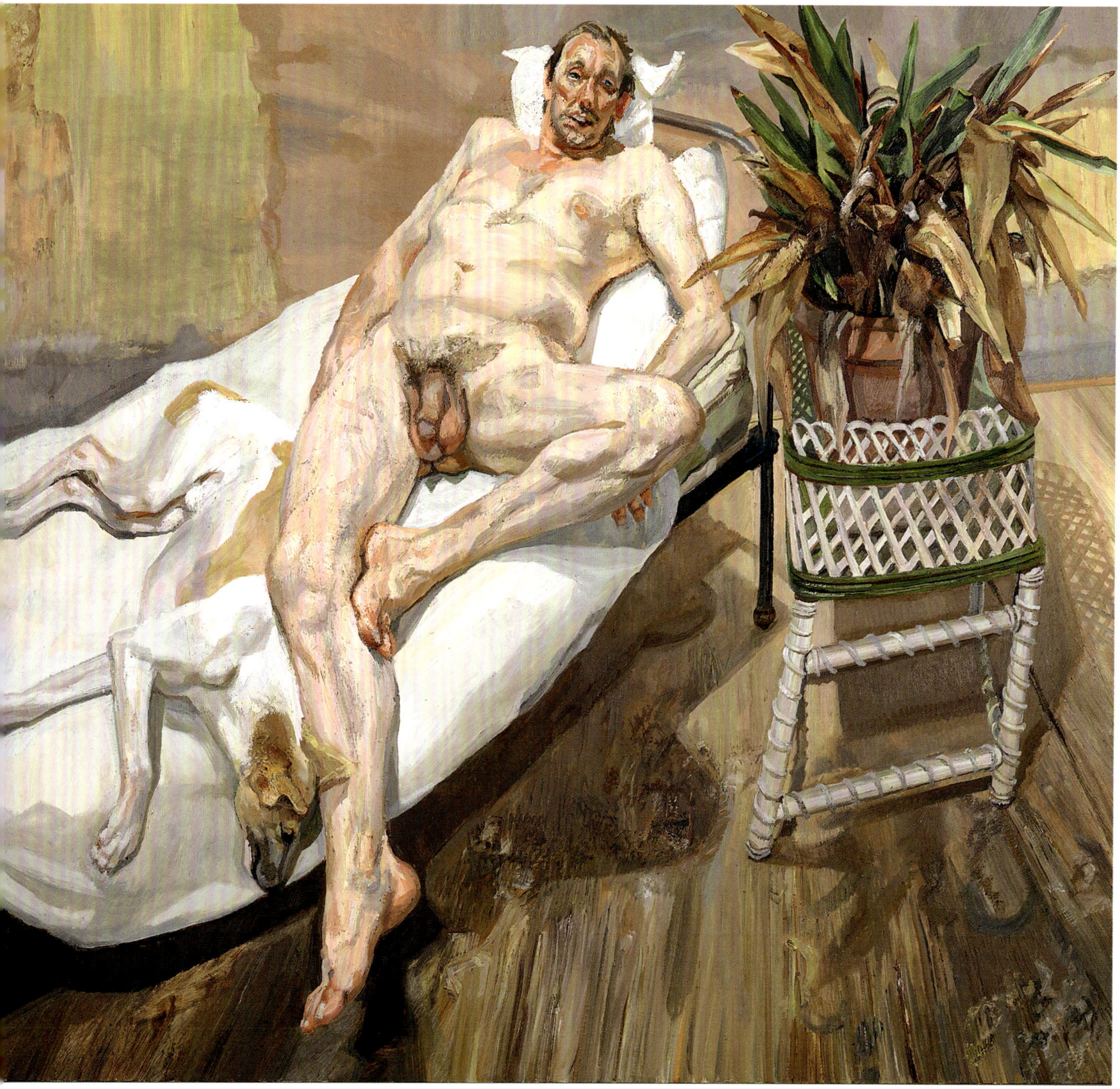

Lucian Freud
David and Eli 2003–4

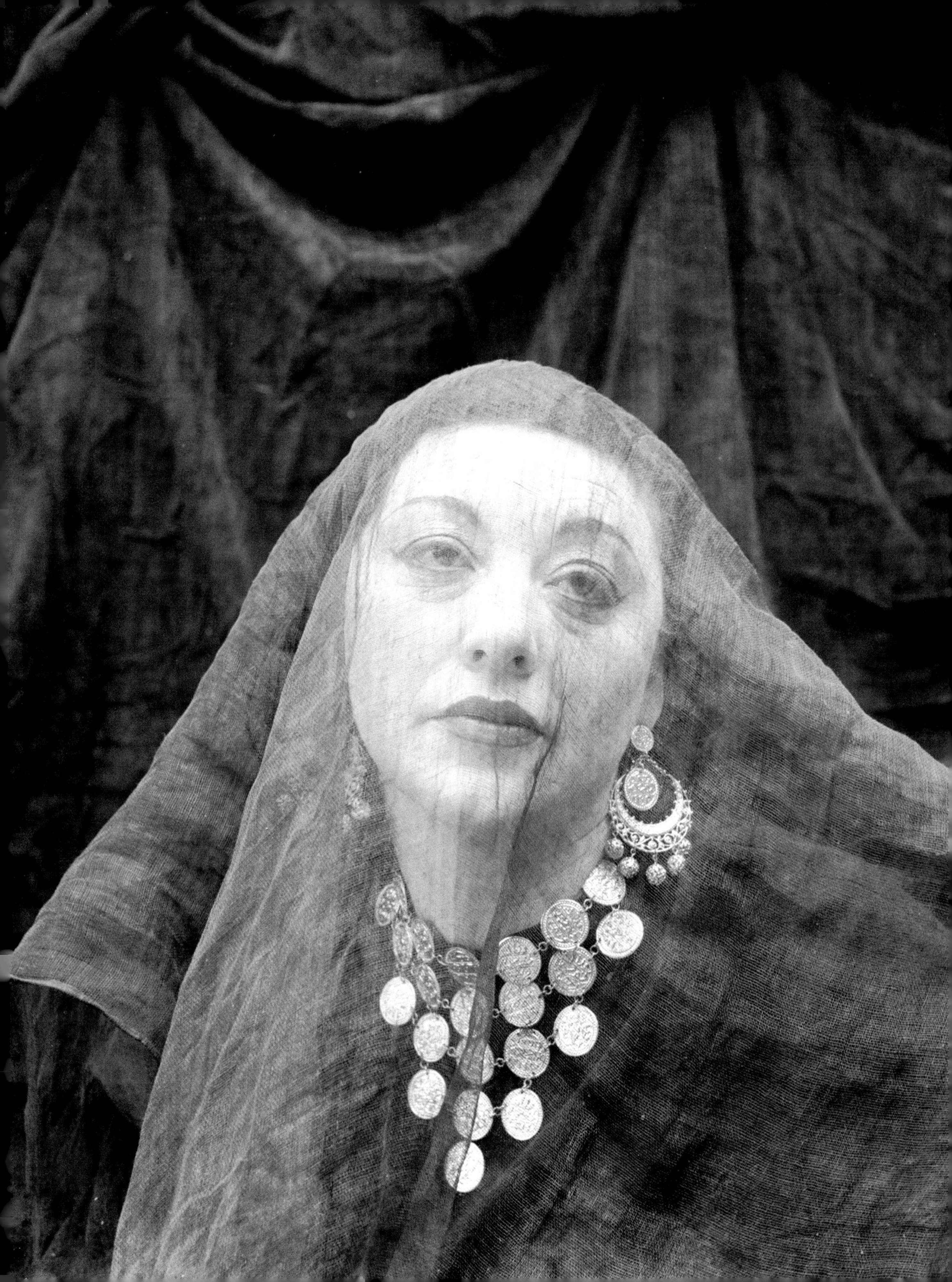

Francis Bacon and John Deakin

Elena Crippa

Francis Bacon's interest in portraiture defined his entire oeuvre, but changed and intensified over time. By the early 1960s Bacon had at least partially reinvented his approach to the genre. If, in the preceding years, he had regularly worked in the presence of sitters as well as taking inspiration from photographic reproductions, he was now exclusively relying on photographic portraits as source material. His engagement with archetypal figures such as the Pope and the businessman had diminished, and his portraits had become more individuated, focusing on a close circle of people he knew intimately. Additionally, from 1959, nudes – until then only sporadically painted by him – became his chief preoccupation. His concerns departed fully from anatomical verisimilitude in order to embrace a more fluid notion of body as flesh.

Working without a model did not lessen the power and poignancy of his figures; in fact the opposite is true, as his figures acquired an enhanced physical presence. Bacon remarked on the importance of memory in summoning not just the features but also the lived presence of a person. He explained that he painted people he knew rather than strangers, despite working from photographs, because: 'What I want to do is to distort the thing far beyond the appearance, but in the distortion to bring it back to a recording of the appearance.'[1] Painting was a process of recalling a presence, violently bringing 'the sensation and the feeling of life over'.[2] As a result, Bacon represents the reality of physical and psychological being as dynamic, as if wanting to awaken or liberate their image from the eternal pose of mechanical reproduction to the gesturality of moving bodies.

By the early 1960s, Bacon had developed a growing interest in the plasticity of his figures, which embodied a growing dynamism. On this subject, the philosopher Gilles Deleuze writes: 'Certainly there is still an organic representation, but even more profoundly, we witness the revelation of the body beneath the organism, which makes organisms and their elements crack or swell, imposes a spasm on them, and puts them into relation with forces.'[3] This is the case with *Portrait* 1962 (p.165), a portrait of Peter Lacy, with whom Bacon was in a relationship between 1952 and Lacy's death, the year of the making of this painting. It is the first of Bacon's paintings in which the internal organs are visible through the skin. There is a strange and unsettling conflation of a seemingly relaxed pose, resting on a sofa, with the menacing quality of the bared teeth, grimacing expression and the bursting-through of bulging internal-cum-sexual organs.

Deleuze described the postures painted by Bacon in terms of their 'matter of fact' nature and, echoing Bacon's own narrative, identified this particular ability to engage with factual reality and tactile experience to the work of Michelangelo.[4] While Michelangelo and Eadweard Muybridge were certainly important references, no other images were as influential to Bacon in the 1960s as John Deakin's

John Deakin
Isabel Rawsthorne c.1952
(printed 2017) (detail)

portraits. Bacon's portraits of his friends in the 1960s depended on the photographs he had commissioned from Deakin, including those of his lover George Dyer (p.175), his friend Henrietta Moraes, and the artist and model Isabel Rawsthorne (p.162). Bacon painted directly from Deakin's photographs in numerous cases, replicating specific details and gestures, as well as echoing deliberately incongruous visual juxtapositions.[5]

The reason why Bacon was particularly attracted to Deakin's photographs may lie in the similarity in the intent of their work, with the two artists sharing a deep interest in the expressive potential of human bodies and facial expressions. In his work from the 1950s and 1960s, Deakin mastered a way of photographing the body that rendered a sense of life swelling and pressing from within. This was achieved through the particular way in which he related to the people he portrayed: intimate close-ups of the face, and stark, frontal compositions of the body, generating what the photographer Bruce Bernard defined as an 'overwhelming feeling of directness'.[6] Deakin's angles, choices of bare environments and relationships between figure and background engender a sense of isolation and matter-of-fact presence of the figures. Figures often look like they have been caught in an unnatural pose, which they are enduring for the camera, or holding positions that seem manifestations of discomfort, pain or insecurity. While there is no evidence that Deakin's work spurred Bacon's renewed engagement with portraiture in the 1960s, Bacon's figures for the 1960s and 1970s shared with Deakin's portraits an intuitive knowledge of individual and collective implicit memories of bodily expressive movements and of the responses they evoke in beholders.

In the late 1960s a further development takes place in Bacon's work and his exploration of portraiture. In *Three Studies of Isabel Rawsthorne* 1967 he first paints figures alongside a portrait (head) nailed to the wall. In a similar way, in *Three Figures and Portrait* 1975 (p.169), Dyer's portrait, framed and nailed to the back wall, is set in a relationship with two other figures bearing his features: one turning into the centre, his spine rising up from the flesh; the other, with sprouting wings, swivelling out to the side. In these paintings Bacon is effectively bringing together the two diverging aspects of any image. On one side is a traditional portrait that, acting like the death masks he painted in the 1950s, is the coming to a still of any gesture and represents voluntary memory, the turning of a person into a static icon, isolated from the facts of life. On the other side are contorting bodies ripe with dynamism, not remembered as frozen images but flashing in one's involuntary memory in all their vitality. It might even be possible to speculate that *Three Figures and Portrait* is a sort of appeal for the memory to reanimate the static image of the artist's lost lover, freeing it back into movement. It is a call to reawaken gesture, to prevent the person's fall into oblivion.

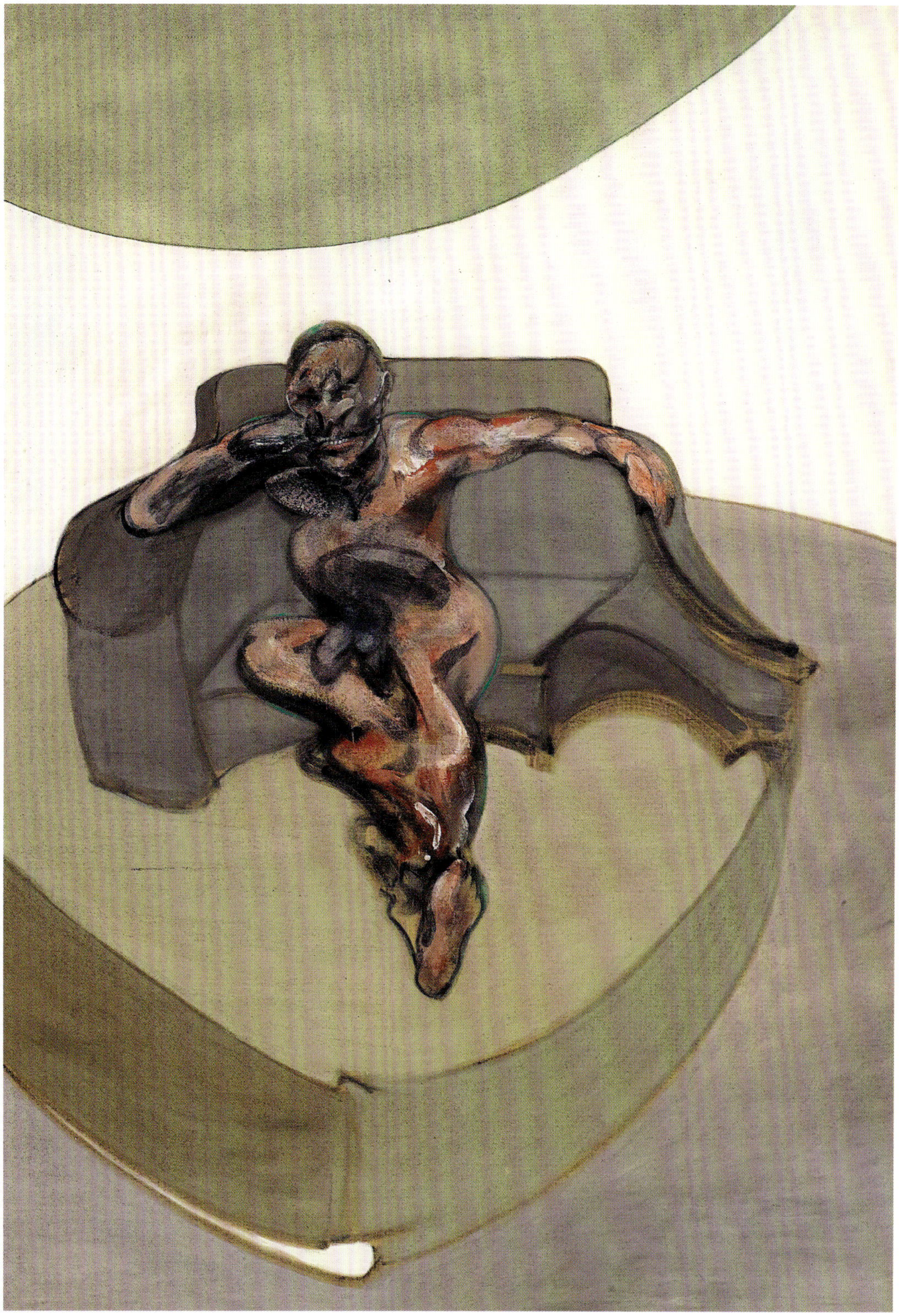

Francis Bacon
Portrait 1962

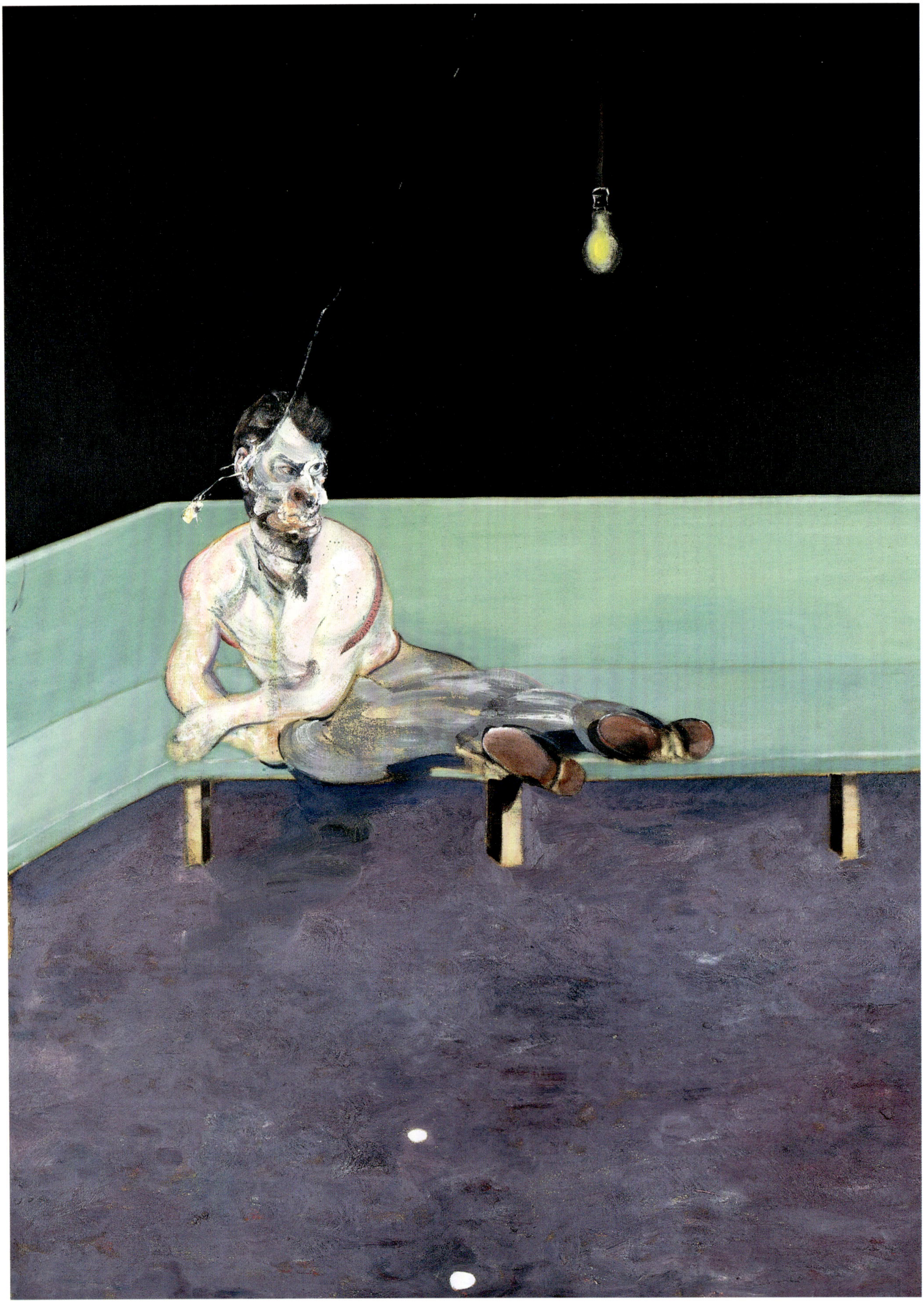

Francis Bacon
Study for Portrait of Lucian Freud 1964

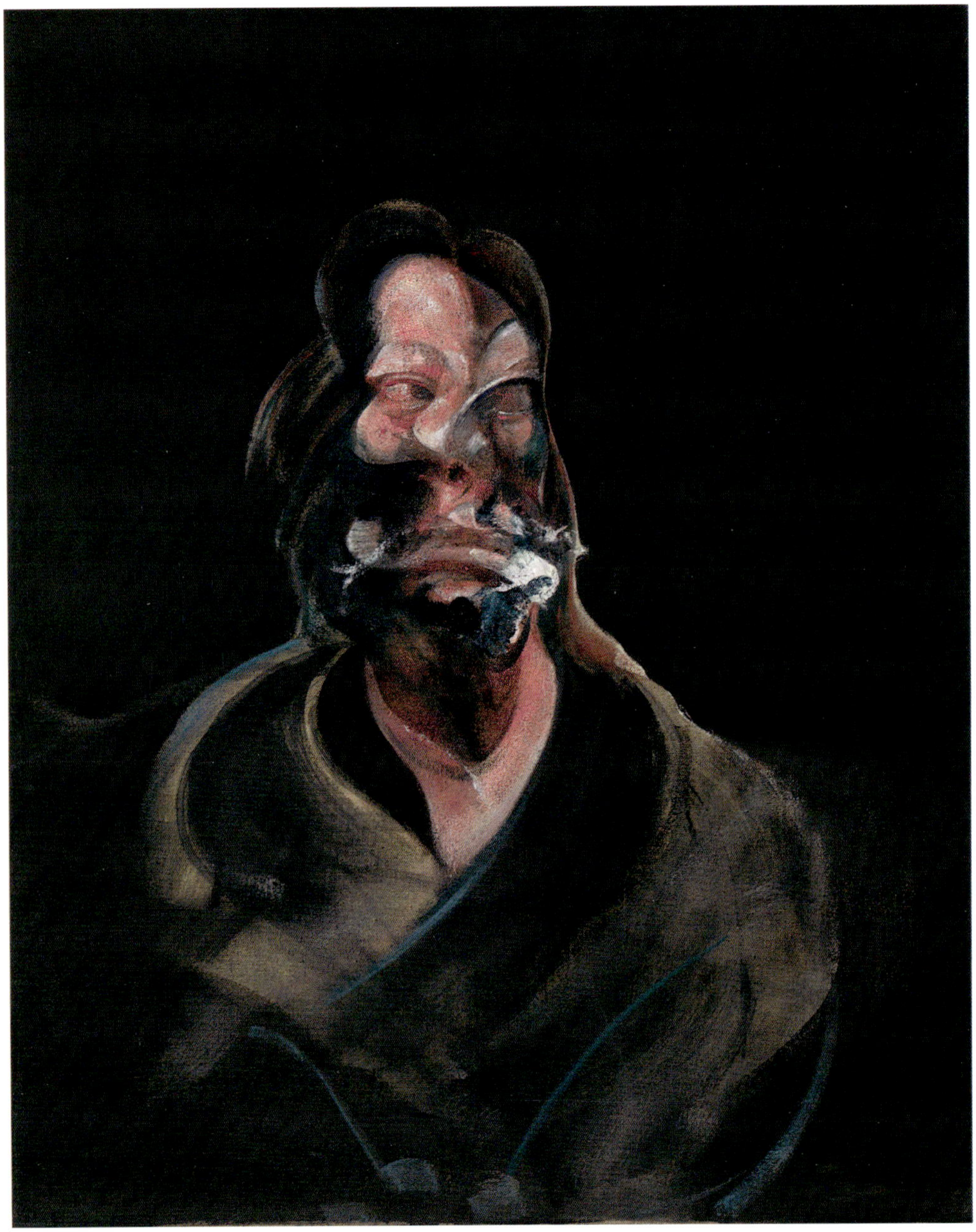

Francis Bacon
Portrait of Isabel Rawsthorne
1966

Francis Bacon
Three Figures and Portrait 1975

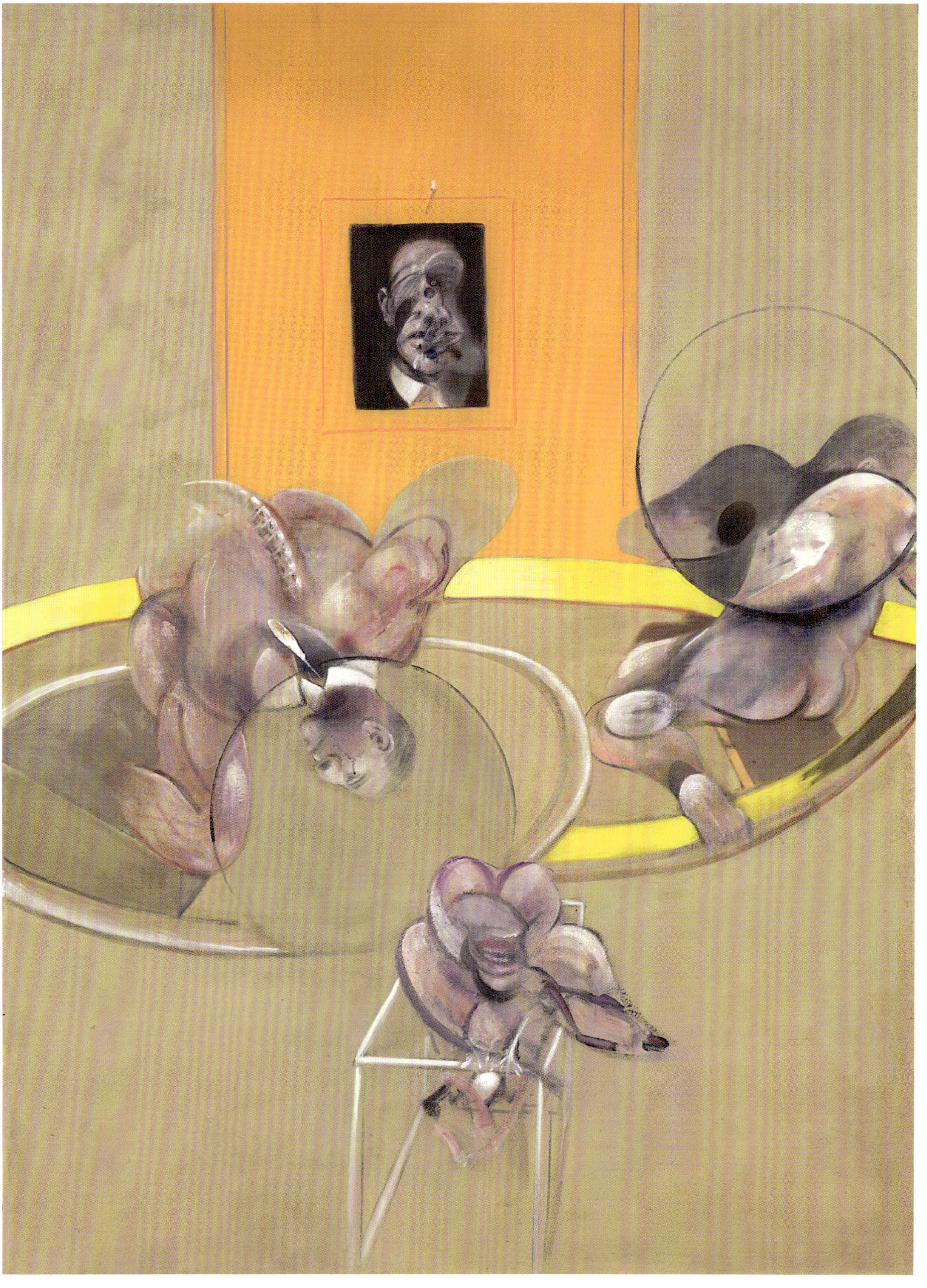

Francis Bacon
Triptych 1974–77

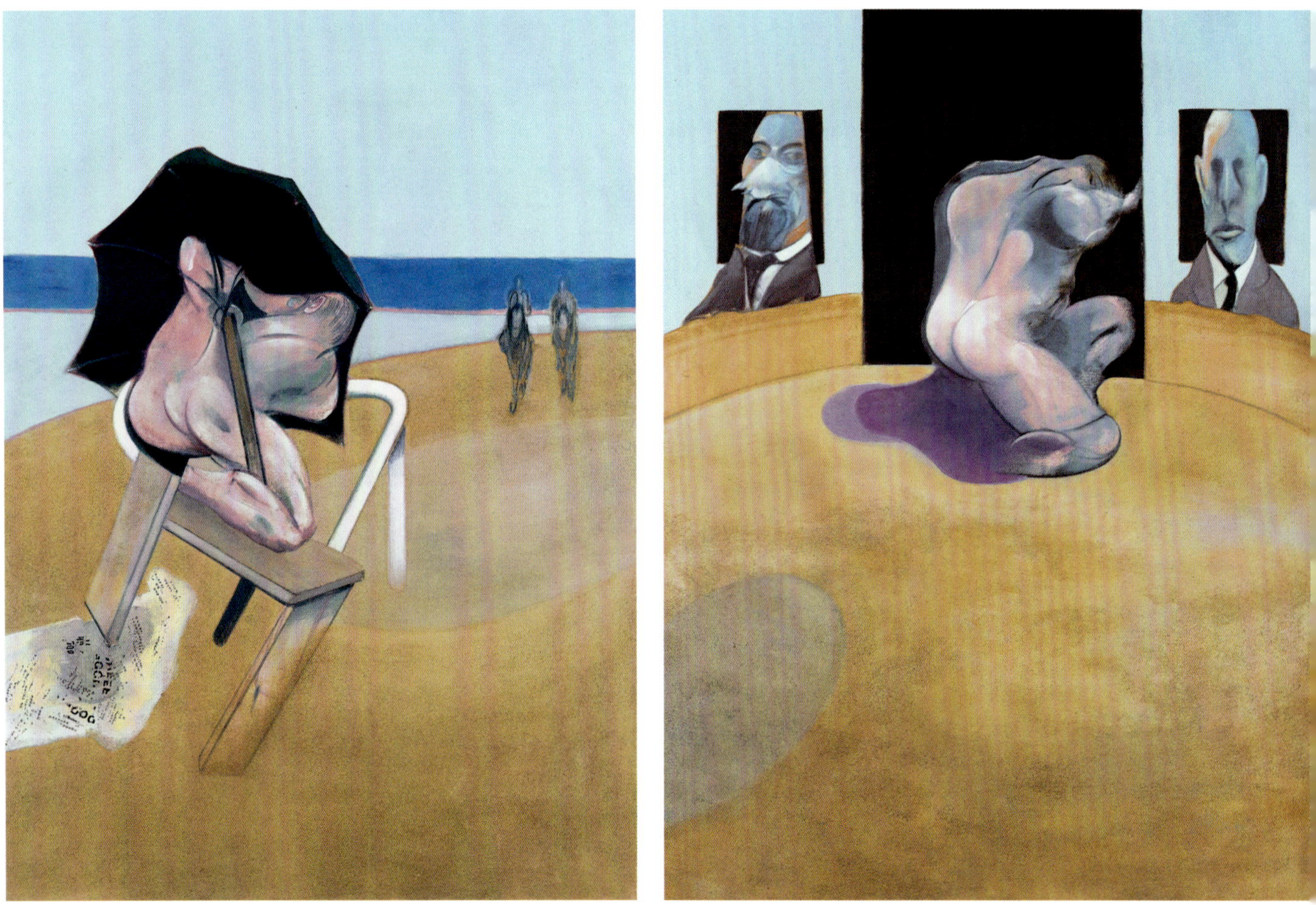

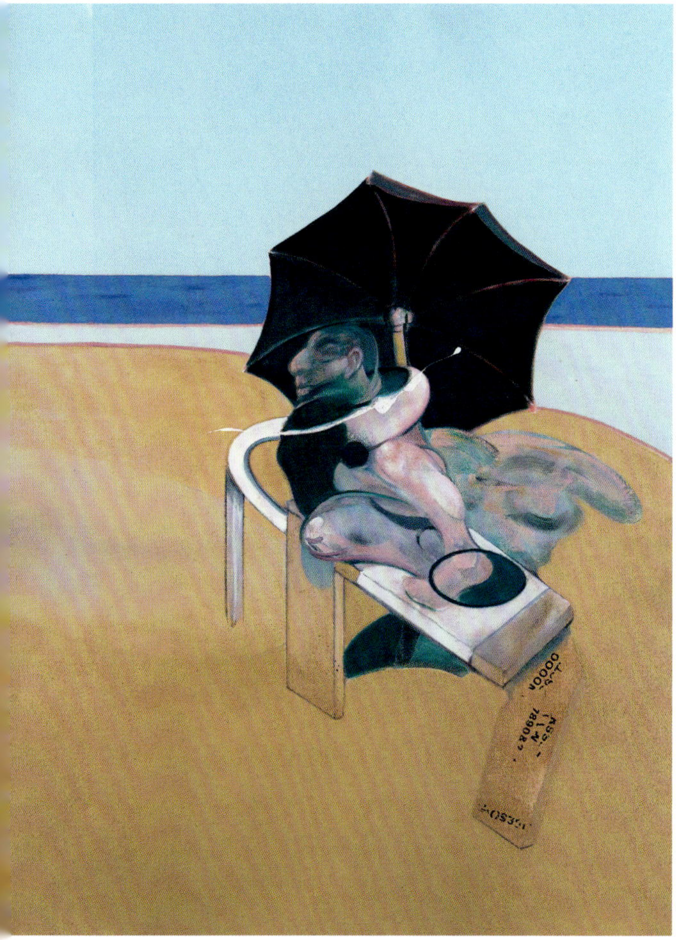

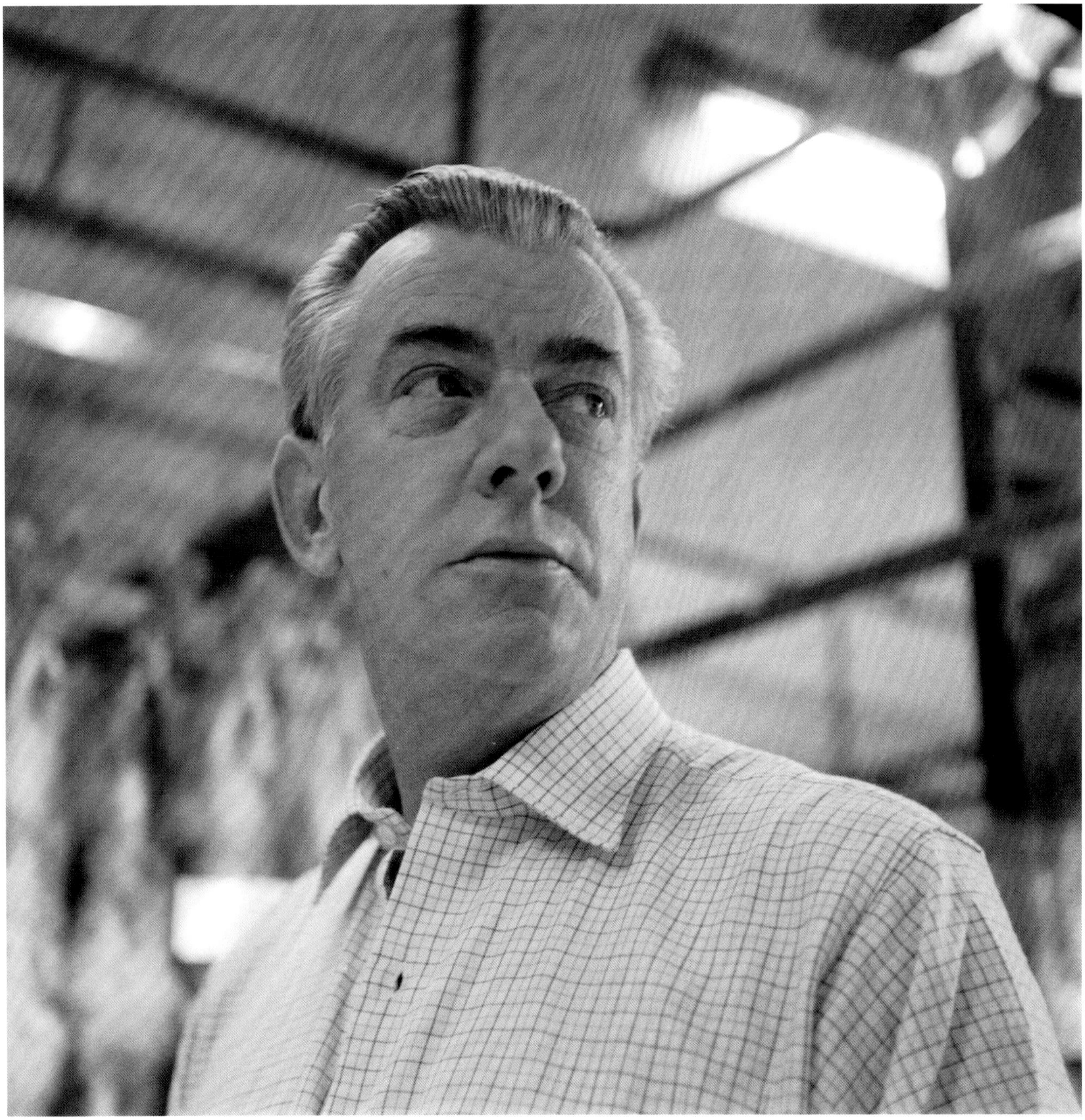

John Deakin
Peter Lacy c.1959
(printed 2017)

John Deakin
Lucian Freud c.1958
(printed 2017)

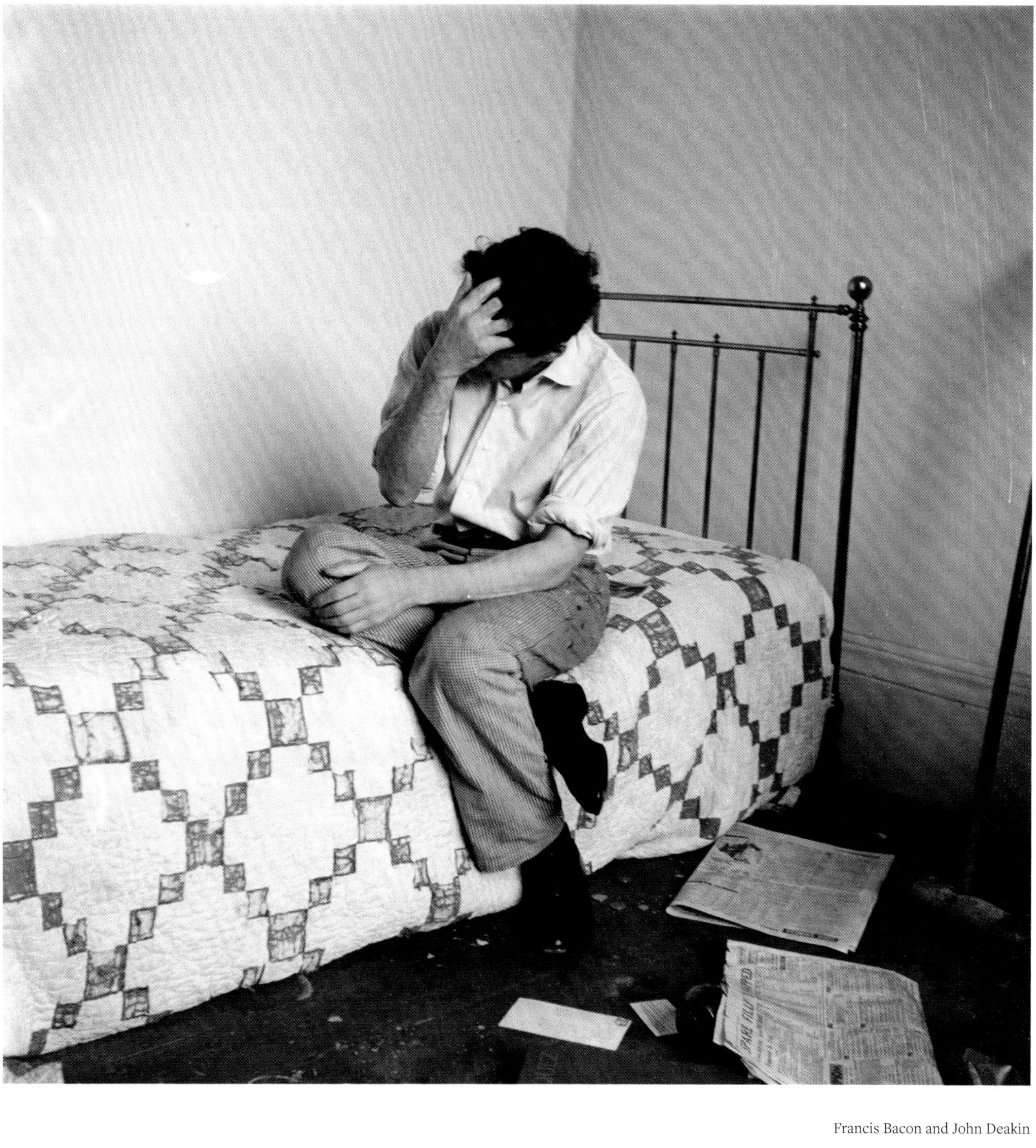

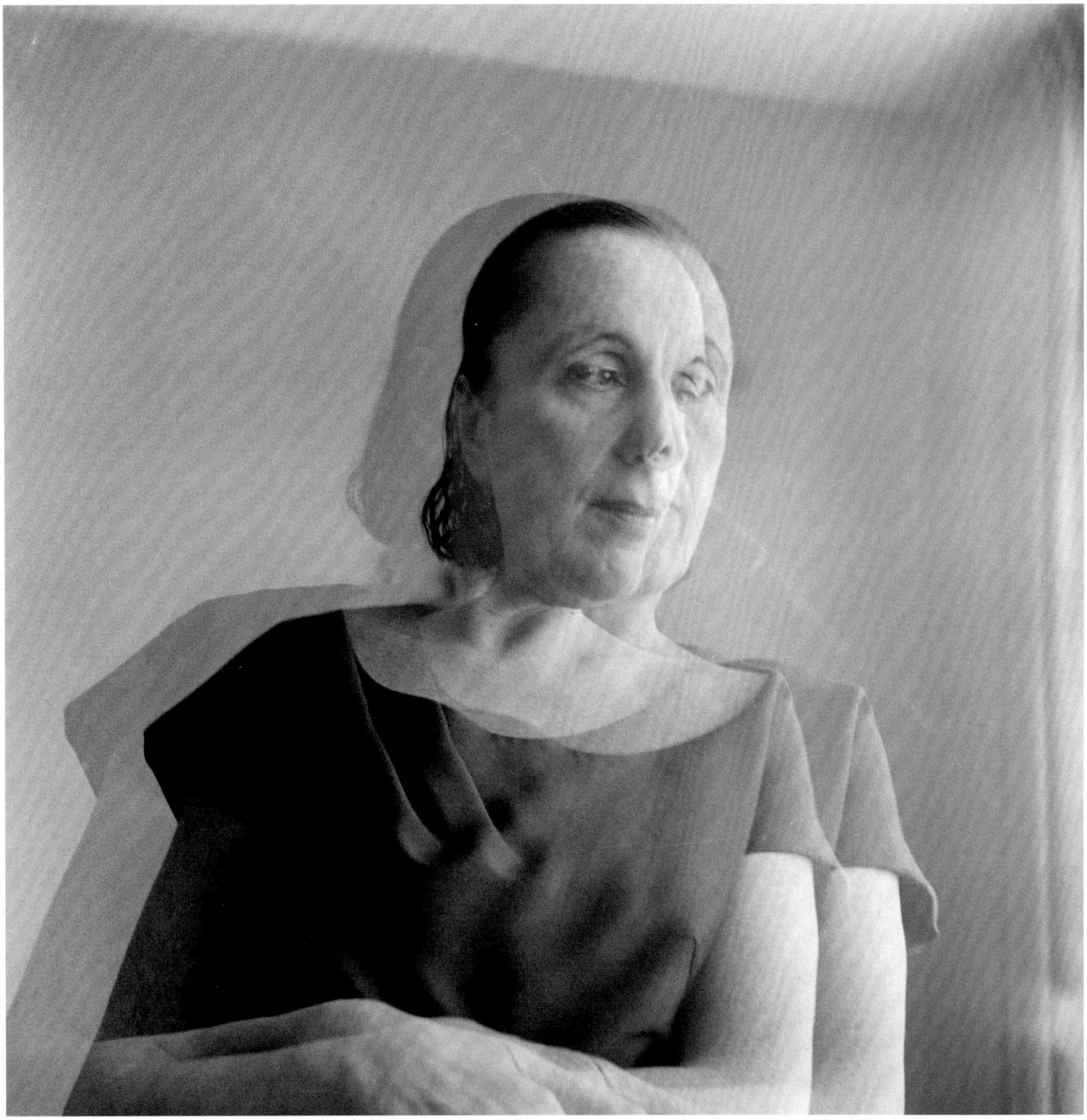

John Deakin
Muriel Belcher c.1965
(printed 2017)

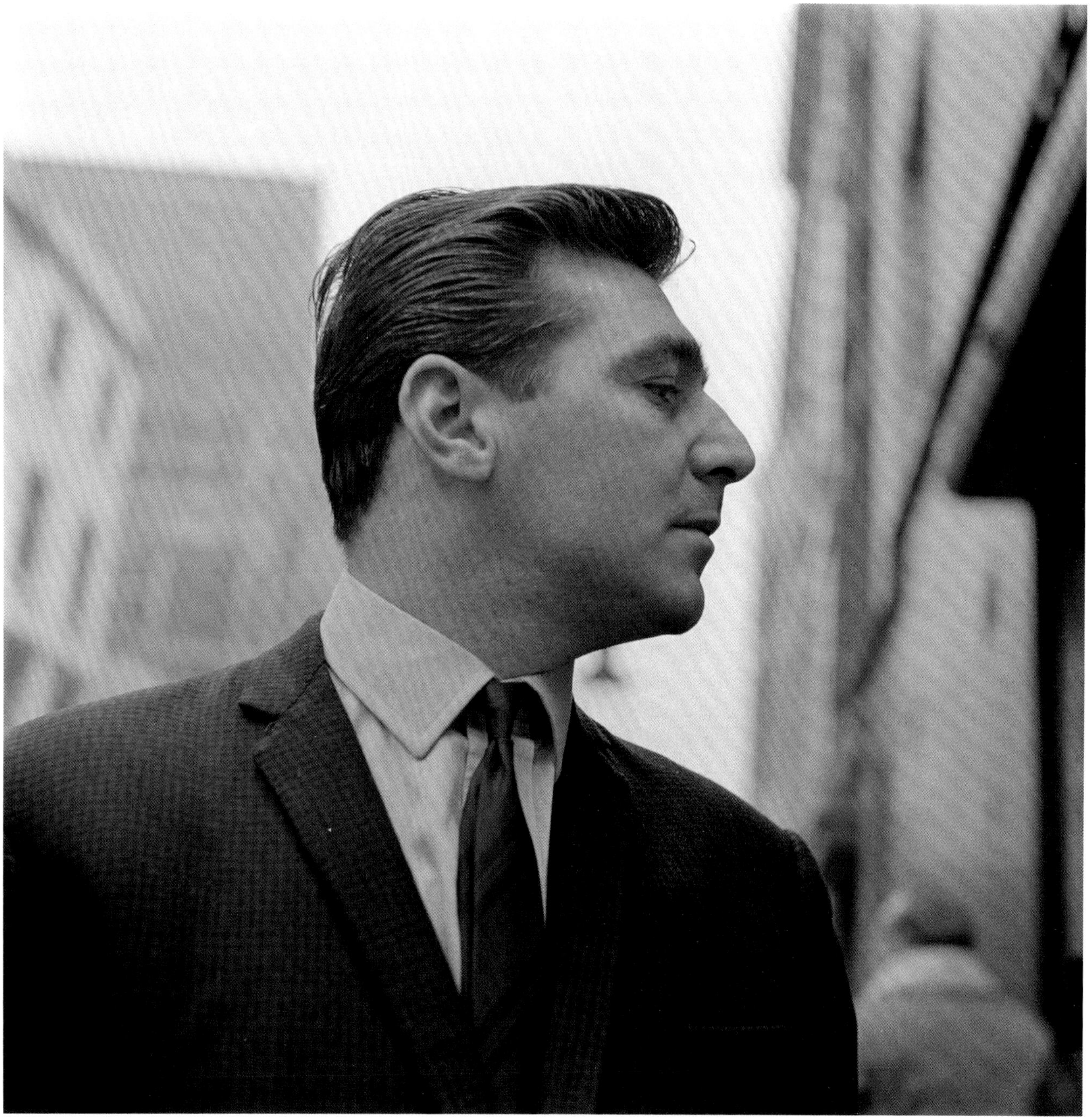

John Deakin
George Dyer c.1963
(printed 2017)

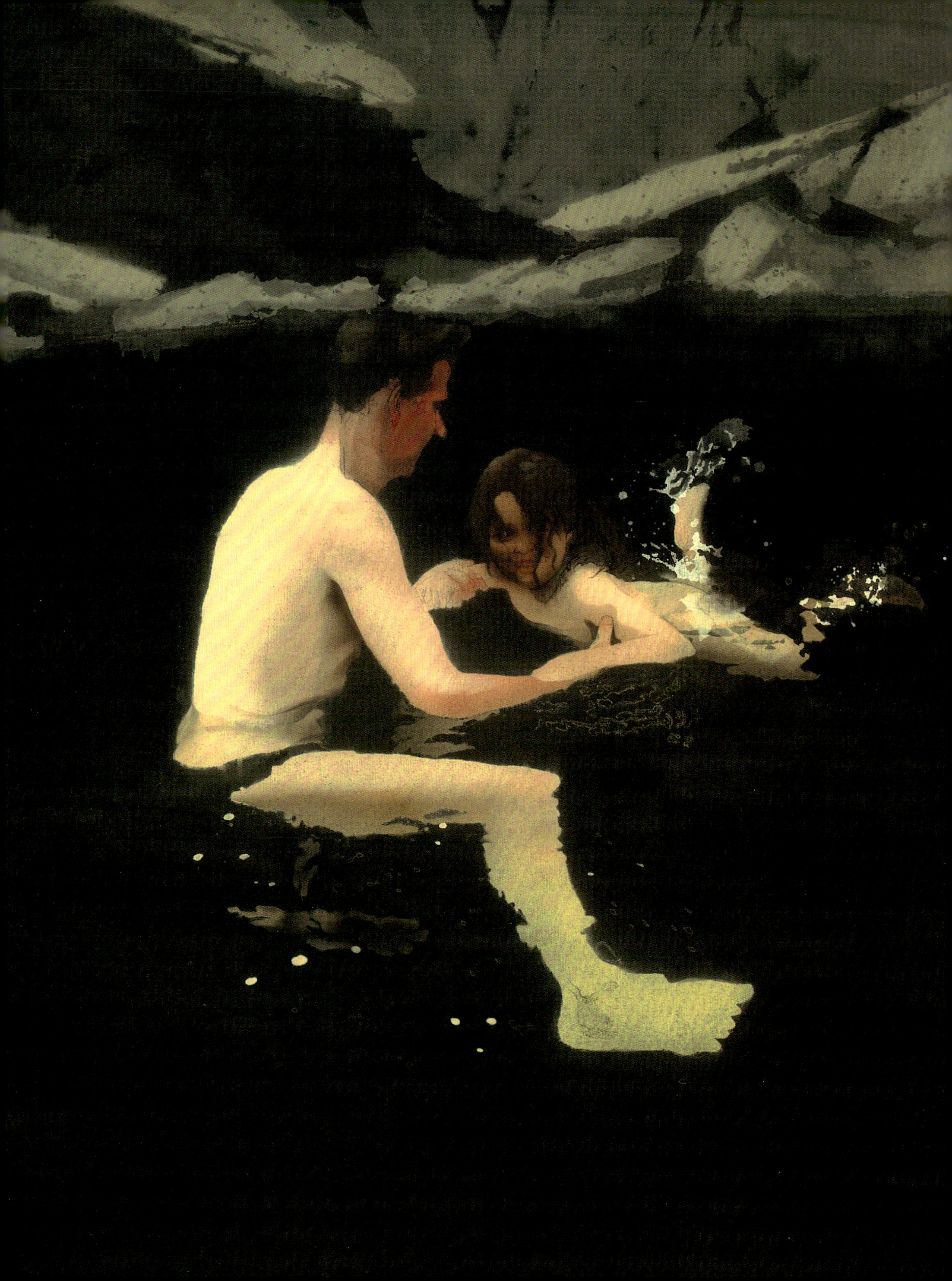

Michael Andrews and R.B. Kitaj

Elena Crippa

From William Coldstream to Lucian Freud, many of the artists who painted figures in the second half of the twentieth century did so by focusing mostly on the body in isolation. Alberto Giacometti and Francis Bacon's stand-alone figures from the 1940s and 1950s were paradigmatic of the human sense of isolation at a time when radical freedom of the individual seemed to be the only possible response in a world lacking in meaning and sense of direction. Conversely, following their student work in the 1950s, Michael Andrews and R.B. Kitaj distinguished themselves by a deep interest in multiple-figure compositions. While still students, they were both inspired by Bacon's use of photography as source material and by his interest in capturing expressions and bodily movement through paint. In their mature work they addressed their interest in the situated experience of inter-subjective life, studying and representing the way in which people behave, interact and coexist. They not only represented individuals in their paintings and drawings, but also brought together groups of figures to tell a story, which could be drawn from the artist's imagination or a literary text or based on historical events with important ethical or political implications. As a result, men and women are painted not only as individuals but also because of the narratives inscribed in their collective body.

Andrews was an acute observer of contemporary life. He enjoyed and was fascinated by social gatherings; occasions on which he could observe people's different behaviour, as he believed people at parties are not doing anything other than being themselves.[1] This intent is evident in *Colony Room I* 1962 (p.179), which portrays the atmosphere of a typical evening in the drinking club in Soho where many artists, poets and photographers used to meet, including Bacon, Freud, John Deakin and Bruce Bernard. Different body languages and postures stand for different ways of engaging with the world, some more controlled and self-aware, others more spontaneous. In *The Deer Park* 1962 (p.180), Andrews continued the theme of party scenes, taking as a starting point his personal experience while completely transcending the specificity of a place. He created a portrait of a transhistorical mundane society, in which a gathering of people, including famous personalities – from the poet Arthur Rimbaud to Marilyn Monroe – are brought together as exemplifying different social behaviours.

Melanie and Me Swimming 1978–9 (opposite) depicts Michael Andrews and his daughter Melanie, then aged six, swimming together in a rockpool. By the time of this painting Andrews had moved from working slowly and painstakingly with oils, to quick-drying acrylic paints, sprayed on to the canvas with a nitrogen-powered gun, resulting in a much more fluid rendering of skins and textures. The painting is based on a colour photograph taken by a friend while they were on holiday at Glenartney Lodge, in Scotland, in the summer of 1976. As with

Michael Andrews
Melanie and Me Swimming
1978–9 (detail)

many of Andrews's paintings, the final image is a combination of real elements and his own memories of the event, developed imaginatively through engagement with the paint itself. While Andrews had by this time abandoned the theme of social gatherings, this painting is nonetheless the image of a human relationship: one that is intimate and that relates to parental love and care, while also metaphorically referring to a child's transition from the protective environment of family life to wider society.

If with Andrews we can speak of an existentialist kind of realism, Kitaj stood for a critical type, not aligned with a specific political movement but motivated by a desire for social reform.[2] As the critic Robert Storr has argued, Kitaj's approach allows us to define him as a 'history painter', but one who created his own pantheon of heroes, populated by characters that mattered to him personally.[3] His paintings addressed not only his personal history but that of his family and, more broadly, the history of the Jewish diaspora and persecution, which affected two of his grandmothers and caused them to flee to the United States. He was also preoccupied with historical and contemporary manifestations of fascism. *To Live in Peace (The Singers)* 1973–4 (pp. 182–3) portrays a gathering of friends at the end of a meal to celebrate Easter in Catalonia, at a time when Spain was still under Franco's dictatorship. Men and women are brought together around a table, in a dream-like atmosphere, giving form to a way of sharing and living together, in a spirit of conviviality and intimacy, that resisted fascist ideology.[4]

Kitaj's encounter with Degas's late pastel drawings in Paris in 1974 fostered a return to life drawing and use of pastels. When he returned to painting in 1980, he did so by reworking drawings until they felt more fully integrated into an overall composition than before, building up layers of paint and adopting a more variable brushwork, as in the case of *Cecil Court, London W.C.2 (The Refugees)* 1983–4 (p.184). The painting's geographic setting – at the time a much-visited street in Central London of rare and second-hand booksellers – merges with his experience as an American of Jewish origins living in the British capital, where he encountered and was touched by individuals who came to the city as refugees. Protagonists are individuals with a history of endurance, who were not merely able to survive, but to preserve their ethical position.

Kitaj met the American painter Sandra Fisher in London in 1971, following an unsettled period marked by upheavals in his private life and low productivity. Fisher played a key role in Kitaj's renewed engagement with his work. *The Wedding* 1989–93 (p.185), painted some six years after their marriage, celebrates their union as well as Kitaj's identification with a particular artistic milieu, through the prominence given to the depiction of Frank Auerbach, Lucian Freud, Leon Kossoff and David Hockney. These were some of the artists who, writing in 1976 for the catalogue of an exhibition he selected for the Arts Council of Britain, *The Human Clay*, he defined as among the most interesting and unique painters in the world, deserving of much more attention than they had so far been granted.[5]

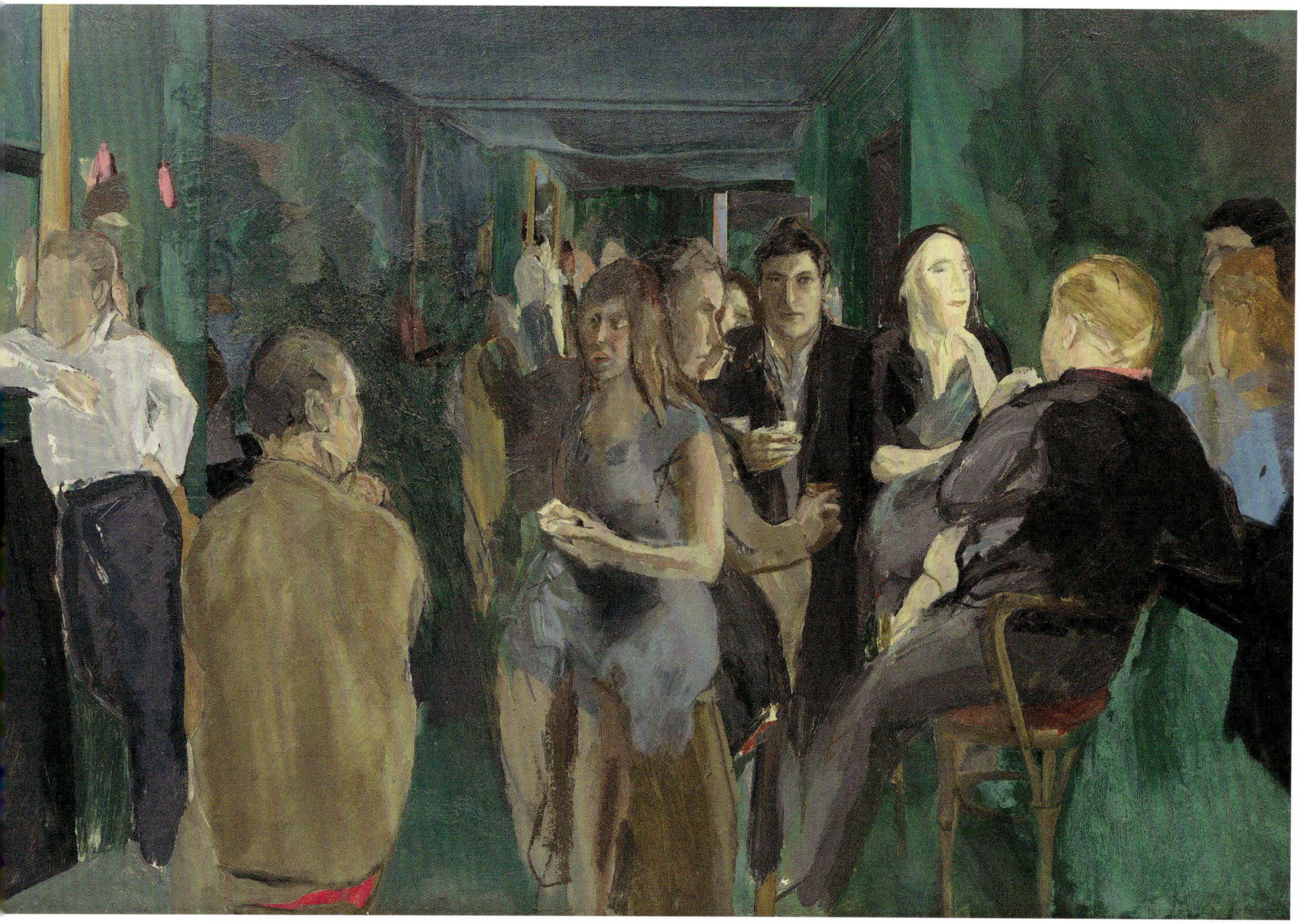

Michael Andrews
Colony Room I 1962

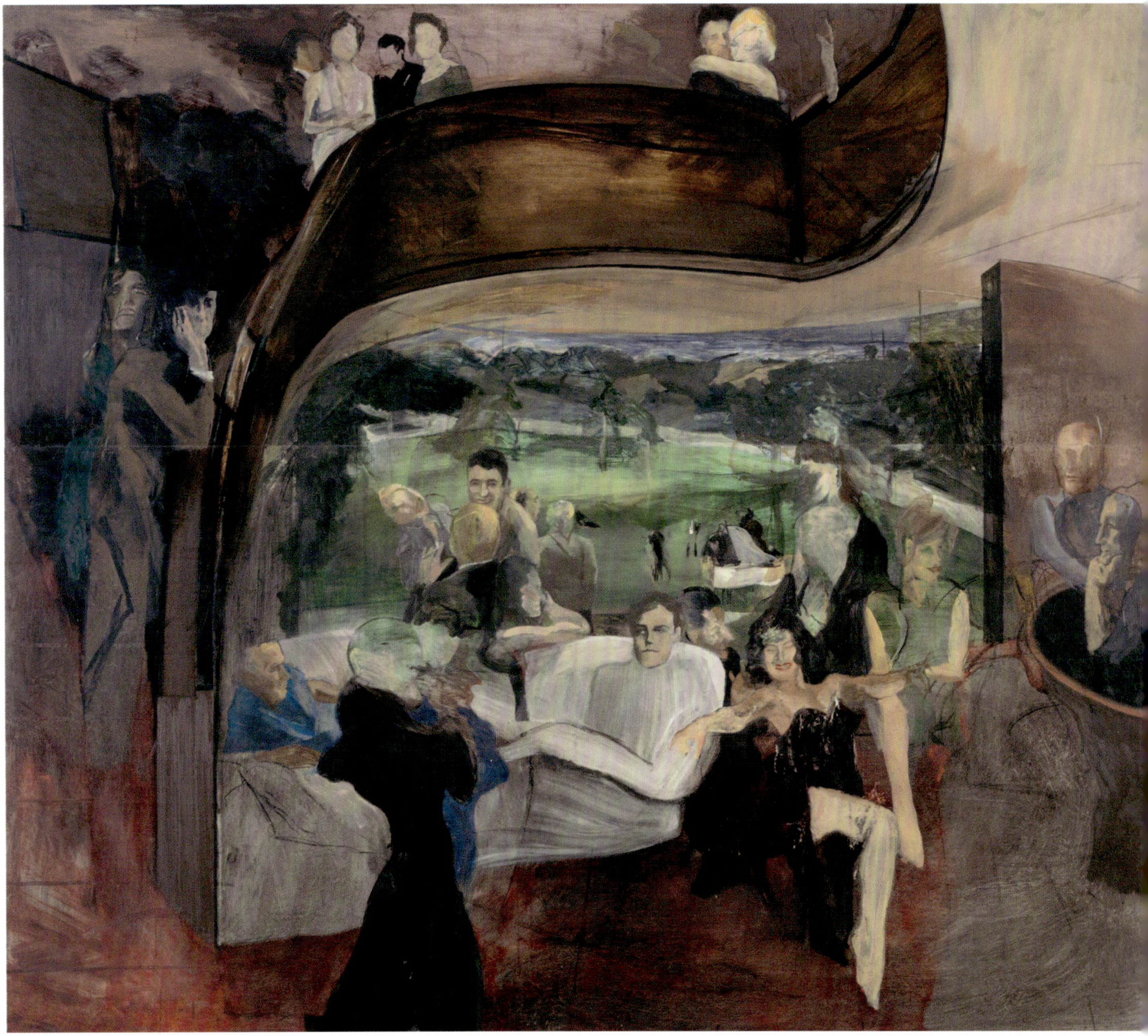

Michael Andrews
The Deer Park 1962

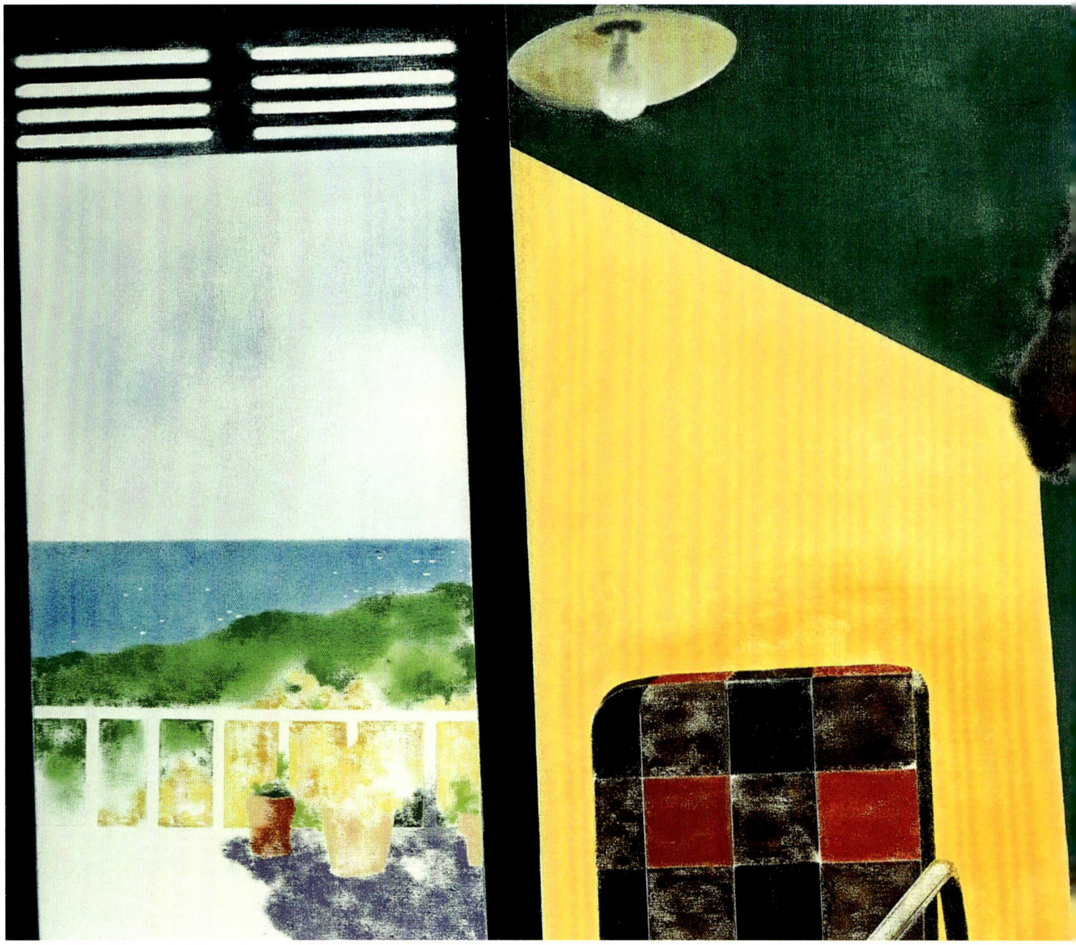

R.B. Kitaj
To Live in Peace (*The Singers*)
1973–4

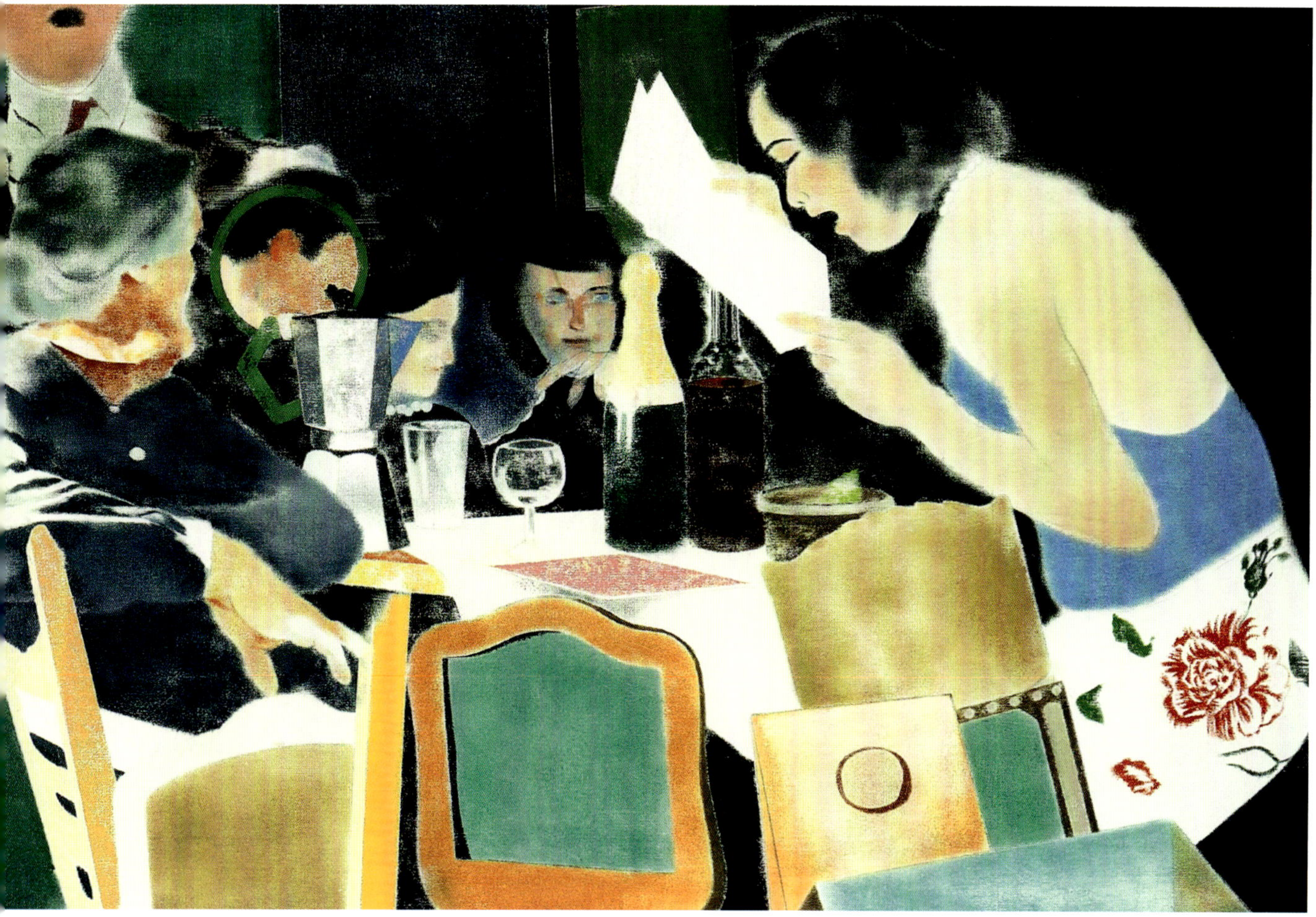

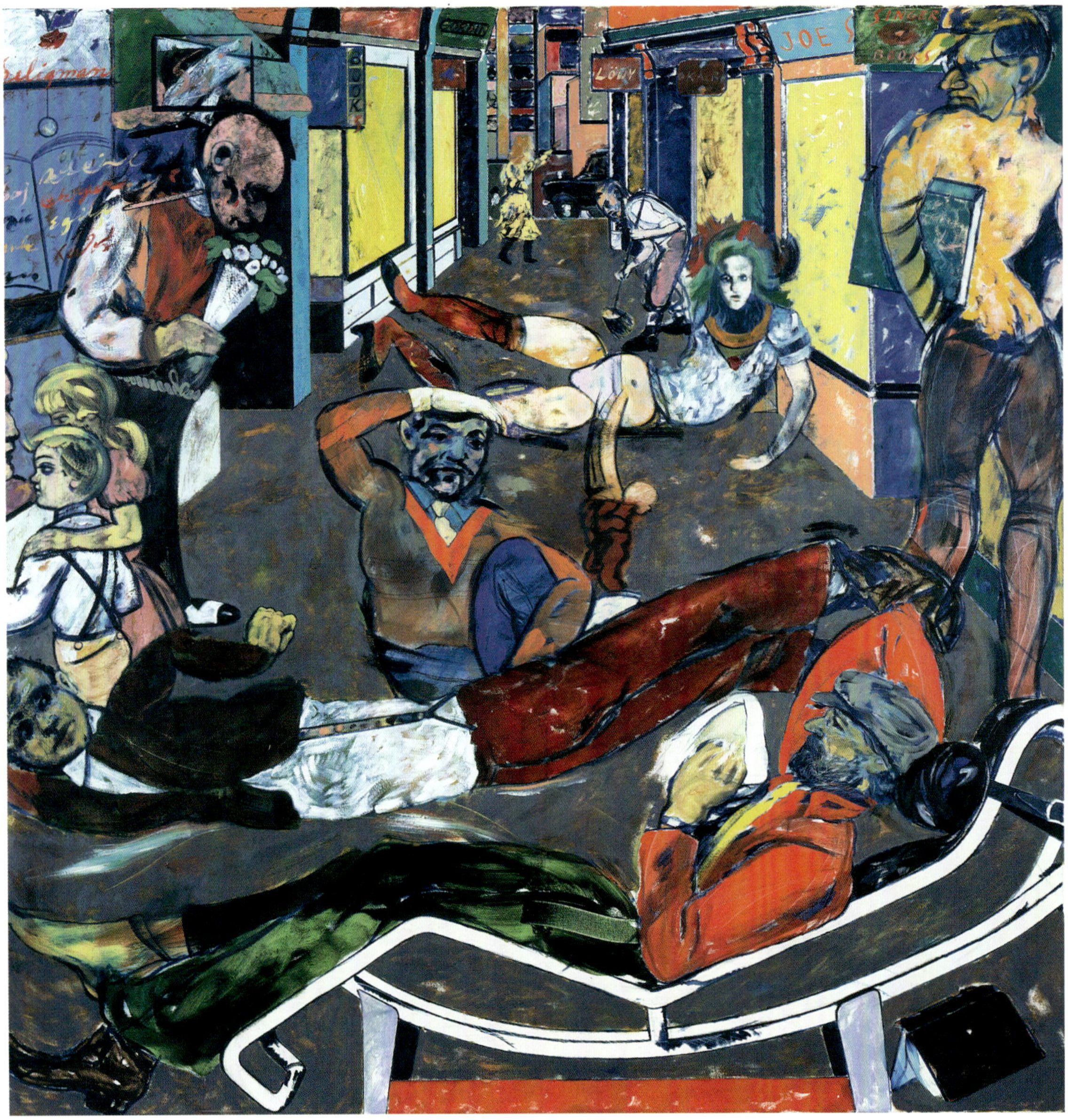

R.B. Kitaj
Cecil Court, London W.C.2
(*The Refugees*) 1983–4

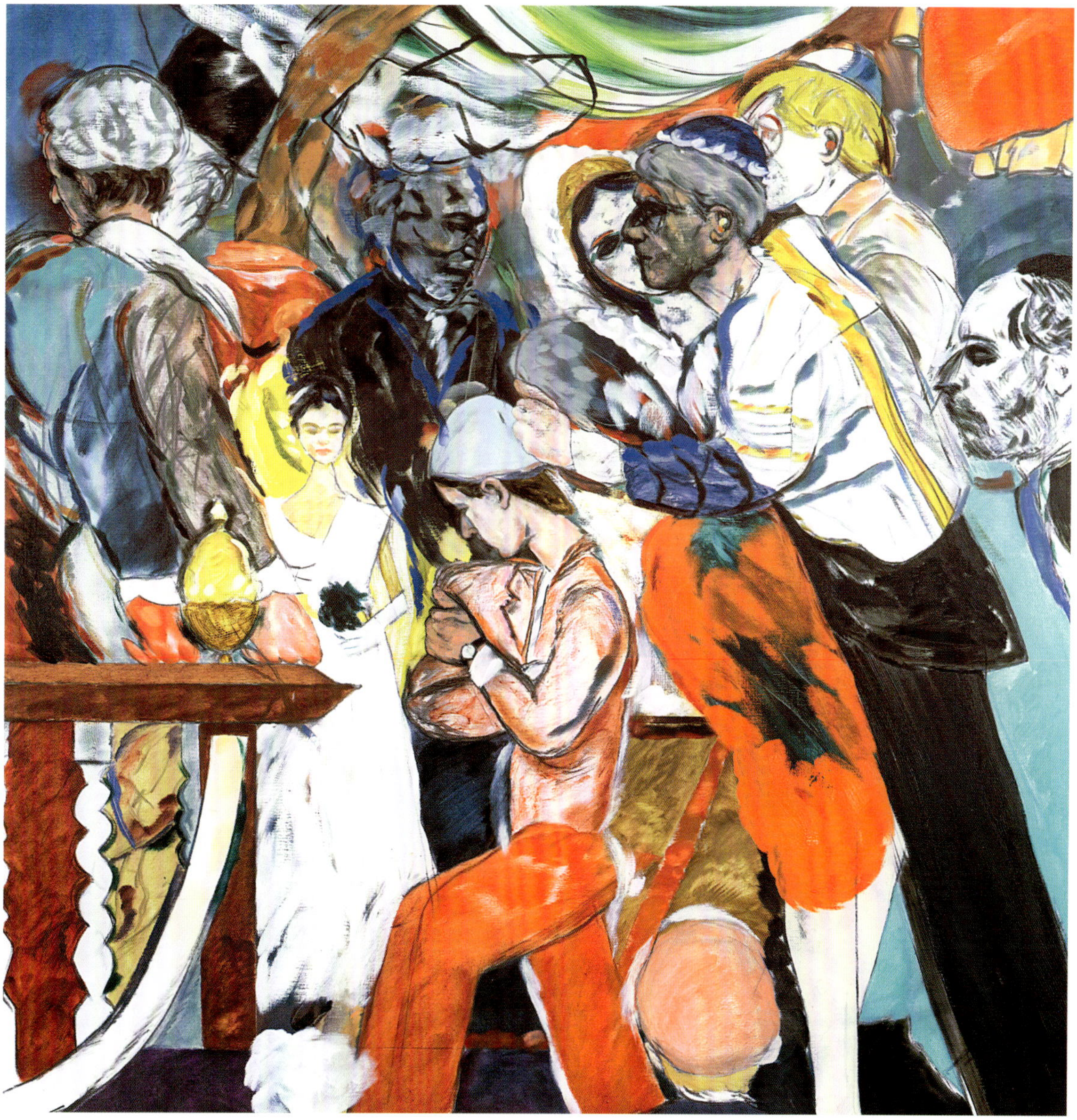

R.B. Kitaj
The Wedding 1989–93

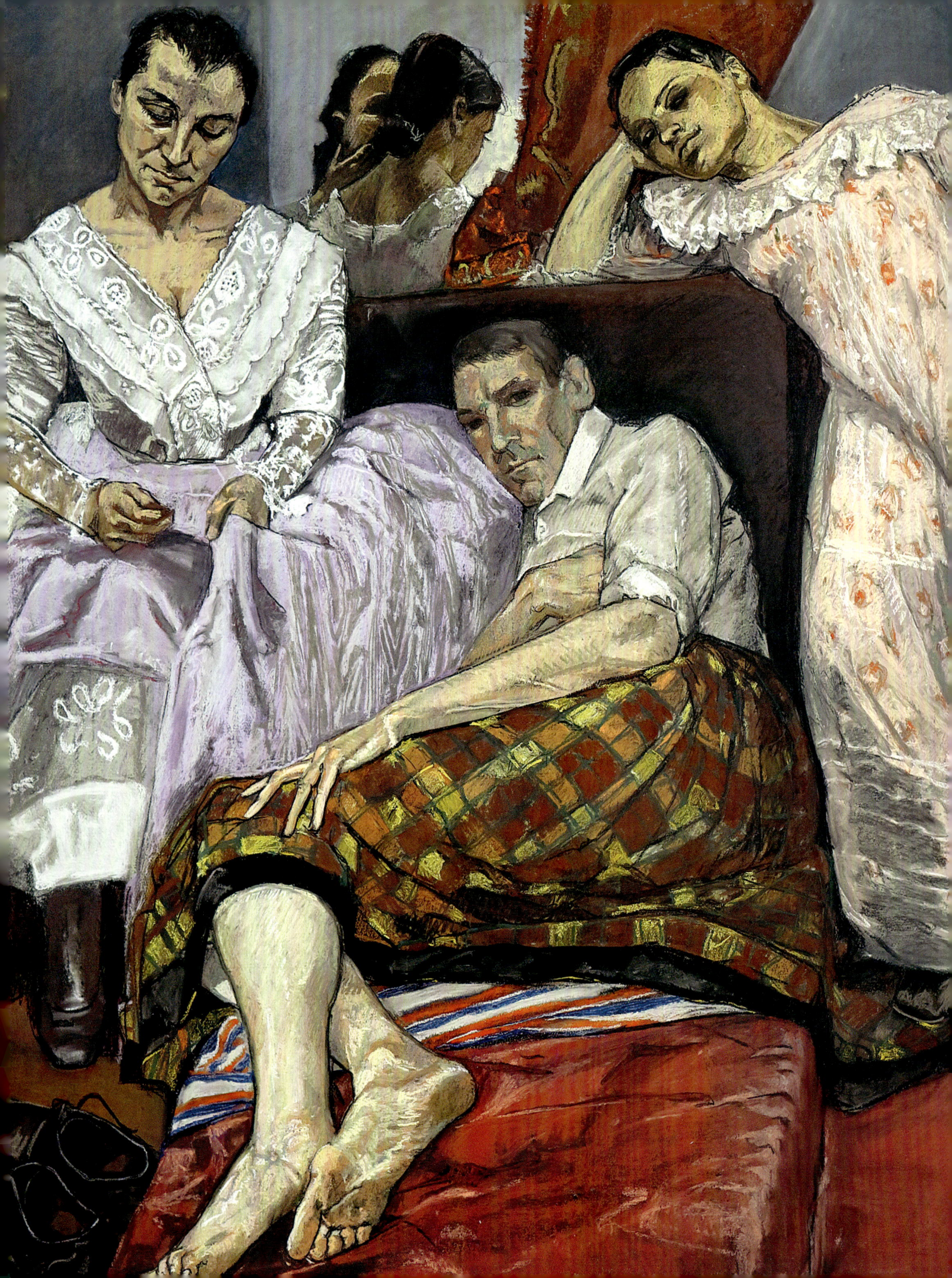

Paula Rego

Katie Campbell

Born in 1935 in Lisbon, Portugal, Rego was sent to England at the age of sixteen to complete her education. She went on to attend the Slade School of Fine Art between 1952 and 1956 under the guidance of principal William Coldstream and alongside fellow students Michael Andrews, Euan Uglow and Victor Willing. Freed from the constraints of the Slade's life room, Rego worked predominantly with collage throughout the 1960s and 1970s, mining her own imagination and immediate surroundings for inspiration. Having returned to Portugal with her then-husband Vic Willing, much of her work from this period tackles wider societal concerns, such as life under António de Oliveira Salazar's authoritarian regime.

In the late 1980s Rego's work underwent a profound change following the death of her husband from multiple sclerosis. The works from this period turn inward to become deeply personal and less overtly political in tone. *The Family* 1988 (p.189) was painted in the final months of her husband's illness and shows a wife and her daughter dressing their invalid husband and father. Rego's work from this time explores intimate, familial relationships within domestic settings. For the first time, shadows appear in her work, grounding the figures we see before us. It was during this time that Rego returned to working from life; in *The Family* her cousin and Willing's carer act as models, and, from then on, drawing and painting from life became central to her process.

The Family radiates the love and pain of the women who must carry the weight of caring for the man in their lives, as a spectrum of emotions, from light to dark, simmer under the surface. Rego conveys the complex way in which such emotions manifest themselves in everyday life. There is an anger to the actions; the wife almost violently grasps the limp arm of her husband, as her other arm seems to smother him, while the daughter stares ahead, disengaged from her surroundings as she blindly goes through the now-familiar motions of assisting her father.

As with all Rego's work, *The Family* is no simple narration of events. It is told and re-told from each of the characters' perspectives while they gaze ahead in different directions as if lost in their own narrative of the scene. The figure of the girl to the right-hand side of the painting underlines how Rego includes not just the views of her characters but also those of the viewer. The girl stands apart from the main trio of characters, her hands clasped in judgement as she gazes on. Her actions echo ours as voyeurs in this intimate family moment, and point to the judgement we make as we look at the story before us.

Rego explores human relationships, like Andrews and Kitaj. She populates her works with her own personal pantheon of characters and is driven by her desire 'to fight injustice'.[1] For Rego, this injustice is the subjugation of women in a patriarchal society, and it is through storytelling that she seeks to convey the truth. She explores the condition of women in society, their interactions and their innermost thoughts, from her own personal, feminist perspective. Her decision to return to a more realist form of painting in the late 1980s, abandoning the fantastical compositions and collage of her earlier work, sees her take on the mainly masculine tradition of painting, one that she constantly subverts.

Paula Rego
The Company of Women 1997
(detail)

Rego's female protagonists do not conform to the idealised female characters of canonical art history; they are multifaceted and human. Women see 'their private world, their dreams, the insides of their heads, projected on such a scale and so immodestly, with such depth and colour'.[2] Rego explores the many different roles women play over the course of their lives, savagely unveiling that which lies beneath the charade. In *Bride* 1994 (p.190) she presents us with an unexpected depiction of a woman on her wedding day. Exhausted, she lies back awkwardly on her marriage bed as if constrained by her own wedding dress to await the night ahead.

Rego is drawn to the dark underbelly of life, unrepentantly depicting the harsh and violent truths that often remain hidden. *Island of the Lights from Pinocchio* 1996 (p.191) is part of a series in which Rego explored early Walt Disney films. Here, she reimagines a scene from Disney's *Pinocchio* 1940, dispensing with any saccharine veneer on the original tale to reveal the truth that lies beneath the mirage of Pleasure Island. We see the moment in which Pinocchio and his companion are transformed into donkeys and sold into slavery. The various stages of their grotesque and violent transformation repeat and flash before the viewer as if seen from a nightmarish merry-go-round.

In *The Company of Women* 1997 (p.186) and *The Betrothal: Lessons: The Shipwreck, after 'Marriage a la Mode' by Hogarth* 1999 (pp.192–3) Rego shatters the glittering mirage of everyday life, reworking the previously banned Portuguese tale *The Crime of Father Amaro* and Hogarth's 'Marriage a la Mode' series, respectively. Both works are searing social commentaries. Rego echoes Hogarth's darkly satirical tone and brings the two tales forward in time to the Portugal of her childhood. The tragedy of the female protagonists' lives play out in front of us: subject to the sway of others, they have no power to take control.

Importantly, these works are the result of commissions from two of London's leading art galleries – the Dulwich Picture Gallery and the National Gallery. Since her appointment as the National Gallery's first Associate Artist in 1989–90, Rego has taken on the 'high art' she had previously shied away from, reworking and taking inspiration from the great masters of figurative painting. Since the late 1980s, Rego has adapted and subverted this masculine tradition to fulfil her desire for storytelling, and in so doing she has led the way for fellow contemporary artists.

Paula Rego
The Family 1988

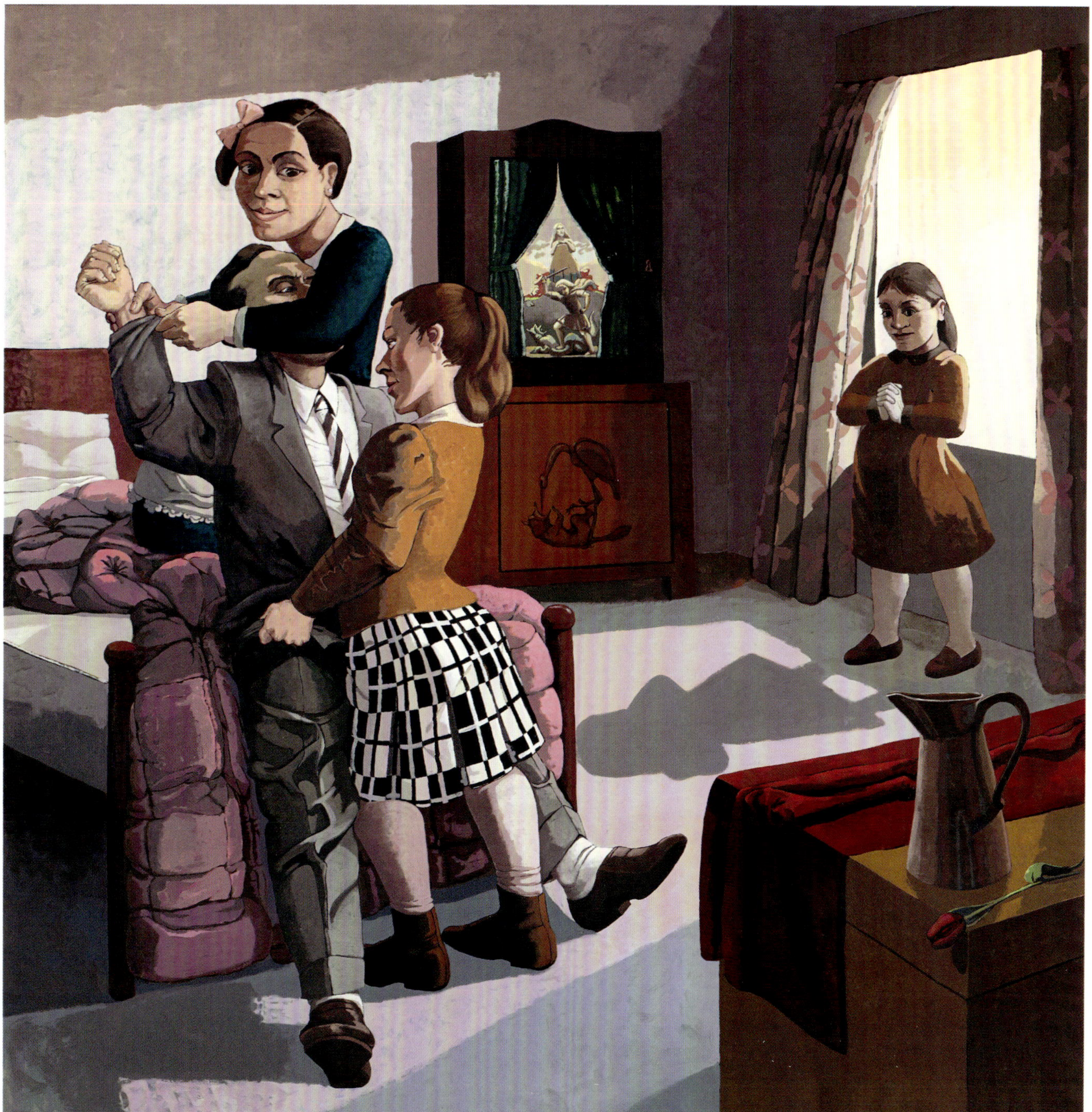

Paula Rego
Bride 1994

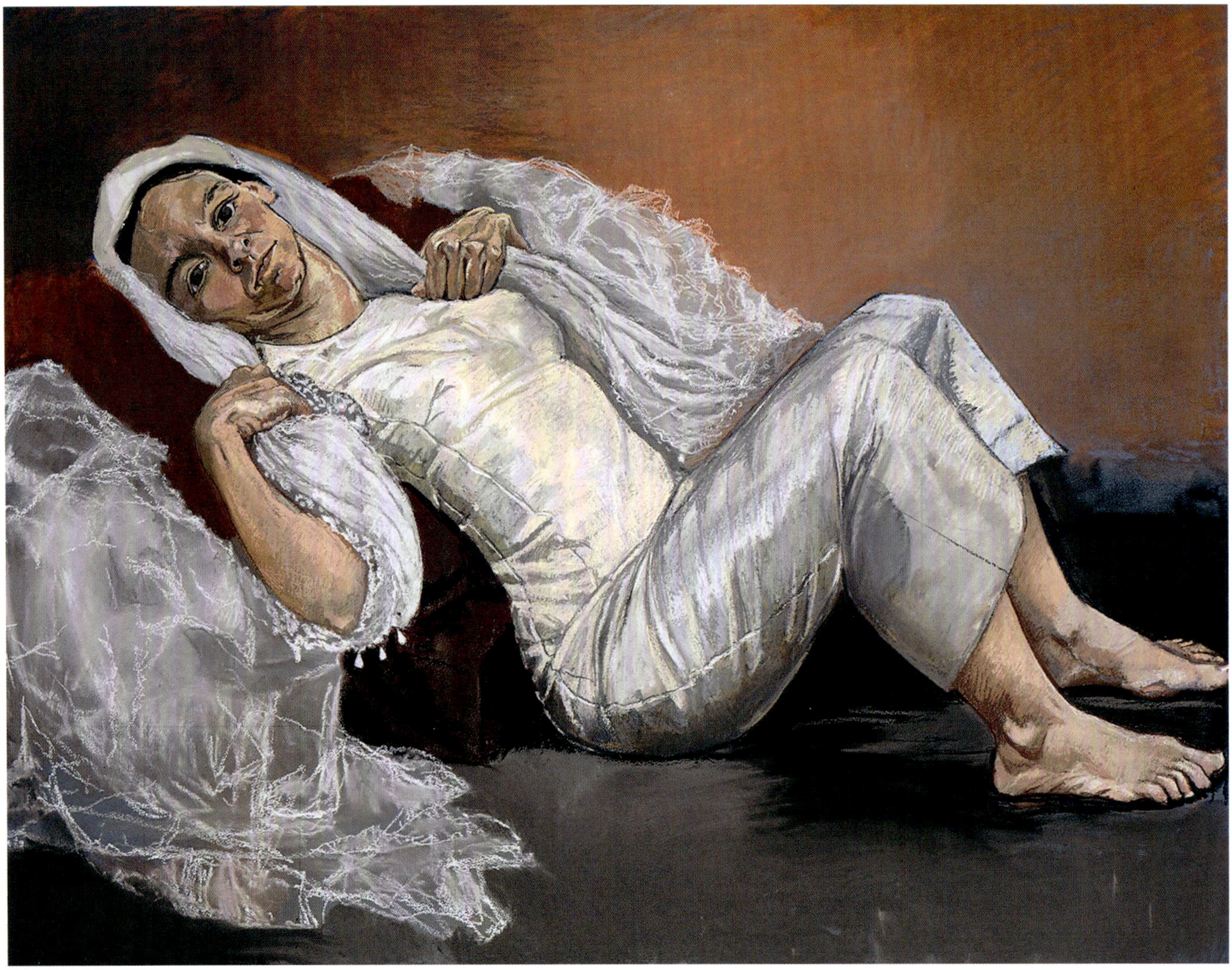

Paula Rego
Island of the Lights from Pinocchio 1996

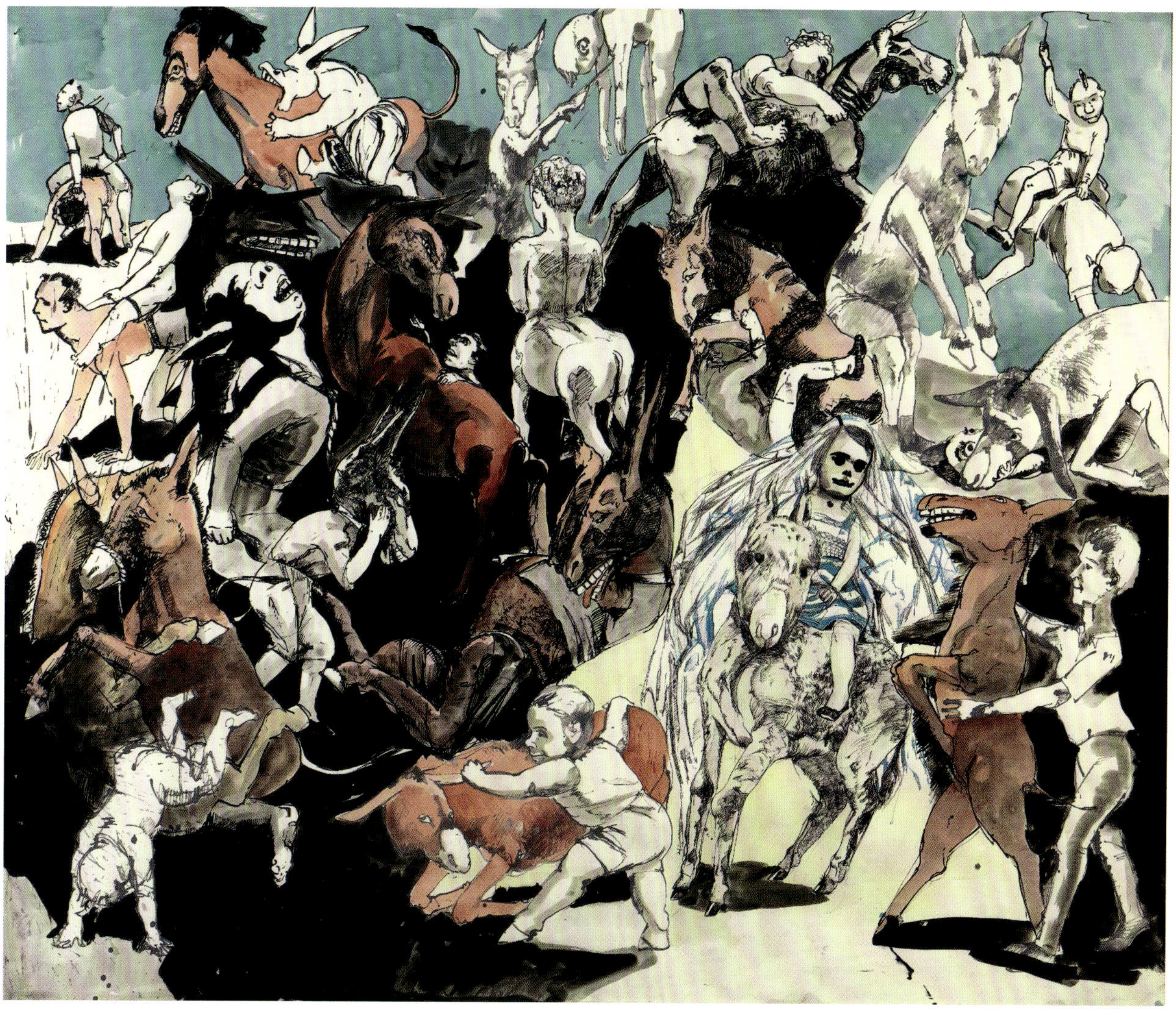

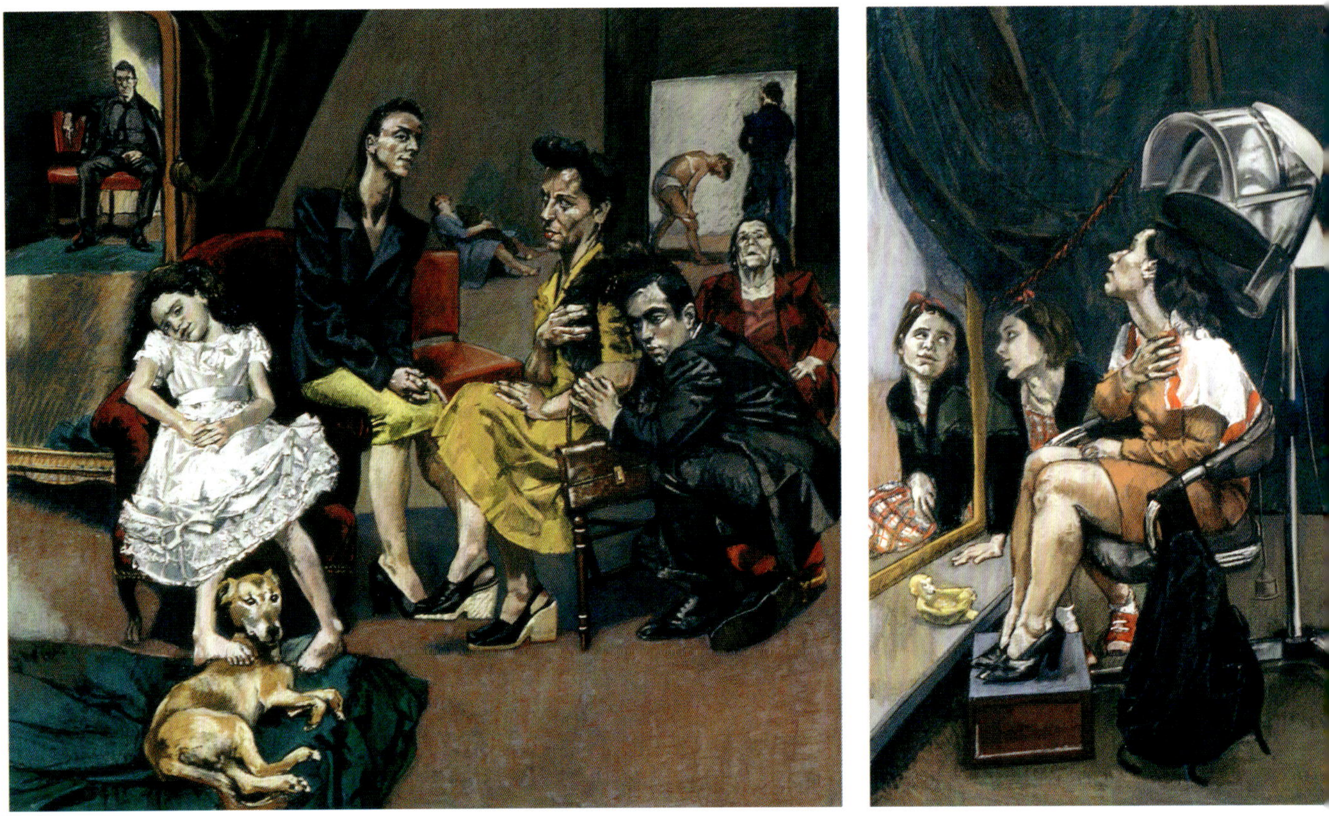

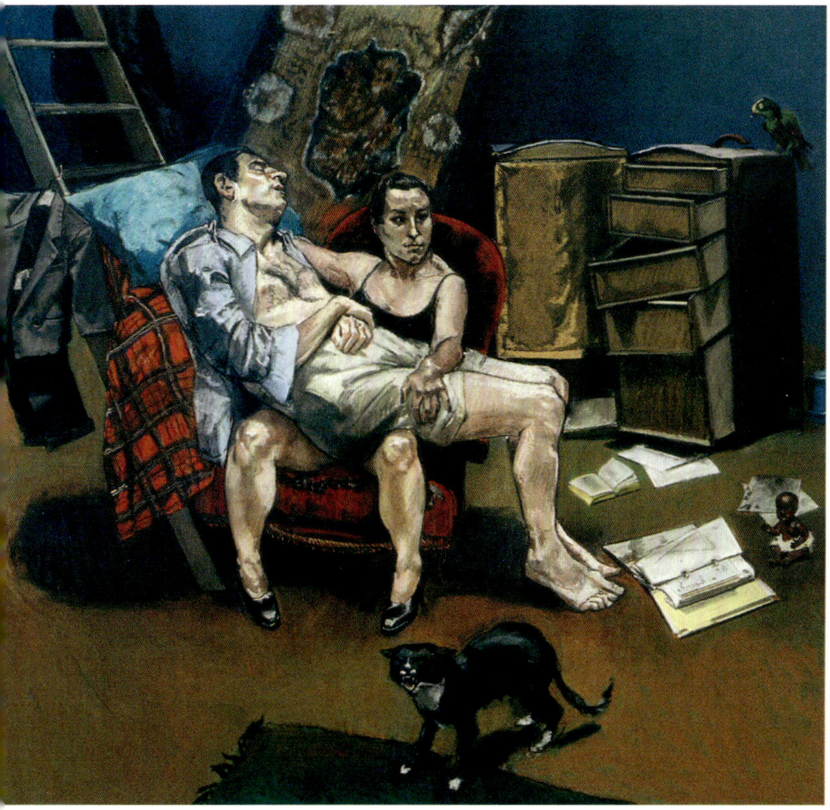

Paula Rego
The Betrothal: Lessons: The Shipwreck, after 'Marriage a la Mode' by Hogarth 1999

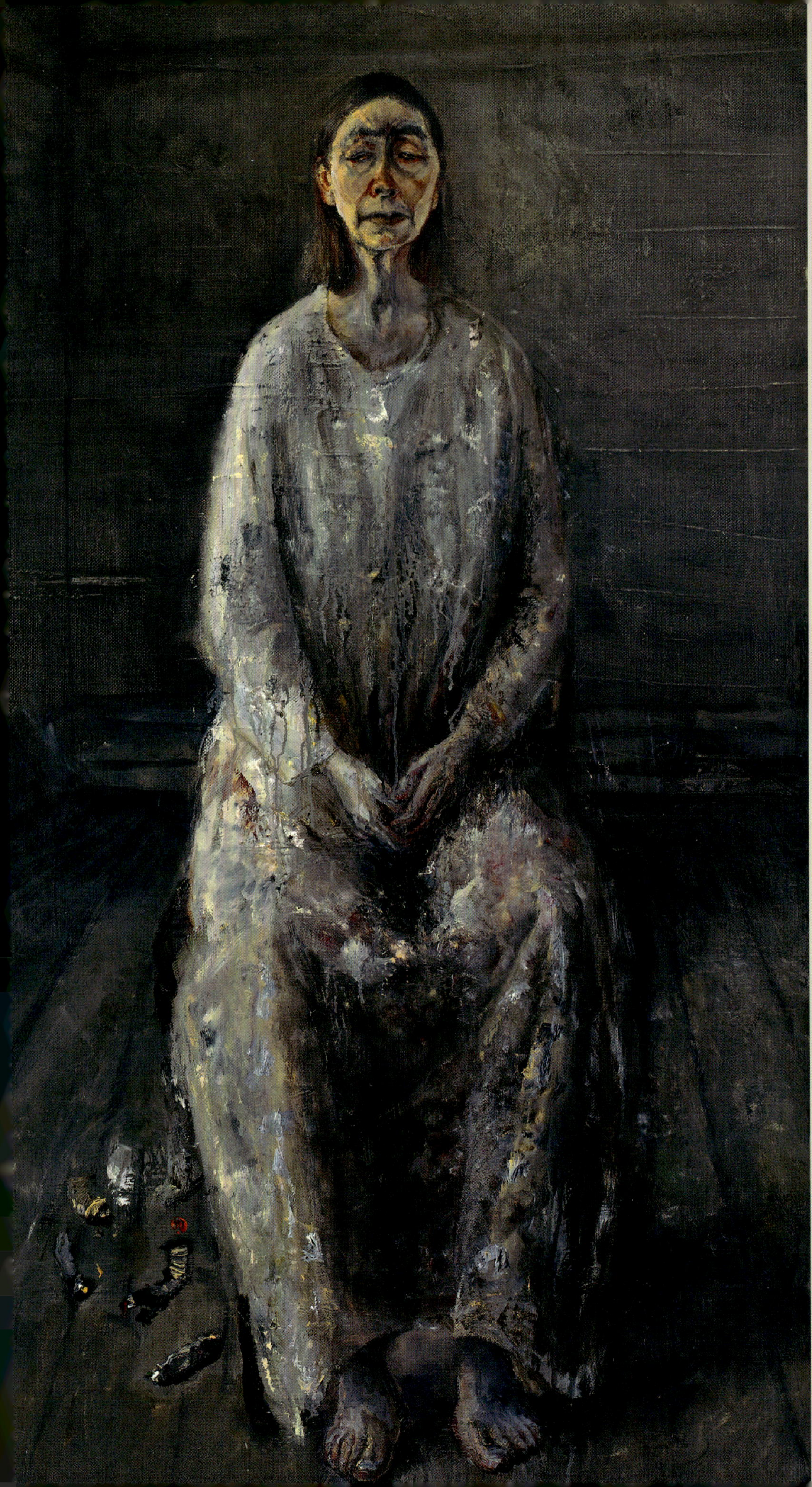

Identity, Self and Representation

Hattie Spires

There are a number of elements that link the artistic practices of Cecily Brown, Celia Paul, Jenny Saville and Lynette Yiadom-Boakye. All of these artists continued working with oil paint during a time when medium-specificity had seemingly been abandoned, and figurative painting was seen as irrelevant to contemporary art production. The human figure is the central concern of these artists, and their portrayal of an embodied sensibility continues the trajectory of those highly influential artists associated with the School of London, who were able to capture the physical and emotional conditions they inhabited when painting their subjects. However their approaches vary from those of their predecessors, and also from each other.

Celia Paul is a direct link to painters of the previous generation. As a student of Lucian Freud at the Slade School of Fine Art and, for a time, in a close relationship with him, she could be said to be a part of the clique that constituted the School of London artists during the 1970s and 1980s. But Paul's work is radically different from Freud's in its empathic gaze. Unlike Freud's unflinching approach that scrutinises his subjects with an unsentimental objectivity and the all-encompassing gaze that pays as much attention to the surrounding environment of the studio as to the sitter, Paul's intimate, quiet portraits depict people as if wanting to bring their inner life to the surface. She paints 'from the inside out';[1] densely rendered individuals are portrayed like orphans, cutting a lonely figure on the canvas. The apparent density of her sitters gives an almost Giacometti-esque gravity to their presence, yet an inner light radiates from each heavily worked figure, a sort of 'halo' emerging from the background and crowning the subject's head.

Both Jenny Saville and Celia Paul share an interest in the work of Chaïm Soutine, and the trope of the butcher is something that Saville has returned to time and again. In *Reverse* 2002–3 (pp.198–9) she offers up her own fleshy, slack-lipped, close-up portraiture. Exuding an almost masculine confidence in her larger-than-life scale and uncompromising, confrontational portrayals of herself, Saville's work verges on sculptural on the picture plane. Her loose brushwork conveys the physical properties of flesh, rendering the painted surface so tactile, so textured, that it evokes meat on a butcher's block – a painterly tendency that has drawn comparisons to the work of Freud in his filigreed, voluminous forms but also, more directly, in Soutine's subject matter in *The Butcher Stall* c.1919 (p.71).

The sense of immediacy transmitted through a Paul painting could only come from an artist who paints a life model. When artists – such as Paula Rego – work from other sources, the effect is mediated. But the physical and emotional state of the painter at work is nevertheless communicated. Rego's facility for storytelling is echoed in the work of Lynette Yiadom-Boakye, whose elegant character portraits evoke a loose sense of narrative. Yiadom-Boakye paints figures not from life but from her imagination, based on composites of images from scrapbooks and drawings that produce a cast of fictitious characters that, once committed to canvas, are difficult to pin down to a particular time or place. Her subjects are always black and often look as though they have been glimpsed resting during

Celia Paul
Painter and Model 2012
(detail)

a dance lesson (indeed, she cites Edgar Degas and Walter Richard Sickert as influences).[2] She deftly asserts black identity and inscribes it within the tradition of Western painting (particularly portraiture) a history of predominantly white, male painters in which black sitters were nearly exclusively cast in minor roles.

Her paintings have allusive titles that help to conjure up the faintest idea of a story in the viewer. In *Coterie of Questions* 2015 (p.204) a young man is perched on a stool. And immediately the brain gets to work: is this an interrogation, and just who is the interrogator? Yiadom-Boakye famously works quickly, executing most of her paintings in a day, improvising as she works to try to capture a particular moment, fleshing out a character from her imagination as a writer might; indeed, she is a writer as much as a painter.[3] Each work is a kind of scientific experiment for the artist, who tries out new layering combinations of paint to build up colour or play with light and shade. Her loose brushstrokes and broken touches of paint allow her to maintain the delicacy of drawing through an economy of line that is reminiscent of Sickert.

Despite its often abstract appearance, the human figure is central to the work of Cecily Brown. She grew up in a house full of art books, some of which to her seemed illicit. Through these books she was exposed to erotically charged, macabre works by Francis Bacon, Lucian Freud and George Grosz, and cultivated an early curiosity in images of the human form, sneaking a peek inside these books as though looking at pornography.[4] Brown describes herself first and foremost as a figurative painter. As she said in 2014, 'To talk about the range of things it means to be human is to talk about the body.' It is the vehicle by which she can scrutinise the world; the 'meat and flesh of life'.[5] Attraction and desire often come to the fore in her work, as can be seen in *Teenage Wildlife* 2003 (p.200) and *Boy with a Cat* 2015 (p.201). Here, figures are on the verge of breaking down to a degree of abstraction, to melt into each other or their painted surroundings through an erotic fumbling.

For Brown, as soon as the figure is removed from the composition, the work simply becomes decorative. What underlies Brown's urge to paint is the same force that impels her peers and those artists who were so influential in plotting this painterly trajectory over the course of the twentieth century and into the twenty-first. It is the same thread that runs through the artists' work from Soutine to Saville: '[in order] to talk about anything at all and all the range of things it means to be human, then it is to be found in the body'.[6]

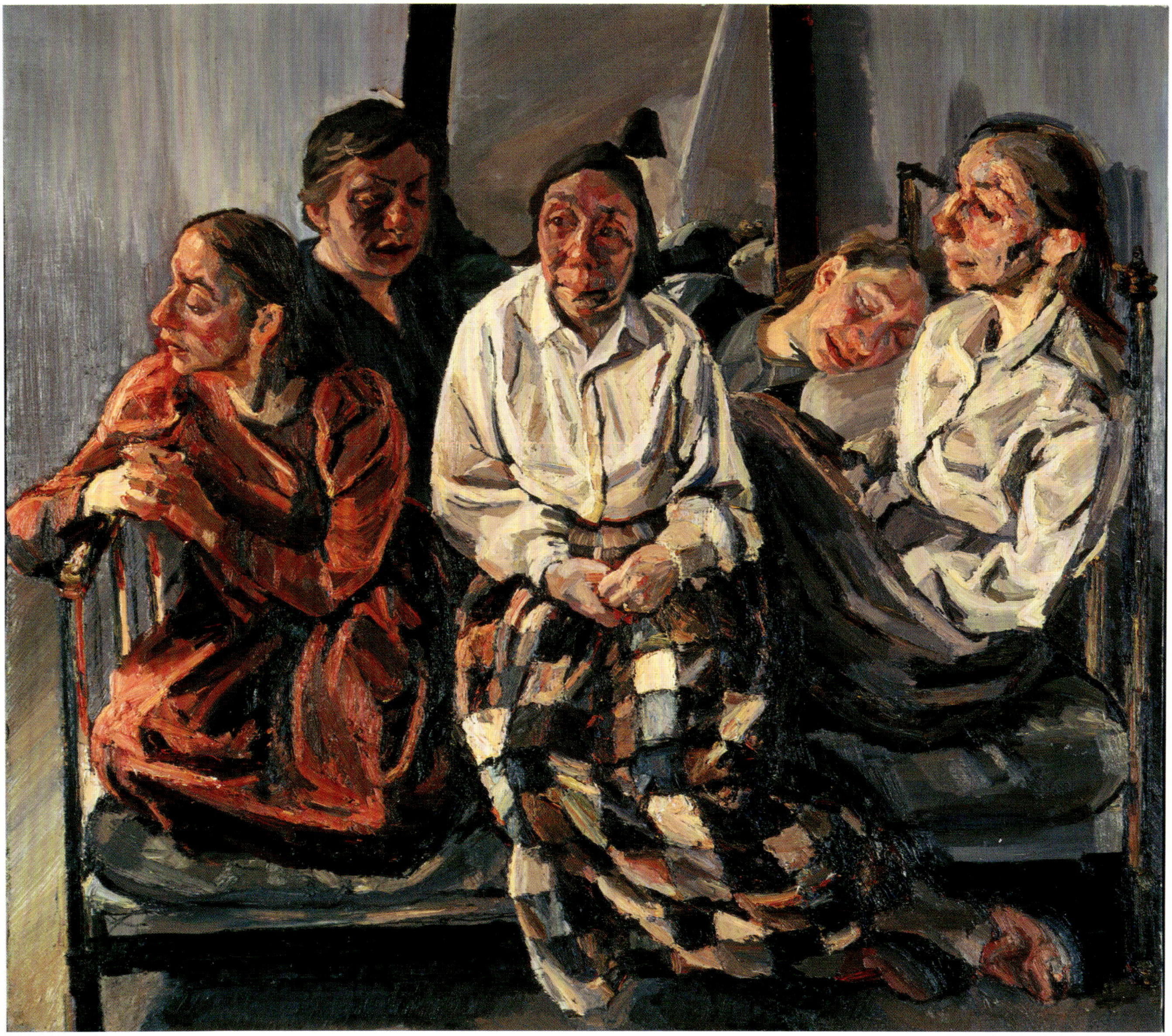

Celia Paul
Family Group 1984–6

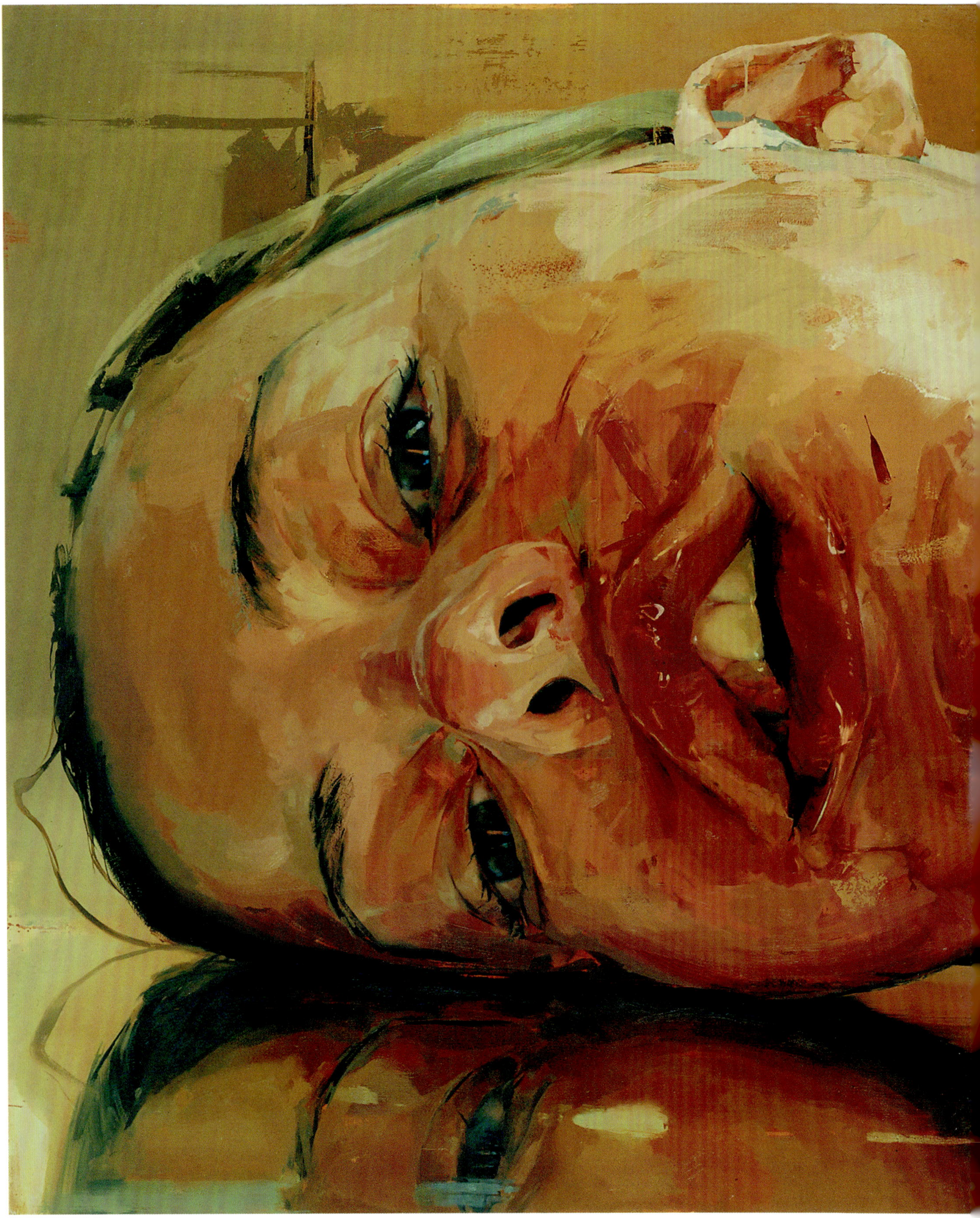

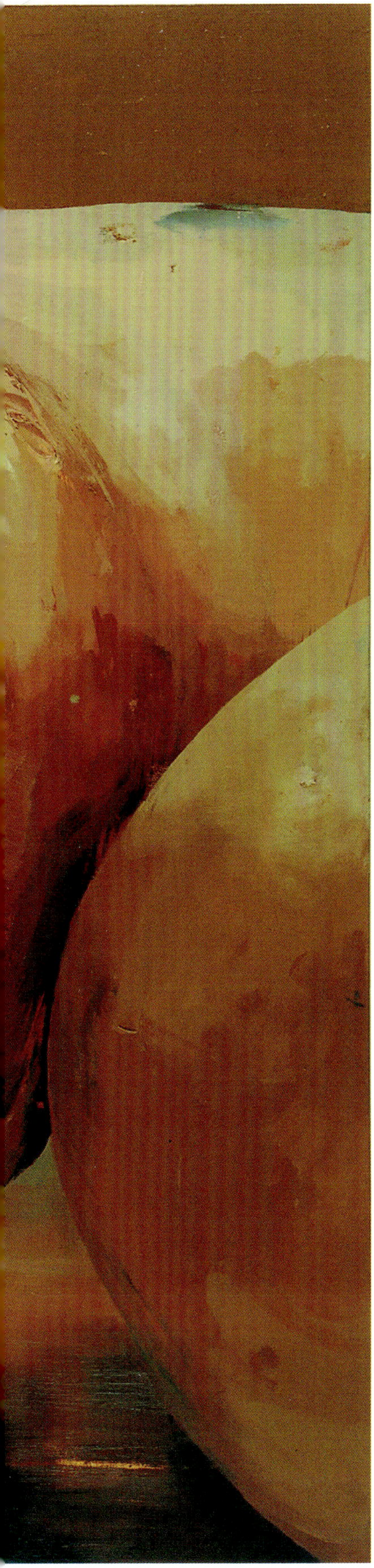

Jenny Saville
Reverse 2002–3

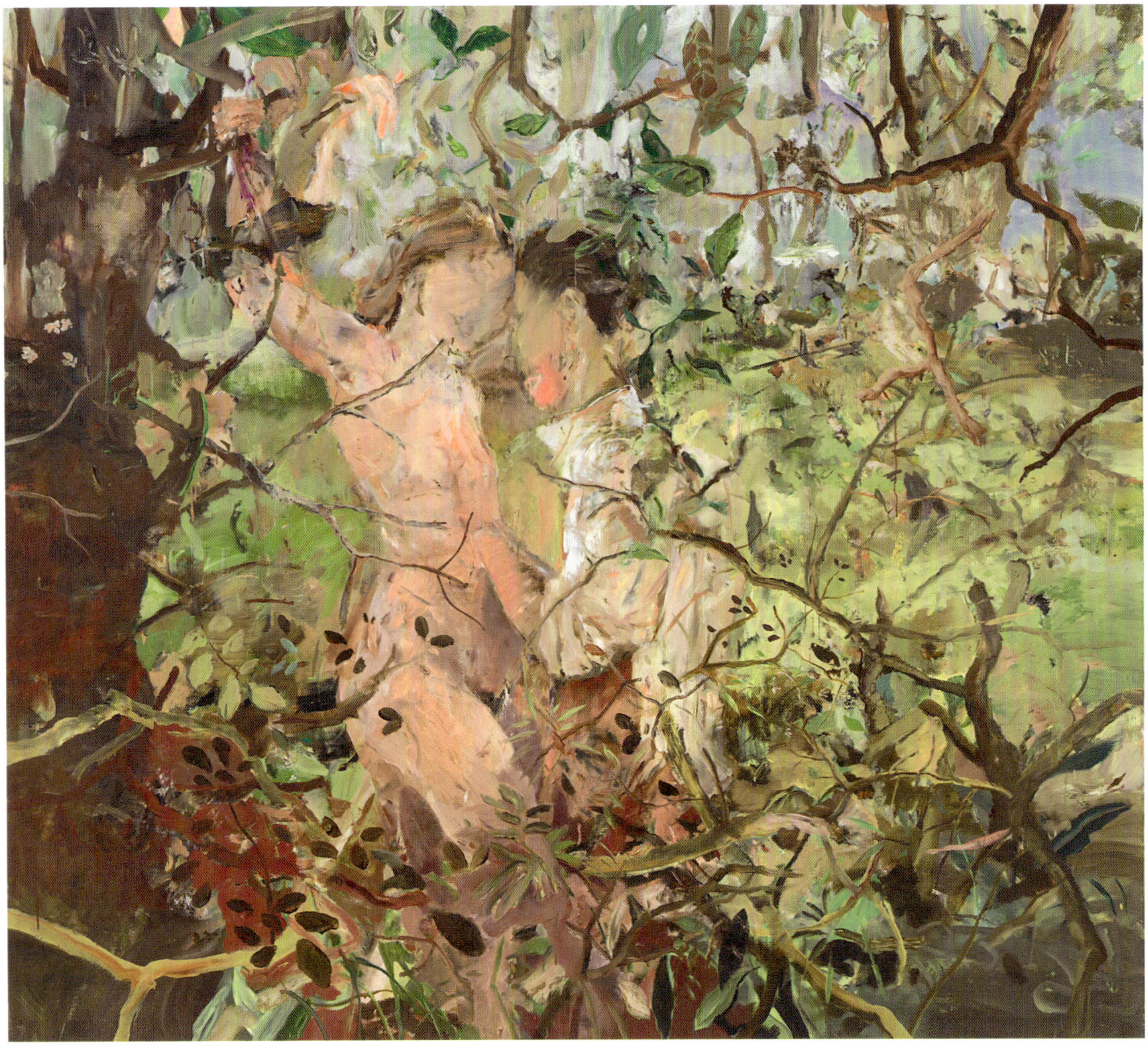

Cecily Brown
Teenage Wildlife 2003

Cecily Brown
Boy with a Cat 2015

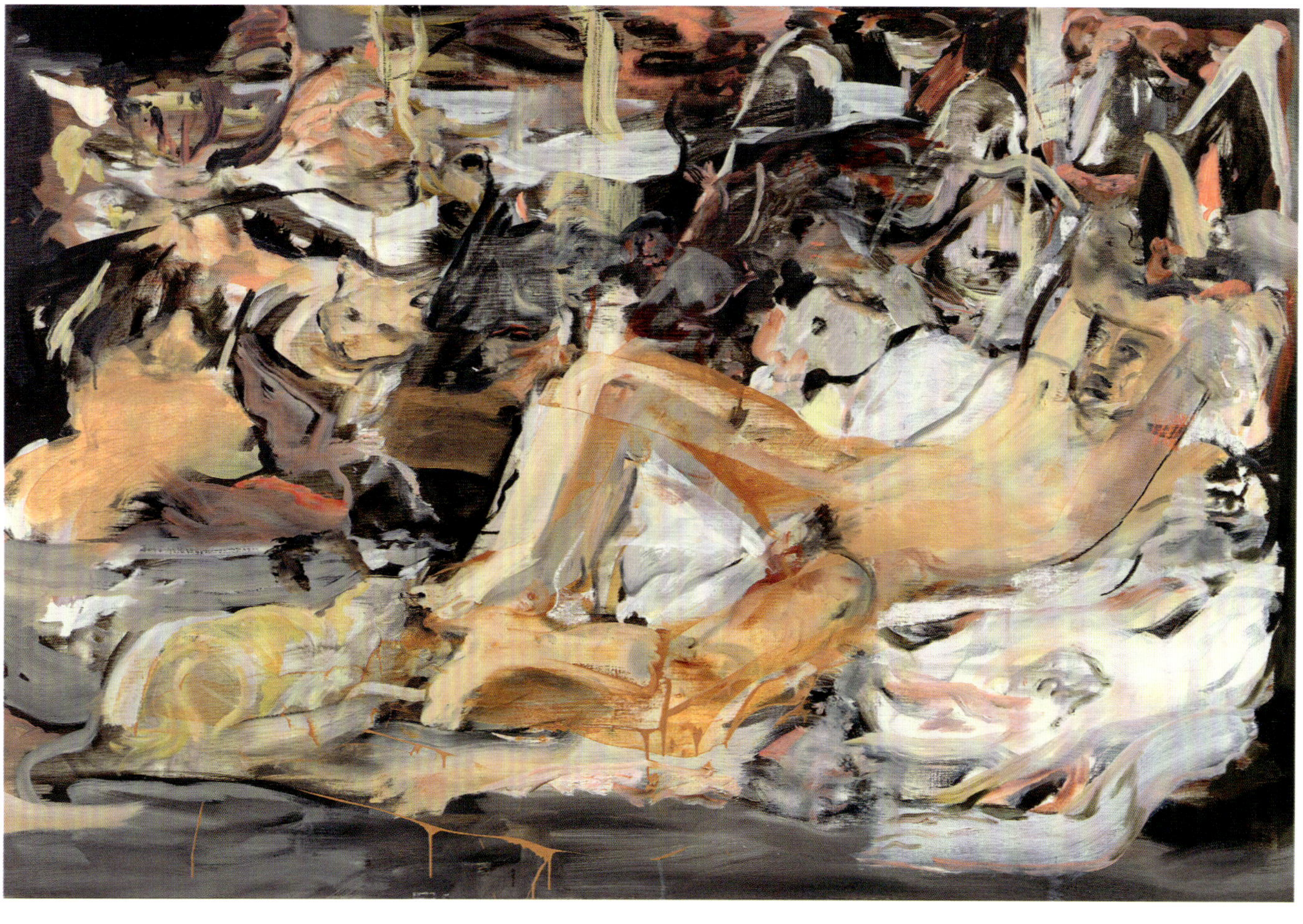

Lynette Yiadom-Boakye
The Host Over a Barrel 2014

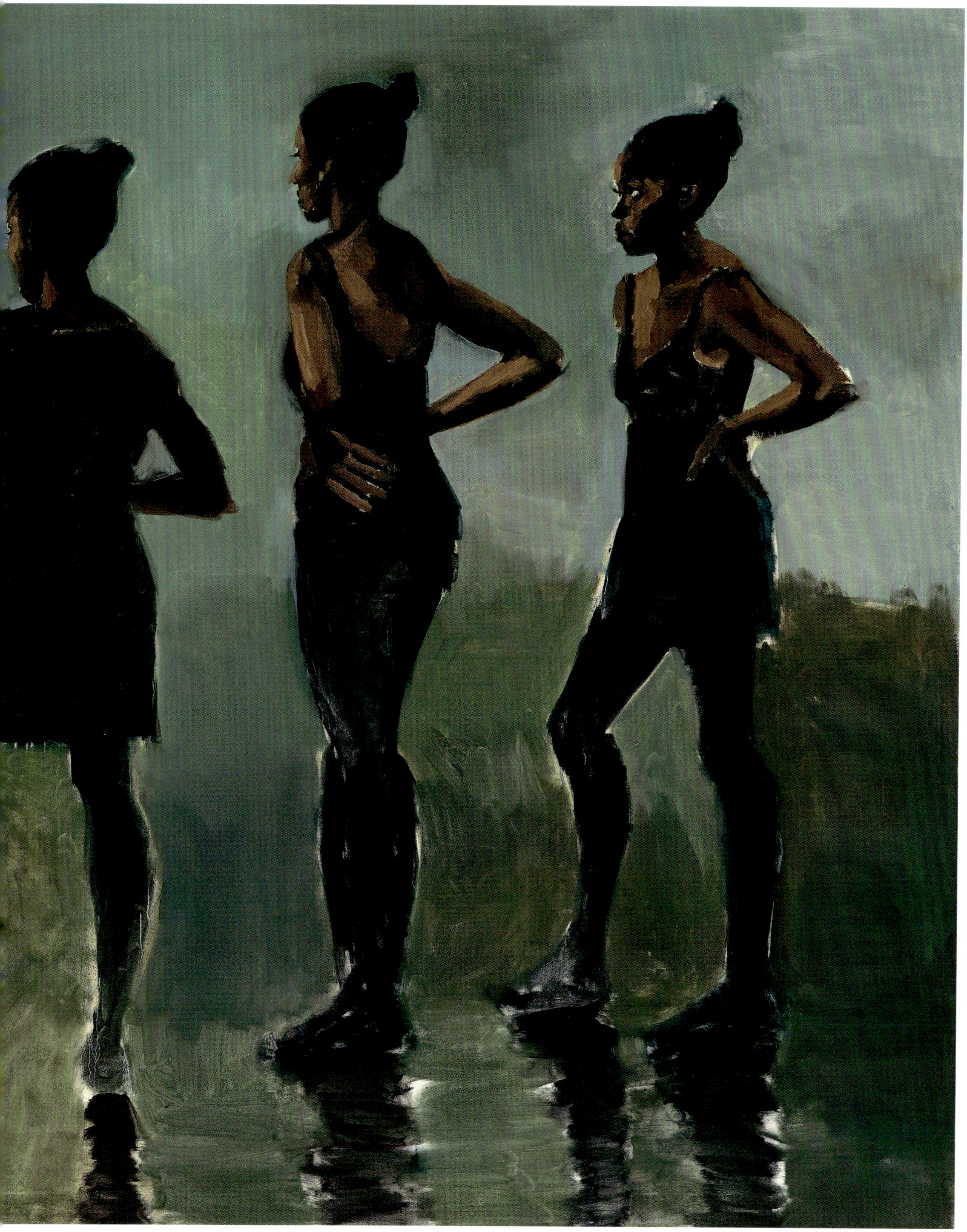

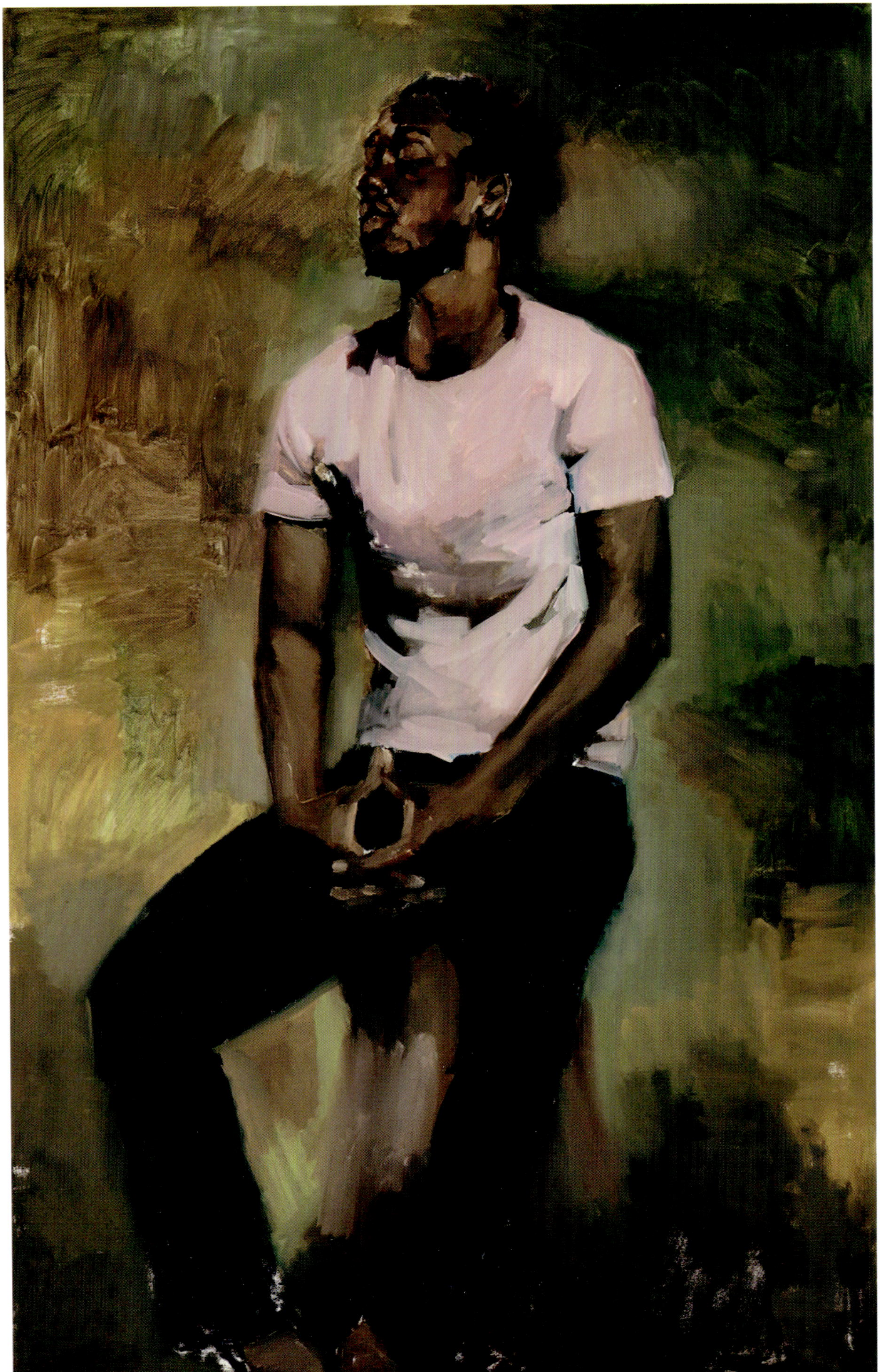

Lynette Yiadom-Boakye
Coterie of Questions 2015

Notes

The Embodied Life of Painting, pp.12–25

1 Richard Schacht, 'Introduction' to Friedrich Nietzsche, *Human, All Too Human, A Book for Free Spirits*, trans. by R.J. Hollingdale, rev. edn, Cambridge 1996, pp.VIII–IX.

2 This is the first verse of W.H. Auden's poem 'Letter to Lord Byron', from which R.B. Kitaj borrowed for the title of his exhibition *The Human Clay*, Hayward Gallery, London 1976. Kitaj's catalogue text discussed the existence of a 'School of London'.

3 See 'School of London', pp.29–30 of this book.

4 Arthur C. Danto, 'The End of Art: A Philosophical Defence', *History and Theory*, vol.37, no.4, 1998, pp.127–43 (p.140).

5 This was already noted by Edwin Mullins, in *FN Souza: An Introduction by Edwin Mullins*, London 1962, p.7. Souza's work has rarely been seen as part of surveys of modern British art. In 1989–90, it was included in *The Other Story: Afro-Asian Artists in Post-War Britain*, Hayward Gallery, London. Curated by Rasheed Araeen, the exhibition aimed to make visible the neglected history of the contribution of British artists of African, Caribbean and Asian ancestry to the modernist aesthetic.

6 'Interview with F.N. Souza, 1994', *F.N. Souza*, exh. cat., London 2008, p.10.

7 On Sylvester's strand of realism see James Hyman, *The Battle for Realism: Figurative Art in Britain During the Cold War*, New Haven 2001, pp.133–4.

8 See Timothy Hyman, 'Introduction' to *Narrative Paintings, Figurative Art of Two Generations Selected by Timothy Hyman*, exh. cat., Bristol 1979.

9 Judith Butler, 'Response to J.M. Bernstein', in Diarmuid Costello and Dominic Wilson, eds., *The Life and Death of Images, Ethics and Aesthetics*, London 2008, p.62.

10 Walter Richard Sickert, 'Idealism', *The Art News*, 12 May 1919, p.217.

11 Frank Auerbach, in Catherine Lampert, *Frank Auerbach: Speaking and Painting*, London 2015, p.176 (originally from Andrew Lambirth, 'Living in the Moment', *Spectator*, 24 October 2009, p.52).

12 See Griselda Pollock, 'Modernity and the Spaces of Femininity', in Griselda Pollock, *Vision and Difference: Feminism, Femininity and the Histories of Art*, London 1988, p.72.

13 This is one of the arguments underpinning Timothy Hyman's *The World New Made: Figurative Painting in the Twentieth Century*, London 2016.

14 Linda Nochlin, 'The Realist Criminal and the Abstract Law I', *Art in America*, no.61, September–October 1973, p.54.

15 'Lynette Yiadom-Boakye in Conversation with Habda Rashid', *Natures, Natural and Unnatural*, exh. cat., London 2015, p.32.

16 Lucian Freud, in conversation with Michael Auping (7 May 2009), in Sarah Howgate, Michael Auping and John Richardson eds., *Lucian Freud: Portraits*, exh. cat., London 2012, p.209.

17 This is how Deleuze describes 'sensation' in relation to Cézanne and Bacon. See Gilles Deleuze, *Francis Bacon: The Logic of Sensation*, trans. Daniel W. Smith, London and New York 2003, p.34.

18 Laura Mulvey, 'Visual Pleasure and Narrative Cinema', in Leo Braudy and Marshall Cohen, eds., *Film Theory and Criticism: Introductory Readings*, New York 1999, pp.833–44 (p.837), first published in *Screen*, vol.16, no.3, 1975, pp.6–18.

19 See John Berger, *Ways of Seeing*, London 1972, and Mulvey, 1999.

20 On the distinction between the nude and the naked see the opening page of Kenneth Clark, *The Nude: A Study of Ideal Art*, London 1956, p.1, and Lynda Nead, *Art, Obscenity and Sexuality*, New York 1992.

21 Pollock, 1988, p.75.

22 For an exploration of paintings transgressing the norm of the representation of women as passively attractive see Charles Harrison, *Painting the Difference: Sex and Spectator in Modern Art*, Chicago 2005.

23 Lisa Tickner, 'Walter Sickert and the Camden Town Murder', in Barnaby Wright, ed., *Walter Sickert, The Camden Town Nudes*, exh. cat., London 2007, p.52.

24 Linda Nochlin, 'Some Women Realists, Painters of the Figure', *Arts Magazine*, vol.48, no.8, May 1974, pp.29–33 (p.29).

25 Leon Kossoff, *Recent Paintings and Drawings*, exh. cat., London 1973, p.5.

26 Maurice Merleau-Ponty, 'Eye and Mind', in Galen A. Johnson, ed., *The Merleau-Ponty Aesthetics Reader: Philosophy and Painting*, Evanston 1993, pp.126–7.

27 Ibid.

28 This section is loosely framed by Jacques Derrida's notion of '*différance*'.

29 Francis Bacon (May 1966), in *Interviews with Francis Bacon*, London 1975, pp.39–40.

30 Melvyn Levy, 'F.N. Souza, the Human and the Divine',

Studio International, vol.167, no.852, pp.134–9 (p.136).
31 Ibid., p.135.
32 See 'Francis Bacon and John Deakin', pp.163–4 of this book.
33 Paula Rego, in conversation with John McEwen, *Paula Rego*, London 1992, p.225.
34 Marion Milner, *On Not Being Able to Paint*, London 2010, p.142.
35 Ibid.
36 Timothy Hyman, *The World New Made, Figurative Painting in the Twentieth Century*, London 2016, p.57.
37 Nochlin, 'Some Women Realists', 1974, p.29.
38 See Caoimhín Mac Giolla Léith, 'Painting Sensation', in *Cecily Brown: Paintings*, exh. cat., Oxford 2005, pp.55–6.
39 See Hilton Als's text in Celia Paul and Hilton Als, *Desdemona for Celia*, London 2016, p.67.

London: Painting in the Time of Modernist Art, pp.26–41

1 Max Weber, 'Science as a Vocation', in H.H. Gerth and C. Wright Mills, *From Max Weber: Essays in Sociology*, New York 1975, p.155.
2 Thierry de Duve, *Kant after Duchamp*, Cambridge, Mass. 1999, p.317.
3 Roger Fry, 'Art History as an Academic Study', *The Last Lectures by Roger Fry*, Cambridge 2015, p.4.
4 R.B. Kitaj, 'School of London', *An Exhibition Selected by R.B. Kitaj*, London 1976.
5 Andrew Brighton, 'Official Art and the Tate Gallery', *Studio International*, 1/1977, vol.193, no.985, pp.41–4.
6 Herbert Read, *Contemporary British Art*, Harmondsworth 1964, p.26.
7 Frank Auerbach, 'Predicament', *The London Magazine*, July 1961.
8 Lynda Morris, 'Tonks, Henry (1862–1937)', *Oxford Dictionary of National Biography*, Oxford 2004 [http://www.oxforddnb.com/view/article/36535, accessed 8 July 2017].
9 Gilbert Spencer, *Stanley Spencer by his Brother Gilbert*, London 1961, p.104.
10 Sir William Coldstream quoted in David Sylvester, *Sir William Coldstream*, Anthony d'Offay, London 1976.
11 David Bomberg, 'The Bomberg Papers', *X*, vol.1, London 1959.
12 Francis Bacon, Interview 6, David Sylvester, *Interviews with Francis Bacon*, London 1980, p.152.
13 Francis Bacon, ibid., Interview 4, p.125.
14 Tate Gallery, *R.B. Kitaj: A Retrospective*, London 1994, p.158.
15 Paula Rego, in conversation with John McEwen, *Paula Rego*, London 1988, p.48.
16 Arts Council England, Grants for the arts: application form, 2017.

Looking at Identity: Bacon, Souza, Freud, pp.42–53

1 Alistair O'Neill, 'Available in an Array of Colours', *Visual Culture in Britain*, vol.10, no.3, pp.271–91.
2 Michael Peppiatt, *Francis Bacon: Anatomy of an Enigma*, London 2008, p.97.
3 Quoted in Michael Peppiatt, *Francis Bacon: Studies for a Portrait. Essays and Interviews*, London 2008, p.181.
4 Quoted in Rasheed Araeen, *The Other Story: Afro-Asian Artists in Post-War Britain*, London 1989, p.11.
5 Such experiences were recorded in contemporary sociological studies like Anthony H. Richmond, *The Colour Problem: A Study of Racial Relations*, Harmondsworth 1966.
6 Francis Newton Souza, 'A Fragment of Autobiography', *Words and Lines*, London 1959, p.8.
7 See David Sylvester, *Looking Back at Francis Bacon*, London 2000, p.22, or Peppiatt, 2008, p.132, for example.
8 Sylvester recognises both intentions, but suggests the microphone as the more likely possibility in Sylvester, 2000, p.22.
9 See Matt Houlbrook, *Queer London: Perils and Pleasures in the Sexual Metropolis, 1918–1957*, Chicago 2006, pp.221–41.
10 Quoted in David Sylvester, *Interviews with Francis Bacon*, London 1999, p.82.
11 Edward Lucie-Smith, 'Three Shows', *New Statesman*, 17 November 1961, p.758.
12 George Butcher, 'London Galleries: The Painting of Francis Souza', *Guardian*, 8 November 1961, p.7.
13 Aziz Kurtha, *Francis Newton Souza: Bridging Western and Indian Modern Art*, Ahmedabad 2006, p.143.
14 Quoted in Araeen, 1989, p.24.
15 William Feaver, *Lucian Freud*, exh. cat., London 2002, p.23.
16 Lucian Freud, 'Some Thoughts on Painting', *Encounter*, vol.3, no.1, July 1954, pp.23–4.
17 Lawrence Gowing, *Lucian Freud*, London 1988, pp.84, 60.
18 Feaver, 2002, p.45.

The Skin of the Day, pp.54–65

1 Virginia Woolf, 'A Room of One's Own', 1929, from *A Room of One's Own and Three Guineas*, Oxford 2008, pp.143–4.
2 Interview with Lynette Yiadom-Boakye by Natalie Bell and

Massimiliano Gioni, in *Lynette Yiadom-Boakye*, exh. cat., New York 2016, p.21.

3 Virginia Woolf, *Walter Sickert: A Conversation*, London 1934, p.25.

4 Francis Bacon, quoted in David Sylvester, *Looking Back at Francis Bacon*, London 2000, p.12.

5 This extends beyond the walls of this exhibition. For example, in both my books on contemporary figurative art, *Painting People* (London 2008) and *Picturing People* (London 2015), and in the painting anthology *Vitamin P2* (London 2011), around two-fifths of featured artists are female.

6 Cecily Brown, quoted in Emily King, 'Larger than Life', *Porter*, 15 (Summer 2016).

7 Woolf, 1929, p.97: 'What genius, what integrity it must have required in the face of all that criticism, in the midst of that purely patriarchal society, to hold fast to the thing as they saw it without shrinking. Only Jane Austen did it and Emily Brontë. It is another feather, perhaps the finest, in their caps. They wrote as women write, not as men write.'

8 Luce Irigaray, 'When our Lips Speak Together', trans. Carolyn Burke, in *Signs*, vol.6, no.1 (Autumn 1980), published by the University of Chicago Press, pp.69–79.

9 Jenny Saville, interviewed by Hunter Davies, *Independent*, 1 March 1994.

10 'Lynette Yiadom-Boakye in conversation with Naomi Beckwith', in *Lynette Yiadom-Boakye*, Munich 2014, p.102.

11 Ibid.

12 Woolf, 1934, p.13.

13 Lynette Yiadom-Boakye, in conversation with Hans-Ulrich Obrist, 2015, audio file available at www.serpentinegalleries.org/exhibitions-events/lynette-yiadom-boakye-verses-after-dusk, recorded to mark her exhibition at the Serpentine Galleries, London (2 June – 13 September 2015).

14 Cecily Brown, quoted in 'Cecily Brown: The Body is Here' by Alessandro Rabottini, in *Cecily Brown*, ed. Danilo Eccher, exh. cat., Turin 2015, p.53.

15 Celia Paul, 'Why do I paint?', in *Desdemona for Celia by Hilton*, exh. cat., New York 2015, p.99.

16 Celia Paul, quoted in 'Celia Paul by Hilton Als', part of 'BOMB: Artists in Conversation', *BOMB* online, 21 December 2015.

The Raw Facts of Life, pp.66–81

1 See Emma Chambers, 'Flesh and Form, Redefining the Nude in the Twentieth Century', in *Nude, Art from the Tate Collection*, exh. cat., Sydney 2017, p.16.

2 On the influence of Soutine on Bacon and Freud see Martin Hammer, 'Found in Translation: Chaïm Soutine and English Art', *Modernist Cultures*, vol.5, no.10, 2010, pp.218–42.

3 David Sylvester, 'The Discovering of a Structure', in *David Bomberg 1890–1957*, London 1967, p.11.

4 See David Alan Mellor, *Interpreting Lucian Freud*, London 2002, p.9.

5 Quoted in Keith Bell, *Stanley Spencer: A Complete Catalogue of the Paintings*, London 1992, p.127.

Francis Bacon and Alberto Giacometti, pp.82–91

1 On different notions of realism in the postwar period see Juliet Steyn, 'Realism versus Realism in British Art of the 1950s', *Third Text*, vol.22, no.2, 2008, pp.145–56.

2 David Sylvester, *About Modern Art: Critical Essays 1948–96*, revised edn, London 2002, p.17.

3 Quoted in David Mellor, 'Existentialism and Post-War British Art', in *Paris Post War: Art and Existentialism, 1945–55*, exh. cat., London 1993, p.53.

4 Giorgio Agamben, *Mezzi senza fine: note sulla politica*, Turin 1996, p.51 (author's translation).

5 Lawrence Alloway, 'Introduction', in *Francis Bacon*, exh. cat., New York 1963, pp.12–13. Alloway extends the comparison to the work of de Kooning, too.

6 Quoted in Catherine Lampert, *Frank Auerbach: Speaking and Painting*, London 2015, p.92.

Francis Newton Souza, pp.92–103

1 George Butcher, 'The Image and Souza', *The Studio*, vol.162, no.823, November 1961, p.179.

2 As quoted in Edwin Mullins, *FN Souza: An Introduction by Edwin Mullins*, London 1962, p.17.

3 John Berger, 'An Indian Painter', *The New Statesman and Nation*, 26 February 1955.

4 George Butcher, 'The Painting of Francis Souza', *Guardian*, 8 November 1961.

5 Francis Newton Souza, *Words and Lines*, London 1959, p.10.

William Coldstream and the Slade, pp.104–117

1 Colin St John Wilson, 'On William Coldstream's Method', in Lawrence Gowing and David Sylvester, *The Paintings of William Coldstream 1908–87*, exh. cat., London 1990, pp.37–47.

2 William Coldstream, 'How I Paint', *Listener*, 15 September 1977, quoted in Lawrence Gowing, 'Remembering Coldstream', in Gowing and Sylvester, 1990, p.11.

3 Entry for 24 March 1953, William Townsend's Journals, University College, London Archive; David Sylvester, *William Coldstream*, exh. cat., Anthony d'Offay, London 1976, p.5.

4 Townsend's journal, 24 March 1953, quoted in Peter Rumley, 'Catalogue', in Gowing and Sylvester, 1990, p.90.

5 William Coldstream, 'Painting Given Subjects: Interview with David Sylvester', *Burlington Magazine*, vol.119, no.889, April 1977, p.271.

6 Richard Kendall, 'Uglow at Work: The Formative Years', in Catherine Lampert ed., *Euan Uglow: The Complete Paintings*, New Haven and London 2007, p.xxxi.

7 Kendall, 2007, p.xxxi.

8 Lampert, 2007, p.120.

9 Andrew Lambirth, 'Euan Uglow', *Artists and Illustrators*, July 1989, quoted in Kendall, 2007. p.xxxii.

10 In a recorded interview with Martin Golding, March 1989, quoted in Kendall, 2007, p.ix.

11 Quoted in Michael Auping, 'Freud from America', in Sarah Howgate, Michael Auping and John Richardson eds., *Lucian Freud: Portraits*, exh. cat., London 2012, p.41.

12 Quoted in Rolf Lauter, *Lucian Freud: Naked Portraits*, exh. cat., Frankfurt-am-Main 2001, p.55.

13 'Then I realised that I very much wanted the figure not to be strengthened by the head, I wanted the likeness, the portraiture, to come out from the figure.' Quoted in William Feaver, *Lucian Freud*, exh. cat., Venice 2005, pp.36–7.

14 As Rolf Lauter has remarked: 'To Freud's mind the human body, in particular the skin, functions as a kind of "membrane" on which we can trace and through which we can sense inner psychological processes.' Lauter, 2001, p.66.

15 Simon Wilson, *Tate Gallery: An Illustrated Companion*, revised edn, London 1991, p.189.

16 David Sylvester, 'Grey Eminence', *New Statesman and Nation*, 27 April 1962, p.609.

17 Interviews between Uglow, Keith Patrick and Catherine Lampert, in Keith Patrick, 'The Basic Idea and Beyond', *Art Line International Art News*, vol.4, no.8, 1989, p.35. Cited in Kendall, 2007, p. xxi.

David Bomberg and the Borough Polytechnic, pp.118–29

1 For a fuller account of Bomberg's teaching see Richard Cork, *David Bomberg*, New Haven 1987, pp.258–86.

2 Cork, 1987, p.263.

3 Typescript of syllabus for a proposed series of lectures on the 'Appreciation of Art: Drawing & Painting', 4 May 1937, Tate Archive, TGA 878.4.23, p.3.

4 'Dorothy Mead, Letter against Perspective', Letter from Dorothy Mead to William Coldstream, 30 April 1959, Borough Road Gallery, Archive, London.

5 Quoted in Catherine Lampert, *Frank Auerbach: Speaking and Painting*, London 2015, p.25.

6 Lampert, 2015, p.60.

Frank Auerbach and Leon Kossoff, pp.130–43

1 See a conversation between Frank Auerbach, Taco Dibbits, Pilar Ordovas and Geoffrey Parton (2013), published in *Raw Truth: Auerbach–Rembrandt*, exh. cat., London 2013, pp.15–16.

2 Quoted in Judith Bumpus, 'Frank Auerbach', *Art and Artists*, June 1986, p.27.

3 Lucian Freud, 'Frank Auerbach's Paintings', *Frank Auerbach and the National Gallery: Working after the Masters*, exh. cat., London 1995, p.5.

4 Paul Moorhouse, '"The Eye Sees More than the Heart Knows": The Work of Leon Kossoff', in *Leon Kossoff*, London 1996, pp.21–2.

5 Andrea Rose, introduction to *Leon Kossoff*, exh. cat., London 1995, p.10.

Lucian Freud, pp.144–61

1 Lucian Freud, in conversation with Michael Auping (7 May 2009), in Sarah Howgate, Michael Auping and John Richardson eds., *Lucian Freud: Portraits*, exh. cat., London 2012, p.209.

2 For an insight into their friendship, see Bowery's interview with Freud: 'Art and Love', in *Lucian Freud: Recent Drawings and Etchings*, exh. cat., New York 1993.

3 Frank Paul, 'Lucian Freud', in Catherine Lampert ed., *Lucian Freud*, exh. cat., Dublin 2007, p.10.

4 Richard Shiff, 'Paint-Walls', in Cécile Debray ed., *Lucian Freud: The Studio*, exh. cat., Paris 2010, p.66.

Francis Bacon and John Deakin, pp.162–75

1 David Sylvester, *Interviews with Francis Bacon 1962–1979*, new and enlarged edn, London 1980, p.40.
2 Sylvester, 1980, p.43.
3 Gilles Deleuze, *Francis Bacon: The Logic of Sensation*, trans. Daniel W. Smith, London 2003, p.160.
4 Deleuze, 2003, p.161, and Sylvester, 1980, p.114.
5 On the specific relationship between Deakin's photographs and Bacon's paintings see Jessica O'Donnell, 'The Street… the Only Valid Field of Experience: Francis Bacon and the Photography of John Deakin', in *Francis Bacon: A Terrible Beauty*, exh. cat., Dublin 2009, pp.88–114.
6 Quoted in Robin Muir, *Under the Influence: John Deakin, Photography and the Lure of Soho*, London 2014, p.10.

Michael Andrews and R.B. Kitaj, pp.176–85

1 Philip Oakes, 'One-Man Party', *Sunday Times* (12 October 1969), p.58.
2 Marco Livingstone, *Kitaj*, 3rd edn, London 1999, pp.15–17, 24.
3 Robert Storr, 'A Draftsman's Painter', in *R.B. Kitaj: A Survey 1958–2007*, exh. cat., London 2015, n.p.
4 Livingstone, 1999, p.29.
5 R.B. Kitaj, 'School of London', in *The Human Clay*, exh. cat., London 1976, n.p.

Paula Rego, pp.186–93

1 John McEwen, *Paula Rego*, London 1992, p.17.
2 Germaine Greer, 'Paula Rego', *Modern Painters*, Autumn 1988, p.34.

Identity, Self and Representation, pp.194–205

1 Hilton Als, *Celia Paul*, exh. cat., London 2014.
2 Rachel Cooke, 'Lynette Yiadom-Boakye: Artist in Search of the Mystery Figure', *Observer*, Sunday 31 May 2015.
3 Zadie Smith, 'A Bird of Few Words', *The New Yorker*, 19 June 2017.
4 Cecily Brown interview, 'Take No Prisoners', by Kasper Bech Dyg, New York City, November 2014. Commissioned by Louisiana Museum of Art.
5 Ibid.
6 Ibid.

Selected Bibliography

Group Exhibition Catalogues and Other Key Texts

Araeen, Rasheed, *The Other Story: Afro-Asian Artists in Post-War Britain*, exh. cat., London 1989.

Arnhold, Hermann, ed., *Bare Life: Bacon, Freud, Hockney, and Others; London Artists Working from Life, 1950–80*, exh. cat., Munich 2014. Texts by Andrew Brighton, Eckhart J. Gillen, Lee Hallman, Invar-Torre Hollaus, Catherine Lampert, Lynda Morris, Tanja Pirsig-Marshall, and Colin Wiggins.

Eight Figurative Painters: Michael Andrews, Frank Auerbach, Francis Bacon, William Coldstream, Lucian Freud, Patrick George, Leon Kossoff, Euan Uglow, exh. cat., New Haven 1981. Texts by Andrew Forge and Lawrence Gowing.

Hyman, James, *The Battle for Realism: Figurative Art in Britain during the Cold War, 1945–1960*, New Haven 2001.

Hyman, Timothy, *The World New Made, Figurative Painting in the Twentieth Century*, London 2016.

Nead, Lynda, *The Female Nude: Art, Obscenity and Sexuality*, London 1992.

Nochlin, Linda, *Bathers, Bodies, Beauty: The Visceral Eye*. Cambridge, Mass.; London 2006.

Pollock, Griselda, *Vision and Difference: Feminism, Femininity and the Histories of Art*, London; New York 2003.

Mullins, Charlotte, *Picturing People: The New State of Art*, London 2015.

A School of London: Six Figurative Painters, exh. cat., London 1987. Text by Michael Peppiatt.

Wilcox, Tim, ed., *The Pursuit of the Real: British Figurative Painting from Sickert to Bacon*, exh. cat., London 1990. Texts by Andrew Causey, Lynda Checketts, Michael Peppiatt, and Tim Wilcox.

Michael Andrews

Feaver, William and Paul Moorhouse, *Michael Andrews*, exh. cat., London 2001.

Michael Andrews, exh. cat., London 1980–81. Texts by Lawrence Gowing, Catherine Lampert, and David Sylvester.

Michael Andrews: Lights, exh. cat., Madrid 2000. Texts by William Feaver and Belén Gopegui.

Wilson, Colin St John, *The Artist at Work: On the Working Methods of William Coldstream and Michael Andrews*, London 1999.

Frank Auerbach

Feaver, William, *Frank Auerbach*, New York 2009.

Frank Auerbach, exh. cat., London 1978. Text by Leon Kossoff and Catherine Lampert.

Lampert, Catherine, ed., *Frank Auerbach*, exh. cat., London 2015. Text by T. J. Clark and reprint of conversation with Catherine Lampert (1978).

Lampert, Catherine, *Frank Auerbach: Speaking and Painting*, London 2015.

Lampert, Catherine, Norman Rosenthal, and Isabel Carlisle, *Frank Auerbach: Paintings and Drawings, 1954–2001*, exh. cat., London 2001.

Wright, Barnaby, ed., *Frank Auerbach: London Building Sites, 1952–62*, exh. cat., London 2009. Texts by Margaret Garlake, Paul Moorhouse, and Barnaby Wright.

Francis Bacon

Brighton, Andrew, *Francis Bacon*, London 2001.

Deleuze, Gilles, *Francis Bacon: The Logic of Sensation* [1981]. Trans. by Daniel W. Smith, Minneapolis 2004.

Gale, Matthew, and Chris Stephens, eds., *Francis Bacon*, exh. cat., London 2008.

Harrison, Martin, *In Camera: Francis Bacon; Photography, Film, and the Practice of Painting*, New York 2005.

———, ed., *Francis Bacon: Catalogue raisonné*, 5 vols., London 2016.

———, ed., *Francis Bacon: New Studies*, Göttingen 2009.

Peppiatt, Michael, *Francis Bacon in Your Blood: A Memoir*, New York 2015.

Sylvester, David, *Interviews with Francis Bacon: The Brutality of Fact* [1975]. 3rd rev. and exp. edn New York 1988.

Sylvester, David, *Looking Back at Francis Bacon*, London 2000.

David Bomberg

Bomberg: Paintings, Drawings, Watercolours, Lithographs, exh. cat., London 1973. Texts by Joanne Drew and David Sylvester.

Cork, Richard, *David Bomberg*, New Haven, CT 1987.

David Bomberg, 1890–1957: Paintings and Drawings, exh. cat., London 1967. Texts by Andrew Forge, Walter Lipke, and David Sylvester.

Lipke, Walter, *David Bomberg: A Critical Study of his Life and Work*, London 1967.

Cecily Brown

Cecily Brown, exh. cat., New York 2013. Text: James Lawrence.

Cecily Brown, exh. cat., New York 2008. Text: Dore Ashton.

Cecily Brown: Paintings, exh. cat., Oxford 2005. Texts: Suzanne Cotter, Caoimhín Mac Giolla Léith.

Cecily Brown: The Sleep Around and the Lost and Found, exh. cat., Köln 2015. Text: Terry R. Myers.

William Coldstream

Gowing, Lawrence and David Sylvester, *Paintings of William Coldstream 1908–1987*, exh. cat., London 1990.

Laughton, Bruce, *William Coldstream*, New Haven, CT 2004.

William Coldstream, exh. cat., London 1976. Text by David Sylvester.

William Coldstream: New Paintings, exh. cat., London 1984. Text by Catherine Lampert.

Dennis Creffield

Dennis Creffield: A Retrospective, exh. cat., London 2005.

Dennis Creffield: Paintings and related drawings, exh. cat., London 1980.

The Gregory Fellows: Neville Boden: Sculpture – Dennis Creffield: Painting, Leeds 1966.

John Deakin

John Deakin: The Salvage of a Photographer, exh. cat., London 1984.

Muir, Robin, *John Deakin: Photographs*, exh. cat., London 1996. Text by Robin Muir.

———, *Under the Influence: John Deakin, Photography and the Lure of Soho*. London 2014.

Lucian Freud

Dawson, David, *A Painter's Progress: A Portrait of Lucian Freud*, London 2014.

Feaver, William, *Lucian Freud*, exh. cat., London 2003.

Gayford, Martin, *Man with a Blue Scarf: On Sitting for a Portrait by Lucian Freud*, London 2010.

Howgate, Sarah, with Michael Auping and John Richardson, *Lucian Freud: Portraits*, exh. cat., New Haven, CT 2012.

Lampert, Catherine, ed., *Lucian Freud*, exh. cat., Dublin 2007. Texts by Martin Gayford, Catherine Lampert, and Frank Paul.
Lucian Freud: The Studio, exh. cat., Munich 2010. Texts by Laurence de Cars, Jean Clair, Philippe Comar, Éric Darragon, and Richard Shiff.

Alberto Giacometti
Alberto Giacometti, Sculpture, Painting, Drawings, exh. cat., London 1955. Text by David Sylvester.
Alberto Giacometti, Sculpture, Painting, Drawings 1913–65, exh. cat., London, 1965. Text by David Sylvester.
Fritsch, Lena, and Frances Morris, eds., *Giacometti*, exh. cat., London 2017.
Moorhouse, Paul, *Giacometti: Pure Presence*, exh. cat., London 2015.
Peppiatt, Michael, *In Giacometti's Studio – An Intimate Portrait*, exh. cat., New York 2010; Italy 2011.
Read, Peter, and Julia Kelly, eds., *Giacometti: Critical Essays*, Farnham 2009.

R.B. Kitaj
Aulich, James, and John Lynch, eds., *Critical Kitaj: Essays on the Work of R.B. Kitaj*, Manchester 2000.
Lambirth, Andrew, *Kitaj*, London 2004.
Livingstone, Marco, *Kitaj* [1985]. 4th rev. and exp. ed. London 2010.
Morphet, Richard, ed., *R.B. Kitaj: A Retrospective*, exh. cat., London 1994. Texts by Richard Morphet and Richard Wollheim.
R.B. Kitaj, exh. cat., Washington, DC 1981. Texts by John Ashbery, Jane Livingston, and Joe Shannon.
Ríos, Julián, *Kitaj: Pictures and Conversations*, London 1994.

Leon Kossoff
Leon Kossoff: London Landscapes, exh. cat., Los Angeles 2013. Text by Andrea Rose.
Leon Kossoff: Paintings from a Decade, 1970–1980, exh. cat., Oxford 1981. Text by David Elliott.
Leon Kossoff: Recent Paintings, exh. cat., London 1972. Text by David Mercer.
Leon Kossoff: Recent Paintings, exh. cat., London 1995. Texts by Rudi Fuchs, Leon Kossoff, Andrea Rose and David Sylvester
Moorhouse, Paul, *Leon Kossoff*, exh. cat., New York 1996.
Wiggins, Colin, with Philip Conisbee and Juliet Wilson-Bareau, *Leon Kossoff: Drawing from Painting*, exh. cat., London 2007.

Dorothy Mead
Dorothy Mead 1928–1975: Paintings and Works on Paper from the Artist's Estate, exh. cat., London 2014.
Dorothy Mead, 1928–1975: Retrospective Exhibition, exh. cat., London 2005. Texts by John Russell Taylor and Philip Vann.

Celia Paul
Celia Paul, exh. cat., London 2014. Text by Hilton Als.
Celia Paul: Identity, exh. cat., London 2011. Text by Catherine Lampert.
Celia Paul: Stillness: Paintings, Works on Paper and Prints, exh. cat., Kendal 2004. Text by William Feaver.
Paul, Celia and Hilton Als, *Desdemona for Celia by Hilton*, exh. cat., London 2016. Texts by Celia Paul and Hilton Als.

Paula Rego
Lisboa, Maria Manuel, *Paula Rego's Map of Memory: National and Sexual Politics*, Aldershot 2003.
Livingstone, Marco, *Paula Rego*, exh. cat., Madrid 2007.
McEwen, John, *Paula Rego* [1992]. 3rd rev. and exp. ed. London 2006.
———, *Paula Rego: Behind the Scenes*, London 2008.
Paula Rego, exh. cat., London 1988. Texts by John McEwen, Bernardo Peinto de Almeida, Ruth Rosengarten, and Victor Willing.
Paula Rego: Jane Eyre, exh. cat., New Haven, CT 2002.
Paula Rego Nursery Rhymes, London 2010. Text by Marina Warner.
Tales for the National Gallery, exh. cat., London 1991. Texts by Germaine Greer and Colin Wiggins.

Jenny Saville
Jenny Saville, New York 2005. Texts by John Gray, Linda Nochlin, Simon Schama, and David Sylvester.
Jenny Saville: Oxyrhynchus, exh. cat., New York 2014. Text by John Elderfield.
Jenny Saville: Territories, exh. cat., New York 1999. Texts by Martin Gayford, Del LaGrace Volcano and Barry Martin Weintraub.
Luckraft, Paul, and Michael Stanley, eds., *Jenny Saville*, exh. cat., Oxford 2012.

Walter Richard Sickert
Baron, Wendy, *Sickert*, London 2001.
———, *Sickert: Paintings and Drawings*, New Haven and London 2006.
Sitwell, Osbert, ed., *A Free House! Or, the artist as craftsman/being the writings of Walter Richard Sickert*, London 1947.
Peters Corbett, David, *Walter Sickert*, London 2001.
Sturgis, Matthew, *Walter Sickert: A Life*, London 2005.
Wright, Barnaby, ed., *Walter Sickert: The Camden Town Nudes*, exh. cat., London 2007. Texts by Wendy Baron, Lisa Tickner and Barnaby Wright.

Chaïm Soutine
Chaim Soutine: 1893–1943, exh. cat., London 1963. Text by David Sylvester.
Chaïm Soutine: Céret 1919–1922, exh. cat., Céret 2000. Texts by Esti Dunow, Joséphine Matamoros and Colette Giraudon.
Chaïm Soutine, Francis Bacon, exh. cat., New York 2011. Texts by Maurice Tuchman and Esti Dunow.
———, *The Impact of Chaim Soutine (1893–1943): de Kooning, Pollock, Dubuffet, Bacon*, Ex. cat., Köln 2002.
Tuchman, Maurice, Esti Dunow and Klaus Perls, *Chaïm Soutine (1893–1943): Catalogue raisonné*, 2 vols., Köln 1993.

F.N. Souza
F.N. Souza, exh. cat., London 2008. Includes interview with Souza.
F.N. Souza: Black on Black, exh. cat., London 2013.
Francis Newton Souza, exh. cat., London and New York 2005.
Mullins, Edward, *Souza*, London 1962.
Kurtha, Aziz, *Francis Newton Souza: Bridging Western and Indian Modern Art*, Ahmedabad 2006.

Stanley Spencer
Bell, Keith, *Stanley Spencer*, London 1992 (reprinted 1999).
Hauser, Kitty, *Stanley Spencer*, London 2001.
Hyman, Timothy and Patrick Wright, eds., *Stanley Spencer*, exh. cat., London 2001. Texts by Adrian Glew, David Fraser Jenkins, Katharine Stout, and Robert Upstone.

Euan Uglow
Campbell, Susan, *Euan Uglow, Some Memories of the Painter*, London 2003.
Euan Uglow, exh. cat., London 1989. Texts by Catherine Lampert, Martin Golding and Andrew Lambirth.
Euan Uglow, Controlled Passion: Fifty Years of Painting, Kendal 2003. Texts by Martin Gayford and Richard Kendall.
Lampert, Catherine, *Euan Uglow, The Complete Paintings*, Catalogue raisonné, New Haven, CT 2007. Texts by Catherine Lampert and Richard Kendall.
Euan Uglow, exh. cat., London 1997. Text by Catherine Lampert.

Lynette Yiadom-Boakye
Gioni, Massimiliano, and Natalie Bell, eds., *Lynette Yiadom-Boakye: Under-Song For A Cipher*, exh. cat., Basel and New York 2017. Texts by Robert Storr, Chris Ofili, Elena Filipovic, Massimiliano Gioni, and Natalie Bell.
Kholeif, Omar, ed., *Lynette Yiadom-Boakye: Natures, Natural and Unnatural*, exh. cat., Moscow 2015. Texts by Habda Rashid, Omar Kholeif, Petra Lange-Berndt, and Lynette Yiadom-Boakye.
Lynette Yiadom-Boakye: Any Number of Preoccupations, exh. cat., New York 2010. Texts: Naomi Beckwith, Okwui Enwezor, and Lynette Yiadom-Boakye.
Verses After Dusk: Lynette Yiadom-Boakye, exh. cat., London 2015. Texts by Amira Gad, Hilton Als, and Glenn Ligon.

Credits

Copyright

Photographic

akg-images p.17
Stefan Altenburger Photography Zurich p.54
Anthony d'Offay London p.134
Arts Council Collection, Southbank Centre, London p.114, pp.128–9
Birmingham Museums Trust p.96
bpk | Hamburger Kunsthalle | Elke Walford p.42
Bridgeman Images p.12, p.33, p.64 top right, p.107, p.151, pp.152–3, p.157, Private Collection / Bridgeman Images p.26, p.112
Courtesy of the British Council Collection. p.53, pp.116–7
Image courtesy Browse & Darby p.113
Christie's Images / Bridgeman Images pp.171–2
Christie's Images, London/Scala, Florence pp.182–3
Jack Cornish Photography p.89
Peter Cox, Eindhoven, The Netherlands p.47
Devonshire Collection, Chatsworth. Reproduced by permission of Chatsworth Settlement Trustees and Bridgeman Art Library p.147
Ferens Art Gallery, Hull Museums, UK / Bridgeman Images p.81
Fine Art Images/Heritage Images/Scala, Florence p.16
Courtesy of the artist and Gagosian. p.64 bottom left pp.198–9,
Getty Images p.167, pp.172–5
Courtesy Grosvenor Gallery p.102
Photo credit: Richard Ivey p.201
Kunsthaus Zürich p.91
London Southbank University p.122
Manchester Art Gallery, UK / Bridgeman Images p.37
Museum of London p.121
Digital image, The Museum of Modern Art, New York/Scala, Florence p.87
Musée d'Orsay, Dist. RMN-Grand Palais / Patrice Schmidt p.64 top left
Courtesy Nottingham City Museums and Galleries p.70
Courtesy of PIANO NOBILE, Robert Travers (Works of Art) Ltd p.69 and p.127
Photo by Justin Piperger p.95, p.98, p.99
Photo: Prudence Cuming Associates Ltd p.82
Photo Scala, Florence – courtesy of the Ministero Beni e Att. Culturali e del Turismo p.58
Photo Scala, Florence p.57
Sotheby's p.165
Southampton City Art Gallery, Hampshire, UK / Bridgeman Images p.80
Tate Images p.22, p.24 (detail), p.39, p.59 top, p.72, p.73, p.85, p.86, p.88, p.90, p.97, p.101, p.104, pp.108–9, p.110, p.118, p.123, pp.135–6, p.138, p.149, p.150, pp.154–5, p.156, p.161, p.168, p.169, p.176, p.180, pp.184–5, p.190, pp.192–3,
Tate Images, Dave Lambert p.71, p.191
UCL Art Museum, University College London p.31
V&A Images p.92
VG Bild-Kunst, Bonn 2017 p.44
National Museum of Wales pp.142–3
Photography Stephen White p.194

Exhibited Works

The works listed below appear in the Tate Britain exhibition. Works are listed alphabetically by artist, and then chronologically. Measurements are given in cm, height before width. Page references to the works illustrated are given at the end of the entries.

Michael Andrews 1928–95
Colony Room I 1962
Oil paint on board 120 × 182.8
Pallant House Gallery, Chichester (Wilson Gift through the Art Fund 2006)
p.179

Michael Andrews
The Deer Park 1962
Oil paint on board 214 × 244.5
Tate. Purchased 1974
p.180

Michael Andrews
Melanie and Me Swimming 1978–9
Acrylic paint on canvas 195.5 × 195.9
Tate. Purchased 1979
p.176

Frank Auerbach b.1931
Head of E. O. W. I 1960
Oil paint on wood 43.3 × 35.5
Tate. Presented by the executors of the estate of David Wilkie 1993
p.126

Frank Auerbach
Rebuilding the Empire Cinema, Leicester Square 1962
Oil paint on board 152.4 × 152.4
The Samuel Courtauld Trust, The Courtauld Gallery (Accepted by HM Government in Lieu of Inheritance Tax and allocated to The Samuel Courtauld Trust, The Courtauld Gallery, in 2015)
pp.124–5

Frank Auerbach
Looking Towards Mornington Crescent Station, Night 1972–3
Oil paint on board 127 × 127
Private collection, courtesy of Clore Wyndham
p.138

Frank Auerbach
St Pancras Steps 1978–9
Oil paint on canvas 168.2 × 137.5
Touchstones Rochdale, Rochdale Arts & Heritage Service
p.139

Frank Auerbach
Chimney in Mornington Crescent – Winter Morning 1991
Oil paint on canvas 143.2 × 133
Private collection
p.130

Frank Auerbach
Head of Jake 1997
Oil paint on board 61.3 × 50.8
Private collection
p.140

Frank Auerbach
Park Village East – Winter 1998–9
Oil paint on canvas 103.2 × 154.3
Amgueddfa Cymru –National Museum Wales
pp.142–3

Francis Bacon 1909–92
Figure in a Landscape 1945
Oil paint, pastel and dust on canvas 144.8 × 128.3
Tate. Purchased 1950
p.85

Francis Bacon
'Study after Velázquez' 1950
Oil paint on canvas 198 × 137
Private collection
p.82

Francis Bacon
Dog 1952
Oil paint on canvas 198.1 × 137.2
Tate. Presented by Eric Hall 1952
p.86

Francis Bacon
Study of a Baboon 1953
Oil paint on canvas 198.3 × 137.3
Museum of Modern Art, New York. James Thrall Soby Bequest, 1979
p.87

Francis Bacon
Study for Portrait II (after the Life Mask of William Blake) 1955
Oil paint on canvas 61 × 50.8
Tate. Purchased 1979
p.88

Francis Bacon
Figure in Mountain Landscape 1956
Oil paint on canvas 152 × 119
Kunsthaus Zürich, 1983
p.90

Francis Bacon
Study for Figure VI 1956–7
Oil paint on canvas 152.5 × 119
Laing Art Gallery, Newcastle upon Tyne
p.89

Francis Bacon
Portrait 1962
Oil paint on canvas 198 × 141.5
Museum für Gegenwartskunst Siegen. The Lambrecht-Schadeberg Collection/Winners of the Rubens Prize of the City of Siegen
p.165

Francis Bacon
Study for Portrait of Lucian Freud 1964
Oil paint on canvas 198 × 147.6
The Lewis Collection
p.166

Francis Bacon
Portrait of Isabel Rawsthorne 1966
Oil paint on canvas 81.3 × 68.6
Tate. Purchased 1966
p.168

Francis Bacon
Three Figures and Portrait 1975
Oil paint, pastel, alkyd and sand on canvas 198.1 × 147.3
Tate. Purchased 1977
p.169

Francis Bacon
Triptych 1974–77
Oil paint, pastel and dry transfer lettering on canvas 198 × 147.5 (each panel)
The Lewis Collection
pp.170–1

David Bomberg 1890–1957
Toledo from the Alcazar 1929
Oil paint on canvas 67.3 × 76.2
Courtesy of Daniel Katz Gallery, London
pp.74–5

David Bomberg
Self-Portrait 1931
Oil paint on board 61 × 51
Courtesy of Daniel Katz Gallery, London
p.76

David Bomberg
The Bridge and the River Tajo, Ronda 1935
Oil paint on canvas 76.9 × 66
Private collection, Ivor Braka Ltd
p.79

David Bomberg
Evening in the City of London 1944
Oil paint on canvas 69.8 × 90.8
Museum of London. Purchased with the assistance of the National Heritage Memorial Fund and the V&A Purchase Grant Fund
p.121

David Bomberg
Vigilante 1955
Oil paint on board 71.8 × 60
Tate. Purchased 1968
p.118

Cecily Brown b.1969
Teenage Wildlife 2003
Oil paint on linen 203.2 × 228.6
Private collection, courtesy of Susan Almrud Art Advisory
p.200

Cecily Brown
Boy with a Cat 2015
Oil paint and pastel on linen 109.2 × 165.1
Collection of Danny and Lisa Goldberg
p.201

William Coldstream 1908–87
Seated Nude 1952–3
Oil paint on canvas 106.7 × 70.7
Tate. Purchased 1983
p.110

William Coldstream
Seated Nude 1973–4
Oil paint on canvas 101.5 × 127
Private collection, Devon
p.112

William Coldstream
Orange Tree I 1974–5
Oil paint on canvas 91.4 × 71.1
Tate. Purchased 1991
p.111

Dennis Creffield b.1931
Isle of Dogs from Greenwich Observatory 1959
Oil paint on board 71.2 × 91.4
Tate. Bequeathed by Margaret Lapsley 2008, accessioned 2012
p.123

John Deakin 1912–72
Isabel Rawsthorne c.1952 (printed 2017)
Photograph, gelatin silver print on paper 50.8 × 40.6
The John Deakin Archive/James Moores Collection
p.162

John Deakin
Lucian Freud c.1958 (printed 2017)
Photograph, gelatin silver print on paper 50.8 × 40.6
The John Deakin Archive/James Moores Collection
p.173

John Deakin
Peter Lacy c.1959 (printed 2017)
Photograph, gelatin silver print on paper 50.8 × 40.6
The John Deakin Archive/James Moores Collection
p.172

John Deakin
George Dyer c.1963 (printed 2017)
Photograph, gelatin silver print on paper 50.8 × 40.6
The John Deakin Archive/James Moores Collection
p.175

John Deakin
Muriel Belcher c.1965 (printed 2017)
Photograph, gelatin silver print on paper 50.8 × 40.6
The John Deakin Archive/James Moores Collection
p.174

Lucian Freud 1922–2011
Girl with a Kitten 1947
Oil paint on canvas 41 × 30.7
Tate. Bequeathed by Simon Sainsbury 2006, accessioned 2008
p.104

Lucian Freud
Still Life with Squid and Sea Urchin 1949
Oil paint on copper 30 × 23
Harris Museum & Art Gallery
p.107

Lucian Freud
Girl with a White Dog 1950–1
Oil paint on canvas 76.2 × 101.6
Tate. Purchased 1952
pp.108–9

Lucian Freud
Baby on a Green Sofa 1961
Oil paint on canvas 53.5 × 60
Chatsworth House Trust
p.147

Lucian Freud
Man's Head (Self-Portrait I) 1963
Oil paint on canvas 53.3 × 50.8
The Whitworth, The University of Manchester
p.144

Lucian Freud
Annabel 1967
Oil paint on canvas 35 × 27
The New Art Gallery Walsall, Garman Ryan Collection
p.148

Lucian Freud
Naked Portrait 1972–3
Oil paint on canvas 61 × 61
Tate. Purchased 1975
p.149

Lucian Freud
The Painter's Mother IV 1973
Oil paint on canvas 27.3 × 18.6
Tate. Bequeathed by Simon Sainsbury 2006, accessioned 2008
p.150

Lucian Freud
Frank Auerbach 1975–6
Oil paint on canvas 40 × 26.5
Private collection
p.151

Lucian Freud
The Big Man 1976–7
Oil paint on canvas 91.4 × 91.4
Private collection, on loan to the Irish Museum of Modern Art
pp.152–3

Lucian Freud
Two Plants 1977–80
Oil paint on canvas 149.9 × 120
Tate. Purchased 1980
p.154

Lucian Freud
Girl in a Striped Nightshirt 1983–5
Oil paint on canvas 30.5 × 25.6
Tate. Presented by Mercedes and Ian Stoutzker 2013 and forming part of the Mercedes and Ian Stoutzker Gift to Tate
p.155

Lucian Freud
Leigh Bowery 1991
Oil paint on canvas 51 × 40.9
Tate. Presented anonymously 1994
p.156

Lucian Freud
Two Women 1992
Oil paint on canvas 153 × 214
The Lewis Collection
pp.158–9

Lucian Freud
Bella 1996
Oil paint on canvas 104.1 × 76.2
Private collection, New York
p.160

Lucian Freud
Sleeping by the Lion Carpet 1996
Oil paint on canvas 227.1 × 120
The Lewis Collection
p.157

Lucian Freud
David and Eli 2003–4
Oil paint on canvas 162.6 × 174
Lent from a Private Collection courtesy of the Faurschou Foundation 2014
p.161

Alberto Giacometti 1901–66
Woman of Venice IX 1956
Bronze 113 × 16.5 × 34.6
Tate. Purchased 1959
p.91

R.B. Kitaj 1932–2007
To Live in Peace (The Singers) 1973–4
Oil paint on canvas 77 × 214
The Lewis Collection
pp.182–3

R.B. Kitaj
Cecil Court, London W.C.2 (The Refugees) 1983–4
Oil paint on canvas 183 × 183
Tate. Purchased 1985
p.184

R.B. Kitaj
The Wedding 1989–93
Oil paint on canvas 182.9 × 182.9
Tate. Presented by the artist 1993
p.185

Leon Kossoff b.1926
Building Site, Victoria Street 1961
Oil paint on board 122.5 × 184.8
Arts Council Collection, Southbank Centre, London
pp.128–9

Leon Kossoff
Early Morning Willesden Junction 1962
Oil paint on board 27.9 × 52.1
Private collector, Europe
p.127

Leon Kossoff
Children's Swimming Pool, Autumn Afternoon 1971
Oil paint on board 168 × 214
Tate. Purchased 1981
pp.134–5

Leon Kossoff
Self Portrait II 1972
Oil paint on wood 56 × 51
Private collector, Europe
p.133

Leon Kossoff
Demolition of the Old House, Dalston Junction, Summer 1974 1974
Oil paint on board 160 × 218.4
Tate. Purchased 1975
p.136

Leon Kossoff
Christ Church, Spitalfields, Morning 1990
Oil paint on board 198.6 × 189.2
Tate. Purchased 1994
p.137

Dorothy Mead 1928–75
Reclining Figure c.1954
Oil paint on canvas 92 × 122
Lent by London Southbank University – from the David Bomberg Legacy, The Sarah Rose Collection
p.122

Celia Paul b.1959
Family Group 1984–6
Oil paint on canvas 165 × 200
Spier Contemporary Collection
p.197

Celia Paul
Painter and Model 2012
Oil paint on canvas 137.2 × 76.2
Victoria and Warren Miro
p.194

Paula Rego b.1935
The Family 1988
Acrylic paint on canvas-backed paper 213.4 × 213.4
Marlborough International Fine Art
p.189

Paula Rego
Bride 1994
Pastel on paper 120 × 160.6
Tate. Purchased 1995
p.190

Paula Rego
Island of the Lights from Pinocchio 1996
Pencil, ink and watercolour on paper, laid on Masonite 150 × 180
Private collector, Europe
p.191

Paula Rego
The Company of Women 1997
Pastel on paper mounted on aluminium 170 × 150
Collection Ostrich Arts Limited on loan to Casa das Histórias Paula Rego/Câmara Municipal de Cascais/Fundação D. Luis I, Cascais
p.186

Paula Rego
The Betrothal: Lessons: The Shipwreck, after 'Marriage a la Mode' by Hogarth 1999
3 works on paper, pastel, mounted onto aluminium 165 × 500 (displayed)
Tate. Purchased with assistance from the Art Fund and the Gulbenkian Foundation 2002
pp.192–3

Jenny Saville b.1970
Reverse 2002–3
Oil paint on canvas 213.4 × 243.8
Collection of Larry Gagosian
pp.198–9

Walter Richard Sickert 1860–1942
Noctes Ambrosianae 1906
Oil paint on canvas 63.5 × 76.5
Nottingham City Museums & Galleries
p.70

Walter Richard Sickert
The Studio: The Painting of a Nude 1906 (also dated 1911–12)
Oil paint on canvas 76 × 50
Courtesy of Piano Nobile, Robert Travers and Offer Waterman
p.69

Walter Richard Sickert
Nuit d'Été c.1906
Oil paint on canvas 50 × 40
Private collection, Ivor Braka Ltd
p.66

Chaïm Soutine 1893–1943
The Butcher Stall c.1919
Oil paint on canvas 55 × 38
Private collection, Switzerland c/o Di Donna Galleries
p.71

Chaïm Soutine
Landscape at Céret c.1920–1
Oil paint on canvas 55.9 × 83.8
Tate. Purchased 1964
p.73

Chaïm Soutine
Polish Woman c.1922
Oil paint on canvas 81 × 65.1
Private collection
p.72

Francis Newton Souza 1924–2002
Jesus and Pilatus c.1955–6
Oil paint on board 92.5 × 122
Jane and Kito de Boer
p.95

Francis Newton Souza
Negro in Mourning 1957
Oil paint on hardboard 122 × 61
Lent by Birmingham Museums Trust on behalf of Birmingham City Council
p.96

Francis Newton Souza
Crucifixion 1959
Oil paint on board 183.1 × 122
Tate. Purchased 1993
p.97

Francis Newton Souza
Nude Holding Breasts 1960
Oil paint on board 121.9 × 91.4
Private collection, courtesy of Grosvenor Gallery
p.100

Francis Newton Souza
Red Sun 1960
Oil paint on board 75 × 75
Jane and Kito de Boer
p.98

Francis Newton Souza
Black Nude 1961
Oil paint on canvas 181.5 × 121
Victoria & Albert Museum. Gift of the Contemporary Art Society, Tate Gallery, London, 1983
p.92

Francis Newton Souza
Citadel 1961
Oil paint on board 68 × 120
Jane and Kito de Boer
p.99

Francis Newton Souza
Two Saints in a Landscape 1961
Acrylic paint on canvas
128.3 × 95.9
Tate. Presented by A.J. Muirhead 1965
p.101

Francis Newton Souza
Two Saints (After El Greco) 1965
Oil paint on canvas 101.5 × 76
Grosvenor Gallery, London
p.102

Sir Stanley Spencer 1891–1959
Patricia Preece 1933
Oil paint on canvas 83.9 × 73.6
Southampton City Art Gallery
p.80

Sir Stanley Spencer
Nude Portrait of Patricia Preece 1935
Oil paint on canvas 76.2 × 50.8
Ferens Art Gallery: Hull Museums
p.81

Euan Uglow 1932–2000
Woman with White Skirt 1953–4
Oil paint on canvas 101.5 × 80.6
Lord and Lady Irvine
p.113

Euan Uglow
Still Life with Delft Vase 1959
Oil paint on canvas 61 × 51
Arts Council Collection, Southbank Centre, London
p.114

Euan Uglow
Georgia 1973
Oil paint on canvas 83.8 × 111.8
British Council Collection
pp.116–17

Lynette Yiadom-Boakye b.1977
The Host Over a Barrel 2014
Oil paint on canvas 180 × 200
Private collection. Courtesy Corvi-Mora, London, and Jack Shainman Gallery, New York
pp.202–3

Lynette Yiadom-Boakye
Coterie of Questions 2015
Oil paint on canvas 200 × 130
Private collection. Courtesy Corvi-Mora, London, and Jack Shainman Gallery, New York
p.204

Index

Note: references in bold indicate pages with artworks; 'n' indicates notes.

First published 2018 by order of the Tate Trustees
by Tate Publishing, a division of Tate Enterprises Ltd,
Millbank, London SW1P 4RG
www.tate.org.uk/publishing

on the occasion of the exhibition
All Too Human: Bacon, Freud and a Century of Painting Life

Tate Britain, London
28 February – 27 August 2018

Museum of Fine Arts, Budapest
5 October 2018 – 14 January 2019

Supported by the All Too Human Exhibition Supporters Circle:
The Garcia Family Foundation
Hazlitt Holland-Hibbert
Victoria Miro
Robert and Matthew Travers, PIANO NOBILE (Works of Art) Limited

Tate International Council, Tate Patrons and Tate Members

A catalogue record for this book is available from the British Library

ISBN 978-1-84976-583-1

Distributed in the United States and Canada by ABRAMS, New York

Library of Congress Control Number: applied for

Project Editor: Emma Poulter
Production: Bill Jones
Picture Researcher: Roz Hill
Designed by Peter Dawson, gradedesign.com
Colour reproduction by DL Imaging Ltd, London
Printed and bound in Italy by Graphicom SRL

Measurements of artworks are given in centimetres, height before width

Front cover: Lucian Freud *Girl in a Striped Nightshirt* 1983–5, see p.155
Back cover: Lynette Yiadom-Boakye *Coterie of Questions* 2015, see p.204

Page 1: David Bomberg *Self-Portrait* 1931 (detail), see p.76
Page 2: Dorothy Mead *Reclining Figure* c.1954 (detail), see p.122
Page 3: Chaïm Soutine *Landscape at Céret* c.1920–1 (detail), see p.73
Page 4: Cecily Brown *Teenage Wildlife* 2003 (detail), see p.200
Page 6: Francis Bacon *Portrait of Isabel Rawsthorne* 1966 (detail), see p.168

MIX
Paper from responsible sources
FSC® C013123

Supporting Tate

Tate relies on a large number of supporters – individuals, foundations, companies and public sector sources – to enable it to deliver its programme of activities, both on and off its gallery sites. This support is essential in order for Tate to acquire works of art for the Collection, run education, outreach and exhibition programmes, care for the Collection in storage and enable art to be displayed, both digitally and physically, inside and outside Tate. Please contact us at:

Development Office
Tate
Millbank
London SW1P 4RG

Tel: +44 (0)20 7887 4900
Fax: +44 (0)20 7887 8098

Tate Americas Foundation
520 West 27 Street Unit 404
New York, NY 10001
USA

Tel: 001 212 643 2818
Fax: 001 212 643 1001

Donations, no matter the size, are gratefully received, either to support particular areas of interest, or to contribute to general activity costs.

Charity Details

The Tate Gallery is an exempt charity; the Museums & Galleries Act 1992 added the Tate Gallery to the list of exempt charities defined in the 1960 Charities Act. Tate Members is a registered charity (number 313021). Tate Foundation is a registered charity (number 1085314).

Tate Americas Foundation

Tate Americas Foundation is an independent charity based in New York that supports the work of Tate in the United Kingdom. It receives full tax exempt status from the IRS under section 501(c)(3) allowing United States taxpayers to receive tax deductions on gifts towards annual membership programmes, exhibitions, scholarship and capital projects. For more information please contact the Tate Americas Foundation office.

Tate Trustees

Tate Foundation Trustees and Honorary Members

Tate Britain Donors to the Centenary Development Campaign

The Annenberg Foundation
The Asprey Family Charitable Foundation
Ron Beller and Jennifer Moses
Alex and Angela Bernstein
The Charlotte Bonham-Carter Charitable Trust
Lauren and Mark Booth
Ivor Braka
The CHK Charitable Trust
The Clore Duffield Foundation
Sadie Coles
Giles and Sonia Coode-Adams
Alan Cristea
Thomas Dane
The D'Oyly Carte Charitable Trust
Sir Harry and Lady Djanogly
The Dulverton Trust
Maurice and Janet Dwek
Friends of the Tate Gallery
Bob and Kate Gavron
Sir Paul Getty, KBE
Alan Gibbs
Mr and Mrs Edward Gilhuly
Helyn and Ralph Goldenberg
Nicholas and Judith Goodison
Richard and Odile Grogan
Pehr and Christina Gyllenhammar
Heritage Lottery Fund
Jay Jopling
Mr and Mrs Karpidas
Howard and Lynda Karshan
Peter and Maria Kellner
Madeleine Kleinwort
Brian and Lesley Knox
The Kresge Foundation
Catherine and Pierre Lagrange
Mr and Mrs Ulf G Linden
Ruth and Stuart Lipton
Anders and Ulla Ljungh
Lloyds TSB Foundation for England and Wales
David and Pauline Mann-Vogelpoel
Sir Edwin and Lady Manton
Nick and Annette Mason
Viviane and James Mayor
Anthony and Deirdre Montagu
Sir Peter and Lady Osborne
Maureen Paley
William A Palmer
Mr Frederik Paulsen
The Pet Shop Boys
The P F Charitable Trust
The Polizzi Charitable Trust
John and Jill Ritblat
Barrie and Emmanuel Roman
Lord and Lady Sainsbury of Preston Candover
Mrs Coral Samuel, CBE
David and Sophie Shalit
Mr and Mrs Sven Skarendahl
Pauline Denyer-Smith and Paul Smith
Mr and Mrs Nicholas Stanley
The Jack Steinberg Foundation
Charlotte Stevenson
Tate Gallery Centenary Gala
Carter and Mary Thacher
Mr and Mrs John L Thornton
The Trusthouse Charitable Foundation
David and Emma Verey
Dinah Verey
Clodagh and Leslie Waddington
Gordon D Watson
Mr and Mrs Anthony Weldon
The Duke of Westminster, OBE TD DL
Sam Whitbread
Mr and Mrs Stephen Wilberding
Michael S Wilson
The Wolfson Foundation
and those who wish to remain anonymous

Donors to The Tate Britain Millbank Project

The Deborah Loeb Brice Foundation
Clore Duffield Foundation
Alan Cristea Gallery
Sir Harry and Lady Djanogly
The Gatsby Charitable Foundation
J Paul Getty Jr Charitable Trust
Heritage Lottery Fund
The Hiscox Foundation
James and Clare Kirkman
The Linbury Trust and The Monument Trust
The Manton Foundation
The Mayor Gallery
Ronald and Rita McAulay
Midge and Simon Palley
PF Charitable Trust
The Porter Foundation
The Dr Mortimer and Theresa Sackler Foundation
Mrs Coral Samuel, CBE
Jake and Hélène Marie Shafran
Tate Members
The Taylor Family Foundation
Sir David and Lady Verey
Sir Siegmund Warburg's Voluntary Settlement
Garfield Weston Foundation
The Wolfson Foundation
and those who wish to remain anonymous

Tate Britain Benefactors and Major Donors

We would like to acknowledge and thank the following benefactors who have supported Tate Britain prior to August 2017.

Abrishamchi Family Collection
Tomma Abts
Raad Zeid Al-Hussein
Dilyara Allakhverdova and Elchin Safarov
Olga de Amaral
Gregory Annenberg Weingarten and the Annenberg Foundation
The Fagus Anstruther Memorial Trust in memory of the late

Hartley Ramsden and Margot Eates
Art Fund
Artangel
Arts and Humanities Research Council
Arts Council England
The Artworkers Retirement Society
Celia and Edward Atkin, CBE
Roland Augustine and Lawrence Luhring
Axel Vervoordt Gallery
Roger Ballen
Charles and Tetyana Banner
Lionel Barber
The Estate of Peter and Caroline Barker-Mill
Corinne Bellow Charity
Big Lottery Fund
Anton and Lisa Bilton
Nicola Blake
Blavatnik Family Foundation
Bloomberg Philanthropies
Oliver Bolitho
Harry and Fabiana Bond
The Charlotte Bonham-Carter Charitable Trust
Mr John Botts
Estate of Louise Bourgeois
Elena Bowes
Frank Bowling, Rachel Scott, Benjamin and Sacha Bowling, Marcia and Iona Scott
Alan Bowness
Pierre Brahm
Ivor Braka
The Estate of Dr Marcella Louis Brenner
The Deborah Loeb Brice Foundation
Rory and Elizabeth Brooks Foundation
Beatrice Bulgari | In Between Art Film
Piers Butler
Jamal Butt
Mr and Mrs Nicolas Cattelain
The Estate of Marigold Ann Chamberlin
Priti Chandaria
Francise Hsin-Wen Chang
Trustees of the Chantrey Bequest
The Chaplaincy to the Arts and Recreation in North East England, Durham
Judy Chicago in honour of Frances Morris
David and Rose Cholmondeley
The Clore Duffield Foundation
The Clothworkers' Foundation
Denise Coates Foundation
R and S Cohen Foundation
Sadie Coles
Connolly
Contemporary Art Society
The Ernest Cook Trust
Douglas S Cramer
The Cranford Collection
Alan Cristea
The Daniel Katz Gallery
Kate-Jane Davie
Mrs Tiqui Atencio Demirdjian
Department for Business, Innovation and Skills
Department for Digital, Culture, Media and Sport
Mr Paul Dickens
The Estate of F.N. Dickins
Braco Dimitrijevic
Anthony and Anne d'Offay
Joe and Marie Donnelly
Peter Dubens
The Easton Foundation
Lonti Ebers
Maryam and Edward Eisler
John Ellerman Foundation
Carla Emil and Richard Silverstein
Tracey Emin
European Union
The Estate of Maurice Farquharson
The Estate of Mary Fedden and Julian Trevelyan
Mr Paul Findlay
The Finnis Scott Foundation
Wendy Fisher
Dr. Kira and Neil Flanzraich, in honor of Anthony d'Offay and ARTIST ROOMS
Eric and Louise Franck
Carl Freedman Gallery / Counter Editions, London
Freelands Foundation
The Estate of Lucian Freud
Amanda and Glenn Fuhrman and The FLAG Art Foundation
Gagosian
Galeria Luisa Strina, São Paulo
Frank Gallipoli
Mala Gaonkar
Georg Geyer
Adrian Ghenie
Glenstone Foundation
Milly and Arne Glimcher
Anna and Ralph Goldenberg
The Estate of Kaveh Golestan, with assistance from Dr. Nina Ansari
Sir Nicholas and Lady Goodison
Antony Gormley
Lydia and Manfred Gorvy
Noam Gottesman
The Granville-Grossman Bequest
Cornelia Grassi
Calouste Gulbenkian Foundation
The Hakuta Family
Paul Hamlyn Foundation
The Ray and Diana Harryhausen Foundation
Sanford Heller in Honour of Sir Nicholas Serota
Barbara Hepworth Estate
Heritage Lottery Fund
The Hintze Family Charitable Trust
Damien Hirst
David Hockney
Hazlitt Holland-Hibbert
Trustees of Lord Howard of Henderskelfe's Will Trust
Sally Hudson
Michael and Ali Hue-Williams
The Estate of Malcolm Hughes
The J Isaacs Charitable Trust
Rasha Said Khawaja
Kikuji Kawada
Dr Martin Kenig
KÖNIG GALERIE
The Estate of Fay Elspeth Langford
David and Amanda Leathers
The Leathersellers' Company Charitable Fund
Agnès and Edward Lee
Legacy Trust UK
The Leverhulme Trust
Ruben Levi
Lisson Gallery
London Art History Society
Galleria Lorcan O'Neill
LUMA Foundation
Lyndsey Ingram Ltd
Mace Foundation
Francisca Mancini
The Manton Foundation
The Estate of Sir Edwin Manton
Salman Matinfar
David Mayor
Lord McAlpine of West Green
Susan McDonald
The Estate of Kenneth McGowan
The Andrew W. Mellon Foundation
The Paul Mellon Centre for

Studies in British Art
Gustav Metzger
Boris and Vita Mikhailov
Sir Geoffroy Millais
Henry Moore Foundation
Les Morgan
Elisabeth Murdoch
National Heritage Memorial Fund
The National Trust
James O'Connell
Outset Contemporary Art Fund
Maureen Paley
Simon and Midge Palley
The Pasmore Estate
Catherine Petitgas
Piano Nobile, Robert Travers (Works of Art) Ltd
Stanley Picker Trust
The Pivovarov Family
David W. Posnett, OBE
Mrs Virginia Powell
Gilberto Pozzi
Massimo Prelz Oltramonti
Andrey Prigov
Emilio Prini
Maya and Ramzy Rasamny
The Robert Rauschenberg Foundation
The Redfern Gallery
Barrie and Emmanuel Roman
The Estate of Eugene and Penelope Rosenberg
The Rothschild Foundation
Edward Ruscha
Keith and Katherine Sachs
The Estate of Simon Sainsbury
Doris Salcedo
Salon 94
Nadia and Rajeeb Samdani
Julião Sarmento
John Schaeffer
Gregor Schneider
Jake and Hélène Marie Shafran
Monir Shahroudy Farmanfarmaian
Stuart Shave
Jack Shear
Dasha Shenkman
Taryn Simon
Andy Simpkin
Lorna Simpson
The Estate of Sylvia Sleigh
Bob and Roberta Smith
Chris Steele-Perkins
Richard Stephens in memory of his father Brian Thomas Stephens
Emile Stipp
The Estate of Michael Stoddart
Mercedes and Ian Stoutzker
T293
Tamares Real Estate Holdings Inc. in collaboration with the Zabludowicz Collection
Aldo Tambellini
Tate 1897 Circle
Tate Africa Acquisitions Committee
Tate Americas Foundation
Tate Asia-Pacific Acquisitions Committee
Tate International Council
Tate Latin American Acquisitions Committee
Tate Members
Tate Middle East and North Africa Acquisitions Committee
Tate North American Acquisitions Committee
Tate Outreach Appeal
Tate Patrons
Tate Photography Acquisitions Committee
Tate Russia and Eastern Europe Acquisitions Committee
Tate South Asia Acquisitions Committee
Terra Foundation for American Art
The Estate of Mr Nicholas Themans
Wolfgang Tillmans
Tomasso Brothers Fine Art Ltd
Phillip Trevelyan
The Hon Robert H Tuttle and Mrs Maria Hummer-Tuttle
Luc Tuymans
Two Palms Press
V-A-C Foundation
Mercedes Vilardell
Marie-Louise von Motesiczky Charitable Trust
Offer and Mika Waterman
The Estate of Kenneth Ernest Webster
Anthony Whishaw
David and Maria Wilkinson
Jane and Michael Wilson
WME | IMG
The Lord Leonard and Lady Estelle Wolfson Foundation
Mr Nelson Woo
Bill Woodrow
The Estate of Mrs Monica Wynter
Yuz Foundation
The Estate of Mr Anthony Zambra
and those who wish to remain anonymous

Tate Britain Corporate Supporters

BMW
BP
EY
Hyundai Card
Hyundai Motor
IHS Markit
Qantas
RSM
Sotheby's
and those who wish to remain anonymous

Tate Britain Corporate Members

Bank of America Merrill Lynch
BCS Consulting
Bloomberg
Christie's
Clifford Chance LLP
The Cultivist
Deutsche Bank AG London
Dow Jones
EY
Finsbury
Floreat Group
Holdingham Group
HSBC
Hyundai Card
Imperial College Healthcare Charity
JATO Dynamics
JCA Group
Linklaters
The Moody's Foundation
Morgan Stanley
Oliver Wyman
Siegel + Gale
Tishman Speyer
and those who wish to remain anonymous